FALLING, FLOATING, FLICKERING

CRIP: NEW DIRECTIONS IN DISABILITY STUDIES

General Editors: Michael Bérubé, Robert McRuer, and Ellen Samuels

Committed to generating new paradigms and attending to innovative interdisciplinary shifts, the Crip: New Directions in Disability Studies series focuses on cutting-edge developments in the field, with interest in exploratory analyses of disability and globalization, ecotheory, new materialisms, affect theory, performance studies, postcolonial studies, and trans theory.

Crip Times: Disability, Globalization, and Resistance
Robert McRuer

Accessible America: A History of Disability and Design
Bess Williamson

Literary Bioethics: Animality, Disability, and the Human
Maren Tova Linett

Disabilities of the Color Line: Redressing Antiblackness from Slavery to the Present
Dennis Tyler

Distressing Language
Michael Davidson

Falling, Floating, Flickering: Disability and Differential Movement in African Diasporic Performance
Hershini Bhana Young

Falling, Floating, Flickering

Disability and Differential Movement in African Diasporic Performance

Hershini Bhana Young

NEW YORK UNIVERSITY PRESS
New York

NEW YORK UNIVERSITY PRESS
New York
www.nyupress.org

Please contact the Library of Congress for Cataloging-in-Publication data.
ISBN: 9781479818440 (hardback)
ISBN: 9781479818457 (paperback)
ISBN: 9781479818471 (library ebook)
ISBN: 9781479818488 (consumer ebook)

New York University Press books are printed on acid-free paper, and their binding materials are chosen for strength and durability. We strive to use environmentally responsible suppliers and materials to the greatest extent possible in publishing our books.

Manufactured in the United States of America

10 9 8 7 6 5 4 3 2 1

Also available as an ebook

For my Stutterer, who taught me what it means to listen

CONTENTS

Introduction

Holding Your Breath

Throughout the following pages, we linger with dead Africans floating face down in the Mediterranean Sea; we watch and listen closely to the gyrating bodies in Spoek Mathambo's music video "Control" (2011); we confront the crawling figure in Wura-Natasha Ogunji's performance piece *Will I still carry water when I am a dead woman?* (2011); and we follow the human-animal hybrids as they slither and lumber through the pages of the speculative novel *Zoo City* (2010) by the South African journalist Lauren Beukes. Through each of these encounters, this book insists on foregrounding black performances as a way to counter the abstraction that results from imperial violence and to remap the body as a messy, transgressive organization of parts unmoored from the typical. Every performance I examine breathes life into a haptic undercommons that reconfigures our bodies, desires, and movements, enabling us to survive the dangerous times that we have been forced to inhabit. The tremendous violence that characterizes contemporary African diasporic life, profoundly altering the very makeup of black bodies, leads me to ask, How can we enact a different kind of black sociality based on differential embodiment and the movements that result? How can this sociality enable us to reimagine the human in ways that move away from individual, discrete, "normal" bodies that seem capable of independent functioning toward alternate corporealities that are hybrid, multiple, reliant on one another, and often seen as "monstrous failures"? What does it mean to respond to Sylvia Wynter's call to invent "new genres of the human" that move beyond Western humanism? How does having a corporeal form that "broaden[s] the possibilities of what it means to be a body" move us away from the straitjacket of the racialized normative? (Miranda 29). Answering such questions requires fluency in theoretical frameworks from across the disciplines. This project is based primarily in African diaspora studies and performance studies, but it also leans on, even as it departs from, disability studies to defamiliarize how we think about bodies. Critical cultural history helps me to theorize black archival absences, and the project lingers in the wings of dance studies to catch a glimpse of what differential movement might look like.

I want to begin with a pedagogical moment—a performance made by a student in one of my classes, titled *Home in Contemporary Black Girls' Bedrooms*. Selome Hailu's video and accompanying narrative essay trace the fraught lines of belonging and home for her as an Ethiopian descendant living in Texas. The performance is divided into three sections connected by a narrative voice-over: "1. I'm going home for the weekend," "2. I think I'm just going to stay at home," and "3. I went back home." I want to focus on the last section, which alternates camera shots of fragmented parts of Hailu's body—her thigh, her hands, and her crossed legs on a bed—with video footage of a group of rural Ethiopian women talking as they work in the fields. These juxtaposed images communicate Hailu's struggle to reside in the fractured space of home between Texas, Addis Ababa, and the rural village of Acheber where Hailu's grandfather was raised and where a favorite uncle is buried. This growing tension manifests itself in her increasing shortness of breath. After a two-hour car drive from Addis Ababa to the foot of the mountain where Acheber is located, Hailu has to hike up the mountain. Exacerbated by cigarette smoke, stress, and the high elevation, Hailu feels the onset of an asthma attack. Irritation, fear, and discomfort weigh down every frustrating and laborious breath as her neck and chest tighten and she starts to lag far behind the others.

It is a chance encounter with three children on the mountain, described in the essay, that changes the way air flows through Hailu's body. She is spontaneously welcomed by the three unknown children who at the sight of her imperiled, belabored breath communicate across oceans of misrecognitions. They yell out the Guragigna word *intabi*, leaving it echoing in their wake. Hailu's father translates, and it is this word that resonates through Hailu, helping her swollen lungs find some reprieve as air starts to reroute itself and bronchial passages slowly expand. *Intabi*—may God take everything ill in you and bring it on to me instead. This moment is an example of what Nathaniel Mackey and M. NourbeSe Philip describe as circle breathing/circle breath. Mackey borrows the idea of circle breathing from a technique used by jazz players to produce a continuous tone, in which the horn player breathes in through the nose while breathing out through their instrument using air stored in their cheeks. The continuous sound is produced, he posits, by "rotating between utopian intimations of assured, everlasting pneumatic amenity and sirening alarm at the precarity to which breath, black breath, is subject" (Mackey, "Breath and Precarity" 17). This haptic oscillation between ability and the inability to breathe articulates the vulnerability of black bodies by revealing situations when the involuntary is shown to be contingent on the world around us. Belabored breath, jagged gasps of air, I can't breathe. The practice of survival. But as NourbeSe Philip reminds us, this practice of survival is relational. Breathing is not only about the circulation of breath through one body, as we all begin life "in a prepositional relationship with air—someone breathes for us" (Philip 32). Each of us is only kept alive because at a certain epigenetic moment in utero, we allowed a woman to labor and breathe for us. Philip calls this circular breathing a "radical hospitality that entails housing the stranger" (34). She thus locates Mackey's "radical pneumatic practice" ("Breath and Precarity" 10) within the black female imaginary. Circular breathing recognizes the labor of all women, whether they be queer, trans, or straight, who fight for survival within systems that hold us down with a knee to the neck. As Zakiyyah Iman Jackson argues in *Becoming Human*, "the black mater holds the potential to transform the terms of reality and feeling, therefore rewriting the conditions of possibility of the empirical" (101), moving us toward what poet Johanna Bruckner describes as a "redistributed sensorium."[1] This redistributed sensorium, where affect moves between individual bodies, creates new possibilities of being with and for one another. It allows for the intimacy of holding another person's breath.

It is important to stress that circular breathing does not reinscribe what Keguro Macharia in *Frottage* calls "hetero-kinship tropes" or a "genealogical imperative" that produces black personhood by "glossing over multiple, conflicting histories of intimate discipline and dissent" (11). Hailu learns that she does not have to fulfill biologic gendered expectations of a wayward diasporic daughter returning "home." Instead, her journey ends halfway up the mountain, before she reaches her ancestral home, in the radical act of hospitality practiced by strangers on a hill. In their evocation of the word *intabi*, she finds not the prescriptiveness of filiation but rather oxygen-rich structures of affiliation. The speaking of *intabi* highlights the vulnerability of black life in particular, for while breathing is a universal necessity, it is harder for some people to breathe in the context of racism and oppression while others use up all the oxygen in the room. Mackey thus writes, "That none of us is guaranteed our next breath is a truth that has to sit alongside another, equally obvious, which is that precarity has been and continues to be unequally distributed, some groups serving, for others, as a sacrifice to it or a shield against it" ("Breath and Precarity" 18).

Despite being a word from a language I do not speak and from an African country not my own, *intabi* opens a discussion about creating African diasporic sociality around differential embodiment and movement. The performative gesture, not only of the children as they embrace a gasping stranger but also of Hailu sharing her video performance with the watching and listening class, uneasily maps out ways of constructing community that, despite mutual unintelligibility, acknowledges the need for ethical relationality. This relationality is not based on the expectation of reciprocity—the children ostensibly have little to gain by hugging a stranger whose jagged breath has become consciously laborious. Instead, black ethical relationality, a circular being/breathing if you will, requires us to navigate our misrecognitions of the historical and geographic forces that bring us together, insisting on the kind of vulnerability described by Sara Ahmed as "a particular kind of bodily relation to the world" (*Cultural Politics* 69).

The location of this exchange, halfway up a mountain, is neither an origin nor a destination. Instead, it constitutes what Katherine McKittrick in *Dear Science* calls a "black sense of place" (106). This black sense of place recurs in each chapter. Here on the hill to Acheber, it does not belong to the children or to Hailu. Rather, it is the air and sky that soak through their pores and in the smudge of dirt that transfers from one girl's cheek to the taller girl's chest. This black sense of place is the "collaborative praxis" that develops between them, where "collective assertions of life are always in tandem with other ways of being (including those ways of being we cannot bear)" (McKittrick, *Dear Science* 106). Place is what grows between.

In "Mama's Baby, Papa's Maybe," Hortense Spillers famously argues that the materiality of racialized violence reduces the black body to splayed "flesh," a meaty substrate characterized by a "zero degree of social conceptualization" (67). Therí Pickens and Nirmala Erevelles use Spillers's essay to demonstrate how the condition of blackness is sutured to the historical process of "becoming" disabled. Impairment is always produced within the context of racial violence and vice versa, for it is when converted into disabled flesh/fungible commodity that "the black body is at the height of its profitability" (Erevelles 42, 30). "Eyes beaten out . . . a left jaw, a right ankle, punctured" (67)—Spillers argues that bodies are not whole or the sum of their parts. The violence of colonialism, global capitalist regimes, and, specifically for Spillers, the Middle Passage "atomizes" racialized wounded flesh without "any hint or suggestion of a dimension of ethics, of relatedness between human personality and its anatomical features, between one human personality and another, between human personality and cultural institutions" (68). Imperial violence has disaggregated us into hierarchical arrangements of bodies that matter and flesh that does not.

The powerful endurance of Spillers's argument lies in her suggestion that the nonrecognition of subjectivity that occurs when one is made flesh might also be a liberatory "insurgent ground" where one can "rewrite . . . a radically different text" of black being (72). As Cristin Ellis writes, "the power of this . . . [wounded] flesh to obdurately persist even after ideology has otherwise denied that being's humanity" suggests a "fluid materiality [that] is at once the condition of possibility for regimes of . . . meaning and a force for their continual upheaval" (162, 165). Similarly, Tiffany Lethabo King writes that to be rendered black flesh "is to be rendered porous, undulating, fluttering, sensuous, and in a space and state at-the-edge and outside of normative configurations of sex, gender, sexuality, space, and time" (23). Flesh, thus, represents an unmaking that allows for multiple, provisional, and strategic potentialities. *Intabi* as a potentiality rooted in the "insurgent ground" of black flesh counters the atomization and abstraction that renders this flesh abject, but not by asking us for a cure or through a valorization of bodily norms that leads to an illusory return to wholeness. All too often, fantasies of wholeness prop up normalizing discourses of racialized ability. Instead, through *intabi* something meaningful emerges between us amid body fragments, a mutual recognition of our reduction to fleshy substrate and the weight of spacetime. Paraphrasing Tanya Titchkosky, the meaning of a wounded blackness resides *between* people as much as it lives within them (3). Amid Hailu's fear, her asthma, her slowness up the mountain, and the unknown young children who see that she can't breathe springs a sense of mutual historical woundings that does not forget the distance between Texas and Acheber, between then and now, between you and me. Rather, by bringing onto me what ails you, I recognize the vibrating relationality implied in the vulnerability that lives between us. Embracing and surviving that which ails *you* thus constitutes both form and method for the innovative and ethical social practices that this book enacts. The resulting black sociality, episodic and performed, provides us a way to rethink and perform black corporeality and movement anew.

"I can't breathe; I will breathe for you" (Philip 39).

This black mutuality insists on geographical and historical specificities as it works against notions of universal, individual rational subjects. Wounded flesh, as Michael Davidson reminds us, is a "matter of . . . site, a series of locations and spaces where political economy, bioregional differences, cultural representations, and medical bureaucracies converge . . . [It is] as much about national and cultural power differentials as it is a matter of medicine and bodies. . . . The discursive and material effects of history, culture, and power converge—along with the embodied and experienced sedimentations of physicality and psychic conditionalities imposed in conditions not of subjects' choosing" (*Concerto* 26, 175). As such, each chapter of this book looks specifically at the historical socioeconomic factors that shape the particular ways in which bodies are wounded and the response to that wounding. For example, Wura-Natasha Ogunji's *Will I still carry water when I am a dead woman?* focuses on crawling and dragging through the crowded streets of Lagos. Ogunji's performance of impairment exposes the crisis of the Nigerian public water system, exploited by companies such as Nestlé that charge more for a single bottle of Nestlé Pure Life water than for a liter of gasoline. The role of women in procuring water every day and the subsequent remapping of the city around water portage add crucial nuance to Spillers's discussion of wounded flesh. This is not the violence of the Middle Passage but rather the violence of global capital's imperial presence in Africa and continued exploitation of people and resources that benefit the so-called First World. In another example, I discuss how Spain continues to invest in SIVE (integrated system for external surveillance), which combines radar, cameras, and patrols in order to stop migrants from crossing the Mediterranean into Fortress Europe. I claim that through performances of floating, Berni Searle's performance *Home and Away* (2003) attempts to counter the violent reduction of the wounded brown and black bodies into red dots on SIVE and other surveillance systems. Thus, I am arguing for performances that are historically and geographically specific, even as they construct an undercommons that forms the basis for reimagined black relationality that connects black bodies across the diaspora.

These performances insist on an envisioning of the body as a collective entity, a morphology, to quote King, "without edges" but still "distinct." I would like us to think about racialized possessive individualism for a moment in order to develop what I call a *politics of conjoinment.* Franco Berardi in *After the Future* (2011) distinguishes "conjunction" from what he calls "connection," a model of relating that dominates in the present. This notion of conjunction, as summarized by Mark Featherstone, is a form of engagement "where self and other meet in such a way that changes both sides of the interaction, and *connection* which . . . comprises a programmatic model of debased sociality where there is no deep engagement or transformative effect upon either person" (261). Berardi writes, "Conjunction is the meeting and fusing of rounded and irregular forms that infuse in a manner that is imprecise, unrepeatable, imperfect and continuous" (*After the Future* 40). My notion of a politics of conjoinment is related less to the alienated condition of late capitalism characterized by the rapidity of info-technologies that affects our being and more to the crisis of being unhuman/property inaugurated by slavery and colonialism. The politics of conjoinment, then, is crucially a response to the technology of fungibility.

Enlightenment epistemologies, where propertied subjects are defined by the willful and independent ownership of their bodies, combined with an individualism that emerges from the liberal democratic state, link what Cynthia Wu describes as "somatic sovereignty to a market-based sociality," thereby creating the "fantasy of possessive individualism" (17). As Tavia Nyong'o writes, "the figure of bodily integrity is itself an ideology of Western humanism" (180). Our current notions of independent, single-bodied atomized subjects acting rationally to further their own best (property) interests result from this inheritance. At the core of this fantasy, as Cheryl Harris has famously argued, is a property interest in whiteness (1713). Harris goes on to argue that the "conceptual nucleus" between whiteness and property, or the common assumption they both share, is "a right to exclude" black and Native peoples (1713). Even after the official end of legalized systems of slavery, African colonialism, apartheid, and segregation, this right to exclude has enabled whiteness to keep abreast of changing notions of property in order to perpetuate racialized privilege ratified by the law. The very idea of an independent, property-owning, universal body with a discrete morphology cannot be separated from the constitution of whiteness itself. To be an individual is to be white, while black and brown folk hover in liminal spaces between fungible objects and what I develop as the not-quite-human in chapter 3. Harris goes on to suggest that the law has "recognized and codified group identity as an instrumentality of exclusion and exploitation; however, it has refused to recognize group identity when asserted by racially oppressed groups as a basis for affirming or claiming rights" (1761). Thus, the denial of black people's status as universal singular individuals has been accompanied by an insistence that their group identity can only be the basis of continued subjugation.

Disability Studies' refusal to privilege notions of subjectivity predicated on autonomy has to be laid side by side with this history of racialized individualism. Erevelles and Rosemarie Garland-Thomson argue that the disabled body, whose supposed "betrayal" of liberal ideals of self-sufficiency and personal responsibility, can point us toward alternate theorizations of dependency and the labor of care as an essential mode of social engagement (Erevelles 178). We cannot ignore the fact that the work of caring is not "natural" and, instead, is embedded in a landscape of social inequity where caretakers are often black and female. I am more interested, however, in a black sociality that shifts our very definition of what constitutes a body. In discussing conjoined twins, Garland-Thomson writes that separating the siblings "expunge[s] the kind of corporeal human variations that contradicts the ideologies the dominant order depends on to anchor truths it insists are unequivocally encoded in bodies" ("Integrating Disability" 13–14). Instead of separating the twins, what happens if we use performance to reconfigure the body past its limits, beyond standard morphologies and beyond notions of sovereign individuals.[2] Without resorting to the traditional collective groups made up of independent participants, we should instead use "bodily variation, pleasure, and desire [to] remap the body, its meanings and its taxonomies for participants and witnesses alike, . . . thus making room for an interpretation of the body as never quite whole, always throbbing with the potential" of insurgent ground (Miranda 92). In other words, we need to enact what I am calling a politics of conjoinment so that, as enabling monstrosities, hybrid darkies, and stuttering freaks, we can emerge from the dark.

"Cranes in the Sky" (2016), a short music video directed by Solange Knowles and her husband, Alan Ferguson, with Arthur Jafa as director of photography, features a series of shots of Solange, dressed in avant-garde costumes against visually arresting backdrops: in one shot, she stands perfectly still as sepia-toned mountains loom; in another, her clothes billow as the wind tries to push her off a futuristic building high in the sky; in yet another, she straddles a tree stump or lies on a white tile floor amid some tall potted trees.[3] Interspersed between these scenes are moving tableaus that Solange creates with other women. Dressed alike, these black women lean on, fold over, and prop up each other. They alternate between quietly staring at the camera and gently undulating against one another to the pulse of the music. Often, these tableaus, with their dressed-alike bodies and similar skin color and hair texture, make it difficult to recognize Solange. Two related scenes in particular create a performative utterance that works against Solange as an individual, exceptional body as they posit a politics of conjoinment. The first occurs near the beginning of the video, where Solange is center stage, wearing a dress made of yarn. Purple threads are wrapped around her breasts and the loops of yarn around her waist. The end of the yarn, snaked around Solange's arm, is held by another woman, whose hand is the only part of her body included in the shot. Solange's solo performance here, the very fabric of fame in which she drapes herself, is not only hers. Should the woman off camera let go of the yarn, Solange's entire dress would unravel. Approximately forty-five seconds later, viewers gasp at the sight of a group of women standing halfway up a brush-covered hill (fig. I.1). These women are connected to one another by a *single* periwinkle dress that references our earlier glimpse of Solange in a yarn dress. Swathes

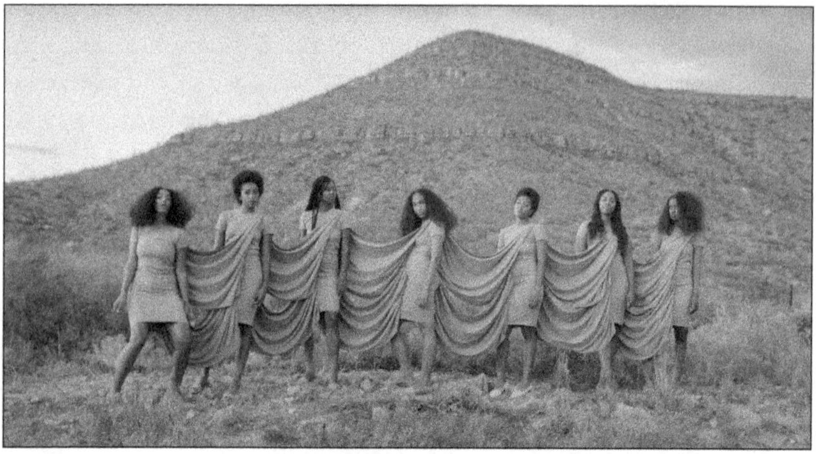

Figure I.1. Solange Knowles, "Cranes in the Sky" (2016) (Screenshot by author)

of cloth bind the front shoulder of one dress to the back shoulder of another; more drapery sewn between the thighs links each woman's lower half to the person in front of and behind them. The women all face different directions; there is no single collective point that arrests their gaze. Though the front of Solange's dress doesn't connect her to another person, her body turns inward toward the rest of the women. She is the head of this conjoined being but not leading, as she can't go anywhere without their participation.

I am not, nor do I believe Solange is, making an ahistorical or universal claim here that we are all connected to one another and share each other's plight. My argument counters the *Miriam-Webster Dictionary*'s definition of *conjoinment* as the joining together of "(things, such as separate entities) for a common purpose." Rather, I am arguing that Solange's performances of conjoinment point us toward what Spillers calls the "living laboratory" of black flesh (68) that refuses blackness as a site of pessimistic negation, instead imagining new ways of breathing, moving, and being that are not merely compensatory. These alternate black (female) morphologies (fourteen-legged, periwinkle, vaginal area connected to ass, and multiple headed) rewrite the boundaries of an atomized body to dismantle both possessive individualism and the group identities used to disenfranchise black people. Despite the crucible in which it continues to be forged, wounded black flesh, to extrapolate Margrit Shildrick's and Petra Kuppers's arguments, represents a condition of possibility, not only a foreclosure or lack (Shildrick; Kuppers, *Disability*). The living laboratory of black flesh "foreground[s] the extent to which the body becomes thinkable when its totality can no longer be taken for granted, when the social meanings attached to sensory and cognitive values cannot be assumed" (Davidson, *Concerto* 4). These somatic test sites also insist that we rewrite the figure of the human, moving away from postulations of independent, agential rational agents toward hybrid bodies that are "unstable, uncontainable site[s]" (Davidson, *Concerto* 225). As I develop in chapter 3, the body as living laboratory demonstrates the "profound and complex linkages, not only between diverse human beings, but between humans and animals and human machines" (Shildrick 157). It facilitates the critical rethinking of gender norms even while articulating the need to redress slavery's and colonialism's violent unmaking of gender. Without making recourse to whole, universalized subjectivities (the "transparent I"), this book embraces the alchemy of wounded flesh and the creative corporeal pedagogy it necessitates. Thus, in "Cranes in the Sky," many women are not wearing one dress. Rather, one conjoined, nonunitary being steps out to insist on new morphologies emerging from the historical substrate of black flesh.

Differential Movement or Flamingo Children

In 2018, a study by Brink et al. appeared in the *African Journal of Disability* in which researchers tested the postural stability of nine-year-old children with fetal alcohol spectrum disorders. The children all attended farm schools or their local primary school in a rural town in South Africa's Western Cape, famous for its wine. The article states without any explanation that fetal alcohol syndrome (FAS) or fetal alcohol spectrum disorders (FADS) is the most common "birth defect" in South Africa, with the Western Cape Province being particularly affected. Nowhere does the article attempt to explain why.

One cannot understand bodies and their movements without unpacking the historical and material conditions that produce them. Brink et al. avoid mentioning the infamous "tot" or "dop" system during apartheid, when South African wine farmers in the Western Cape paid their workers a percentage of their wage in second-rate wine. Leslie London et al. describe the "dop" system as "the institutionalization of alcohol as a medium of remuneration of, and social control over, employees" (109). The formal use of wine as remuneration/reward has declined since the 1990s, but unofficial practices that have insinuated their way into cycles of agricultural labor and leisure mean that the consequences of enforced addiction are still keenly felt. The study noted that finding future samples of children with FASD was "feasible." The children were asked to stand on one leg on a portable pressure-sensitive mat with Matscan software, allowing both for "real-time" and "offline" viewing of the children's plantar pressure distribution and the position of their pelvis and abdominal core. The rules were simple; I am sure the children perceived this as a fun game. You only get two tries. Stand on one leg. Your raised leg can't touch your standing leg or the floor. Look at this picture three meters away. Your arms must hang freely at your sides. Open your eyes. Close your eyes.

The study's findings allow me to introduce what I describe throughout this book as differential movement. The male control group took longer to achieve postural control because they performed the task differently from the boys with FASD. On the other hand, as expected, girls with FADS, who approached the task in the same way as the control group of girls did, took longer to achieve postural control than the control group did. The findings implicitly implied that if the boys without disabilities approached the problem of postural stability in the same way as the boys diagnosed with FASD did, the latter group would demonstrate their lack of postural stability. In other words, differentially embodied boys and girls would be shown to lack postural stability, thereby confirming their diagnosis. Such children are more likely to fall, to be unable "to control the orientation of the body segments" because of those "nonlinearities of neuromuscular control" referred to as "postural sway" (Brink et al.).

What if we were truly to insist not on a hierarchy of abled-bodied and disabled movement but rather on an array of various movement strategies based on differential embodiment? Rather than a study that simply reinforces the idea that children with FADS have less control over their bodies than "normal" children do, what happens if we center different ways of approaching the problem of balance and test, if we have to test, *for* postural sway? Instead of asking children to stay still, flamingo style, on one leg, can we instead value their ability to bend and contort the pelvis? Let's see who can orient their body segments in various nonlinear ways. Who can bend one leg while hopping on the other? Who chooses to look at the other children instead of a picture three meters away? Postural sway would move from being a limitation, a sign of deficient functioning caused by alcohol poisoning, and become instead another way of moving through the world that defies expectations. Children with FADS would be able to achieve some movements that other children cannot, and vice versa.

Retheorizing wounded flesh in global contexts requires thinking about how bodies don't stand still with perfectly isolated muscles, how they fall, crawl, float, and spasm. These movements are not compensatory, nor are they the best we can do given the limitations of our body. The way my friend signs a credit card receipt with stiff fingers curled into themselves is not praiseworthy because she has transcended the limitations of her body. Rather, as Kalpana Seshadri suggests, perhaps we can see the black "(disabled) body *as* movement—as life that is always already movement, . . . hyper-aware of its interconnectedness, . . . its potentiality" (197–98). Thus, movement provides us with a way of "not of transcending the body but of thinking through it" (Davidson, "Concerto" 619). Through the incorporation of differential embodiment, disability opens up a space for alternate choreographies that better articulate the haptic reality of permeable bodies, global violence, and the aftermath of slavery and imperialism. Hailu's asthma causes her to lag behind the rest of the group—a seeming failure to keep up. But, perhaps, her pace up the mountain and her wayward steps are precisely what is needed *both* by her and by the rest of the group in order to alter the spacetime of the mountain.

Let us briefly consider Ravel's *Concerto for the Left Hand*, a piece that requires the pianist to use only their left hand. As Davidson writes, "the technical difficulty of one-hand playing [can be seen] as a compensatory response for the missing hand, a response that requires the pianist to imitate the full pianistic range, coloration, and dynamics of the nineteenth-century virtuoso style" ("Concerto" 616). But what happens if, instead of one hand being limiting or something to overcome, the inclusion of particular limitations into the very conceptualization of the composition creates whole new constellations of possibilities? (Davidson, "Concerto" 616). If we insist on the inextricability of differential embodiment and black sociality, our imagining of the concerto form and its performance would have to change. Instead of the historically white audience for a genre based on the exclusion and exotification of blackness, what if the musical composition itself was written for and by those who are marginalized from dominant aesthetic practices? What would the concerto look like? Would it be a concerto at all?

Africans across the diaspora have seldom had a platform for aesthetic practice, especially around issues of differential embodiment and movement. Referring to Shakespeare's *The Tempest*, Sylvia Wynter writes that the play is structured around the epistemic absence not only of "Caliban's woman [Ariel] . . . but also of . . . Caliban's endogenous desire for her" ("Beyond Miranda's Meanings" 361). In other words, Western epistemologies and performance rely on the aporia that is the black woman, foreclosing any possibility of desire for her. But merely recovering her and writing her in does little to change the exclusionary and hierarchical order of Western man with its foundational myths of universal, agential subjects. Wynter and later Katherine McKittrick suggest that instead of another foundational myth, what is needed is a "frame of reference which parallels the 'demonic model' outside the 'consolidated field' of our present mode of being/feeling/knowing, as well as of the multiple discourses, their regulatory systems of meaning and interpretative 'readings,' through which alone these modes, as varying expressions of human 'life,' including ours, can effect their respective autopeosis *as such* specific modes of being" (Wynter, "Beyond Miranda's Meanings" 364). Wynter calls for alternate technologies of articulation located on a shifting, indeterminate ground that work against dominant conceptions of the disaggregated, universal rational human who is white, male, and able-bodied. What if one such "demonic ground" is differential embodiment and movement—the materiality of wounded flesh and its patterns of performance—whose very divergence from the normal provides alternate modes of being capable of imagining not only a piano concerto for one hand but a musical form that departs from the range, coloration, and style of piano concertos and nimble-fingered (white) pianists themselves?

Alex S. Porco's "Throw Yo' Voice Out: Disability as a Desirable Practice in Hip-Hop Vocal Performance" argues that despite hip-hop being deeply implicated in racist capitalist structures, part of its revolutionary potential lies in its insistence on disability as central to its aesthetic and cultural vernacular form. Porco begins his essay with Ice T.'s comments about Run DMC's Darryl McDaniels's spasmodic dysphonia (a condition in which the larynx spasms, causing the voice to periodically give out). Ice T. laments, "You're a rapper. Your tool is your voice. . . . If you lose your voice, it's like being a piano player and losing your fingers. . . . How cruel is that? That's the worst thing that can happen to you" (Villeneuve, in Porco). Rather than agreeing that a spasming larynx, like missing piano fingers, is a tragedy in need of a cure, Porco posits that "vocal disability" might actually be a beneficial resource in hip-hop performance that disrupts the prescriptive insistence on vocal smoothness and agility that characterizes the modern commodity. The grain of the voice foregrounds the extralinguistic aspects of vocal performance that should not be reduced to a symptom of (racial) trauma. To reduce disability simply to trauma, Porco argues, "diminish[es] the importance and positivity of play, style, and pleasure (including humor) for the hip-hop artist and listener, respectively." Instead, Porco concludes that hip-hop as a form of vernacular theory "*flips the script* on disability, transforming a physical condition and social stigma into a desirable aesthetic value."[4] Thus, for example, asthma sufferers Fat Joe, Coolio, and Raekwon are renown for the aspirated timbre of their vocalizations. Their aspirated timbre signals what Daphne Brooks theorizes as the "black voice" of dissonance and disappointment (191), where disability is embraced as part of a new constellation of possibilities that centers differential embodiment, sonic disruption, and alternate breathing practices.

In *Sister Mine* by Nalo Hopkinson, once-conjoined twins Makeda and Abby are living with what it means to be surgically forced into individual bodies. Both bodies are left injured by the procedure, and their dependence on each other, rather than being mitigated by separation, takes on different forms. The surgery has left Abby unable to walk without crutches, and she requires Makeda's assistance to accomplish physical tasks. Makeda, for her part, has lost her "mojo" or magic and is totally reliant to others for access to the spiritual realm. This scenario encapsulates what Eunjung Kim calls "curative violence," which arises from the "everyday failure to imagine the uncured body as a mode of being, . . . [as well as from] how transnational flows of knowledge about systemic disability management and historical relations contribute to such violence" (*Curative Violence* 228). Curative violence is twofold: it denies the possibilities of differential embodiment and movement even as it perpetuates disabling violence in the name of a cure. *Sister Mine* refuses the idea of a cure as the opposite of a persisting disability. Curing the sisters by insisting on individual, discrete morphologies changes their relationship to a heterosexual, somatic ideal, but its violence scars the body, requiring the navigation of another set of painful conditions.

Both sisters, in particular Makeda, exert considerable effort looking for their mother, who crossed over into the spiritual world at the scene of their birth. At a certain moment in the novel, the two girls find their mother and realize that their difficulty in locating her has partly been their failure to recognize her. Their mother has assumed a nonhuman form: "The creature was some dark colour; black or maybe midnight blue. Its body was streamlined; fat in the middle, tapering at the neck end. . . . That rubbery, slimy thing that smelled of wet algae wasn't the mother I'd dreamed of. That thing couldn't be anyone's mother" (Hopkinson 224–25). Mother as seal, as long-necked creature with flippers and eyes like saucers: this is differential embodiment at its most fantastic. But maybe not so fantastic when I think about how I could barely recognize my father as various types of cancer spread through his body—the large bobble-head with giant ears, concave chest, and those same eyes like saucers. The familiar made strangely monstrous in order for us to see anew. This is a back and forth crossing or flickering across the multiple borders that separate human from animal and life from living death.

For Makeda and Abbey, finding their mother demands that they accept and welcome her differential embodiment, and this acceptance requires alternate ways of communicating, in particular through movement. Makeda watches as her sister and her mother, "one on land and one in water, one stumbling for lack of balance and the other wheezing for lack of breath, dance[] with each other at the shoreline" (Hopkinson 225). This moment results in an abrupt italicized break in the text where Makeda remembers and dreams about the first time she saw her "crippled sister" dance. As these memories permeate the present encounter between mother-as-seal and sisters, the past and present fold together in unexpected ways. When Abby was nine, Makeda remembers, she insisted that she could sing with her body: "And my crippled sister threw down her crutches and began to dance. She ceased being a little girl constrained by braces and crutches. Her body moved in its own language. Suddenly, her shorter leg wasn't disabling her. It was *the crook of a comma*, the illustrative pause in a devastatingly meaningful statement spoken in movement. It was the length and shape it needed to be" (Hopkinson 226; emphasis added). Seal/cripple/mojo-less "claypicken":[5] swimming/dancing/dreaming. Performances of conjoined bodies as "lattice[s] of agencies rather than primarily self-authored closed system[s]" that imagine new ways of moving as we breathe life into our blackness (Z. Jackson, *Becoming Human* 163). You hold my breath.

The Crook of a Comma. Stoppage That Is Passage. There Is a Stutter Happening.

I don't know how to use commas correctly. I can't seem to unlearn an early lesson when a teacher told me that commas represented those moments when you pause, when the sentence requires you to take a breath. Sometimes my breathing is appropriate as I inhale before the coordinating conjunction. At other times, my commas are wildly errant as thoughts, sentences, histories, and time overlay each other and I am gasping for breath. After all, as Jennifer Brody writes, punctuation as a nonverbal, gestural "excess" informs "our quotidian movements and missteps by stopping, staying, and delaying the incessant flows of information to which we are subject" (7, 6). Breath as an arbitrator of time. Throughout this book, I argue that linear progressive time has little value when thinking about differential embodiment and movement. In chapter 6, for example, I develop Michelle Wright's notion of "epiphenomenal time," in which the past manifests itself in the present moment (42). "Epiphenomenal time" allows us to explore spacetime horizontally, incorporating the multivalent memories and views of contingent, conjoined beings. As Julius Fleming Jr. writes, such a "radical grammar of the present—of the here and now—[is] pivotal to black people's efforts to exist and imagine otherwise" (588).[6] It disrupts progressive teleological narratives of an imagined time prior to injury folded neatly on top of the time after a cure when the rehabilitated body, as Kim argues, becomes a "sign of decolonized and sovereign statehood under capitalism" (*Curative Violence* 8). Whether we call it epiphenomenal time or crip time or black queer time, rethinking temporality insists on our varied bodies occupying a present moment saturated with a past and future that loops, stops, drools, lingers, and rushes. It is the time that it takes someone with asthma to make it up the hill to Acheber.

It is also the time it sometimes takes my son to get out a particular word and the time it takes me to listen quietly. *Stuttering time.* I watch strangers fidget, rush, trip over themselves to get to the end of *his* sentence. They are missing the avalanche of commas, the extraordinary ellipses, the dot-dot-dots that differential embodiment insists on. My son's stuttering results from neurophysiological differences. His stops and starts do not require another to fill in the words for him; nor do they require "fixing" in speech therapy so that he can keep up with the ebb and flow of "normal" conversation. Instead of seeing his stuttering as an impediment to communication and speech, what happens if we envision his particular muscular tensions, rhythms, and patterns of words as an alternate world-making practice based in black sociality and epiphenomenal time?

Sean Cole's piece for *This American Life*, titled "Time Bandit," focuses on the composer and performance artist JJJJJerome Ellis. Ellis tells Cole, "Stuttering is not bound to my body. . . . It is a phenomenon that occurs between me and whoever I'm speaking to. I like to think of it like it's something that we share." Thus, instead of Ellis being the person who stutters, he recasts the interaction so that the weight and rhythm of language is shared: "There is a stutter happening," he tells us. During his performances, Ellis tries not to resort to a strategy that most people who stutter have been taught to use: the substitution of one word that is difficult to say with another that flows a little quicker. He describes being deeply unhappy after a performance because he substituted the word "distúrbio" with the word "break" when talking about the "timing and fluency" of speech. What he wanted to do, what he wanted his audience to do, he states, is wait.

> SEAN COLE: Wait for the word.
>
> JJJJJEROME ELLIS: Wait for it. But it was especially—especially *d*'s. They can be really painful. (S. Cole)

Waiting for a word in the silence stretches time. Ellis tells his audience to use the time of his glottal breaks to reflect or to remember or to honor the suffering of others. He gives us small spaces within language to breathe. Ellis's and my son's embodied aesthetic practice requires another form of listening that opens out possibilities for communication not usually available to nonstutterers. Such speech insists on our disorientation, on us reworking how to relate to one another. Their words, stops, repetitions, and silences require us to step out of time with them, to slip the yoke, to painfully limp and to balance delicately and joyously on jagged edges.

Alternate world-making is not easy or painless. At an event for the Michael and Tami Lang Stuttering Institute, a little girl described her stuttering as the fluttering of hummingbird wings in her throat as words cascade nonstop out her mouth. While the audience seemed to think this was a pretty metaphor, I found it particularly terrifying—a throat scratched up by rapidly beating feathers. My son, on the other hand, feels as if he is drowning. The words are ensnared somewhere deep inside him until, catching his breath, he releases them. Then there is the painfulness of the sound *dddddd* for Ellis as his body freezes, face tight, eyes wide.

In the video performance *Life of Life*, Ellis collaborates with Alice Sheppard to create a powerful sound, text, and dance collage. Sheppard's dancing body is contained by the three walls of a cardboard box located in a field with tall grass and trees. Sheppard twists, inverts herself, heaves, and angles her body in beautiful ways, testing but never escaping the box's narrow confines. Careful not to break through the imaginary fourth wall of the box, her arm, now her feet, later her rounded shoulders push against the cardboard constraints. Her movement is accompanied by Ellis's solo singing and later the lush, melodic sounds of his saxophone. *Life of Life* is based around two newspaper advertisements for runaway slaves (one from Jamaica, the other from Pennsylvania). Both these archival advertisements identify the runaway slave in question as having speech impediments, as "having a stoppage in his speech." Sheppard's dancing is obscured at certain points by visual images of this archival material, which is initially awkwardly slapped over the footage of her moving body. Later, the performance shifts between Sheppard in the box and the print ads for runaway slaves. In the spaces and movement between the two, questions arise about fugitivity and what Ellis, using Saidiya Hartman's work, calls the "opacity of black noise"

(Ellis, Hartman, and Hunt). "Black noise," according to Saidiya Hartman in "Venus in Two Acts," refers to "shrieks, the moans, the nonsense, the opacity, which are always in excess of legibility and of the law and which hint at and embody aspirations that are wildly utopian, derelict to capitalism, and antithetical to its attendant discourse of Man" (12). The black noise that Ellis foregrounds, the "stoppage in his speech," exceeds not only the runaway advertisement as a gesture of the law but also the confines of the sentence. Inspired by M. NourbeSe Philip's work on the Zong, Ellis writes the lyrics of his songs by rearranging the words from the advertisements. In this way, he wrests away the utilitarian erasure of black life that these documents accomplish by insisting on the possibility of generating alternate meanings that are not bound by the archival document, the cardboard box, the prosaic sentence. What he says is crucially impacted by how he says it. The stutter, Ellis tells us, is a form of fugitive speech: "not just because it feels like when I am stuttering . . . that my voice leaves me, . . . escapes me, but also because it feels to me that the stutter itself escapes certain norms and structures and strictures of speech and verbal exchange" (Ellis et al.). Ellis sings the following words that, as they appear on screen, supplement and exceed normative strictures suggested by the cardboard box:

> The law pretends to stutter,
> the law pretends to stutter,
> the stutter is coffee for the runaways,
> the stutter is reward, the stutter is passage,
> the stutter is a high chariot, the stutter is a scar on speech,
> the stutter is a house for speech, the stutter is a horse for speech
> The stutter has run away from any government
> Stoppage that is passage that's stoppage that's passage. (Ellis and Sheppard)

The stutter, then, is the time of black fugitivity or "epiphenomenal time," an uneven oscillation between arrested movement and the free fall of words, between uninhabitable enclosed spaces and the power of dance that creates black sociality. And I, like Shelley Jackson in *Riddance*, "love this [thick] music" of black noise, "in which the tension between being unable to say and being unable to stop saying . . . that is most characteristic of the stutterer's speech [is] elevated to an aesthetic principle" (157). My son and I argue about reading, we paint quietly together, and we love each other in stuttering time.

A Note on Disciplinarity: Melting

In "On Being Area-Studied," Macharia uses as his entry point Neo Musangi's articulation of his queerness through the word *tala*. Musangi writes, "The thing that I am they call *tala*. . . . But *tala* is not even a name. It is a description. . . . To think of *tala* is to imagine a state of being and not being. Neither this nor that. This and that but not. I live as a description" ("On Being Area-Studied" 184). Macharia astutely points to what the use of indigenous words can elicit for us African scholars in the Western academy: an "instinctive recoil that says 'native informant'" (184). *Tala* can function as insider information that validates Western identitarian categories by providing analogous indigenous terms. It allows Queer Studies to largely dismiss contemporary Africa (with the possible exception of South Africa) as plagued by homophobic postcolonial state formations that obscure their supposedly more progressive precolonial past. *Tala* then can be celebrated as a reclamation of that queer identity *for* contemporary Africans by the Western episteme. Simply adding indigenous African examples to established fields such as Disability Studies falsely suggests that all examples from "other" parts of the world are stable and equivalent; in other words, this Kenyan example is posited as the same as this Ethiopian example in its value and across time and can therefore simply be added to dominant philosophical frameworks.

Tala for Musangi and Macharia is not so much inside information as it is an interrogation of the terms by which personhood and sociality have traditionally been defined. *Tala* flags the impossibility of translation, the incommensurability of terms, and the necessity to think about black queer relationality in ways that are not only located in the West. Similarly, beginning this book with *intabi* (a word that arises from a pedagogical moment from an African culture not my own)[7] demands a politics of relationality made historically and geographically concrete. By using *intabi*, I wish to complicate the universalizing dictates of Western identitarian categories. The reclamation of other languages with vastly different worldviews unsettles the undergirding imperial assumptions of individualism, with its identitarian categorizations where Otherness spectrally defines the universal subject. *Intabi* asks what queer, black diasporic, and disability studies have to "unlearn about [their] geohistories to encounter [the term] on shared ground? What fluencies would [these disciplines] . . . have to give up to enter into conversation with [*intabi*]?" (Macharia, "On Being Area-Studied" 185). The use of indigenous African words engages with the limits of various disciplinary formations, insisting on disparate configurations of time, space, the body, and movement that allow us to create an impossible black sociality that must be constantly renegotiated. *Intabi* provides oxygen to an extended bronchial network that links Hailu's swollen air passages to my son's stuttering to the hundreds of seropositive women in KwaZulu, Natal, my home, where HIV rates are among the highest in the world, without making any of them the same. The postcolony, as Achille Mbembe reminds us, is ultimately "a timespace characterized by proliferation and multiplicity" that exceeds historical and geographical limits (Höller). Guragigna, English, and Zulu; mountain, subtropical hills, and coastline; asthma, stuttering, and HIV—it "might be precisely . . . in the folds of multiple entangled temporalities, that [alternate knowledges] have the best chance of resisting 'the repetitions of colonial epistemes' that . . . 'rework' themselves into even the most unruly and dissident discourses" (Currier and Migraine-George 298).

I am not arguing, via *intabi*, that ethnicity is somehow more real than the social construction of race is. As Nyong'o in his citation of Alexander Weheliye insists, "No matter how far into the margins of representation one goes, no matter how deep into the history and prehistory of racial capitalism, one never arrives at any retrievable 'positive conception' of ethnicity from which to posit a pure lineage, freed of ambivalence" (180). Ethnicities are never redemptive or original; *intabi* is not a word that springs intact from an authentic cultural milieu. Instead, it is the word remembered by a young Texan woman in her negotiation of diasporic memory, belonging, and estrangement. It is an epistemology created out of her embodied response to an ancestral landscape, history, reconstructed ethnicities, and strangers on a hill.

Intabi is also not a metaphor, as Michael Davidson writes, that "politely ask[s] ['real' impaired persons] to step offstage once the metaphoric exchange is made" (*Concerto* xxi). Blackness does not stand in for disability, and disability for the alienation and disenfranchisement of blackness. Instead, my project thinks through disciplinarity itself—what Anjali Arondekar and Geeta Patel call its "historical freightedness" (153) as well as what kinds of knowledge our particular investments in field formations produce. Therí Pickens in *Black Madness: Mad Blackness* writes about how disciplinary fields have become increasingly segregated. For instance, Disability Studies as a field has benefited from the intellectual and activist work done by Black Studies and Women's Studies, and as such, race and gender are woven into the very warp and woof of the field. Pickens argues that despite this, "the principles of critical race studies tend to have a penumbral presence because disability studies rarely engages whiteness as a social position and often thinks of Blackness as a contribution rather than part of its construction" (7). This is part of the more general devaluing of blackness and Black Studies in its various iterations, a legacy of Western thought. What is needed, I would argue, is not so much an acknowledgment of the erasure of blackness and an indebtedness to the theoretical interventions of Women's Studies or Black Studies, for example (though this would be a good start). I am suggesting, as Arondekar and Patel do, that we need to rethink our disciplinary practices as messy performances of translation that resist the United States' and certain European countries' "hold as a homing device to which [alternate] . . . epistemologies [are] continually orientated" and profitably marketed (Arondekar and Patel 153).

I often wander into the busy crossroads where disability studies, queer studies, and race studies chafe against each other. But rather than attempting to arrive at a way to theoretically synthesize these unwieldy fields, I concentrate on those alternate and often untranslatable mappings of race, sexuality, differential embodiment, and movement that are often overlooked. Following in the footsteps of scholars like Moya Bailey and Izetta Mobley, I am interested in those "black feminist texts . . . [that] can provide a methodological map for the integration of disability, race, and gender, even when disability is not named as such" (22). As Julie Livingston reminds us, "disability's meanings are often buried in places with few markers" (7). I therefore focus on performances of the black body that take into account "sites [*not*] marked explicitly as about disability" (Kafer 9), as well as sites traditionally overlooked in the weighted calculus of intellectual value. These sites such as the often-lewd routines of Angolan kuduro street dancers posted on YouTube or the court proceedings that narrate conflicting stories of how the political detainee Ahmed Timol "flew" out a window to his death allow me to unearth the injury of history as it permeates the present and devastatingly reinvents itself in today's global economy.

Part of the chafing that comes about when I set various fields in conversation with one another is a profound tension that winds throughout this book, namely, the potentially exploitative and dangerous, as well as generative, relationships enabled by performances of disability as they rub against the creative acts of living with disability. Juxtaposing painful muscle spasms with "voluntary" virtuoso performances of spasmodic dance moves, for example, might give a reader pause: Am I saying that these are the same? After a talk and a workshopped choreographed performance piece about horizontality that ended with me and a group of five other dancers prone on the floor of a lecture hall, I was approached by a white friend of mine in a wheelchair. As I dusted my clothes off, my friend struggled with how direct to be with his criticism. "But you get to stand up and go home," he stated as I buckled a delicate shoe strap around my ankle and stood up, all one and a half meters of me towering over him in his wheelchair. "You are . . . um . . . upright," he wryly noted after searching for the word. I was immediately ashamed. I had made horizontality seem like play-acting with my words and movement. I had inadvertently replicated a binary between voluntarily performing and the enforced horizontality of surplus populations who are always overshadowed by the specter of death.

My friend's question exposed the limits of performance as a frame and as a method, especially if we consider performances of differential movement as an *imitation* of disabled movement by able-bodied subjects. Performance, he was arguing, reduces and erases the lived experiences of disability, further continuing the ontological dominance of the normate body that mimics disability. As I develop particularly in chapter 4, examples of this kind of blatant "cripping up" or the appropriation of disability do occur. But rather than decide that because of these various discouraging instances, performance as a field has little to contribute to Disability Studies, what happens if we assert that performance allows for differential embodiment and movement by insisting on disparate epistemological and ontological positions that are always in relation to one another? As Eliza Chandler and Megan Johnson write, reducing all performances of disability as imitation rests on ableist understandings of the "always-already neutrality encased in the normative body" (387). Chandler and Johnson, by way of Carrie Sandahl,[8] develop that traditionally only the able-bodied "neutral" body has been seen as capable of letting go of all its affective particularities in order to perform physical difference. My friend's astute question assumed that it was the "neutrality" of my particular body that enabled my imitation of horizontality, whereas his marked body would disallow him to similarly perform horizontality. Leaving aside for the time being misperceptions of my able-bodiedness, my friend's potential performance of horizontality versus mine would reveal not the imitation of narrowly defined performative parameters of horizontality but rather a wide array of what constitutes differential embodiment and movement. Similarly in chapter 1, I discuss how the beggars in Sierra Leone's creative ability (not disability) to navigate their daily lives, to bathe, clean, use cellphones, and fuck, disrupts humanist notions of the autonomous, capable body, in which humanity is associated with verticality or being upright. I compare their abilities alongside the difficulty that Ogunji and Pope.L have crawling and lurching down a street. Rather than the "neutrality" of their able-bodiedness enabling a more dexterous performance that imitates the creativity of "real crawlers," Ogunji's and Pope.L's repertoires of movements work productively alongside the Sierra Leonian beggars. Their movements expand repertoires of privileged movement already remade by the disorienting corporeal practices of survivors of polio in Sierra Leone.

Implicit in the critique of performance as derivative of disabled people at best and exploitative at worst is the idea of the original or real as temporally prior to an inauthentic copy. The "real" disabled person as original precedes the imitative performance as copy. This temporalization is based on "the assumption that a character cannot be built from a position of physical difference" (Sandahl, "Tyranny" 260). This tends to overlook the work that differentially embodied performers so skillfully produce, whereby they do not imitate normative culture but instead reimagine repertoires of embodied movement. Chandler and Johnson use the example of the British comedian and theater actor Jess Thom, cofounder of Touretteshero,[9] and her performance of Samuel Beckett's *Not I* to analyze how disabled actors can expand performative vocabularies. *Not I* is a short modernist play with two characters: Mouth, a disembodied mouth suspended high above the stage that talks constantly, and Auditor, a silent presence who stands to the side of stage. Mouth delivers the urgent monologue of the play at frantic speeds, requiring a verbal dexterity made that much more challenging by the Beckett estate's insistence on faithfulness to Beckett's written words. Thom's performance includes several of her vocal tics that reorient Beckett's play itself. Chandler and Johnson write, "Though her tics interrupt the flow of Beckett's words at varying intervals (and as varying intensity and duration), the staccato nature of Thom's tics do not detract from the fragmented aesthetic of the original text. Rather, there is a generative dialogue that emerges from the dance between the scripted text and Thom's unscripted vocal interjections. . . . Thom's imitation sidesteps the requirements of the 'neutral body' in actor training traditions. Instead, Thom's rendition of the play embraces the creative possibilities that emerge from centering disability, disability aesthetics, and accessibility (395)."

Performances of disability thus are not simply imitations of lived experiences of disability. They are not indexes only of loss and limitation but also critically about radical, disruptive ways of reimagining *all* embodiment as the basis of (black) community. Polio sufferers navigating down stairs, a performer spasming in a music video, an actor with Tourette's syndrome whose vocal tic often includes the word "biscuits"—recognizing the generative richness of these moments means also never losing sight of the danger of cultural appropriation. Moving, listening, and speaking along this razor's edge of innovation and appropriation necessitates a radical politics of black sociality in which ability and disability are constantly reorienting themselves in relation to one another and in which differential embodiment and movement form the foundation for an impossible yet as-necessary-as-breathing radical fugitivity.

This book is also indebted to dance studies, as the concept of "choreography" undergirds much of my discussion on differential movement. Choreography sometimes operates as a mode of theoretical practice or as a signifier of dance. It stands in for the ways we move through space, and crucially it is a tenuous and trembling embodied encounter between space, stillness, pain, dexterity, and (non)virtuosic movement. In *The*

Choreographic, Jenn Joy writes that "to engage choreographically is to position oneself in relation to another, to participate in a scene of address that anticipates and requires a particular mode of attention" (1). Joy describes this address as a "precarious encounter" or "dialogic opening" across a landscape strewn with violence. Importantly, this opening occurs not just between you and me but also between the art that "is not only looked at but also looks back" (1). Hailu being embraced by strangers is choreography on a hill but also in the classroom as I encounter the performance piece that she created and it encounters me as audience. These historically contextualized openings, Joy summarizes, are characterized by a series of "stutters, steps, trembles and spasms," a melting of "exhausted limbs" that "open[s] up more promiscuous and irrational, sensual and critical possibilities for the making and writing of art" (1, 13, 4). Borrowing the notion from Boris Charmatz, Joy foregrounds choreography as a melting where one sinks slowly into an encounter. As limbs grow heavy, the body moves voluntarily and involuntarily to assume the shape of its surroundings and the edges of where I end and you begin to blur. Melting centers disorientation and uncertainty. It is a complicated encounter that runs "contrary to the pedagogy of sitting [as well as seeing and thinking] straight" (Joy 13).

In "Choreography as a Cenotaph: The Memory of Movement," Gabrielle Brandstetter points out that choreography also stages an encounter between a material performance and that which is no longer being present, between life and death. She writes, "This space between the material and the immaterial world opens and closes by means of the gesture of turning, by the torsion of the body which 'holds open the door to the grave'" (103). Turning toward each other and falling out of movement, we melt into the space of the encounter—the car as an African Uber driver navigates the streets of Paris, a back alley in Angola, an empty bullfighting arena, a mode that shifts between life and death. By recognizing how differential bodies melt, stumble, labor, and disappear, choreography as precarious encounter helps establish what Rachel C. Lee calls "the nonsovereignty and nonautonomy of biological life processes and species-being" (160). Choreography recomposes and refigures the self, challenging our understandings of normally embodied humans and animals. It puts together the body in different ways, surprising us as we arrive at "unexpected innovation and embodied understanding, . . . demonstrating the inexhaustible [in]capacities of . . . bodies" (DeFrantz, "*This Is America*").

As I rub each of these various disciplines uncomfortably against each other, I would be remiss not to mention Macharia's theoretical deployment of the word "frottage." In *Frottage: Frictions of Intimacy across the Black Diaspora*, Macharia wishes to "privilege conceptual and affective proximity: the rubbing produced by and as blackness, which assembles into one frame multiple histories and geographies. . . . Frottage . . . suggest[s] diaspora as a multiplicity of sense-apprehensions, including recognition, disorientation, compassion, pity, disgust, condescension, lust, titillation, arousal, and exhaustion, . . . the frictions and irritations and translations and mistranslations" (5, 7). Macharia borrows the term "frottage" from queer sexual and artistic practice, centering queerness as a methodology. The haptic performance of chafing and rubbing together that reveals the traces of what has come before allows Macharia to theorize a black queer diaspora that does not congeal around the fantasy of black like-mindedness or genealogical sameness. Tiffany Lethabo King also writes about "Black thought, movement, aesthetics, resistance, and lived experience . . . as a form of chafing and rubbing up against the normative flows of Western thought" (2). Putting the concept of frottage together with differential embodiment and movement, I want to ask what would rubbing together feel like, if I experience the chafing of my own skin while also assuming responsibility for the condition of yours (*intabi*)? What is frottage if I understand you and me not to be separate bodies but conjoined, differentially embodied beings? Something more than either one of us emerges from the multiplicity of sense-apprehensions and from our difference that forms the basis of our accountability for one another. Eli Clare's gorgeous writing in *Brilliant Imperfections* also reminds us that frottage might too quickly become another word that privileges normative movements. Clare insists on recognizing differential movements by those of us who can't rub against each other but instead tremor and spasm. They describe a scene of intimacy as they lie with their partner, exhausted after a long day:

> Your hands twitch, twitch again, on my skin. I answer with a tremor, starting as always behind my right shoulder blade, descending my arm. My touch vibrates into you. Your hands twitch and curl over me, trigger-

> ing a cascade of tremors. Slow, slow—my muscles don't lock. Tremors rise to meet twitches, call and response. I've had lovers tell me how good my shaky touch feels, tremors likened to extra caresses or driving over a gravel road, their words an antidote to shame. But until now, I had never felt the pleasure they describe. Your twitches spread across my skin—tingle, echo, dance. (19)

This is the imaginative ebb and flow of sociality that allows something dangerous and beautiful to emerge. A call and a response across and through our differences. A differentially embodied choreography of intimacy in which we rub, chafe, tremor, spasm, and fly in each other's arms. Each chapter in this book is organized around verbs. Floating. Flickering. Falling and Crawling. Spasming and Passing Out. Shaking. Thinking. Unhinging. As McKittrick reminds us, "viewing black texts as verbs rather than nouns, engendering interhuman relationalities, asking the groove and the poem for theoretical insight" are all ways of reimagining black sociality (*Dear Science* 52). These verbs are a call and response between the senses (breathing, seeing, feeling, hurting) and between a vast array of texts (literary, visual, choreographic, haptic, and autobiographical). The chapters meander, veer off course, breathe, circle, always circle what it means to be black, differentially embodied and living in a time of grief and anger. They insist on what Bailey and Mobley call a "radical liberatory corporeal politics that imagines and makes space for truly free Black bodies of all abilities" (26).

Falling and Crawling

Chapter 1 begins with Boris Gerrets's visually arresting film *Shado'Man* (2013), which documents the life of the Freetown Streetboys, a group of disabled men and women residing in Freetown, Sierra Leone. The visually arresting film, I argue, perpetuates the myth of human rights as a marker of progress with the Global North leading the way for disability rights. Instead, in this chapter, I wish to decolonize African disability studies by asking how scholars, performers, activists, and cultural practitioners can theorize a disorienting politics of moving that contests the normalization of verticality. What kinds of embodied reimagining arise when we beg, squat, crawl, lean, and fall? The chapter situates the queer

American/Nigerian artist Wura-Natasha Ogunji's piece *Will I still carry water when I am a dead woman?* in its multiple iterations, alongside work by the queer African American William Pope L. and various accounts of quotidian performances of the polio-disabled in Sierra Leone. If, as Telory Davies states, to be horizontal is both "an aesthetic modality" and "an egalitarian political gesture" (46), then verticality or uprightness should no longer be figured as an essential index of human value.

I purposively do not use Deleuze-Guattarian notions of rhizomatic assemblages in this chapter as I remain deeply invested in the politics of citation. As Alexander Weheliye writes in *Habeas Viscus*, "the challenges posed by the smooth operations of western Man since the 1960s by continental thought and minority discourse, though historically, conceptually, institutionally, and political relational, tend to be segregated, because minority discourses seemingly cannot inhabit the space of proper theoretical reflection" (9). While many people have widely adopted Gilles Deleuze and Félix Guattari's notion of the American western frontier as an idealized landscape of rhizomatic, horizontal connections, assemblages, and ruptures that function as modes of cultural and political liberatory "becoming," I have chosen to cite other sources for two reasons. Consider the following, famous and deeply disturbing passage from *A Thousand Plateaus* about a "rhizomatic West, with its Indians without ancestry, its ever-receding limit, its shifting and displaced frontiers. There is a whole American 'map' in the West, where even the trees are rhizomes" (Deleuze and Guattari 19). Through descriptions of the West as an expansive (physical and symbolic) terrain, largely open to whites for the taking due to the inadequate claims of the indigenous people who live there, the passages recapitulate the logic of settler colonialism. Rather than rhizomatic deterritorializations offering liberatory possibilities, we see through judicial orders the violent horizontal extensions of imperialism as it forcibly deracinates native peoples. Scholars such as Alex Trimble Young and Tiffany King thus conclude that simply applying Deleuze-Guattarian concepts of rhizomatic assemblages uncritically to conceptualize liberatory projects does so at the expense of Native people (Byrd; A. Young; T. King).[10]

Instead, in chapter 1, I insist on African diasporic movement practice as theory. I thus reach toward vocabularies that emerge from the performative movement itself and that enable theorizations of conjoined black sociality that answer back to, rather than rely on, settler logics of expansion. The chapter thus revolves around new kinds of sociality that emerge from conjoined, not-quite-human bodies moving differently across city landscapes. I focus on the gendered dynamics of horizontality, Egungun traditions, and the inherent vulnerability of prostrated bodies. Can the imagined possibilities that arise from such performances include a queer erotic intimacy with the ground? Ogunji's piece also draws attention to the shortage of potable water in Nigeria and the failure of this oil-rich country to establish an efficient infrastructure for delivering this water to its citizens. Using the fact that women are the primary procurers of water in Nigeria and that they carry these heavy loads on their head using a special gait, I stress how Ogunji's performance helps make women's embodied labor visible. I also discuss how the spiritual, evoked by Ogunji's reference to Egungun masqueraders, requires us to fall or "drop[] into the blaze of the unknown" (Dent and Thompson 8) as we meaningfully engage with the sacred. The chapter ends with a critique of horizontality as only an index of black death. Looking at the South African political prisoner Ahmed Timol's dive and "horizontal" fall out the window of an interrogation room, I consider the extent to which we can reclaim the horizontal as an alternate mode of black sociality that reimagines our lives as well as our deaths.

Floating

Chapter 2 begins with a powerful short film by Creative Interruptions called *Unburied* (2019), about a migrant taxi driver in a European country, listening as the radio announces the number of corpses recently found washed up on Europe's shores. These are the often-nameless men and women from Syria, Eritrea, South Sudan, Libya, and Tunisia who attempt and fail to cross the Mediterranean Sea in order to enter into the European Union. The film mourns the dead through an "intersensorial mingling," a sensory form of scholarship that forms part of what Eunjung Kim calls "necro-activism." The dead are not merely symbols around which we have to organize our calls for justice. Instead, they "enliven and depend on the labor of the living [in order to enact our] interconnected futures" (Kim, "Continuing Presence" 15). The dead and the living are conjoined in a way that demands imaginative ways of thinking through black sociality and that reconfigure the black body. The chapter discusses how the bodies of migrants crossing the Mediterranean are abstracted, in particular by European border-surveillance systems that reduce the body to what Denise Ferreira da Silva in *Toward a Global Idea of Race* calls the "transparent I" (a transcendent universal rational subjectivity). In order to counter this abstraction that has lived on after slavery and colonialism, I propose intersensoriality or a haptic sociality using the work of Fred Moten and Stefano Harney, Rizvana Bradley, Katherine McKittrick, and Christina Sharpe. I specifically move the conversation of a haptic undercommons away from the model of transatlantic slavery to instead revolve around saltwater and the differential movement of floating. The bulk of the chapter develops this idea of a haptic undercommons in performances that feature submerged bodies and the sea or dead bodies at the water's edge. I focus on the "colored" South African artist Berni Searle's performance piece *Home and Away* (2003), in which she floats in the Mediterranean as a voice-over whispers, "I feel, you feel, we feel. . . ." The chapter concludes with a discussion of vitreous opacities, commonly known as "floaters"—dark shadows, spots, strands, squiggly lines that appear in one's field of vision. Floaters, I argue, constitute another form of differential embodiment and movement that allows us to look at the dead and see that which we would otherwise be blind to.

Flickering

In chapter 3, using the performances of the South African Nandipha Mntambo and the journalist/novelist Lauren Beukes's novel *Zoo City* (2010), I attempt to catch sight of the flickering oscillations between human and animal in order to reimagine black value through a sociality that does not make recourse to liberal humanism.[11] The flickering between the human and animal also crucially reveals the jagged edges of human ontology, allowing us to follow Rosemarie Garland-Thomson's charge to explore what types of "knowledge might be produced through having a body radically marked by its own particularity, a body that materializes at the ends of the curve of human variation" ("Integrating Disability" 20). As a counterpoint to Robbyne Kaamil's award-winning yet deeply troubling video *Animal Captivity Is Slavery* (2015), made for

PETA, I focus on Mntambo's video performance *Ukungenisa* (2009), shot in an abandoned bullfighting arena in Mozambique. Mntambo, who was trained as a taxidermist and whose work arranges cowhides into humanoid shapes, wears a cowhide bustle made from cow ears, faces, and tails sealed in resin and polyester mesh for the performance. She performs as both bullfighter and bull in tightly choreographed sequences that unsettle human-animal distinctions, not in order to claim that animals are just as valuable as people but instead to unsettle our belief that normatively embodied humans are the epitome of value. I continue this discussion in my study of *Zoo City*, which imagines a science-fiction world where human criminals are conjoined with animals as punishment, creating a subclass of humans called "zoos." These differentially embodied zoos are examples of the politics of conjoinment, what Cristin Ellis in *Antebellum Posthuman* calls a "mutuality of being" (151) as they expose as chimera the fantasies of whole, singular, independent actors. I pay close attention to the murder in the novel of a transgender sex worker and her brown sparrow, showing how the severing of relationality, of the conjoined, is key to the extraction of value from black bodies. The chapter ends with an epilogue on Nigerian Ruby Amanze's mixed-media drawing *That low hanging kind of sun . . .* , which depicts an African mermaid figure and the character of Twin, a conjoined body missing its head.

Spasming and Passing Out

In chapter 4, I look specifically at Spoek Mathambo's video "Control," a cover of Joy Division's "She's Lost Control," and the controversial Die Antwoord's short film/video "Umshini Wam" to develop whether spasming and passing out can constitute alternate modalities of movement. In "Umshini Wam," Die Antwoord depict themselves as wheelchair-bound and juxtapose images of their faces and bodies with those of people who are living with various illnesses. Ninja (Watkins Tudo Jones) sporadically passes out throughout the video, his wheel spinning in the air as his chair capsizes. Spoek Mathambo depicts the spasm passing through the Cape dance troupe Happy Feet like a contagion as the dancers fall against each other. Can the spasm (real and enacted) interrupt teleological time to insist on bodies that are always in and out of control?

Does the performance of suddenly passing out with the body limp, its vulnerability on display, signal an opportunity for, or the foreclosure of, black sociality?

Both Die Antwoord's and Spoek Mathambo's work is replete with images of differentially embodied, racialized subjects who roll, spasm, and pass out to the relentless beat of popular music. On the one hand, it would be easy to dismiss both performers if the "authenticity" of performances of disability rests solely on an essential politics of black disabled bodies. While it is important that differentially embodied people represent themselves, can performances of differential movement and embodiment by nondisabled people advance an insurgent politics? In other words, can nonessentialized performances of disability work not to reinforce notions of self-mastery but instead to open up new ways of being black and embodied in the world? Die Antwoord, I argue, traffic in discourses of Otherness, or what David Hevey in *The Creatures Time Forgot* calls "enfreakment" (53), to compensate for what they feel is a crisis of the legitimacy of whiteness in South Africa. Die Antwoord legitimizes ableism by exploiting the fungibility of difference as a market commodity. Their performances demonstrate how the aesthetic depiction of differential movement can parody disabled people, reinforcing the universal, able-bodied subject.

On the other hand, Spoek Mathambo's "Control," in its performance of the "spasm" that runs through a group of dancers, insists on the importance of differential movement and embodiment in thinking through wounded black flesh. The spasm, even as it rehearses a particular mastery of one's body, also necessitates a surrendering to uncontrolled movement. The spasm is what Melissa Blanco Borelli calls a "productive corporeal interruption" (58) as it pushes the body beyond willful performance toward a surrender to unexpected movement that emerges from the performance itself. Spoek Mathambo also places the spasm in the context of African spirit possession and mediumship. Unlike Die Antwoord, who appropriate disability without acknowledging from whom they are borrowing, Spoek Mathambo anchors the spasm within specific histories of disabled performers and African spiritual practices in order to reimagine the black social body. He thinks through the effects of violence on the black body while evoking an array of rituals of healing from various religions. The end result is brief glimpses of a nonidentitarian community, based on the body's vulnerability when it falls out of time, and the embodied ritual that gathers up the spasming body and holds it close—a palm is pressed against another's forehead to calm a seizure, a young boy's head is doused in water as in baptism.

Shaking the World

Chapter 5 uses Chris Abani's novella *Song for Night* and the Angolan popular music and dance form kuduro to meander through a conversation about liminal bodies, (un)death, and differential movement. Instead of the floating dead of chapter 2, this chapter pays respect to the walking dead or zombies as My Luck, a mute child soldier separated from his platoon in *Song for Night*, retraces his steps across a war-ravaged landscape after being killed by a landmine. Each chapter of *Song for Night* is organized around a sign or gesture that the platoon uses to communicate as all their vocal cords have been severed. For example, dreaming is "Hands Held in Prayer over the Nose," and silence is a "Steady Hand, Palm Flat." Rather than this sign language being a rudimentary approximation of speech, I argue that signing is an embodied sensuous interaction that establishes black sociality through differential embodiment and movement. This signing is part of the platoon's larger choreographic repertoire, in which the soldiers clear the earth around landmines with bare feet and naked toes and playfully tap rhythms on the barrels of their guns. The beauty and power of differential movement are encapsulated best in the novella by a single scene when the child soldiers encounter a group of "half-people holding onto life" (Abani, *Song* 50) and witness a group of differentially embodied children dancing in a circle. A young girl with one leg teases that she can do better, and when challenged, she throws away her crutch and jumps into the middle of the circle, moving as though she were "an elemental force of nature" (Abani, *Song* 51). In this scene of a "small fire sprite shaking the world" (Abani, *Song* 51), we see the power of differential embodiment and movement emerge as the substrate of black sociality. This sociality does not transcend the deathly frictions of war or the pain of injury. Instead, the girl's one-legged dance is an example of what I call "imaginative excess": creative acts that are not examples of the ahistorical enfreakment, discussed in chapter 4, but instead give rise to black sociality based on a critical defamiliarization of scripted performances in order to generate new meaning. These acts allow for profoundly political ways of interacting with a historical landscape of imperialism and war. Moving from novella to popular dance form, I turn to the Angolan dance and music form kuduro as it resides at the intersections between (un)death, war, differential movement, and embodiment. Kuduro as an Angolan music and dance type successfully incorporates both differentially embodied dancers and the embodied vocabulary of amputees to create a performance style that imaginatively exceeds the strictures of the world around them. Paying close attention to particular dance steps, or *toques*, such as lying dead or making ugly faces, I detail how kuduristas signify on life after the devastation of colonial and civil wars, which have resulted in many of them being differentially embodied. Kuduro is also fundamentally a spatial performance practice that while drawing attention to the segregation of Luanda also remaps the city and thus attempts to imagine a future of greater equity.

Unhinging

Chapter 6 is an experiment in unhinged thinking situated within neurodiversity. Thinking and writing, I argue, is not the product of an individual brain whose firing synapses snappily produce great thoughts. This book is not evidence of the dexterity of my scholarship or how smart or dumb I may be. Instead, it is a product of what Mel Chen in "Brain Fog: The Race for Cripistemology" terms a "decolonizing cripistemology" (182)—a way of producing knowledge that is haptic, collaborative across difference, and sometimes painfully embodied. Unhinging myself from disciplined thinking in various ways such as writing scenes with dialogue meant to be performed by the reader, I begin by showing how my attempts to write the chapter collaboratively with various colleagues "failed." As McKittrick notes, cowriting opens doors between disciplines, diverse neural pathways, racial identifications, and ancestral memory and is "a form of life that cannot be totally capitalized on and is therefore slightly in excess of work as we know it. . . . Working in friendship could be a way to work outside of productivist demands" (*Dear Science* 73). My "failure" to cowrite the chapter shows how real the demands on production are for differentially embodied/women of color in the academy.

But it also draws attention to how much my various colleagues, despite not cowriting the chapter, influenced the shape, texture, and depth of my thought. Their poetry, their refusals, their sea-creature emojis, their laughter, and their exhaustion saturate this chapter that is anything but a solo performance.

In order to develop the value of collective, undisciplined, and incoherent thinking, I turn to Rivers Solomon's *An Unkindness of Ghosts*, in which the main character is described as neuroatypical. Readers repeatedly diagnose her as autistic. Thinking through diagnostic categories, I move away from pathologizing the way she thinks, insisting on the generative possibilities of what I call "neurocacophony"—different kinds of thinking that interact noisily and sometimes painfully. Aster's individual way of thinking—her practical literalism—must work alongside, for example, her friend Giselle's contradictory metaphoric leaps, angry absences, and acts of arson in order to solve the mystery of her mother's demise and the ship's deterioration. Singular, individual modes of cognition are not enough, nor do these various modes come together harmoniously. Rather, cognition is collectively embodied in affective, cultural performative rehearsals of knowing that are riotous, messy, undisciplined, and painful. This cripistemology/neurocacophony, the novel argues, is absolutely necessary to surviving violent racial and gender oppression and to mapping new ways of being and moving. The chapter calls for a "noise riot": the creation of embodied, nonproductive, multivalent, blurred, and crooked thinking in order to claim the "demonic" ground necessary for a black sociality located in the epiphenomenal present.

1

Falling and Crawling

Eli could not accept this. Again and again, he tried to teach Jacob to walk upright. A human child walked upright. A boy, a man, walked upright. No son of Eli's would run on all fours like a dog."
—Octavia Butler, *Clay's Ark*

Introduction: Moving Out of the Dark

Boris Gerrets's visually arresting film *Shado'Man* (2013) documents the life of the Freetown Streetboys, a group of disabled men and women residing in the areas around the junction of Light-foot Boston and Wilberforce in downtown Freetown, Sierra Leone. The film begins in the dark with a creaking of wheels, the staccato rhythm of crutches, the sound of body parts scraping along the ground. We begin to see limbs, bodies, and before long, what appears to be a veritable army of the disabled emerge from the darkness. *Shado'Man* is filmed entirely at night, and the only illumination provided is from nearby streetlights, passing cars, the glow of cellphones, and, occasionally, beams fixed to Gerrets's cameras. Throughout the film, the stories of Lama and David, both blind, Shero and the pregnant Sarah, and Alfred and Suley are woven together to create a bleak story about familial and social abandonment, dire poverty, and a violent urban landscape. An IDFA review labels the film a "mega-urban dystopia" about "the most disadvantaged members of society." The film's "impressionistic results," the review continues, "will appeal to programmers of the more adventurous festivals and those specializing in human-rights issues" ("Shado'Man").

What makes *Shado'Man* particularly visually striking is Gerrets's choice to film almost entirely in the dark. On the one hand, the difficulty the viewer has in seeing clearly draws attention to David's and Lama's lack of sight, emphasizing the visceral quality of their blindness and the thickness of night and shadow. However, Gerrets is also obviously concerned with shining light on that which has been neglected, unseen, and overlooked. He writes in his director's note,

> Something in their world reminded me of the universe of Beckett: the cosmic darkness of a stage, the absence of life's ornamentations, the waiting for a salvation that won't come, a sense of timelessness; and that fact that, like in a Beckett play they have their tragedy written on their body. . . . As they live as outsiders at the periphery of society, I feel that their lives reveal our human condition more truthfully. . . . If film is indeed shadow and if shadows heal, can the film restore the human dignity of which the protagonists have been deprived? (Gerrets)

Many of the ideas that circulate in the preceding passage replicate a liberal discourse of tragic Africans, waiting for their "human dignity" to be restored, ostensibly by Gerrets's camera. The stark contrast between us (the civilized West) and them (Africans without a history, "timeless") replicates what Benedicte Ingstad in "The Myth of Disability in Developing Nations" calls "the myth of the hidden disabled" (757). Due to tribal Africans' primitive cultural beliefs, we are told repeatedly, they hide or lock away their disabled, as they believe them "evil," "possessed," less than human, and "shameful." Thus, Emmelie Andregård and Lina Magnusson tell us that some children who are differentially embodied are called *debulpikin* in Krio, meaning "devil" or "demon child" (2623). Their essay explicitly concludes that "traditional beliefs can cause discrimination and have a negative impact on people with physical disability" (2623). There is no denying that those who are differentially embodied can be met with cruelty, prejudice, and sequestration. But to assign this only to non-Western cultures and to generalize such behavior as "cultural" tradition retains the inherent superiority of the "rational" West as the beacon of "humanitarian" light that illuminates the dark corners of the globe. As Diana Szántó notes in her powerful book *Politicising Polio: Disability, Civil Society and Civic Agency in Sierra Leone*, "the insistence that 'culture' is blocking the exercise of rights by disabled people may be used to wage a deadly war against life-worlds not totally compatible with present forms of 'predatory capitalism'"

(191). Factors such as dire poverty, the lack of access to medical care and knowledge, the privatization and/or absence of public services in Sierra Leone, and the disruptions of familial support structures due to regimes of war take a backseat to explanations of an unsophisticated cultural prejudice. Disability becomes part of neoliberal development agendas in which "individualised, short-term, one off interventions [are prioritized], targeting disabled individuals rather than their communities, let alone society as a whole" (Szántó 176). The same structural inequities that have been inherited from imperialism and that benefit the West today are left quietly festering. Applying human rights discourse to disabled Africans has furthered these inequities by privileging the moral superiority and modernization projects of a global necropolitical regime of predatory capital. It is no accident then that the homepage for *Shado'Man* contains an epigraph from George Berkeley (1685–1753): "Esse est percipi. To be is to be perceived." Gerrets hopes that his film brings the story of the "hidden" disabled out into the light as he reveals the concealed humanity of the Freetown Streetboys. In doing so, he perpetuates the myth of human rights as a marker of progress with the Global North leading the way for disability rights.

Rather than shining a spotlight on disabled people who supposedly would otherwise be kept in the dark by the supposed ignorance of people in the Global South, I hope in this chapter to decolonize African disability studies by raising a series of questions: How can scholars, performers, activists, and cultural practitioners theorize a politics of moving differently through an urban landscape? What are the connections between the ground beneath their bodies and a vibrant population of the lurching, crawling, and falling as they navigate large urban cities in Africa? How do the poetics and politics of a horizontal differential embodiment and movement contest the normalization of verticality? Instead of thinking of every act of falling, leaning, and crawling as an opportunity to, in the parlance of self-help books, "get back on one's feet," I wonder what can be gained from lingering on the ground and using alternate kinetic modes as performances of disorientation that depart from verticality. I argue that modernity's emphasis on spectacles of ceaseless, upright motility discounts differential embodiments and ways of moving, presenting these bodily forms as "heroic" but ultimately "inferior." This chapter focuses on several disorienting modes of moving that depart from verticality: begging, squatting, crawling, leaning, and falling. Each of these modes constitutes a vibrant performative cultural practice that refuses Western humanitarian discourses of rights based on the human, even as it demonstrates vibrant ways that Africans reimagine their bodies, the ways they move and the spaces they occupy. In order to do this, this chapter zig-zags across the African diaspora. We look at Sierra Leone, Nigeria, South Africa, and the United States, moving awkwardly from real-life performances of the polio-disabled and the murdered to performance pieces by the award-winning queer African American and Nigerian artist Wura-Natasha Ogunji's *Will I still carry water when I am a dead woman?* (2011) and William Pope.L, the self-proclaimed "Friendliest Black Artist in America."[1] This juxtaposing of different sites is partly due to the predominance of interventionist rights-based reports and the dearth of performative texts on disability in African countries. Importantly, it also allows me to situate various African countries within a global necropolitical economy. By toggling between the quotidian performances of polio-disabled beggars in Sierra Leone, the artwork by Ogunji and Pope.L, and Ahmed Timol's historical horizontal fall out of a window, I investigate how black sociality might be imagined through differential embodiments and movements based on horizontality. As Telory Davies states, to be horizontal is both "an aesthetic modality and an egalitarian gesture" (46). While verticality or uprightness has long been figured as an essential index of one's value as a human being, I would like to posit instead a new kind of sociality that emerges from conjoined, not-quite-human bodies moving differently across shifting sociogeographic terrains.

Squatting and Begging

Imagine us making our own film, also set in Sierra Leone, about people living with polio. Perhaps it is the beginning of 2009, and we are in a two-story house on Walpole Street, a polio-squat.[2] Dawn sees a group of a hundred or more squatters, most of them survivors of polio, readying themselves for the day. Many have their own spaces, there are magazine pictures on the wall, a family has claimed a space over there, and elsewhere a baby sucks on her fingers, watching her mother intently. Her mother wears worn-out calipers that often cause her pain. Her crutches lean against the wall as she fixes her hair. Another man crawls with his phone in his mouth toward a communal bucket of water used for bathing. This bucket was filled last night by a nondisabled family member of one of the other squatters. The staircase behind us is steep, missing steps, and we watch a man make his way to his wheelchair, using wooden slats that have previously been laid down.[3] There is a rhythm to the morning preparations, a complex interplay of dependency, fierce determination and creativity, exhaustion and pain in these "self-organising polio communities" (Szántó ix). As it is Friday, this community of squatters is readying itself for the collective performance of begging.

For Muslims, the blessings derived from offering charity, either *zakat* or *sadaqah*, are multiplied when given on Jumanah (Friday).[4] Even in cities that also have a large Christian population, like Freetown, Sierra Leone, this Islamic tradition of *zakat* and *sadaqah* has resulted in Fridays being the day when beggars flock to town. Those people who on any other day would walk by find themselves digging into their pockets for change to distribute to beggars who crowd the pavements and street corners. Amputees on crutches and in wheelchairs (who predominantly tend to be war veterans), people with congenital diseases, former child soldiers, and our large group of polio survivors from Walpole Street and other squats rub shoulders with raucous street sellers, *okada* (bike) and *poda poda* (minivan) drivers, and their passengers as the city breathes dustily around them.[5]

So thoroughly intertwined is the idea of disability and the public performance of begging that the creole words for "cripples" (*cripulden*) and "beggars" (*dregmanden*) are often interchangeable.[6] These disabled are not hidden in the shadows, only emerging in the dark, but instead form an integral part not only of the city's economy but of its physical and political landscape. While excluded from official systems, as Szántó argues, "the territorialized sub-systems of the squats are not cut-off from the mainstream. In fact, they are connected by a multitude of links to the 'mainstream' and its public spaces, beginning with the street" (72). The street thus becomes a public-facing stage for differentially embodied creative performances of begging. This is painstaking labor as the beggars work to instrumentalize the spectacularization of their differential embodiment. The possible evocation of able-bodied guilt, mixed with obligation, disgust, terror, and perhaps true compassion, hopefully will inspire the necessary generosity that will feed the beggars for a day or two.

Polio sufferers tend to be conjoined, a community of disabled and nondisabled who prefer to beg in large, gender-segregated groups. Those who live and beg alone are seen as "selfish" and even more vulnerable to the vicissitudes of the city. Mariama from the Hastings building explains, "Some people do not take the opportunity to live with disabled *compins*, they do not think about it. They do not have love for their fellow disabled; they do not even go close. So they cannot benefit, because they stay alone, they do not associate and they cannot get the benefit that comes with it" (Szántó 62). The solidarity and support that comes from living and working together, protecting each other from violence, and providing aid depending on different (physical) capabilities far outweighs not only the conflicts that can arise but also the benefits of keeping to oneself what one earns while begging.

People in Sierra Leone sometimes feel profound discomfort at what Mirey Ovadiya and Giuseppe Zampaglione describe as "well organized networks of beggars" (13). The deputy mayor of Freetown, for example, tells Szántó, "As soon as you group them together, like mind thinks alike. . . . There should be a way of integrating them in a way that they cannot keep together" (63). I would argue that this discomfort stems from the powerful potential inherent in the beggars' conjoinment, in their development of a collective identity. This collective identity doesn't revolve only around differential embodiment but also around poverty. The polio-disabled share the experience of contracting a sickness when young that changed their bodies, the way they move, and the way they live. The disruptions of the war meant many that polio sufferers wandered destitute around the countryside, eventually landing in Freetown, where they encountered not only other polio sufferers and disabled people but also the numerous displaced underprivileged in what is one of the poorest countries in the world. Ovadiya and Zampaglione reiterate, "Poverty is both a cause and consequence of disability. . . . Studies indicate that disability and poverty are mutually reinforcing; poor people tend to be disproportionately disabled and disabled people are disproportionately poor. Disability is both a cause as well as a consequence of poverty" (5). Thus, in strategically taking over abandoned buildings or displaying twisted limbs while congregating at street corners to beg for alms, these networks of beggars place their disability and poverty side by side. Their suffering, they insist, stems not only from polio but also from inadequate housing, the breakdown of health systems, and the privatization and erosion of essential services such as clean water and sanitation.

Polio-disabled people in particular have had to work harder to make their plight known, as they meet few of the criteria for international and governmental aid. Despite the failure of the state to immunize, prevent against, and treat polio, polio survivors do not fit neatly into categories of victims and perpetrators established by postwar compensatory structures such as international nongovernmental organizations (INGOs) to aid Sierra Leoneans. Governmental authorities also are uncertain about how to respond to the "ambiguous status of polio-disabled people—being not precisely compensable victims but still belonging to a vulnerable category" (Szántó 22). Unlike the wounded soldier with missing limbs whom I discuss in chapter 5, the polio survivor is often seen as a victim of fate rather than war. This ambivalence around the differentially embodied polio survivor means that the polio-disabled are often overlooked by the state and aid organizations. Yet their creative, collective informal mobilization has secured them a space within national and international discourse such that their squatting and begging within larger structures of authoritarian violence are largely tolerated and sometimes marginally supported.

The drastic reduction of cases of poliomyelitis has been one of the success stories of preventative vaccination, whether administered in the form of oral drops containing the attenuated live virus or the inactivated injected vaccine. The deep distrust between the "First" and "Third" World countries, a largely white medical establishment and black peoples, and the rich and the poor comes as a surprise to no one. What is astounding is the success of international collaborative efforts to eradicate the disease in the Global South. With the exception of Nigeria, Afghanistan, and Pakistan, the spread of poliomyelitis is thought to be largely controlled. How, then, do we account for the estimated ninety-eight thousand polio-disabled in Sierra Leone? This is where the less obvious ramifications of civil unrest and war start to become evident. Alongside the death and injury of citizens, the war in Sierra Leone disrupted medical services, resulting in several long-term effects.[7] Ovadiya and Zampaglione summarize, "As a result of conflict, . . . essential services, supplies, and logistics are damaged including the provision of clean water and sanitation, food, key infrastructure, as well as networks of communication. Essential preventive services such as disease control, immunization and supplementation programs, and campaign activities are thwarted. Further, as surveillance systems break down, the incidence and spread of disease cannot be tracked and treated adequately in a timely fashion" (10). The particular physical vulnerability of women affected with polio led to many becoming pregnant as a result of the sexual violence by soldiers.[8] Children with polio were orphaned, and with their support networks gone, those who survived often found their way to Freetown. The ramifications of civil unrest are far reaching and long term. Thus, the increased numbers of the polio-disabled and their inadequate treatment should be considered a direct consequence of the necropolitical postcolony and the mechanisms of civil war.

Poliomyelitis commonly occurs in young children between the ages of three and six. Usually contracted when children are exposed to the enterovirus through contaminated fecal matter, the virus attacks the nervous system, often causing severe pain and paralysis of limbs. Szántó describes the onset of the disease, as related to her by Manish or Abubakkar Sidiki. Born in 1985 in a small village, Manish describes how one day he fell and couldn't get up. "He walked, ran and played like other children until the disease struck him. Then, he fell down and the next thing he knew, he was not able to get up anymore. . . . He could [still] play, using a stick to drag himself around" (Szántó 14). As polio sufferers age, there can be a progression of muscle weakness, often accompanied by severe fatigue and increasing muscular and joint pain (sometimes known as post-polio syndrome). Mobility without assistance becomes increasingly more difficult. Given devastating poverty, many polio sufferers lack access to corrective surgery and assistive devices that help with mobility.

Such devices, Andregård and Magnusson conclude, are extremely important to the participants of their study. They interviewed some 425 households, and both nondisabled and disabled people alike repeatedly stated how important mobility was for the polio sufferer. The interviewee K notes, "Not all persons with disabilities are working or earning money. So let these things . . . be affordable for us. Most of our colleagues have gone back to [crawling on] the floor because orthotics are not available to them. So I am begging, let these things be affordable for us again" (Andregård and Magnusson 2622). Another participant in the study describes being house-bound for many years as he did not have assistive devices, which, he told interviewers, were really important to him: "Being able to stand up straight instead of crawling on the ground, and to move freely and dress neatly gave increased dignity . . . in society" (2622). Even though prolonged use of these devices caused the interviewees pain, participants nonetheless prioritized the maintenance and repair of their devices.

Implicit in these discussions is an emphasis on being upright as a marker of one's humanity, as a way to be more dignified. The story of Raymond and Pierre Jaccard provides an interesting case in point. Primarily working with lepers in Cameroon and later expanding to the polio-disabled, Raymond Jaccard along with his brother, Pierre Jaccard, developed a simple, adjustable prosthesis, made from local resources such as wood, roofing material, and laces. The prosthesis, adjustable to accommodate the shrinkage of limb stumps, does not differentiate between left and right limbs; nor does it allow for the articulation of knees and ankles. In a documentary titled *The Bare-Handed Prosthetists*, Raymond Jaccard narrates, "When you see a mother dragging herself along the ground because she has two diseased legs, God is also suffering as he sees this mother crawling along the ground. He created mankind to stand upright." Inspired by the Jaccard brothers, Belgium's humanitarian aid programs in the Democratic Republic of Congo also have focused on the production of corrective footwear. As Patrick Devlieger and Jori De Coster write, "The activity of fitting children with the device was thought to be humanizing, given that it enabled children to adopt an upright position in their mobility, replacing a mobility that hugs the ground (often mediated by hand and/or knee aids). Crawling rather than walking was seen as dehumanizing by the missionaries and also by the Congolese people themselves who compared this kind of mobility to that of the snake" (6). Devlieger and De Coster write of the relationship between body, shoe-clad foot, and the ground as a "dance of animacy," insisting that disability "appears as a set of alternative ways in which this triad, body-shoe-ground, is articulated, and is an inherent part of the humanization of humans" (9).

Even while anchoring my discussion in the very real plight of people with limited mobility, I would like to question this association of uprightness, of the normativity of the vertical, with the putative dignity of the human. What openings for differential embodiment and movement can arise if instead of putting everyone back on their feet, we accept the disorientation of the horizontal and move toward the not-quite-human? Rather than dismissing the horizontal, can we imagine ways of moving for our polio survivors that do not revolve solely around achieving uprightness but instead around material access to health care, housing, sanitation and comfort, and other ways of moving with dignity? Instead of Manish's fall being the onset of tragedy, can this moment be theorized as a pivotal disorientation that allows us access to the unknown? This chapter asks what happens if instead of avoiding particular moments of disorientation, we embrace their difficulty.

In "The Body as Archive," André Lepecki details the black body's ability to embody a history of racial subjugation. Rather than a traditional notion of a paper and artifact repository, he identifies the body as an archive in "its constitutive precariousness, perceptual blind-spots, . . . muscular tremors, memory lapses, bleedings, rages, and passions" (Lepecki, "Body as Archive" 34). Similarly, Darieck Scott in *Extravagant Abjection* reprises Frantz Fanon's use of muscle tension (present in several of his works) to describe that disorienting moment when the colonized body oscillates to the rhythm of a traumatic past.[9] Scott writes that Fanon's muscular tension "inheres in a nexus between bodily sensation and perception, and in the structure of consciousness itself. Thus, 'tensed muscles' represent a form of bodily (un)knowing that recognizes its existence in a history of defeat while instancing its unconscious preparation to meet and resist that defeat" (25). Fanon's disorientation then forces him to foreground the materiality of his racialized being in time and space. His body has exploded and then reassembled into another configuration marked by his Otherness, and he must respond to the new terrain by feeling and responding to the weight of racist history with new conceptualizations and methods of movement. Fanon thus falls to his knees and crawls.[10]

For many people, to trip, fall, crawl, and spasm as Fanon does is to err—which must be prevented at all costs. Black communities, particularly in the United States, have historically associated verticality with racial-uplift ideology. A veritable chorus of voices from Booker T. Washington with his bootstrap philosophy to writers such as Maya Angelou

("And Still I Rise") to Rastafarian musicians chanting Babylon down by asking us to "get up, stand up" have all championed notions of rising, elevation, and uplift as the means of progressing racially beyond the dark abyss of history. In contrast, falling and lying prone on the ground connote a feminized position of failure, an abject surrender to the myths of black subservience, vulnerability, and inferiority.

Horizontality or Fanon's downward mobility, instead of being a source of shame, as Jason King argues, elicits "alternative ways of imagining how to act, look and be black, unabashedly incorporating socially unacceptable behavior" (38). These queer imaginative acts recuperate disorientation through the political, cultural, and aesthetic value of wayward, errant movement. Whether these movements be the spectacular "death drops" and "dips" of New Way voguing or crawling under the radar or being on the down-low or lying down in protest, such imaginative kinetic acts undercut the illusion of a self-regulated, autonomous Enlightenment subject through familiar and unfamiliar repertoires of resistant mobilities. "While standing up tall and proud may be inseparable in the popular imagination from (political) virility and potency, . . . [falling, crawling, and being low can] confirm . . . that there is also an erotics of . . . downward mobility. Every day more and more people are choosing to fall off the ladder, opting out of its treacherous game of balance and negotiation. There is an erotic appeal to the practice of falling, a stylized sexiness at its core" (J. King 40). Of course, the erotic appeal of falling revolves around King's language of choice. His use of "choosing" and "opting" suggests a certain voluntariness around alternate movement practices that elide the reality of many black people such as the polio-disabled for whom differential movement practices are necessities. I wish to think through the pleasure of alternate movement without ignoring the material difficulties and pain that accompany such practices for many people. Thus, for example, the erotics of one's thighs tightening in a squat and the pleasure of arriving at alternative movement strategies should not obscure that the squat is necessary to avoid the excruciating pain of bending. An example of this occurs in the work of the performance artist Bill Shannon, whose interventions in public space are based on his experiences living with a hip condition (Legg-Calvé-Perthes disease) that makes it difficult to walk. Shannon writes, "When I noticed my own alternative solutions to everyday task[s] such as carrying books while climbing stairs or picking up a cup without bending over I instinctively realized that thinking creatively and looking inwardly for answers was the way for me to survive. . . . I believe this type of daily creativity and self-reliance cultivated creative problem solving." Shannon's pleasure in his own creative solutions, in his ability to take his everyday experiences and turn them into performative public interventions, must be foregrounded even as we contextualize his art within the constraints of living in disabled environments that privilege certain types of bodies and relegate pain to the realm of the private.

Carrying Water Even When I Am Dead

I place the squatting, begging, lurching, and crawling of groups of polio-disabled alongside Wura-Natasha Ogunji's *Will I still carry water when I am a dead woman?* The piece provides me an opportunity to explore horizontal differential movement that imaginatively creates a diasporic black sociality. Ogunji's performance (which begins individually and morphs into collective movement) raises a particular set of questions, not just about differential movement and embodiment but also about feminized labor, our embodied relationship to the terrain, and Nigerian negotiations between the secular and the spiritual. The movements I focus on in this chapter allow black bodies to speak against the spectacularization of modernity. This modernity insists on vertical, progressive movement and more often than not fails to recognize all those who imagine their relation to the earth differently. Ogunji's performances of disorientation suspend both normative Western flowing movement and also the assumption of quotidian able-bodied negotiations of space. Instead, she favors embodied practices rooted in African diasporic and disabled choreographic vocabularies that embrace falling, contact with the earth, and being low. Bodies that take risks, fall, lean, quiver, and crawl to the offbeat require us to think about how the social practice of movement can shape our imaginings of equitable ways of living with difference.

On March 19, 2011, the cameraman Jelili Atiku and curious onlookers watched Ogunji lower herself onto the unpaved Erinfolami Street in Ejigbo, Lagos.[11] The ambient sounds of the audience, children playing, people chatting, and the occasional car vrooming by somehow am-

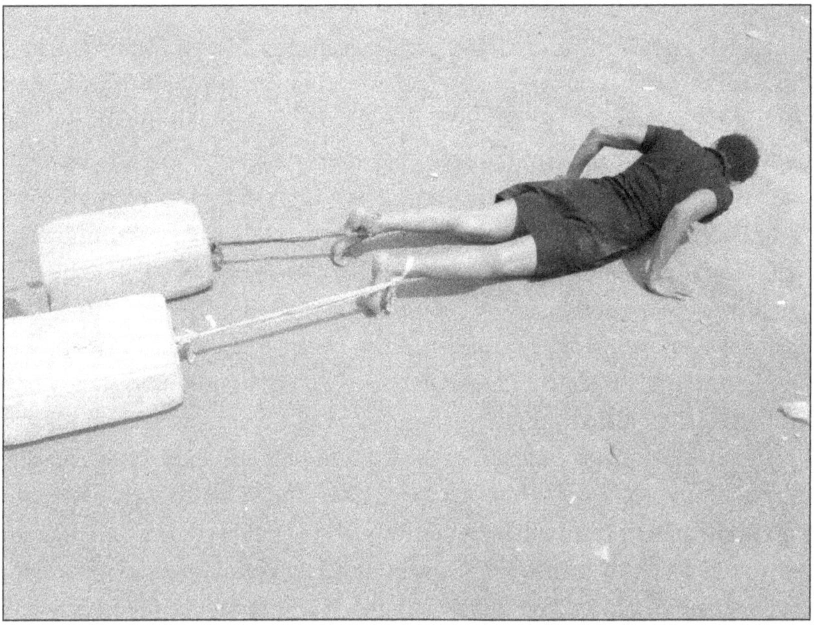

Figure 1.1. Wura-Natasha Ogunji performing *Will I still carry water when I am a dead woman?* in Lagos (2011) (© Wura-Natasha Ogunji; camera: Jelili Atiku; screenshot by author)

plify the slow pull-scrape of Ogunji's body as she drags herself down the road, arms first, head raised, belly flush against the dirt (fig. 1.1). Her face is painted with various white markings. Tied around each of her ankles is a plastic gallon container of water. The plastic containers rasp against the bumps in the road. The cords securing them to Ogunji's ankles tighten and pull as she attempts to drag the water forward. The crowd gets sparser, and one of the containers starts to leak, leaving a thin wet trail behind her. The occasional grunt and her increasingly labored breathing and movements speak to her growing physical discomfort as she struggles to get down the road. Eventually this discomfort prompts her to use the terrain itself to continue. Her hands find stones, indentations, protrusions that she uses to drag herself forward. She eventually pulls herself onto a rise in the road and stops.

In later performances that build on the initial piece, Ogunji collaborates with six similarly masked and costumed women to prioritize conjoined bodies.[12] Like a crowd of beggars with polio, these women navigate the city en masse by dragging behind them water kegs, tied to their wrists and/or ankles. Ogunji describes how dragging the kegs altered her ability to walk. Maryam Kazeem quotes Ogunji as saying, "Walking required my entire body. Were we even walking? It felt like something else." Stills and video of the performance show the women's bodies at various angles to the ground as they lean forward to pull. Each step is offbeat and laborious, and the body, while not horizontal as in crawling, departs from and questions verticality. Especially as the performers' exhaustion grows, walking begins to resemble the stiff-legged lurch of someone with crutches or a prosthetic limb. A performer sways as she attempts to collect herself. Another puts a hand out to steady herself against a parked car. The group becomes smaller as several women fall away. In the end, there are two women left, and every step forward appears torturous. It is almost a relief when the video footage stops and the performers presumably can relinquish the gallon containers that are so much work to transport. Ogunji and her collaborators' exhausted performances of horizontality challenge not just the performers themselves but also the audience as complex visual and visceral, aesthetic and political meanings accrue over time and space.

Ogunji's performances raise a particular set of questions in this chapter. What is the Western normative subject's relationship to the ground, and do black/differently abled bodies resist verticality through disorienting, slowed-down performances of horizontality? Given the transnational nature of Ogunji's performance, what are the politics of potable water, focusing not so much on corporations such as Nestlé that are working hard to amass resource rights and dominate the global water market but instead on the everyday labor performed by Nigerian and other African women to procure water for household tasks? Finally, how does Ogunji, through her deliberate evocation of Nigerian masquerades such as Egungun, "recontextualize . . . the sacred and profane as [she] performs the arduous (if not impossible) task of hauling water kegs through the city" (Ogunji, "*Will I still carry water . . . ?*").

Ogunji's performance is *not* a traditional Yoruba or Egungun masquerade. Rather, via a process of surrogation and circum-Atlantic travel, *Will I still carry water . . . ?* occupies a vortex of behavior, a "spatially induced carnival, a center of cultural self-invention through the restoration of behavior" (Roach 28). This vortex allows Ogunji to use the vocabularies of different performance traditions such as Yoruba cosmologies and staged protests to create a spectacle that resonates in several registers. Ogunji seizes on and remixes these different public memories and uses of space, thinking through relations between geography and the dead. As Noam Leshem writes, "If popular geopolitics focuses [on how the body engages with the material and discursive environs], . . . what, then, is the role of the [living] dead body, in its corporeal form and more specifically through its spatial and material representations, in this everyday order of power" (36)?

Ogunji's performance resists the prescriptiveness of flowing, independent, and upright movement by slowing down time. Her performances are laborious, in fits and starts, and painfully slow. André Lepecki would point to this aspect of her work as evidence of what he terms the "still-act."[13] The still-act is not simply the cessation or abdication of movement. Rather, it is a method of moving that inserts stillness into a performance in order to change the way the performer and audience experience time and to challenge preconceptions about movement (Lepecki, *Exhausting Dance* 15). A still-act suspends time by interrupting the flow of capital production and "refus[ing] the sedimentation of history into neat layers. The still-act shows how the dust of history, in modernity, may be agitated in order to blur artificial divisions between the sensorial and the social, the somatic and the mnemonic, the linguistic and corporeal, the mobile and immobile" (Lepecki, *Exhausting Dance* 15). While useful, Lepecki's notion of stillness needs to be rethought, especially when applied to disabled/African diasporic lexicons of gesture and movement. As Margaret Ames notes about directing a performance troupe with various abilities, stillness is not something all dancers are able to achieve. She writes, "Disability often makes impossible the feat of quieting the multitude of reflexes, and discharges of internal activity externally. Stillness is a controlled neurological act as much as dancing is. Disability often externalizes internal processes of spasm, fluctuation of tensions and decision at play with indecision" (178). Steve Paxton, for example when describing the dancing of Emery Blackwell, notes how "extension and contraction impulses in [Blackwell's] muscles fire frequently and unpredictably, and he must somehow select the right impulses consciously, or produce for himself a movement image of the correct quality to get the arm to respond as he wants" (16).

Given the necropolitics of the postcolony and the precarity of black life, stillness can evoke the specter of morbidity. The increasingly common spectacles of dead black bodies lying in the street insist that perhaps what is necessary to counter the prevalence of black death is *not* stillness but the notion of a syncopated horizontality that disrupts time through the insertion of improvised polyrhythms or "offbeats." These offbeats depart from the metronomic flow of time that usually accompanies vertical articulations of limbs with an upright spine. Syncopation instead insists on the horizontality of blackness and disability, where one leans, falls, crawls, and surrenders to the gravity, history, and spirit of a place. As Davies reminds us, for those of us with impaired mobility, "life's daily movement is a constant series of touches, leans, counterbalances, and the help of human and technological supports" (56). The performance artist Alicia Grace, who lives with ME (myalgic encephalomyelitis), describes her movement as "dancing with lassitude" or "dancing without promptness," where "the timing of the performances" is "based on the rhythms of [her] body rather than fitting into the rhythms of the market place of performance" (26). What Thomas DeFrantz calls "progressive minoritarian performance practices" ("Book Review" 190) can allow for movement that imagines inventive ways of relating that resist hegemonic capital flows and the fungibility of black bodies. This practice is embodied in the synchronized lurch, crawl, and active lying on the ground that enables beggars staging their polio-disabled limbs to disrupt the pace of life around them in their call for a more just polity. Such African diasporic and disabled modes of kinesis underscore the vulnerability of the body to police bullets, tremors, spasms, and exhaustion while also formulating alternate movement practices that undermine the necropolitical forces of capital.

Ogunji's moving examples of a polyrhythmic horizontality fully engage with the historical body and landscape. At certain times during her performance, Ogunji stops crawling when she reaches a certain level of exhaustion or when she attempts to alleviate the tightening of the ropes around her ankles. She turns on her back to adjust the water kegs, looking up at the sky for a moment before continuing her dragging crawl. She relies on the ground to support her weight. In other performances, one participant stumbles and rests against a parked car for a moment. Another bends down slowly to remove her shoes. Reliant on each other to keep going on in the slow and syncopated procession, the women move as if they have shackles on their feet. This is no accident; Ogunji uses movement to conjure up an African American history of slavery and chain gangs, her body bearing the weight of water keg as phantom shackle. Descriptions of shackles around the ankles and feet appear repeatedly in various accounts of slavery, and what is consistent throughout are accounts of the slow negotiation of pain, the demands of labor, and the weight of the shackle with every step.[14]

Nathaniel Mackey also links temporality with the limping dragging crawl, arguing that the slave's altered gait, like the limp of the Fon-Yoruba orisha of the crossroads, Elegba, insists that history is not the linear march of time. Rather, the stutter step embodies the offbeat as time pauses, pulses, drags, stops, and starts, altering progressive time as it strays outside the ordinary. Mackey writes, "A master of polyrhythmicity and heterogeneity, [Elegba] suffers not from deformity but multiformity, a 'defective' capacity in a homogeneous order given over to uniform rule. . . . Impairment taken to higher ground, remediated, translates damage and disarray into a dance" ("Sound and Sentiment" 40). Or as Jason King puts it, disorientation necessarily characterizes black performance with its "uncanny balance and rhythm" (41). The unpredictable and spectacular drop or downbeat and lift up, the sudden losing of one's way only to realize that there is no single way—this is the resistance of disoriented mobility. Thus, Ogunji's and the other performers' inability to walk upright and purposefully in a straight line and in step, their offbeat dragging/pulling/straining and groaning, refuses a sanitized history where the past has been left behind in a movement "forward." In its drag/crawl that falters, restarts, and stops again, *Will I still carry water . . . ?* profoundly alters the speed of the spectacle. Time unravels as the women's choreography remaps the city. In their centering of nonnormative movement practices, the performing bodies decelerate the pace of the urban landscape. Just as in the case of differentially abled beggars, BMWs impatiently slow and honk as they maneuver around the group of performers; passersby are diverted, and some choose another path. The women slowly move but never arrive. There is no end point to the performance other than the process of motion, the scrape against the ground of one elbow at a time, and the tentative groping of hands and feet. Wandering replaces the straight line of progress. *Will*

I still carry water. . . ? does not end with the successful completion of a journey but rather at an arbitrary spot in the middle of nowhere. As Chris Thompson writes, "in accepting the awkwardness of human gropings and longings, the snail pace promises at some point to arrive not at a particular location but at the state of grace that comes only from the pragmatic commitment to push forth" ("Afterbirth" 84).

Crawling to Remember

In some ways, Ogunji's work builds on a prior series of crawls performed by the African American performance and visual artist William Pope.L. Their performances of crawling, lurching, and falling reflect differences, not only in their artistic visions but also in their gender and geopolitical locations. Their reappropriations of public space, what it means to be a black man in the United States versus a diasporic black woman in Nigeria, and the different performance traditions that they draw on necessitate that we place these performances in conversation with each other. It also requires that we acknowledge how difficult these conversations actually are—as difficult as an asthma attack while climbing up a hill. Both artists, however, insist on differential embodiment and movement as a response to necropolitical governance that renders black lives vulnerable to "spatial and corporeal destruction" (Leshem 36).

During the late 1970s, Pope.L began a series called *eRacism* that included over forty performances consisting of "crawls," varying in length and duration. In direct contrast to Ogunji, these were not ensemble performances. Instead, as Pope.L's lone body inched painfully forward, the performances emphasized the atomization and alienation of being a black man in white America. The first of Pope.L's crawls was the *Times Square Crawl* (1978), in which, dressed in a business suit, he painfully inched his way down a stretch of West Forty-Second Street that before redevelopment was home to numerous homeless camps and a thriving drug trade. It was during this crawl that Pope.L first began to articulate what he termed "giving up verticality" (Bodinson and Cannon). The most well-known of his crawls is *The Great White Way: 22 Miles, 9 Years, 1 Street* (2001–9), in which, dressed in a Superman costume, he strapped a skateboard to his back. His inverted use of a mobility device that could have made his movement quicker, if not easier, calls to mind a turtle on its back, feet churning uselessly in the air. Dressed in the costume of American masculinist ideals, Pope.L articulates the ongoing crisis of black gender inherited from slavery. Like a brace keeping his back rigid or the symbolic weight of oppression, the skateboard ensures his horizontality. It took nine years for Pope.L to make it down Broadway, as each attempt lasted only as long as he was able to withstand the painful exhaustion, the often bone-chilling temperatures, the city dwellers inconvenienced by his snail's pace, and spectators angry at the discomfort engendered by a crawling black man. As Lepecki writes, "Pope.L's crawls inevitably challenge the presumption of free movement as a given of citizenry by revealing how certain subjects have a very different relationship to mobility, verticality, circulation, and ground, since they all stumbled and (as Fanon points out) were *fixed* by a speech act" (*Exhausting Dance* 98).

Pope.L carefully chose the routes of his crawls, not only for their importance in ensuring the smooth flow of capital but also because these areas were often targeted by "revitalization" initiatives. Under the guise of making public spaces "safer," these "revitalization" initiatives continue to remove the homeless, addicts, and other supposedly unproductive and delegitimized users of public space. This population of discarded people, much like the disabled beggars who crowd Sierra Leonean or Nigerian city streets, are actually a vibrant community remaking public space. With Pope.L's own family members experiencing homelessness, drug addiction, and alcoholism and thus targeted by these initiatives, he sought, via an interrogation of his own privileged position as a funded and employed artist, to generate a kinetic practice that confronts audiences with the disenfranchisement of black subjects. He thus consciously surrenders his verticality even as he is careful to maintain a distinction between the voluntarily "giving up" of verticality and being coerced into horizontality. Choosing horizontality for Pope.L meant a corporeal opening of his body to danger as he enacts the black body's inherited vulnerability to white power. Darcy English quotes Pope.L as stating, "To undergo that threat to his/her bodily/spiritual categories—that person would learn something. I did . . . now I crawl to remember" (266). This remembering is not just a reorientation of body to earth, but in its articulation of the legacy of slavery, it also provides an ironic foreshadowing of our contemporary period, when black bodies lie dead in the streets for hours. Pope.L's embrace of the discomfort and vulnerability of the horizontal thus allows him to embrace his blackness, which he stunningly defines as a "have-not-ness" or a "lack worth having" (English 259). This pained gesture of crawling exposes the myths of stereotypic masculinity that have ungendered the black body even as they claim that this inheritance of disenfranchisement is always worth having.

Stefano Harney and Fred Moten theorize this mode of engagement as a "being together in homelessness," where an artist works alongside a squatter, addict, punk, and beggar in an "interplay of the refusal of what has been refused" (96). They ask, "Can this being together in homelessness, . . . this undercommon appositionality, be a place from which emerges neither self-consciousness nor knowledge of the other but an improvisation that proceeds from somewhere on the other side of an unasked question?" (96). This being together can then, as Jack Halberstam puts it in the introduction to Harney and Moten's book, "reshape desire, reorient hope, reimagine possibility and do so separate from the fantasies nestled into rights and respectability" (11–12). Diving into the unrespectability of horizontality, into belabored movement dismissed as "disabled," Pope.L like Ogunji embraces a politics of conjoined differential embodiment and movement that pushes against the devaluation of the necropolitical body.

Pope.L uses overt signs of exertion and exhaustion, such as labored breathing, to perform his corporeal vulnerability, his liminal status as the living dead, his homelessness. He gasps, swallows, and pants, smelling and absorbing the breath of the city that creeps up through vents, drains, and cement. His breath mediates between the environment and the material self. The act of breathing, then, contests ideals of a unitary, bodily whole self. As Helen Sharp insists, "[The] movement of breath between the world and me seems to become the conduit for perceptual shifts that reverberate through my materiality so that time and spatiality are reconfigured. In this encounter I no longer sense myself to be a subject in separate relation to other objects out there in the world" (*Encounters* 25). Later, in her posthumous dissertation, she elaborates, "I am not so much looking at the world as becoming in relation with it through each movement of breath. . . . I breathe in the world" ("Profane Halo" 62). Pope.L's labored offbeat breathing viscerally connects him to the city's landscape as he slows down the city's rhythm, reconfiguring time and space as he breathes in the city. Like Ogunji inhaling dust and exhaust fumes, Pope.L's labored breathing reanimates his relationship to the world around him.

Both Ogunji and Pope.L are very aware that horizontality has traditionally been seen as a coerced feminized disability, while the vertical is associated with masculinist autonomy and the self-possessed, able-bodied human. One need only remember Stokely Carmichael's infamous response during the Student Non-Violent Coordinating Committee (SNCC) staff meeting in Waveland, Mississippi, in 1964, when he stated that "the only position for women in SNCC is prone" (Richardson 186–87).[15] The privileging of phallic uprightness bolsters particular forms of masculine authority so that the verticality of surrounding police officers, for example, comes to stand in for their virile masculinity. The way Pope.L's costumes function within his performances actively dismantles these associations of verticality with authority. As he crawls, the friction dirties and tears through his Superman costume and business suit. This attire, clearly representative of iconic masculine physical exceptionality, mythic heroism, and corporate conformity, takes on different meanings when worn and worn out by a black man who has given up his "upward mobility" and submitted to the vulnerability of horizontality. Embracing his blackness (his lack worth having), Pope.L rejects normative masculinity, reclaiming the horizontal. His is an intimate embrace of a racialized terrain as an essential "choreopolitical" performative reworking of subjectivity.

During Pope.L's crawls, his suit incurred emotionally charged responses from various passersby. Without his suit, perhaps Pope.L would simply have been one of those "other black men," dismissed, ignored, and overlooked except when observed through crosshairs. One particular crawl took place in Tompkins Square, a site where Mayor David Dinkins had recently implemented a policy of forced removal of people "squatting" in the public park, making it their home. During the performance, an older black resident of the East Village expressed concern upon encountering a horizontal Pope.L being filmed by a white cameraman. According to English, this onlooker interpreted the scene as an example of a black man subjugated by a white man; the "resident sought compassionately to receive Pope.L within a maximally expansive blackness that drew him across class lines" (English 279). Disregarding the white cameraman, the resident stepped into the camera's frame to ask Pope.L, "You all right, brother?" to which an exhausted and preoccupied Pope.L barely responded (English 275). The resident interpreted Pope.L's terseness as a dismissal. Indignant and angry, the resident enlisted another black onlooker for support, and together they approached Pope.L again, this time to ask, "What are you doing showing black people like this?" (English 275). English transcribes the following dialogue from the recording of the performance:

> POPE.L: Listen, you guys give me another half an hour and I'll sit down and talk with you over a Coke, but right now—
> RESIDENT: Explain what? You running down the street like this in a goddamn suit? I wear a suit like that to work!
> POPE.L: Listen, I'm *doing* work. I'll explain it to you later.
> RESIDENT: No bitch, you're going to explain it to *me* now . . . No? All right, then we're going to break the camera. (278)

The resident's initial feelings of racial affiliation are replaced by anger and mistrust when he realizes that Pope.L is aesthetically representing the destitution of many black and disabled peoples by voluntarily embracing horizontality. The initial affiliation he felt with Pope.L as a black middle-class man recedes under the realization that Pope.L is refusing the prescriptions of behavior in which the able-bodied black bourgeoisie, in attempts to distinguish and distance themselves from lower-class blacks, embody an upright respectability. Pope.L's breach of middle-class unity also exposes the gendered basis on which such alliances rest, signaled by the legitimizing suit that both he and the resident wear to work, namely, a masculinist authority based on capitalistic notions of productivity. As English points out, "By threatening the emasculation/feminization of the nonascendant," the resident "simultaneously invokes and reinstates the familiar figure of the representative autonomous, unambiguously straight, middle-class black man as a kind of built-in stabilizer for the black body politic writ large" (280). By making clear that he is choosing horizontality over verticality, Pope.L ruptures the tacit heterosexist, masculinist alliance that the resident hoped to form. As a final response to this rejection, the resident falls back on one of the ultimate assertions of straight masculinity: the threat of violence. By promising to break the camera and "knock" Pope.L "off the street," the resident, in an affirmation of the hegemony of phallic verticality, distances himself from the queered, feminized black body lying on the street.[16]

The black man's threat to knock Pope.L off the street, I would argue, is an essential part of the performance. Pope.L's lone crawl highlights the alienation and atomization of individuals under capital. But the evocation of this singularity is belied by the active, complex intervention of another black man who recognizes himself in the abject figure of a crawling Pope.L. The performance thus needs and relies on other black participants to flesh out its commentary on black sociality. It consolidates itself around fractured conversations across difference that dismantle the possessive individualism of liberal humanism and illusions of independent, free-flowing movement. Ogunji also attempts to rework her racialized and gendered subjectivity through the crawl. As a queer woman, her vulnerability, as she lies belly down on the ground, increases the difficulty of her performance. I cannot help but feel that the implicit danger (she has no police protection, just a cameraman, during her initial performance) is part of what prompted the change in her performance from crawling to dragging, from a lone woman lying on a dirt road to a group of masked women moving with each other, while being surrounded by male performers keeping away traffic.

I would argue that both Ogunji and Pope.L queer their intimacy with the ground. Ogunji and Pope.L disrupt the putative naturalized feminine position of the prone and notions that the earth is insentient by thinking through pleasure and desire in nonnormative ways. While I have no access to what kind of pleasure the ground beneath them generated, perhaps some of their heavy breathing is not just about pain but pleasure. Gloria Naylor's *Bailey's Café* allows me to explore these queer vectors of desire and the pleasure that stone, dirt, and cement generate as they scrape beneath belly and tender nipples. Naylor rewrites the story of the biblical Eve's expulsion from Eden with her Eve, who is expelled from Pilottown by her Godfather for a "game" she plays with the neurodiverse Billy Boy. Eve lies pressed to the ground while Billy stomps up dust around her:

> The best toy is your imagination and with us, the only toy. . . . And I felt the warm earth against my warm flesh, pressed so hard into the ground

> I could hear my heart beating in my ears—beating in time with that last throbbing warmth of the sun in the packed dirt under my stomach and thighs. . . . *Stomp, Billy, stomp.* . . . The tremors on my arms, legs, thighs. I part my thighs ever so slightly and arch my pelvis hard into the soil—there, yes, now I can feel it even down there. So close to the earth—the tremors. *Stomp, Billy.* (Naylor 85–87)

Eve's arching her pelvis into the soil asks us to consider what Juana Rodríguez calls "the urgency of confronting alternative forms of racialized queer female sexuality . . . that inform a much wider range of sexual power relations" (20). Especially when thinking through sex and disability, sexual pleasure encompasses an entire range of fantasies, longings, and perverse practices that expand the realm of erotic to include, I would argue, the feel of the ground against breasts, pelvis, and thighs as one drags oneself down a dirt road. It lies in Billy Boy's "sweating and baying at the clouds" as he stomps the earth, making it vibrate (Naylor 87). Ogunji's crawling centers alternate forms of pleasure that are part and parcel of a queer disabled erotic practice that recognize the pain and abjection of disability even while reinvesting with value nonnormative fantasies and practices. Using Sylvia Wynter's work, Kathryn Yusoff writes that in "the struggle against forms of propertied relation with the inhuman, different intimacies developed with the earth" (36). Rather than accepting imperialistic aggression that voided subjects by emptying out their haptic relations with land (35), black and brown people have insisted on erotically engaging with dirt and soil. The garden plot where slaves grew food, pouring libations onto the earth for the ancestors, spilling blood, or "kissing the earth before rebellions" as "an oath-act" (37)—this is the historical genealogy of an indigenous blackness that centers intimacy with the ground.

Pope.L's and Ogunji's crawling bodies, through their reconfiguration of queer desire and black sociality, also intervene in traditional geographies. Disobedient uses of public space such as stopping and redirecting traffic or fucking the ground are emancipatory spatial practices that resist traditional geographies. Putting into conversation disability studies' foundational claim about "disabling" environments and black/feminist geographers such as Doreen Massey, Katherine McKittrick, and Judith Madera, Ogunji and Pope.L enact McKittrick's claim that "traditional geographies . . . *require* black displacement, black placelessness, black labor, and a black population that submissively stays 'in place'" (*Demonic Grounds* 9). McKittrick invokes the work of Édouard Glissant to argue that the geographies produced through European practices of transatlantic slavery and colonialism produce a form of "sociogeographic madness" in which the "landless black subject is . . . anchored to a new world grid that is economically, racially, [able-bodied] and sexually normative, or seemingly nonblack" (*Demonic Grounds* 3). Put simply, racialized and ableist hierarchies don't just exist in space; they create and are created by the biopolitical governmentality that is necropolitics.

Bodies that are excluded from the category of citizen-subject and the not-quite-human demonstrate how "cultural politics, power relations and contested meanings . . . intersect in the making of deathscapes" (Leshem 35). For example, observers note that the majority of those who are differentially embodied in Lagos "are left to fend for themselves, usually at the 'mercy of nature,' roaming around *our* streets" (Kurawa 1805; emphasis added). A small minority of the differentially embodied are housed in institutions or vocational centers supposedly for "rehabilitation." Isiaka Maaji, a former beggar who now builds tricycles, motorbikes, doors, and windows, is one of the people interviewed for a newspaper article in the *Nigerian Echo* about turning Nigeria's disabled from beggars to workers. He tells the interviewer, "We encourage people like us to learn skills they can do to become self-reliant to support themselves and their families, because being *in the streets* as beggars is a disgrace to all of us" (Yusuf). Therefore, part of the supposed abjectness of disability is constituted by *where* the disabled are forced to become visible in order to survive. The spectacle of the disabled roaming around "our" streets fixes and spatializes social hierarchies. The disabled person's use of public spaces stages the distinction between legitimate consumers/productive citizens and a surplus population whose only value lies in the commodification of their injury or difference—an insight both Ogunji's and Pope.L's performances pivot around.

In *Black Atlas: Geography and Flow in Nineteenth-Century African American Literature*, Judith Madera writes that traditional geographies "from Henri Lefebvre to Fredric Jameson" represent space as a surface on which a linear progressive time is inscribed to create "a kind of *vertical* history" (6; emphasis added). She calls instead for an understanding of place as active, imaginative, and historical and of synchronous place-based histories that "run aslant of temporal encapsulations" (8). By exposing what she terms the "geographic consequences . . . of official histories" (15) with their normative temporalities, Madera suggests the development of black countergeographies through polyrhythmic, heterogeneous performances that render visible official productions of space, even while counterinvesting black embodied choreography and space with new meanings. Thus, while Ogunji's horizontality draws attention to racialized and gendered surplus populations produced by the violent structures of the state, it is also, like Pope.L's refusal of the gentrification of Tompkins Square, "part of a counterpractice of civil disobedience that takes aim at the view, so often mobilized in the name of revitalization, that 'deviant' uses of public space impede the flow of life as it is meant to be lived" (English 263).

Still Carrying: Water and the Sacred

Ogunji states on her blog that *Will I still carry water . . . ?* was inspired by the "daily task of carrying water at [her] cousin's house": "I observed how this particular work was largely something that me and my female cousins performed" (Ogunji, "Will I still carry water . . . ?"). Her crawl, then, also forces our attention to a global economy of feminized labor and the gendered politics of water. Corruption and mismanagement have brought the public water system in Nigeria to a standstill.[17] Water is delivered in pushcarts, even to the middle class. Only the wealthy, with their own wells and generators, can presume that water will flow out of the tap when it is turned on. Global industries such as Nestlé have stepped in to exploit this underdevelopment and have thus greatly inflated prices for potable water. Consider for a moment that one bottle of Nestlé Pure Life is more expensive than a liter of gasoline in Nigeria and far exceeds the daily income of many Nigerians. In response, Nigerians have turned to other sources, buying their water every day from formal and informal vendors, queuing at community water points, or walking to and from rivers, streams, and ponds with makeshift containers. Nigerian women are primarily responsible for the onerous task of household water provision. Studies of Lagos in 2005 by the United Nations report that women are twice as likely to collect water than men.

In 11 percent of households, children procure water, with girls being more likely to do so than boys (Akiyode 41).[18] These women and girls are highly likely to encounter sexual and other types of harassment as they navigate public space.

Ogunji sets out to demonstrate that women's labor is often invisible, specifically as it relates to water portage. Indeed, responses to the piece confirm this. Ogunji and her collaborators initially elicited many comments and queries from onlookers about the strength required to drag the kegs and the rationale for the performance. One spectator thought the women were being punished and that the punishment was too harsh. Whether they should be punished and what possibly could have warranted such public humiliation is left unsaid. Another witness dropped a hundred-naira note on Ogunji's shoulders. Very quickly, however, as Ogunji and fellow performer Wana Udobang note on their blogs, most of the townspeople began to ignore them. Udobang writes,

> About twenty minutes into our somewhat two mile journey, people stopped looking, stopped caring, they just went about their business. Some of us moved faster than the others, so at the beginning we would stop and wait for the others to catch up. Again just the way the puzzled observers stopped observing, we stopped waiting, and during the very few times we did, I noticed the impatience and agitation in each performer's body language, the sudden realisation that each woman had their own load to carry to the finish point and thus the feeling of a certain lonliness [*sic*] through the journey.

Their laboring bodies gradually begin to disappear, fading into the background along with the numerous other women traversing the city, carrying out arduous household chores such as water procurement, laundry, and child care. The performers become, in the words of Daphne Brooks, "spectacularly opaque," hypervisible and yet erased by a "kind of shrouding" that paradoxically yokes "corporeal unveiling" with "the (re)covering and rehistoricizing of the flesh" (8). During one of Ogunji's performances, a passerby hastily squeezes past performers and cameras, paying them scant attention even as she interrupts and participates in Ogunji's taped performance. On this woman's head are several large bottles of water, packed in a metal bucket.

The primary way that water is carried is on the head, with most women being able to carry up to 60 percent of their body weight in this manner. This method of transporting heavy loads depends on how one walks and interacts with the ground. As Willems et al. explain, "These women employ a gait mechanism by which they increase a pendulum-like conservation of mechanical energy with each step" (360). They appear to be gliding, as if on water. The woman in the video walks briskly, expending very little energy on external work (the force needed for the center of mass to overcome ground reaction forces, for example) and even less energy on internal work (such as respiration or muscle contraction).[19] The skilled economy of her movement, when juxtaposed with Ogunji's piece, highlights the difficulties the performers face as they continue to struggle with their containers of water shackled to their ankles and wrists, like fetters. But whether moving with ease or difficulty, all these women, performers and laborers, are largely ignored. The indispensability of women's labor is matched only by how much it is taken for granted. By drawing attention to the process by which women's embodied labor becomes opaque, Ogunji's work pushes spectators and fellow performers toward alternative reading practices. She reveals to the spectator/performer, via their own responses, their resistance to recognizing the value of women's labor and the toll this lack of recognition exacts, such as feelings of isolation, loneliness, discomfort, and pain. Ogunji's performances remind us that the price of certain types of labor is not just written *on* the body but also paid *by* the body.

Ogunji's performance demands new forms of spectatorship that are relational, rather than individual. Rather than thinking about performance from an immobile perspective that congeals simplistic ideas of being "within" the performance or "outside" it, Ogunji's work renders performance as a social form that can only exist within a social context where actor and audience continually shift. As we have seen, during the performance, the various performers watch each other and the crowd, and the crowd intervenes at various times by walking around the women or calling out to them or asking questions or ignoring them. Speaking specifically about Yoruba masquerades (a key precedent for Ogunji's performances), Margaret Thompson Drewal writes about performance traditions that are so participatory as to render the distinctions between spectator and performer largely irrelevant. The community watching the performance possesses some learned and embodied knowledge or competence in the performance tradition of the masquerade and spontaneously interacts with the performances (M. Drewal 119). The dropping of money on Ogunji's shoulders is actually part of the performative responses elicited by masquerades. That particular man read her performance as a masquerade and, mobilizing his improvisational abilities, responded and intervened in the performance to become part of it.

The term *egungun* refers to any masked figure or masquerade that houses forces affecting the living. Roughly translated as "powers concealed," egungun represent Orisa and/or the ancestors (H. Drewal 18). The egungun ensemble is an exquisite shell made from multiple layers of fabric and beadwork that becomes animated only when the masker enters the costume and transforms into the particular ancestor or deity that the ensemble evokes. The ensemble is thus a portal to another world that allows the spirit to enter and the human to transform. The ensemble transcends time, sending the bodies of the maskers into liminal states between here and there, now and then. The cloth forms are often conceptualized and sewn in ways that alter or obscure human features, such as enclosed faces that are invisible to the audience or eyes that open to the sky (Clausius 6). These costumes are well tended but not revered. The egungun society can choose to remake them if they are worn-out or if they need to reflect changing societal concerns. The costume acquires meaning primarily through performance. Not everyone can become egungun. An egungun society is composed of a group of men and women whose ancestry gives them the right to inhabit a particular ensemble. However, it is men who predominantly do the masking. Women form a chorus that sings praise poems (oriki) and recites genealogies.

Ogunji's decision to mask herself and a group of female performers thus intervenes in the particular gendering of egungun performance. By wearing a costume of African fabric and covering her face with a mask, Ogunji draws attention to how women's performances of labor get relegated to the realm of the mundane and the quotidian. The sacred and the spectacular, the whirling dancer who creates a "breeze of blessing," for example, become the province of the male, despite the fact that egungun themselves challenge simplistic gender binaries. Ogunji claims a space for women's performances of labor by using many of the performative traditions of egungun masquerades. She does *not* attempt to perform actual masquerades, but she does revisit them, drawing aesthetic parallels between the various performances to insist on the value of women's spiritual and physical labor. Thus, for example, attendants separate and protect traditional egungun maskers from the surrounding crowd except when the crowd participates in scripted ritualized ways in the masquerade. Similarly, the women in *Will I still carry water . . . ?* are assisted by male attendants who ensure that the women are not obstructed in any way. The men direct traffic around the performers as well as shoo away passersby who threaten to disrupt the women's movement. Ironically, these same vigilant attendants often overlook women briskly walking by; the woman carrying water on her head almost brushes against one of the performers, and another woman presses her child close to her side to avoid a near collision. In a sense, this becomes a key aspect of the performance: the attendants' assessment of what disturbs the logic of the performance and what is contiguous to it. Women's domestic work is folded into the masquerade in a reiteration of the very logic that Ogunji's performance is critiquing.

The corporeal language of *Will I still carry water . . . ?* carries added significance when we consider the choreographic concerns of traditional Yoruba masquerades. For the Yoruba, the performer's power lies in his ability to call spirit into being, to contribute to the creation of a reality that is both tangible and hidden. Through the performance, the skilled masquerader can render unseen forces momentarily visible and thus open the door between the worlds. He does this by falling into the dance. Margaret Drewal cites the following verse that appears in Ifá divination texts:

> He [made a sacrifice].
> He did not die.
> He started to dance,
> He started to rejoice.
> He started to praise his Ifá priests
> While his Ifá priests praised Ifá.
> As he opened his mouth [to sing],
> He uttered forth his song to Ifá,
> As he stretched his legs,
> Dance caught him. (123–24)

The successful dancer thus sacrifices himself, falling into the rhythm of the drums and the arms of the dance. As Drewal writes, "This catch-as-catch-can approach to dancing means . . . that the dancing often appears rough and ragtag; the dancers sometimes seem off-balance" (124). Rarely do masqueraders perform in unison—they seldom even face the same direction. Each one is left to interact and respond to the role to the best of his abilities. When the dancer, overtaken by rhythm, looks as if he is about to fall, knowledgeable bystanders intervene by grabbing and holding him to keep him safe. This collaboration between bystanders and performers unanchors their respective positions in relation to the performance. Spirit and dance are created and re-created in the ebb and flow of this collaboration.

Ogunji's *Will I still carry water . . . ?* captures the essence of this fall, this "dropping into the blaze of the unknown" (Dent and Thompson 8). By falling and crawling, or by constantly teetering on the edge of falling, she re-creates the moment when the masquerader falls into the dance's embrace. The breathtaking disorientation that characterizes her spectacular black performance, as Jason King states, exemplifies the "highest form of orientation" in its "uncanny balance and rhythm" (41). To begin to fall is to relinquish control to the historical strata of the ground. It is to surrender to the horizontal in a meaningful engagement with the sacred.

Coda: Room 1026

Horizontality traditionally is associated with death. The image of Michael Brown lying facedown on the street in Ferguson, Missouri, for over four hours after being shot by the police painfully illustrates a very familiar concatenation of brutalized black body, horizontality, and public space. Brown's body resonates for me with the images of hundreds of prone, dead bodies, killed by the South African apartheid state. Seventy-three anti-apartheid activists died between 1963 and 1990 while being held by the South African police. But what if rather than imagining dying as an end, we foreground African diasporic spiritual notions to complicate notions of horizontality and death to include notions of flight?

I turn to the twenty-second name on the list of seventy-three dead: Ahmed Timol, a member of the South African Communist Party whose death occurred four days after his arrest and detention on October 27,

1971. The repetition of the descriptor "horizontal" in the testimony is striking. J. L. de Villiers, the magistrate presiding over the original official inquest held in June 1972, ruled that Timol committed suicide by jumping out of a tenth-floor window of the infamous John Vorster Square (now the Johannesburg Police Station). The inquest was reopened by Justice Billy Mothle in 2017, more than forty years later, with testimony including that of Paul Erasmus, a former security officer who admitted that torture was "standard procedure," and Salim Essop, who described being held by his ankles over a tenth-floor stairwell during detention at the John Vorster police station (see Kennedy). The court officially recognized that members of the security branch had murdered Ahmed Timol. Since most of the men actually responsible for the murder have since died, the inquest was largely symbolic, an attempt to memorialize anti-apartheid activists, many of them brutally tortured in Room 1026 (the so-called truth room), before being similarly murdered.

The inquest found the former police officer Joao Rodriguez guilty of perjury both in 1972 and in 2017. At both inquests, Rodriguez insisted that he had nothing to do with Timol's death. In his original testimony, Rodriguez tells us that when he tried to stop "the Indian" from opening the catch and diving through the window, he fell over a chair and thus was unable to prevent Timol's "suicide." His testimony reads, "The Indian already had the window open and was diving through it. When I tried to grab him I fell over the chair, I could not get at him" (Bizos 31). Gen Buys, another collaborator, described the event as follows: "In the office on the tenth floor here was the most relaxed atmosphere that could be expected in such circumstances. Ahmed Timol sat calmly on a chair. There were Security Police men with him. At a certain stage two of them walked out of the room. Suddenly Timol flew up and aimed for the door. The one Security Police man jumped up and ran to the door to stop him. But the Indian then rushed for the window and dived through. Nobody frightened him. The autopsy will show this" (Myburgh).[20] The words the security officers use to describe Timol's movement are significant, especially given autopsy reports that detail Timol's prefall injuries. According to the pathologist Shakeera Holland, Timol had facial injuries and wounds that might have been caused by blunt objects such as a hammer. He also had fractured ribs, extensive damage to his brain, and tears in liver and lung tissue. Many of the bruises on his body were patterned and clear, unlike the irregular bruises that would result from a fall. There also seemed to be extensive damage to the lower right calf that was probably sustained prefall (Venter). How could a man who was so seriously injured "fly up" and "dive through"?

The now-retired state prosecutor Ernie Matthis, who was working on the fourth or sixth floor of John Vorster Square that day, recollects that by chance he glanced out the window only to see a body falling "horizontally" with head pointing toward the highway. Rushing to the window, he looked down to see Timol "lying prone" close to the curb with one arm extended over his head. Looking up, he did not see an open window or any officers trying to prevent a suicide ("Timol Inquest").

What does it mean that Timol's injured fugitive flight was "horizontal" and that he lay prone, his cheek lovingly mangled by the cement of that infamous square? On the one hand, Timol's horizontality is one of death. His prone position on the ground is not what Mark Auslander in his discussion of Black Lives Matter protest strategies calls the "trope of dramatized subordination." Rather, this horizontality is a painful reminder of the disposability of black life. Yet Timol does not lie on that ground alone, for we are here to mourn him and others like him. His death, like his life, is testament to the power of reimagining ways of moving and alternate sociogeographic terrains within the constraints of power.

Jesse Torrey in *A Portraiture of Domestic Slavery in the United States* (1817) describes an incident in which Anna or Ann Williams (he does not mention her name), destined for sale in Georgia, jumps out of the garret window of Miller's Tavern.[21] The fall of three stories leaves her with a shattered spine and broken wrists and elbows. Wanting to see the "mangled slave," Torrey gains permission from her landlord and owner to visit her as she lies on a bed on the floor. He finds the garret crowded, not just by Anna, who has displaced her set bones so that she is "perceptibly crooked," but also by a young man hobbled and manacled, a black woman with a scar on her head from repeated beatings with a wooden stick, and the woman's infant. The latter three were captured and awaiting sale despite being legally free. This is yet another torturous room designed to extract everything but the truth. Her suicidal fall, Anna purportedly tells Torrey, stemmed from her confusion and distraction: "They brought me away with two of my children, and would'nt let me see my husband—they did'nt sell my husband, and I did'nt want to go;—I was so confus'd and 'istracted, that I did'nt know hardly what I was about—but I did'nt want to go, and I jumped out of the window;—but I am sorry now that I did it;—they have carried my children off with 'em to Carolina." The illustration that accompanies this story, designed by Torrey and discussed by Yusoff in *A Billion Black Anthropocenes or None*, shows the woman awkwardly hovering in the air (fig. 1.2). The proportions of house, window, street, trees, and body are distorted. Anna's body couldn't possibly fit through the garret window, which appears significantly smaller than her. She is depicted as "falling" slightly to the left of the nearest window, almost as if she is walking on air. Her shadow looms large over the entire face of the top floor. She is utterly alone as an ominous dark cloud looms overhead.

The skewed perspective of the print is not a sign of the artist's lack of skill. Rather, the distortions suggest the out of space/out of time nature of Anna's escape. Despite what may have motivated Torrey's design, the hovering/flying/diving Anna refuses the horizontality of black death. Instead, as she falls away from the enclosed space of the garret, her body the shape of a boomerang, she attracts the light, pushing back the encroaching shadows of black death. She is too large to be contained by the buildings around her, and her fall insists on rewriting how the forces of the world act on the black body. Her fugitive actions demand that we invent new laws of geometry, gravity, and proportion. Anna's survival tells us that the epistemic, ontologic, and material rooms of power that attempt to contain her, like Room 1026, are simply too small to house the errant trajectories of black freedom. As Yusoff writes, "In the geophysics of this image of the suspended woman, gravity is both the problem and the solution, rendering her invulnerable, held in the possible, awaiting a different tense of being. A different future" (95). The narrative of a woman "held in the possible" relies partially on the fact that Anna survives. Thirteen years after her fall, she files a petition for freedom in 1828, claiming that George Miller and his son held her unjustly in slavery, and she eventually wins legal freedom for herself and her children. The testimony of doctors who treated her and others like her trapped in Miller's Tavern played a significant role in convincing the jury to grant her her freedom.

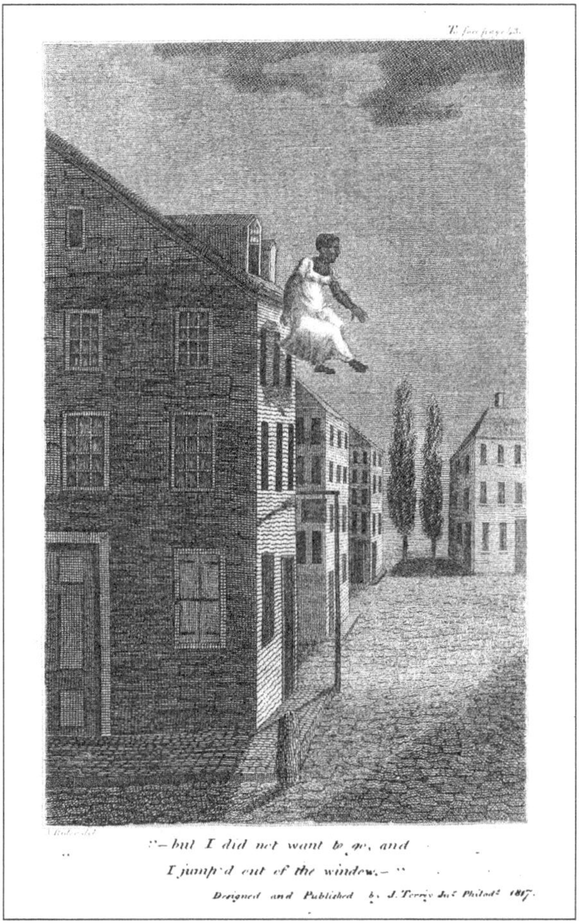

Figure 1.2. "—but I did not want to go, and I jump'd out of the window.—" (Designed and published by J. Torrey Junr Philada, 1817; illustration: A. Rider del)

Anna Williams teaches herself how to move differently, painfully. She survives the fall. Ahmed Timol does not. But perhaps Timol's fall out the window, as he surrenders to gravity, is a similar call for another tense of being. This alternate temporality reclaims the horizontal for black sociality, insisting not only on another way of being (free) but also on *another way of dying*. For it is the dead whose bodies, in their conjoinment with ours, animate the living.

2

Floating

Between sunrise and the midnight curfew, we honed a sense of loss in keeping with Ethiopia's elaborate tradition of mourning— . . . what the call-and-response of keening entailed, how grief was embodied and embroidered, how the timeline of loss was calculated. And inevitably, we also developed a heightened political sense of loss—how the state . . . disposed of its disprized citizens, how it exercised authority over the living and the dead.
—Dagmawi Woubshet, *The Calendar of Loss*

The dead, through their differential embodiment and the specific ways they move, make unique demands on the living, morphing us into something more than individual bodies. Conjoined with the living, the people drowned in the Mediterranean are connected to us not only by the ways that they float, sink, and saponify but also through entangled tendrils that I develop as "intersensorial spillings" or the haptic. These intersensorial spillings counter the abstracted mathematics of dead bodies advanced, for example, in Europe's surveillance systems as it polices its borders against African immigrants and refugees. By drawing our attention to the action of floating, the dead insist not only that we rethink the ways we move and imagine bodies but also that we reconfigure black sociality around the conjoined live body and bloated corpse. The floating dead demand that we breathe our air into their lungs.

Prologue: Intersensorial Spilling

Commissioned by Creative Interruptions in collaboration with the independent race equality think tank Runnymede, the short film *Unburied* (2019) was written and directed by Sally Fenaux Barleycorn. The six-minute-long film is a masterful demonstration of what Steven

Connor in his talk titled "Intersensoriality" calls "intersensorial spillings and minglings." These spillings and minglings work against a more traditional hierarchy of the senses, for example, the privileging of the visual in race studies. They also refute what Connor calls a "radial model" in which each distinct sense communicates a different set of information back to a centralized, individualized self, who then processes the experience. Rather, as *Unburied* demonstrates, the "senses communicate with each other, in cooperations and conjugations which are irregular and emergent. This complexion of the senses knits itself together anew with each new configuration" (Connor). Intersensorial spillings are always geographically and historically located—black sociality has acquired specific sounds, smells, and tastes that have accrued over time. The tendency toward high blood pressure, the repressed yell when your grandmother snaps your head back hard like her grandmother as she braids your hair, the pucker in your mouth as you learn from older cousins to eat green mangoes covered in chili powder and salt—these are learned, passed down, cumulative. These historical intersensorial spillings "twine[] about a happening like ivy around a wall" (Benjamin 108).

Barleycorn deliberately evokes the intersensorial in order to think through the violence of abstraction that haunts black death. In particular, her use of sound disrupts traditional film techniques, in which the aural and the visual directly correspond. Instead, she uses the texture of sound to conjure worlds beyond the frame of the screen but also to suggest events that cannot be articulated verbally or shown visually. These events cannot be processed and depicted using linear time or continuous geographies. Instead, the gaps in time, the lack of explanation, and geographical incongruities as the road ends and becomes the ocean insist that the only way to understand the horrifying deaths of the Mediterranean crossing is by occupying the "'strange horizon' where sensory modes meet and cross over" (Barker 241).

The film begins inside the car of a young black woman as she drives through streets. Smooth music by Nu Epoque fills the car. As the woman drives, her face is half in shadow. Now and again, we see her more clearly as the taillight of a motorcycle or a building light shines on her face. Shots of her face are interspersed with images of her hands on the steering wheel and her illuminated dashboard. She turns the volume up when the news comes on the air. The radio tells us in Spanish that it is 6 a.m., but it is the kind of street-light-illuminated dark that could just as easily be the middle of the night. The reporter's voice, as she reads the news, captures the full attention of the driver and the viewer. We move from hearing about mundane issues of Barcelona speed limits to more pressing ones about student protests and then finally to news about the Mediterranean. The announcer's crisp voice reports, "An empty vessel had been discovered near the Mallorcan coast. Considering the type of boat, its dimensions and size, sources estimate that there must have been between 150 and 300 people on board from sub-Saharan Africa. Since the first of January 2019, 508 people have died in the Mediterranean." The woman grows visibly more uncomfortable as the reporter continues. She shifts in her seat, she takes a deep breath, she looks out the window, and the car starts to feel like the small, enclosed space it is.

As the voice goes on to relay more statistics regarding Mediterranean fatalities, the camera zooms in on the woman's tight face and the tears in her eyes. The voice on the radio begins to reverberate and distort. Instead of the viewer hearing the radio announcer's voice as it really is, the distortion we hear reflects the woman driver's response to the news. The radio fades away, and all we hear now are the noises that someone inside the car would experience, an exhale as the driver tries to breathe through her tears, breathing, the sound of tires on tar. The camera cuts between the woman driving and stopping at lights become more frequent, making the viewer feel as though the car is moving faster. The driver roughly wipes away her tears; she keeps driving and, as she drives through what appears to be a tunnel marked with graffiti, her breathing gets louder and momentarily sounds like the ocean. The woman eventually stops at what appears to be the deserted end of a road and throws her head back as she cries. Flinging open her door, she stumbles out, and we hear her sobbing. The screen goes black as the following words appear, each line adding to the one before: "During the filming of this movie, 70 people drowned in the Mediterranean Sea attempting to reach Europe. 35, 597+ migrants have been killed due to EU policies since 1993. Hundreds are still dying every single month using the most dangerous migration route in the world." The plight of the drowned is inseparable from that of the young taxi driver. She is conjoined with them, con-

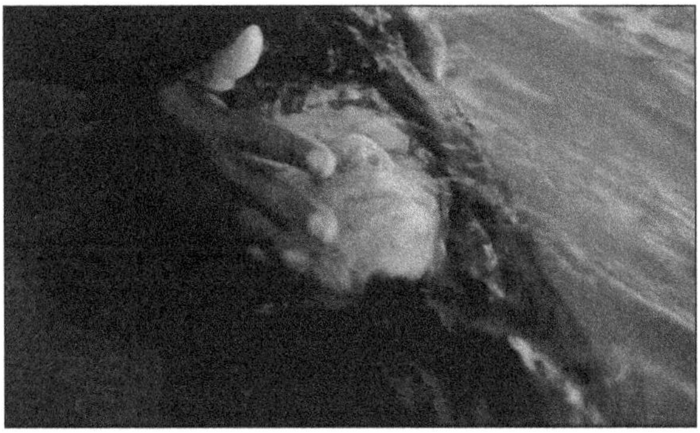

Figure 2.1. Sally Fenaux Barleycorn, *Unburied* (2019) (© Runnymede Trust and Creative Interruptions; screenshot by author)

nected by intersensorial threads that continually reweave the loose net of black sociality.

The sound of the ocean gets louder and louder, and the woman's sobs turn into a guttural off-screen scream of anguish. The next shot is of the Mediterranean as someone walks into the sea. As the waves heave, we begin to see bare-chested men, standing waist deep in the water as they look over the expanse of water. Each shot reveals more and more people standing in the water. The film focuses on their hands: this man prays with his palms together; another has his hands raised in Muslim prayer; a woman dips her hands along the surface of the water. We begin to see hands rubbing against what appears to be log sculpture of some sort bobbing in the water. The sound of the Sey family singing fills the soundtrack before we see them singing as they hold each other, as the waves threaten to knock them about. More hands touching the log, and we eventually see that it is a sculpture of a face of a drowned body made by Olga Govtvian (fig. 2.1).

Men and women, touching each other, send the sculpture off across the Mediterranean. With the camera at water level, we watch it float until it is lost from view. A woman wades after it, crying before she stops. The film appears to end as its dedication appears on a black screen: "To all the black bodies unburied in the seas of the world." Yet this is a false ending, as the film reopens on the beach. It is now morning; the sun has risen, as everything is more clearly visible. The same men and women sit and stand on the beach, passing kola nut from one pair of hands to another, emulating West African funeral rituals, in which the kola nut is passed as friends and family remember the dead. The film ends again. This beginning and ending again of the film speaks to the conjoinment of the drowned and the living. The dead refuse to be buried; they continually insist on their concatenation with the living. The living, in recognition of this, embrace and surrender to the sea essential parts of themselves.

No one directly speaks in the film. We hear the announcer speak on the radio, we read the filmmaker's words on the screen, and groups of voices sing. The film forces us to experience a landscape and history that cannot be separated into any single sense modality. The oversaturation of color as the film plays with light and dark, the continual shifting between sound that does not correspond to the visual, the visual that refuses linear narratives—all enact a landscape of grief, loss, and life. Kimberly Mair cites Jean-Luc Nancy when he describes sleep as "the abyss and the plunge, the density of deep water and the descent of the drowned body sinking backward" (18). Rather than sleep, to remember and mourn our dead is to experience this haptic plunge, this descent, the incommensurability of loss within one's own body. The driver's scream of anguish that occurs off-screen stages a disorienting encounter not with the abstraction of loss but with the painfulness of living connected to others. The intersensorial, as it loops, severs, and sutures geographic and historical worlds, insists on incomprehensible loss that can only be mourned through performative modes of witnessing. The film insists that the living's need of the dead is matched only by the dead's need for us to remember. Rubbing the sculpture and leaving the drowned unburied by casting them afloat represent an intersensorial black social engagement that enables us to get back into the car and keep on driving through the city haunted by past death and the dead yet to come.

Dagmawi Woubshet in *The Calendar of Loss* writes about how "loss govern[s] time and temperament" in Ethiopia (ix). Describing not only the brutal violence of the Derg's communist regime, in which more than a million Ethiopians died, but also the later devastation caused by the AIDS epidemic, Woubshet insists on what he calls a "poetics of compounding loss" that does not "recount, respond to and reflect upon singular events of mourning, but instead explicitly underscore[s] . . . the serial and repetitive nature of the losses they confront" (3). This is not just the loss of those who have already passed but also the loss yet to come. The taxi driver in *Unburied* breaks under this compounding political sense of privation. The intersensorial spilling of her grief points toward the inability of "experts" to calculate loss through quantitative data. The numbers of the dead announced on the radio and the film's black screen, which tells us how many people died crossing the Mediterranean during its making—these all sink under the weight of compounding loss.

Rituals of grief (the film *Unburied*, the voices of the dead that disrupt the surface of the text, this book itself) do not reduce the dead body to a symbol around which the living organize their sociopolitical claims. Instead, staring into the abyss of the "horizon of death" (Ferreira da Silva, "No-Bodies" 231), this chapter is a form of necroactivism, what Eunjung Kim describes as a "technology of resistance" that emerges in those moments when the dead demand that the living acknowledge their "material" and "spiritual presence" ("Continuing Presence" 4). Making space for such presence does not only serve the dead. Instead, our very aliveness or animation is derived from their presence—the dead "enliven and depend on the labor of the living to demand their justice and their interconnected future" (Kim 15). Living and dead are entangled, conjoined, somatically inextricable. As Woubshet writes, "For the living, there is no constituency as formative as the dead" (ix). The conjoinment of dead and living constitutes a crucial form of differential embodiment. The dead as constitutive of the living body moves us away from liberal Enlightenment notions of individuated bodies that rest on Western biopolitical notions of being and nonbeing. As Kathryn Yusoff reminds us, the "division of matter into nonlife and life pertains not only to matter but to the racial organization of life as foundational to New World geographies. . . . The language of materiality and its division between life and nonlife, and its alignment with concepts of the human and inhuman, facilitated the divisions between subjects as humans and . . . inhuman matter" (5, 9).

The drowned bodies of black and brown migrants are marked as nobodies, as nonbeings, through performances of the global nation-state's indifference. Denise Ferreira da Silva calls this "the most insidious power effect of raciality, the logic of obliteration, which is inscribed in the very production of racial subaltern subjects as the "affectable I" ("No-Bodies" 234). This logic of obliteration transforms the racialized dead into fungible "things," into the "social scientific instruments of racial truth" (Ferreira da Silva, "No-Bodies" 232) of casualty statistics, red dots and iron ballast. Floating through the racialized objects that produce humanity as always white, I wish to grab hold of the enlivening corpse, to claim her as integral to my life and to black sociality. The conjoined bodies of the living and dead enable a continued search for what Tiffany Lethabo King calls an "utterance and grammar outside of . . . the narrativity of the liberal subject or human" (21). While traditional disability studies would not include the floating dead in their idea of differential embodiment, black feminist studies allows us to reconsider a conjoined personhood in which the ancestors are necessary in animating the living. *To be alive is to insist on a concatenation with the corpse.* It is to embrace the horizon of death, to pull it in like Zora Neale Hurston's great fishnet and drape it over our shoulders as "so much of life [lies] in its meshes" (184).

My argument in this chapter is divided into three parts. First, I examine how the drowned bodies that are the casualties of Mediterranean crossings are considered, especially in light of surveillance technologies. Looking at Eurosur (European external border surveillance) and specifically Spain's "integrated system for external surveillance," or SIVE, I theorize the red dot on a radar screen that encapsulates the worldview that produces what Ferreira da Silva calls the "transparent I." The transparent I constitutes a transcendental form of subjectivity that reduces the people in its crosshairs to disposable labor and corpses to be processed (identified, disposed of, returned). It robs us of our sensuous and resistant relations with the dead. The second part of the chapter elaborates on the theoretical apparatus introduced by *Unburied* to counter this abstraction. Using Rizvana Bradley, Fred Moten, and Christina Sharpe, I argue for the importance of intersensorial spilling and mingling, or what others have called "hapticity" as a performative method of imagining black sociality across the diaspora that counters necropolitical abstraction and reduction.

The third part of the chapter looks specifically at instances of performance that insist on floating as a mode of differential embodiment and movement. The dead move in many ways. They apparate, throw things, pop up suddenly behind you. They also sink and float, as we have already seen in Runnymede's commissioned short film *Unburied* and over and over again in news coverage of the fatalities of black and brown people who fail to make it across the Mediterranean alive. The second half of the chapter thus thinks about floating as a form of differentially embodied movement that remembers the dead even as it insists that the living revalue slowness, directionlessness, and a sensory engagement with water.

I thus turn to the South African Berni Searle's *Home and Away* (2003), a performance of floating in the Mediterranean that is at the heart of this chapter. *Home and Away* is a six-minute multiple-screen video performance produced by Montenmedio Arte Contemporáneo Foundation in Vejer. Two screens are projected opposite each other. The opening sequence displays a gray-blue sky with a refracted sun on the left and ocean water on another screen. Searle, dressed in a black top and reddish-pink skirt with a white overlay, floats on her back into the screen (figs. 2.2–2.3). Her body, as Liese van der Watt writes, "becomes a glistening sculpture of sorts, its corporeality enlarged and altered by the billowing mass of fabric, wet and animated and glowing with a life of its own" ("Tracing" 78). Eventually, what looks like a mass of seaweed or black ink enters the frame, spreading beneath Searle's floating body, gradually darkening the water and fabric. There is no music. One hears the wind and waves breathing. Thirty seconds into the piece, a whispered voice-over by Searle begins, "I love . . . you love . . . he loves . . . we love . . . you love . . . they love." On one screen displaying the ocean's surface, the frame is gradually filled by the wake of a boat moving away from shore. After approximately three and a half minutes, Searle repeats the declension, replacing the verb "love" with the word "feel." "I feel . . . you feel . . . he feels . . . we feel . . . you feel . . . they feel." The piece ends with another repetition, this time with the verb "leave." "I leave . . . you leave . . . they leave." Searle demonstrates the centrality of hapticity to counter the material and epistemic violence to which black people are subjected. Her performance of both the living and the dead as they float and feel, arrive and leave, foregrounds the intimacy of black sociality, differential embodiment, and movement that does not ignore difference. Instead, to quote Christina Sharpe, she performs "from and into a 'we' that [is] black and global and that recognize[s] the conditions—specific to each geographical location—and a set of phenomena that disproportionately and overwhelmingly affect black people everywhere" ("And to Survive" 172).

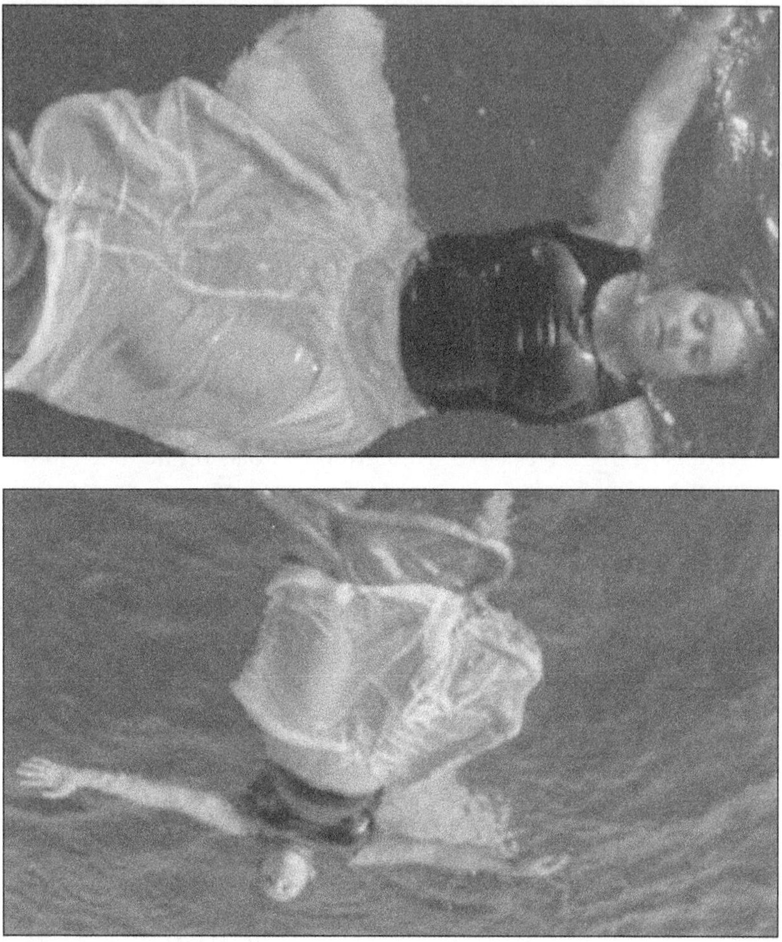

Figures 2.2 and 2.3. Berni Searle, *Home and Away* (2003) (© Berni Searle, NMAC Montenmedio Arte Contemporáneo, Vejer, Spain; screenshot by author)

Part One: Red Dots and Blocks of Ballast

In April 2015, the world's eye suddenly focused on large numbers of migrants from Syria, Eritrea, South Sudan, Libya, and Tunisia, desperately fleeing the political violence and proxy wars of the "First World" and trying to cross the Mediterranean Sea and enter an economically depressed European Union. The past decade had seen over a thousand migrants, passengers on such vessels, reported dead or missing, their bodies washing up on various beaches in Spain, Turkey, Greece, and other countries in Europe, trapped in fishing nets or rocks at the bottom of cliffs, randomly scattered across the sea. The sudden interest in the plight of Africans crossing the Mediterranean was due in large part to several wrecks of overcrowded vessels with high casualty rates, in particular a wooden shipping boat that began floundering some seventy-seven nautical miles off the coast of Libya, eventually capsizing and sinking with hundreds of people trapped below deck. Trisha Thomas of the Associated Press writes, "Their conditions were reminiscent of slave ships plying the seas in the 18th century—the migrants had clearly been trapped, unable to move." There were 457 body bags full of commingled human remains recovered from the wreck of the Libyan coast, twenty-eight people survived, two hundred people were trapped in the engine room alone. Body no. 421 was that of a young man whose remains were placed in a metal container before being put into a wooden coffin. This arithmetic of value and valuelessness, what Woubshet calls "a leitmotif of inventory taking" (4), has become the main legacy of their death. This inventory taking obfuscates their relationality to each other and their inextricability from us.

The Strait of Gibraltar is the narrowest waterway between the coasts of North Africa and Europe.[1] One can stand on specific parts of the coast of Africa and see Europe with the naked eye, a fact that has generated considerable panic as the EU fortifies its external frontiers and ceaselessly patrols what has come to be seen as Europe's Achilles' heel. Refugees cross these patrolled waters mainly in two kinds of small crafts, the precarious patera or the fast, inflatable boat called the Zodiac, after its brand name. For Europe, the patera and the Zodiac have come to stand for the threat to "civilization" posed by the racial other. As David Álvarez writes, these migrants and their boats have become reminders of the proximity of the undesirable "worlds of Islam and of Third World underdevelopment" through "the instrumental conflation of clandestine migration with drug trafficking and more recently with Islamist terrorism" (120). The Strait zone has become heavily fortified in an attempt to keep out these migrants and refugees. Those who reach the shores alive are met with various state responses that run the gamut from conditional hospitality to Italian declarations of nonpersonhood. All these responses, no matter how seemingly generous, are part and parcel of an escalating politics of securitization generated by Europe's fear of being invaded and having its putative whiteness imperiled (as the racialized body is always from someplace else).[2]

Thinking through the various iterations of capital across "global spacetime" requires me briefly to think through the business of Europe's external border surveillance system. As migrants shiver on the beach and watch the lights come on in Europe across the Strait,[3] European states continue to invest in Eurosur (European external border surveillance system) and all that is connected with it. Spain's "integrated system for external surveillance," or SIVE, combines radar, cameras, and patrols. Reading the SIVE map requires understanding how various boats and migrants move. "A sinuous, zigzag path [on the radar screen] means it could be a *patera*," a guard tells the economist Ruben Andersson (9). How fast the red dot moves tells the guards a great deal. If it moves laboriously across the screen, it could be a *cayuco*, a large wooden boat carrying up to a hundred passengers. If the red blip moves quickly, it could be drug smugglers or a handful of migrants in a Zodiac. When the dot moves closer to the shore, high-definition or infrared cameras zoom in to identify the craft. If it is a vessel bearing migrants, patrol boats are deployed to intercept the craft. The time/space moment of interception is marked by the crosshairs symbol. SIVE cannot locate dead bodies.

I would like to dwell for a moment on this red dot on a radar screen; this pulsing pixel is a perfect instantiation of the rational that produces what Ferreira da Silva calls the "transparent I," that form of subjectivity that has easy access to the transcendental. Traditional Western scholarship, Ferreira da Silva argues, has privileged this transparent I, an abstracted form of subjectivity constituted as rational, self-determined, singular, and universal. The framing of migrants as red dots on a grid is the consequence of the project of rationality, which disembodies and rationalizes the world. Thus, the destruction of migrants becomes the elimination of a blip on a coordinate—the apotheosis of map-thinking.

Andersson writes that "clandestine migration," with its radar cameras, patrol boats, international coordination centers, intelligence networks, and aid agencies, has become a veritable "illegality industry," in which "a migrant boat has become a source of risk sold on to the industrial investors," with "'junk' risk . . . outsourced [onto] African forces and the migrants they are paid to target" (7–11). In this cycle of capitalist accumulation, we see an illustration of Ferreira da Silva's aggregation of historical moments—a time/space that is not linear but that reassembles what has happened and what is to come.[4] Indeed, this speculative economy of risk and death on the open waters echoes what Ian Baucom, in *Specters of the Atlantic* (2005), has called "an ocean-crossing network of loans, debts, bonds, and bills of exchange, an archipelagic eddy of circulating [promissory] money" (112). But whereas circum-Atlantic slavery relied on the calculated risk of buying and selling loans that relied on the credibility of American and Caribbean factors,[5] the system of contemporary risk management on the Mediterranean produces and profits from the illegality of migrants who attempt to cross the Strait by increasingly perilous means. Necropolitical labor is defined by Jin-Kyung Lee in *Service Economies* as "the ultimate labor commodity or worker, something or someone to be thrown out, replaced, and/or (both literally and figuratively) killed after or as the labor is performed. If we extend this notion of necropolitical labor, . . . the Nazi uses of dead bodies or body parts for medical and other purposes, or the contemporary organ trade" constitute "a posthumous labor" (6). The migrants' necropolitical labor lies in their fueling of Europe's profitable surveillance machinery—their bodies are only valuable insofar as they attempt to cross into Europe and the speculative finance capital invested in preventing them from doing so.

The technologies at work in this oceanic economy form a historical aggregate. The conversion of the bodies of these migrants into abstract red dots has its roots in earlier practices in which universal subjects converted the material bodies of black and brown peoples into blocks of iron ballast.[6] Consider, for example, the case of the *São José–Paquete de Africa*, which sank in 1794 on some submerged rocks less than three hundred feet off the shore of Cape Town, South Africa, near the now-affluent area called Clifton Beach. The ship was able to signal for help with a cannon blast, and the captain, crew, and half of the captives were rescued. Two days later, these captives were resold into slavery. The remainder of the slaves, some 212 Mozambicans, drowned. Jaco Boshoff, a maritime archaeologist with the Iziko Museum, realized when he discovered iron blocks in the wreckage that the vessel was not a Dutch merchant ship but instead was a Portuguese slaver filled with human cargo. The blocks were used as ballast, enabling the crew to stabilize the ship and control the ship's height in the water by counterbalancing the weight of human cargo. This weight fluctuated as slaves starved, died, and disappeared overboard. As Paul Gardullo, curator at the Smithsonian's National Museum of African American History and Culture in Washington, DC (NMAAHC), states, "The more cargo that you have that is living, the more ballast you need because live cargo moves and is not as heavy as, say, tubs of molasses. . . . Ballast becomes a signature for slaving, and a direct corollary to human beings" (Cooper). Each pound of ballast, then, stood for a single pound of flesh. Of the slaves who drowned, we have no other trace. No corpses. No bones. Just inert blocks of iron ballast that stand in mute testimony to the weight of captive bodies lost under the surface.[7]

Contemporary technology used by SIVE cannot detect corpses as they are too insignificant in mass and size. The corpses are insignificant to larger projects of national security in which individual deaths are seen as evidence of individual risks rather than as a legacy of structural inequities inherited from slavery and colonization. Thus, for example, while Cristina Cattaneo and Prefect Vittorio Piscitelli led a large-scale forensic effort to identify victims from the April 2015 wreck during a costly initiative called Melilli5 that lifted the sunken boat to the surface, identifying the bodies received "zero funding" from the government (Amade and Casartelli 744). While it was deemed necessary to bring the boat up to the surface to prevent the continual surfacing of decaying remains, who these corpses were and to whom they were attached was of little importance. Many of the bodies had been immersed in water for so long that they had undergone saponification, in which soft tissue and fat form a soapy white coating called "adipocere" or "cadaver wax." After a few months, the coated body begins to break into pieces, dissolving distinctions between individuals. A graveyard in Catania, Sicily, houses a plaque with the identification numbers of three drowned migrants. Their bodies were conjoined, their bones and teeth indistinguishable from one another (Amade and Casartelli 750).

Under Western common law, there are no rights of personhood conferred to the dead. The body in most cases becomes the property of the nearest blood kin. In other words, the floating corpse/body fragment makes visible the property relations that already structure the lives and deaths of these black and brown migrants. Relationality between the dead and the living gets transformed into an overt property relation.

But what if we think of the corpse's capacity to perform black sociality or affinity? Debra Levine insists that claiming the saponified corpse/fragment "enable[s] a political location for the dead to speak the conditions of their own finitude by creating an ensemble composed of the materiality of corpses and the animative capacity of the living." She summarizes: "The reformulation of affinity conceived and practiced as performance opens a temporal and relational framework of prosthetic politics that allows bodies to speak their death even after the end of life." This conjoined black sociality intervenes in the law's reduction of the corpse as owned by blood kin. It also resists the state's control over the meaning and value of our disprized black bodies, both alive and dead.

Given the lack of DNA, the washing away of fingerprints by the sea, and absent dental or any other biomaterial records, the Melilli5 forensic team collected personal effects, placing them in plastic bags with the same identification number as on the coffin or plaque. The list of personal effects painfully counters the abstraction of the red dot. There is the spoonful of dirt wrapped and carefully stored in a pocket, a photograph sewn into the lining of a jacket, a boy's report card in his pocket. Cattaneo, using European embassies in Eritrea, Somalia, and Ethiopia, put out a call to anyone searching for their loved ones who might have been on board the capsized ship. She asked families to make their way to Rome or Milan with any information. Members of more than fifty families came to seek their dead, despite distance and expense. As Sharon Holland reminds us, "Bringing back the dead . . . is the ultimate queer act" (103–4). Thirty-one of the dead were named as they in turn wrapped the living up in their monstrous embrace.

Part Two: The Language of Seagulls

The dead speak. *I stand here in the dark behind the dunes. The temperature is dropping, and I can feel my shoulders start to fold inward. The man next to me stills even his breathing when the lights begin to come on across the Strait. At first, it is a few yellowish circles here and there, then there are bursts. Or perhaps we are both imagining them as the water swells in front of us. The White Sea, the Middle Sea, the crossing. A baby in his mother's arms mewls as he opens his eyes. She runs her palm along the fuzz on his scalp in a moment of fierce pride. Her future. Future sucks listlessly at a soaked rag. He is unnaturally quiet. She has prepared him for this night's desperate sojourn. "We do what we have to do," she told her sister earlier as she rubbed brandy along the boy's gums, the inside of his cheeks, and the soles of his feet.*

There are fewer of us than at the start. The brother and sister, after the sister woke with her right eyelid swollen and a trail of angry red bumps around her mouth, have turned back. It was a sign, they said to each other. They are still alive. Unlike us.

The air smells of burnt paper. Those of us who didn't leave our documents and ID cards behind burnt them a couple of hours earlier. Decarded. Discarded. We are all of us, beautiful drops of life caught in "transnational circuits of harm" ("Continuing Presence" 17). We move clumsily between coercion and consent, our limbs stuck to this web.

Just as there are many predatory creatures, this crossing is not a solo performance. It feels strange to be tethered, bound to strangers who will never become kin. Your cough can result in my eviction, my ability to float the difference between your son living or drowning. Conjoined. I resentfully drag the bowlegged man to the boat as he attempts to pray one last time—the quicker everyone gets on, the sooner we can be off. Later, when I drown, I wonder if his completed prayer could have saved us. God can be very exacting.

My sensuous remembering, on the other hand, is very inexact. A mediocre performance in the face of the repeated fury and teeth of slavery, colonialism, and its afterlife. But some lies are necessary. They are as vital as breathing if we are to move beyond the way you process, bury, store, or send back our bodies to the place we felt we had no choice but to leave. We are the disposable populations, the waste, the saponified unrecognizable "thing." We are remnants as our bodies sink into opacity. We are the words spoken by gulls.

If the aforementioned technologies and economies are about a process of bodily abstraction and alienation, then the performances in this chapter allow us to recover the haptic and affective dimensions of historical aggregates. In contradistinction to the red radar blip and the iron ballast, the mixed-media performances of Berni Searle exemplify intersensoriality, what Stephanie Springgay calls "a corporeal pedagogy, where inter-embodiment functions as a pedagogical practice that shifts our understanding of self and other . . . to one premised on [a haptic] relationality" (19). In other words, these performances and images reclaim and rework the red dot and iron ballast of abstracted, burdened subjectivity, positing our queered bodies not as receptacles for meaning but inherently *as* meaning. Rather than a recovery of individual subjectivity, these performances gesture toward conjoinment of being and nonbeing, the living and the dead, in order to create an embodied black sociality that enfranchises the dead and embraces the bloated corpse.

Christina Sharpe, in *In the Wake*, writes of an unnamed, overfilled ship with over five hundred passengers that caught fire, capsized, and sank approximately half a mile from the coast of Lampedusa. Sharpe is struck by the repeated use by the media of the word "human cargo" when attempting to calculate the financial loss that the capsized ship represented: "The addition of the word *human* to *cargo* does nothing, here, to ameliorate the ghosting these ships do of transatlantic slavery or the afterlives of slavery or the afterlives of property" (*In the Wake* 55). To counter the continuing violence of abstraction, Sharpe picks carefully through reports, searching for details that contest the anonymity of body bags and human cargo, what she terms "the violence of abstraction represented, for instance, in the 'ditto ditto,' or 'Negro woman,' 'Negro man,' 'meagre girl' in the ship manifest and plantation ledger" ("And to Survive" 179). Her attention is arrested by what bystanders mistake as a gaggle of seagulls (Eritrean migrants shouting for help as they flail in the water), a "sea of heads" and arms, the story of a dead young woman whose baby was still connected to her via its umbilical cord. She uses these sensory moments as a form of "wake work," as a kind of "mapping, survivor testimony and counter narrative [that] might counter forgetting, erasure, the monumental and that ditto ditto in the archives" (*In the Wake* 59). Sharpe's "wake work" is not an insistence that nonwhite bodies be included in the category of the transparent I, with its putative universal subjectivity materialized in this chapter by the red radar dot. Instead, like Ferreira da Silva, she situates her truth claims within the affective body, that being associated with irrationality and exteriority, "subjected to both natural . . . conditions and to other's power" (Ferreira da Silva, *Toward a Global* xv). Sharpe dares to imagine what it would look like to theorize a world floating in the undercommons, as Saidiya Hartman reminds us, "to tell a story [whose content and form proves] capable of engaging and countering the violence of abstraction" (Saunders 5). What would thinking look like, if instead of arising from the transparent I, theory arises from collective affectable bodies, attempting to dismantle our racial subjugation even as we strategically navigate transparency? What if I could write using the language of seagulls? As Paul Stoller explains, "To accept sensuousness in scholarship is to reject the conceit of control in which mind and body, self and other are considered separate. . . . To accept sensuousness is . . . to lend one's body to the world and accept its complexities, tastes, structures, and smells" (*Sensuous Scholarship* xvii). Sensuous scholarship is historically and culturally sedimented, more performative than representational. It decenters the individual humanist subject as it forms a repertoire with which to experience, understand, and theorize the world.[8]

This idea of a repertoire of embodied performances, connected not just to specific historical and geographic moments but to large arcs of black life, necessitates a departure from traditional, linear, and progressive notions of history. Linear thinking—overreliant as it is on cultural difference defined within early twentieth-century accounts of racial subjugation—has ignored "the links between various incarnations of capital across the fabric of global spacetime" (Ferreira da Silva, "Fractal Thinking"). It has allowed for the theorization of colonial violence as isolated moments, as singular crises without precedent. In order to think seriously and nonlinearly about Sharpe's ghostings and the afterlives of slavery and property—in order to understand the affective dimension here—one needs to turn toward what Ferreira da Silva calls "poethical" or "compositional" thinking, in which events are imagined as four-dimensional or more. Time (Einstein's fourth dimension) is folded into the three dimensions of depth, width, and length. This fourth dimension of time is not linear but rather a dense moment occurring within a particle-level plenum, where "*what happens* . . . is always already a reassembling of what has happened before and of what has yet to happen" (Ferreira da Silva, "Fractal Thinking").[9] In other words, each moment is an aggregate of historical moments as it expresses "what has already passed, and what is yet to come" (Ferreira da Silva, "Fractal Thinking"). This aggregation of historical moments refutes the notion of a refugee "crisis" in the Mediterranean. Instead, the so-called crisis is a continuation of the forces of primitive accumulation that have necessitated global forms of (human) capital and alienated labor. Thus, the phenomenon of the Mediterranean refugee crisis must be compositionally conceived as part of a spatiotemporal constellation that includes the transatlantic slave trade. As such, slavery is not over and done with but instead repeats itself in a global cycle of capital accumulation, founded on the fungibility of black and brown bodies.[10]

Such "compositional" thinking necessarily includes the haptic, what Stoller calls "sensuous scholarship" that enables us to listen to the plaintive and angry cries of drowning men and women that connect them to each other and to seagulls. In "Haptic Geographies: Ethnography, Haptic Knowledges and Sensuous Dispositions," Mark Paterson argues that senses are not individual experiences but rather "historically [and culturally] sedimented bodily dispositions and patterns of haptic experience that become habituated over time" (779). These sensuous dispositions are more performative than representational, decentering the individual humanist subject as they form a repertoire with which to experience, understand, and theorize the world. Paterson's careful reading of the historical and cultural particularity of the haptic refuses to either individualize or universalize such sensations. The haptic is *not* some romantic call to recognize the universality of all humanity, nor does it suggest that each person's pain, for example, is unique. The haptic is fundamentally about how bodies relate to one another in specific times and spaces—our race, class, gender, and sexuality condition our experience of the visceral. The haptic, as Allison Hayes-Conroy and Deborah Martin write, "recognizes a multiplicity of ways in which minded-bodies are constantly developing, moving, shifting and working," even as they are shaped by "social cues and sedimented experiences of social difference" (278, 273).

Rizvana Bradley, in her introduction to the special issue of *Women and Performance* on the haptic, details the importance of tactile and textured somatic epistemes that force us to question the sociologic of race even as they create racial structures of feeling. The haptic, she suggests, crucially is about "the worlds and imaginations that have both conditioned and surpassed the body in and of performance ("Introduction" 129–30). As such, she builds on the argument laid out by Stefano Harney and Fred Moten in *The Undercommons: Fugitive Planning and Black Study*. Focusing on the specific structures of feeling generated by being dispossessed, displaced as a commodity (i.e.. enslaved), Harney and Moten deploy the term "hapticality" to describe a speculative practice that constitutes an unlocatable undercommons, arising from the shared history of the "hold." They argue, "The hold's terrible gift was to gather dispossessed feelings in common, to create a new feel in the undercommons. . . . In the undercommons of a new feel, another kind of feeling became common. . . . [It was] a way of feeling through others, a feel for feeling others feeling you. This is modernity's insurgent feel, its inherited caress, its skin talk, tongue touch, breath speech, hand laugh. This is the feel that no individual can stand, and no state abide. This is the feel we might call hapticality" (Harney and Moten 98). The haptic, then, is a visceral way of experiencing *both* the material ties of modernity that link black peoples *and* the imaginative worlds that these ties engender. This hapticity resides in the somatic conceptions of a tightly packed space gathered through interactions with the built environs, bodily fluids, ocean water, and the touch of skin against bone as we lay against each other in the bottom of the hold. It is compositional, intersensorial, a constellation of the past and a harbinger of things to come.

The work of Berni Searle in *Home and Away* reminds us that Harney and Moten's haptic undercommons is not only about the hold of the slave ship and transatlantic slavery. Instead, their undercommons encompasses the larger crisis of capital, in which "blackness is an unspeakably intelligible trait within the practice of geographic violence" that "knits together destructive force and human life through the prism of coloniality" (McKittrick, "On Plantations" 953). Searle's necroactivist work, even as it moves us away from singular notions of originary blackness, insists on recognizing the "dead and dying black body" as a way of refuting linear progressive intellectual and spatial politics as well as theorizing the performative connections between the living and the dead. Her performances, through compositional thinking, enable us to theorize the undercommons as a resistant practice that includes the internal migrations of continental Africans over land and also the passage in the bellies of those ships that transported slaves toward Africa. Harney and Moten astutely link the accumulative cycle of finance capital underpinned by the slave trade to the coerced migrations of indentured laborers from India, China, and Java and to the boats crossing the Mediterranean (92). "Modernity," they write, "is sutured by this hold" (93).

Yes, the hold is the terrible belly of the slave ship, but it is also what Moten has famously theorized as the multidimensional moment of the "break" (*In the Break*). It is the fragmented, crumpled spaces where the angles are irrational, where one feels not one's own dispossession but the dispossession of others who are feeling for you. The hold is "entering again and again the broken world, to trace the visionary company and join it" (Harney and Moten 94).

However, the danger of the way that the "hold" has been taken up is that it can underemphasize the numerous movements of black and brown bodies within and toward the African continent and, instead, center the undercommons around the transatlantic crossings of the slave trade. For example, even as Harney and Moten write of all the various transportations of speaking commodities such as Chinese indentured laborers to the Caribbean, they assert that modern logistics "was founded in the Atlantic slave trade, founded against the Atlantic slave" (92). The performances of Berni Searle, in particular, quietly eddy against such an unintentional privileging of transatlantic slavery, instead asking us to think about the forced movement of slaves across the Indian Ocean, within the African continent, and toward the African continent itself. Rather than privileging transatlantic slavery, Searle allows us to glimpse a new kind of haptic world characterized by the migration and displacement of black and brown peoples during late modernity. As I have argued extensively elsewhere, while the transatlantic trade was the largest forced migration of Africans, the trans-Saharan trade of nearly eight million slaves and the Indian Ocean and Red Sea trades of more than four million slaves should not be overlooked (Hershini Young, *Illegible Will*). South Africa was a complicated landscape, with slaves hailing from Madagascar, India, Sri Lanka, Batavia (modern-day Jakarta), and later Mozambique. Much of Searle's work addresses this genealogy, reshaping the notion of the undercommons by focusing on multiple displacements and relocations not just from but also *to* Africa.

Searle's maternal great-grandfathers from Mauritius and Saudi Arabia were brought as slaves to South Africa, where they married "Cape Malay" women, resulting in Searle's identity as a "coloured" woman.[11] Like most black genealogies, Searle's family history is produced through forgetting and rememory. She thus states, "Apart from my physical features, very little connects me to . . . [my Mauritius/Saudi Arabian] heritage, one of the tentative aspects being food. . . . This effectively means that the local or potential indigenous part of me can be traced by looking at my lineage of my maternal and paternal great-grandmothers, i.e., women" (Gqola 128). Forging a connection between herself as an artist and the women who came before her, many of Searle's performances revolve around the language of food and cooking. Using spices to expand the notion of the undercommons and to theorize the complex patterns of coerced movement toward Africa, Searle created what perhaps is her best-known work, the *Colour Me* series (completed between 1997 and 2000). Using the spices used to create the distinct style of food known as Malay cooking, Searle documents how food and spice perform the cultural work of articulating a black/Asian diaspora. She navigates what Pumla Gqola calls the "histories of 'grotesque' spectacle and 'exotic' Oriental that attach to dominant historic representation of African and Asian bodies in creative and epistemic regimes which support diasporisation" (134). Her work refuses to privilege origins, complicating the blackness of the South African Capetonian. Such a reorientation of the undercommons demands from us a dive into a plenum where the haptic sutures together nonlinear time and deep space. What we are left with is compositional, fragmented, and multidimensional necroactivism, residing in the break.

Part Three: Differential Movement—Floating

Originally a sculptor who received her MFA from the University of Cape Town, Berni Searle uses lens-based media—photography, video, and film—along with her own body to create moving installations about her complex South African ancestry, narrative, and history. A six-minute multiple-screen video performance produced by the Montenmedio Arte Contemporaneo Foundation in Vejer, *Home and Away* (2003) was filmed along the Strait of Gibraltar. Searle's performance, compositional thinking at its finest, coaxes the viewer through voice-over and video, movement and stillness, toward recognizing an undercommons forged by body and water that gestures toward the future, even as it reiterates the past. The swell of saltwater and the way her body works to stay afloat foreground how feelings are sedimented in social bodies that move differently through global spacetime.

In an interview with Rory Bester, Searle tells us that the Cuban performance artist Ana Mendieta is a major influence in her work ("Interview"). Though Searle does not directly mention it, Mendieta's 1974 video performance *Untitled (Ocean Bird Washup)* is striking in its exploration of similar themes as *Home and Away*. The silent performance shows us a floating Mendieta, covered in white feathers, struggling against waves that buffet her body about. As she tries to stay afloat, we see the feathers become waterlogged and her struggle to breathe. She eventually succumbs to the force of the waves that sweep her onto the sand, where she is left ensnared in the branches of a dead tree. Noting the similarities between the two artists, Liese van der Watt writes, "Like Mendieta who left traces of her body in the American landscape, the image of Searle's body becomes a document—a trace—of previous actions and performances" ("Disappearing Act"). Searle's manipulation of both photograph and film creates a system of layers that she claims "are derived from and located within a grid of power relations . . . embedded in everyday life and culture" (Bester 108). To wit, the majority of her work focuses on her body or particular aspects of its corporeality. The black female African body, like the black slave body, has traditionally been subjected to what Ayo Coly calls "colonial 'scientific pornography'" (653) or what Hortense Spillers calls "pornotroping" (67). The black female becomes an object to be studied, classified, and exposed even while that act of exposure operates within a violent libidinal economy that ungenders her, reducing her to vulnerable flesh that is ripped apart, violated, and written on. The contemporary African artist, then, has to struggle with how to depict this "discursively overburdened" (Ayo 654) black female body without resituating the body within the visual field of the pornotrope.

How does one engage with the African body in productive ways that do not simply reiterate the colonial gaze of objectification/sexualization? Searle does this in each of her works by using her racially opaque body to think through the discursive processes by which her body is made. Working with the idioms of staining, tracing, and imprinting, her *Profile* series (2002), for example, in which her cheek holds the memory of patterns pressed against it, explores how her body has been racialized by colonial and apartheid governments, as well as by postapartheid regimes. Searle's body registers and alludes to this racial classification in the *Colour Me* series (1998) and *Snow White* (2001), in which she is buried under spices or white flour. These themes resonate in *Discoloured* (1999), in which her hands and parts of her torso are stained with henna and ink, and in *Night Fall* (2006), in which she rolls down a mound of grape skins, staining her skin and dress wine-red. Throughout each of these works, her careful documentation of her body's transformation creates sensuous performances that navigate between various media such as photography, video, and installation.

Searle's insistence on her body being produced through mediation of various historical genres of interpellation and looking comes through in her resistance to performing in front of a live audience. She says, "My works have a definite performance character to the extent that they invoke movement and indeterminacy. But there is an assumption that because it's performative, I perform. I have been asked on a number of occasions to do performances. The problem with 'performing' is that I am more directly and easily consumed or exoticised, which I'm trying to avoid. Mediating the 'performance' through lens-based media provides me with options to reconstruct myself in the process" (Bester 108). Searle articulates what José Muñoz calls the "burden of liveness," a "reified link between performance and liveness" where the "story of 'otherness' is one tainted by a mandate to 'perform' for the amusement of a dominant power bloc" (*Disidentifications* 189, 187). Muñoz develops that the mandate for "crude materiality" that haunts black performance becomes a surrogate for political and historical representation as it rewrites the temporality of the artist of color. For to be always "live" is to be stripped of both a past and a promised time that comes after. It is to be consumed in a single bite of fictive pristine authenticity. Searle insists that it is necessary to "dislodge" herself "from a theoretical apparatus that positions her as only legible as a live and immediate presence and not as a historicized and representable entity" (Muñoz, *Disidentifications* 191), so she layers her performances. She resists the illusion of easy (sexual) accessibility that live performance can generate in audiences eager to consume black bodies. Her photography inserts a layer of mediation between her body and the gaze of her audience, and these optic relationships are further complicated in her video work, in which her use of multiple screens short-circuits the standard centering of the audience's attention on a single frame. These video works disrupt the objectifying gaze as the viewer becomes unsure how the narrative unfolds, what we should be focusing on, and which screen we should be looking at. Searle uses these processes of mediation, not only to push back at how audiences view her as an artist but also to resist biologically based narratives of her identity. Her race and gender, she insists, are produced through the processes she self-consciously performs, and access to the black body is necessarily indirect and complicated. There are no bodies that are easy pickings here: neither her own as an artist nor the black pornotroped female body produced by technologies of race.

Thus, *Home and Away* is both a three-screen video of Searle's performance and her surroundings and a series of related photographs, *Waiting #1–6*. Searle's videos and photographs do not merely document her live performances. Nor are her original performances authentic private rituals that just happened to be captured on film. Rather, Searle constructs the "private" performance as a means to resist transparent documentation through the play of embodied absence and felt/heard/seen presence in her work. Searle's work, thus, does not simply indexically trace and record her body. Instead, as Joanna Walker writes, "like the conductor or choreographer, [Searle] is present in a mediated form of self-expression" that proposes not only a body that is "playfully unstable" but also the instability of identitarian categories such as race and gender. As Searle states, her creative "processes attempt to convey something about . . . intangibility or a flexibility and a state of flux, which is central to . . . [her] view of occupying multiple identities that are constantly changing" (Murinik 77). The colliding and interaction of various surfaces—skin, spices, henna, photographic frame, video screen—allow for the emergence of complex self whose outside surfaces do not index interiority so much as force the viewer into a haptic engagement with them. In other words, the haptic moves the meaning of the body away from singular subjectivity toward one of polymorphous black sociality.

In *Against the Closet*, Aliyyah Abdur-Rahman asks what it would mean for "racial embodiment and experience, if instead of belonging to the realm of the external, the phenotypical, the material and instead of heavy-handedly fueling the operative forces of compulsory interpellation, race moved inward and operated for the racialized subject primarily from an internal site of instinct, impulse, intuition, longing" (3)? This is a queer "architecture of race" (Abdur-Rahman 3) that does not rely on the pursuit of individual subjects, hitherto denied. Instead of our feelings for one another, the intimacy sparked by performance allows for the emergence of a changing, hybrid, and differentially embodied black sociality with a history and a future. The dark undifferentiated mass that moves under Searle, threatening to subsume her, suggests a rising to the surface of this sociality. This black ink, woven together with the whispering voice-over inciting us to feel the sound of the ocean and boat and glimpses at a coastline insisting on geographical specificity, coaxes the viewer toward recognizing how feelings are sedimented in social bodies that move differently through global spacetime. This performative interplay, the watery weaving of sea, land, collective body, and boat, forms what Nguyen calls an "oceanic spatiality" that dismantles traditional land-based nationalism and global hierarchical space and posits new forms of temporality (66). Rizvana Bradley, talking about Mediterranean crossings, offers a similar theorization. She writes, "I want to think about the sea, and even more the boat, as figures that animate new possibilities for . . . [compositional] thinking . . . and [that] compel . . . us to rethink how we conceive not only of geographical categories, but of biological categories as well" ("Poethics"). In the affective encounter between sea, boat, and body, a terrible, disorienting wild new world is created.

Searle's performance is terrifying in many ways. This, after all, is a performance of vulnerability in which her seemingly lone body lies on its back under a sky, floating as others pass by. Her eyes are burning, her feet and hands grow more wrinkled, she is unable to protect herself from vicious seagulls. There is the cold wetness, the excruciating slowness of the performance, the tangle of skirts that could drag down her legs if she is not careful, her fear of being left behind, the dread conjured by an errant wave that could force her to swallow saltwater, to choke. Above all, there is the specter of exhaustion, that at any moment she will not be able to do all the things required of her to complete this performance and stay afloat. There is the fear of drowning. Ocean spatiality is always mediated by death. In colonial epistemologies, black people, as Achille Mbembe writes, are understood as undifferentiated, "meaningless corporealities," characterized by their disposability ("Necropolitics" 35). The majority of bodies found floating in the Mediterranean Sea or dead on Europe's shores have no personal documents and often are far from family that could recognize them.[12] Sowande Mustakeem argues in *Slavery at Sea* (2016) that during the Middle Passage "the sea became a constant 'zone of death'" (5). The ocean was not just "*where* the story of slavery transpired as black bodies were ferried beyond coastal ways and into unknown lands, but . . . it also became a central conduit for *how* bondage unfolded and consequentially devastated lives" (Mustakeem 14). The "relentless rhythm" of the slave ships as they transformed the seas into zones of death and the African captive into fungible commodity is best articulated, as Stephanie Smallwood writes, using the slave vernacular term "saltwater." A term describing those slaves who survived the Middle Passage to disembark for the first time in the "new" world, "this fragment of the slaves' language put a name to the crooked lines (social, cultural, epistemological) that shaped their Atlantic world, . . . illuminat[ing] what *forced* migration entailed" (Smallwood 7–8).

Here, then, is a complex genealogy of coerced movement theorized and performed around the term "saltwater" that transforms the sea not only into a zone of death but also into the location and method by which bondage devastates African lives. As Nguyen writes, the sea is "not merely a physical setting, but rather a crucible, a place and an experience that destroys and produces, that molds and transforms" (70). It is "saltwater" that holds the bloated corpses fished out of the Mediterranean at increasing rates. It is "saltwater" that also defines the experiences of migrants once they reach the shores of Spain. The passage across the sea is never over, as new African migrants continually wash up on shore or arrive to take their place alongside those who remember the crossing. "Saltwater" gives birth to a terrible intimacy, to the cohabitation of the dead and the barely living.

Searle's compositional performance of floating on ocean water could be thought of as a transtemporal flotilla, linking, for instance, those who drowned when the *São José* sank in 1794 to present-day Africans trafficked and coerced across the Mediterranean. Returning to the words of Harney and Moten, Searle's floating body replaces iron ballast with a haptic performance that insists on the "capacity to feel through others, for others to feel through you, for you to feel them feeling you" (98). Her performance insists on an undercommons forged by the sea. She reveals the sea to be both *where* captive bodies are found and also the *method* by which they are formed. Searle, as a Coloured South African woman floating in the Mediterranean, is remade through oceanic spatiality. Her history encompasses slave journeys and ancestral coerced passages from Saudi Arabia and Mauritius to South Africa in the past and also incorporates contemporary journeys to and across the Mediterranean, made by both the living and the dead. The oceanic undercommons reworks her individual subjectivity, resulting in a black social body that feels for and with its members.

The corpse will begin to sink unless it dies face down in the ocean. In the watery depths, the dead body begins to decompose. The bacteria release gases such as ammonia, hydrogen, methane, and carbon dioxide that act like flotation devices, urging the body back to the surface. Here the gassy corpse floats until most of the built-up gases are released and the body sinks again, only to rise once more as the cycle continues. These bodies normally surface face downward. Since most of the bacteria are produced in the gut and chest cavity, these areas are the most buoyant. The limbs and head create drag, rotating the corpse so that the torso floats facedown as the limbs dangle beneath it. Images of the corpses that litter the Mediterranean show African bodies floating in this manner.

In 1969, R. L. Allen and David Nickel from the Department of Zoology at Ohio University observe that "the generally low degree of floating ability among [living] Negroes (males in particular) . . . indicate[s] some biological differences that might account for this" (404). Looking at lung capacity, organ size, morphology, basal metabolism, and other factors in palpably racist ways, Allen and Nickel conclude that the lack of buoyancy of the black male means that he cannot learn how to swim with the same ease as his more buoyant Caucasian counterpart. The authors' argument is underpinned by the assumption that floating is important only in its facilitation of learning how to swim. In other words, in a hierarchization of movement, floating is seen as second to the ultimate accomplishment of swimming.

In many ways, floating is seen as a disempowered horizontality, the epitome of a feminized helplessness. One is vulnerable when floating, not in charge, at the mercy of waves and currents that take you where they will. Swimming, on the other hand, despite there being many ways to swim, is often thought of as purposively moving in a particular direction. The swimmer moves through the water, not directed by the sea so much as by a desire to reach a particular destination or to accomplish a particular task. Hence, one swims to the shore or swims laps across the pool. Floating, on the other hand, is seen as the absence of purpose. One simply floats to wherever the water takes you. This drifting motion disrupts the centered purposive focus usually associated with the visual image. The video footage shows Searle drifting out of the camera frame. She then appears at another edge of the image and drifts until she moves out of the frame again. The floating determines the ways that we as viewers engage with her image: the camera is not focused on following her body but rather insists on a methodology that centers an oceanic drift. Thus, we are not precisely denied access to her appearance, but we are also not allowed a voyeuristic consumption of her corporeality.

However, floating requires the expenditure of considerable muscular energy to ensure that one is not overturned or submerged. Breathing deeply is important, as lungs filled with air help with buoyancy. While it may appear that Searle is simply allowing the sea to cradle her, she is working hard.[13] Even though she does not expend energy to move in any particular direction, she uses smaller muscular movements such as undulating arms to keep herself on her back above the surface. She gives an occasional kick as the waves threaten to take her under due to the dragging of her legs. As such, floating can be seen as a kinetic practice that utilizes different muscular vocabularies that value incremental motion rather than directional progress. By floating, then, Searle insists on the validity of other forms of movement based on different abilities. She communicates feelings of discomfort, exhaustion, weighted limbs, wetness, and the freedom of being adrift.

Searle's floating contrasts with the rapid movement of a boat leaving a wake on the parallel screen. Whereas in the floating scene, the camera is decentered from Searle's body as the object of focus, here the camera is rigidly trained on the wake and the shore. The rapid movement draws attention not only to the directionless, almost circular pattern of her floating but also to the seeming contradiction between slow and fast movement. Searle's performance insists on the importance of slowness. Not in a rush to move in any one direction, she floats a few feet in one direction and then is carried back or in a slightly different direction by the waves. She is getting nowhere fast. Her floating embraces slowness as a critique of fast-paced globalization.[14]

My childhood reluctance to keep up with my white classmates in South Africa on public outings would be met with an affected, laughter-eliciting American drawl from one particular "friend" as she repeatedly misquoted a line from her favorite movie, *Gone with the Wind*: "I swear, you are slower than molasses on a cold day."[15] It was only years later, after moving to the United States, that I saw Victor Fleming's movie, which my father had mercifully forbidden me to watch. Identifying where the quote was from, I realized breathlessly what that "friend" was performing in her careless drawl and her collapsing of the "slowness" of the slave Prissy with my clumsy brown African body. She brought together stereotypes about the indolence of transatlantic slaves with the torpor of African natives in zones "too hot for habitation" (Wynter, "Unsettling the Coloniality" 279). This slowness of black (former) slave and native African has been used paradoxically both to signal their lack of suitability for hard (manual) labor and to make them ideal candidates. Inherent in the civilizing mission, then, is the necessity of speeding up black people, of inculcating efficient, capable movement with a purpose. Kemi Adeyemi suggests how slowness can enable "an expanded range of available movements" that "refus[e] . . . a consumption style endemic to (assimilation under) . . . capitalism" (557). Discussing a friend, Alex, who can't dance like she used to, because her knees and feet hurt, Adeyemi suggests that valuing slowness opens up a space for her friend to *not* dance at a club. Instead, by engaging more with the black queer women off the dance floor, Alex recalibrates the "neoliberal order that not only governs and rewards the physical ability to 'keep up' but relatedly circumscribes the range of connections . . . that people can have to those around them (Adeyemi 557). Floating on the edges of a dance floor instead of diving into a throng of moving bodies, differential bodies adjust temporal expectations by recalibrating the speed at which we move.

Vitreous Opacities, aka Floaters

The worst part of embodiment is being unseen.
—Akwaeke Emezi, *Freshwater*

I do not mean to set up a false dichotomy between one side (the transparent I) that renders invisible through abstraction black bodies (alive and dead) crossing the Mediterranean and another, more enlightened side, sees these bodies clearly. Keeping with the idea of floating as differential movement, I would like to consider float*ers* as a differential way of seeing. According to the National Eye Institute, "floaters" or "vitreous opacities" are "small, dark, shadowy shapes that look like spots, thread-like strands, or squiggly lines. They move as your eyes move and seem to dart away when you try to look at them directly. They do not follow your eye movements precisely, and they usually drift when your eyes stop moving" (National Eye Institute). Dark spots, lines, and squiggles: a kind of ghostly vision that edits out certain things, overlays others, and blurs clear sight. Floaters are part of a differential viewing practice that stems from what Mel Chen in "Brain Fog: The Race for Cripistemology" calls a "decolonizing cripistemology"—a way of producing knowledge that is haptic, collaborative across difference, and fuzzy or unclear (182). Floaters disrupt clear fields of vision by palimpsestically superimposing geometric shapes and lines and dark or light patches. The illusion that the (video) camera can document what is really happening, that one can see things as they really are, runs counter to my insistence on differential embodiment and movement. Sometimes, we are able to catch a glimpse of what is truest in what Teju Cole calls performances of "deep shadow and blur" as dark spots float, like dead bodies, across liquid expanses.

What we believe doesn't just color how we see but also determines what we are able to see. As Osagie Obasogie writes in *Blinded by Sight: Seeing Race through the Eyes of the Blind* (2013), "*Seeing is not believing.* Rather, to believe, in a sense, is to see" (xvi). Insisting that social relations produce visual experiences, Jonathan Crary writes, "What determines vision at any given historical moment is . . . the functioning of a collective assemblage of disparate parts on a single social surface. It may even be necessary to consider the observer as a distribution of events located in many different places" (6). The floaters that haunt the edges of our sight are not obstacles to sight but rather an embodied manifestation of the politics of belief. Floaters suggest that sometimes the best way to see things is out of the corners of our eyes.

Juan Medina's *In Plain Sight* (2006) is a famous series of photographs that has helped publicize the crisis of Mediterranean migrants. Medina, transfixed by what he describes as "one of the most horrific, cruel and important immigration movements of our time," has spent many years documenting the arrival of African migrants to the island of Fuerteventura, the closest of the Canary Islands to Africa ("Juan Medina—Cruel Sea"). In one of Medina's most famous images, titled *Cruel Sea*, the setting sun washes over an idyllic beach. In the distance, a couple walks along the shore. They are backlit so we only see their slightly blurred outline as they head off to the right of the image. In the foreground of the image lies the sharply focused body of a drowned migrant wrapped in mylar. The gold/silver of the mylar reflects the light, and the body shines like a fallen star (fig. 2.4).

Often after gazing on images of black death, such as the dead body on the beach, I feel a strain behind my eyes, what Frantz Fanon in *The Wretched of the Earth* called a "muscular demonstration" that is both a source of serious discomfort and a political refusal (56). My vision becomes blurred as floaters drift across my field of vision. When I attempt to focus on them, they move away in the direction that I focus on. Instead of treating floaters as in need of a cure (a vitrectomy), what happens if we maintain the discomfort of not seeing "straight"? As Paterson reminds us, not all haptic sensations are pleasant. In fact, damaged bodies in pain, under strain, differently abled, diseased, or aging produce different sensory repertoires within specific environments. Angela Naimou writes that the case of African migrants has resulted in "the historical straining of the optics of legal personhood" (229). These migrants, according to Naimou, appear on the shores of Europe as the "not-quite-afterimages of unending wars elsewhere" (227). As not-quite-afterimages, they expose the fact that the relative peace and wealth of certain countries rests on the brutalization and suffering of racialized bodies and the extraction of resources, always taking place somewhere else. By bringing this violence to the shore, these migrants rupture the surface of Europe's myth, generating instead a fleshy surplus that opens out the possibility for new sets of material negotiations, refuses the editing out of certain bodies and perspectives, maintaining a multisensory way of viewing. Rather than move away from strain and the clumping of the eye's vitreous as it becomes more liquid with age, acknowledging floaters as an intersensorial practice constitutes an important intervention. The altered vision caused by floaters becomes a speculative practice that centers bodies that would otherwise be relegated to the margins, allowing us to squint across space and time.

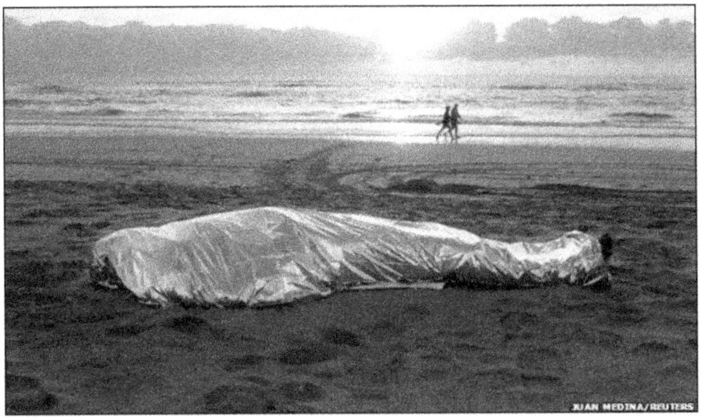

Figure 2.4. Juan Medina, *Cruel Sea* (2006) (© Juan Medina, Reuters)

That Medina's photograph depicts white European indifference to the suffering of people deemed as nonpersons seems obvious. Instead of constructing a unified image by editing out ghostly distortions and irreconcilable ghost images, Medina, like Obasogie, insists that social relations produce visual experiences. Medina foregrounds the obscured body that history has repeatedly attempted to erase. The passersby, in their indifference, make the body's invisibility legible. The death of that African, whose materiality is hidden from view by the pristine blanket, is precisely what helped give rise to the ability of tourists to enjoy their leisure time in the first place. The beachgoers who normally would be the subject of the photograph are relegated to a blurred backdrop. By rendering the couple on the beach indistinct and slightly out of focus, Medina bares the processes by which belief and sight are made possible. He attempts to undo the processes of seeing that render black bodies disposable through differential viewing practices. Through floaters.

The image in figure 2.5 appears on the website of the Vision Health Institute as it discusses whether eye floaters are serious and whether patients should come in to see them. Each panel depicts an example of what someone with floaters would see. There are amoeba-like squiggles, bright lights, streaks of white. The composition of this image appears to invert Medina's *Cruel Sea* photograph. This is an idyllic scene of white bathers at a beach, with no troublesome black migrant bodies to disrupt their pleasure. However, in the top left-hand corner of Vision Health's image, over there at the periphery of whiteness, a cluster of black dots

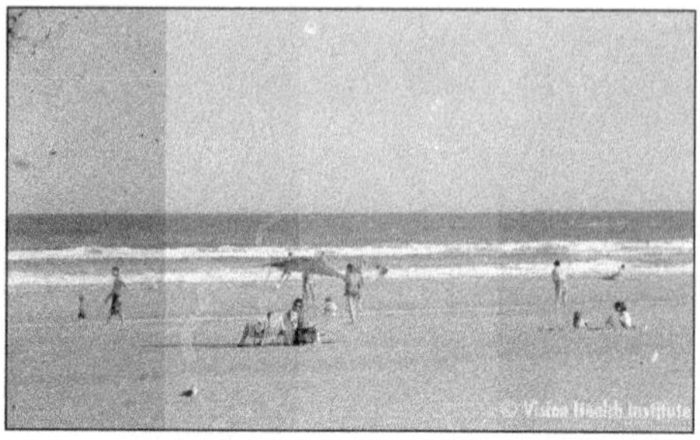

Figure 2.5. Image of eye floaters from the Vision Health Institute's website (2015) (© Vision Health Institute; screenshot by author)

floats closer, encroaching on the image. If we read this "medical" image as an ontological map, the black dots "are at the outer edge of humanity in proximity to death and decay, . . . the 'horizon of death'" (T. King 80). Normal vision, then, is one in which racial violence embodied in the transcendental I obliterates black presence, in which space is emptied out of any threatening black and brown presence. The violence that results in the removal of black presence of any kind is completely elided. Of the black dots hovering at the edge of the image, the Vision Institute tells us not to fear. This dark threat is not serious. Attempting to reassure their presumed white viewers, they insist that the black dots are not real, just a figment of an anxious imagination floating across the lens of the eye.

I would argue that these black dots are a surfacing of black life and death. In their "flutter, kinetics, and flight," blackness invades the so-called healthy eye, exposing the processes of violence that enable images of landscapes absented of people of color in the first place (T. King 77). The shifting black dots, unlike the red dots of surveillance systems, are the fleshy pulses of black sociality, insisting on recognizing the violence of raciality that reduces black bodies to no bodies. Instead, like Patricia Williams snatching off her head rag, the black dots question and demand, "Don't I exist for you? See me! And deflect, goddammit" (*Alchemy* 235).

3

Flickering

As critics such as Sylvia Wynter, Denise Ferreira da Silva, Alexander Weheliye, and Kathryn Yusoff have argued, claiming black humanity is fraught with contradictions when we consider that liberal humanism functions as the very tool that enabled our disenfranchisement/dispossession in the first place. This tradition of scholarship has long argued that the inclusion of racial bodies into the category of the human does little to change the category of the human that uses the Other as the horizon-limit of the transcendent I or privileged space of the universal. To place this genealogy in conversation with Disability Studies, this chapter turns to the human-animal hybrid. Such a turn is not an insistence that black life occupy a position of value above the animal in a distancing of black life from animal life. Nor is it located in animal-rights rhetoric that insists that animals should have the same rights as humans. Instead, my exploration of the positionalities of animal and human recharts and reclaims the value of black life, not as anchored in claims of humanity or animality but rather as embedded in notions of embodied relationality that encompass true difference. By exploring monstrous notions of human-animal hybrids, the chapter moves past discussions of posthumanism to an ontology of radical difference from which the value of black life stems.

In *The Alchemy of Race and Rights*, Patricia Williams uses the case of *Pierson v. Post* to compare the perspective of the doomed wild fox with that of her great-great-grandmother. She writes, "In reviewing those powerfully impersonal documents, I realized that both she and the fox shared a common lot, were either owned or unowned, never the owner. And whether owned or unowned, rights over them never filtered down to them; rights to their persons were never vested in them" (156). She continues this comparison between black person and animal later as she concludes the book with a story about polar bears and being invisible to white people. She writes about these white people, "They come trotting at me with force and speed; they do not see me. I could force my presence, . . . but I would be smashed in the process" (222). She tells us about the eleven-year-old boy Juan Perez, son of a black welfare mother, who climbed the walls of the polar bear enclosure to swim in the moat at the Brooklyn Zoo. The polar bears, "fearful in tremendous awakening," maul Juan Perez to death (234). Subsequently, the polar bears are put to death, and the presiding priest at Juan's funeral, dismissing Juan's mother's pain, self-righteously asserts that perhaps the polar bears' actions actually saved Juan from what would surely have been a valueless life of crime (235). What Juan and the polar bears share is their lack of value, their disposability, their invisibility, and the fact that they exist in a "constricted referential universe" (159) that hoards rights, protecting white universalism and black invisibility, animate-inanimate object status and separations between human and animal.

Williams's anger at the end of the book results in her confronting a group of boys who push her off the sidewalk as they are unable to see her. Furious, she bares her covered head and ferociously demands their respect. The text wavers at this point, and we slide into an icy world of polar bear lunacy where Williams becomes the polar bear with vicious white teeth and white-fur invisibility. This invisibility, the way her body morphs into that of the polar bear and the way the polar bears become her, testifies to the inherent complexity of being. She claims her value as a black woman not by saying that she is more important than polar bears or by recognizing her lack of value by juxtaposing it with the way animals are treated. Rather, she assumes a radical commonality between bared head and bear teeth, between polar bears' demands that their caged territory be respected despite being owned and her insistence that those teenagers see her and deflect. She is both fox and slave, Juan Perez and polar bear, black woman, still not free, and owned animal. She establishes relationality across embodied choreographies of difference, insisting that rights-based discourse be unlocked from narrow definitions of what it means to be human. Williams demands that we flood trees, rivers, and crazy professors "with the animating spirit that rights mythology fires in this country's most oppressed psyches, and wash away the shrouds of inanimate-object status, so that we may say not that we own gold but that a luminous golden spirit owns us" (*Alchemy* 158). This animating spirit, as Kathryn Yusoff writes, is a "call across categories, material and symbolic, corporeal and incorporeal, intimacies cut across life and nonlife" (203). This animating spirit, this call, moves this chapter as I attempt to imagine black value through a sociality that extends beyond narrow notions of the human. This chapter traces those moments when human and animal choreographies lean, push off, lift, carry, and drop each other in order to provide us with a way to claim the value of black life without resorting to the liberal binaries of human and animal. Using the works of the South African Nandipha Mntambo and the journalist/novelist Lauren Beukes's *Zoo City* (2010), I focus on the flickering oscillations between human and animal that push past both terms to reimagine black value through sociality.

Animal Tales from Aardvark Girl: I can smell the leaves, taste them caught between my back teeth. As a matter of fact, I can taste and smell everything, the meat that the man in the elevator ate for dinner (it was stringy, unspiced) and the loneliness of that woman in the front seat whose hair smells like library book pages. I resist the urge to drop to my hands and knees and crawl, sniff sniffing the trail on the ground as it leads to between her legs. I want to stick my snout against her juicy thighs and the cool plastic of the seat, using my aardvark tongue to hollow her out, scooping up her fluid so that it runs down my throat.

Contemporary popular culture, in particular graphic and paranormal romance novels, appears to affect what at first glance seems to be a transspecies democracy based on nonnormative embodiment.[1] The abundance of feline girls with tails, postapocalyptic boys with antlers, and devastatingly handsome men with dragon eyes or wolf claws who "mate for life" would make it seem as though the disruption of the human/animal hierarchy is commonplace. Take, for example, Vertigo's limited series *Sweet Tooth*, launched in 2009 and written and drawn by Jeff Lemire. An apocalyptic pandemic released on the world is suspected to have given rise to human-animal hybrids such as Wendy, the pig-girl, and Sweet Tooth, a deer-boy with antlers and a deer face. Whereas for the adults like Dr. Singh in the series, these hybrid human-animals represent a grotesque and tragic consequence of a world gone wrong, Lemire suggests that these human-animal hybrids are a way of representing an alternative to "an irreparably screwed-up humanity," a way of thinking about what a new race or a new species means for "mankind" (Jensen). Yet, despite Lemire's stunning drawings and innovative plot, there is a limit to this hybridity. His characters are still humanoid; they follow mostly human cultural norms and walk upright. Similarly, the hybrid shifters in romance novels are always human at key points in the narrative: for example, during sex. Human-animal hybrids in popular culture are limited to those animals that lend themselves to anthropomorphization or onto which human qualities can be projected: the loyal Alpha wolf, for example, or the avenging panther. As Michael Chaney would have us notice, the animal is located at the "vanishing point of the human" (131–32). The human always emerges as superior—their "infinitely pliable" surfaces allow for animal-human embodiment, but at any point of significance, the human emerges to confirm their higher status (Chaney 133). To wit, one almost never sees a representation of a human-animal that walks on all fours. It is almost as if the very definition of human is embedded in one's upright stance as a bipedal individual subject.

As in the instance of Patricia Williams, something different happens in the human-animal hybrids in the work of Nandipha Mntambo and the human-animal "aposymbiots" in Lauren Beukes' *Zoo City* (2010). These performative and literary texts unravel the project of the "normal" human who relies on the animal as its supposed ontological and physical negation as they flicker between various embodiments. This flickering or oscillating nonnormative human-animal embodiment does not function as a mask behind which the human resides. Instead, it reveals the body as relational, capable of open-ended meanings that disrupt the ontological superiority of the human while insisting on new modes of being black. The triangular configuration of race (specifically blackness and brownness), the animal, and the human is a messy one. This chapter makes it even messier, as through a methodology of oscillating between human and animal embodiment, we theorize black value without making claims for black humanity.

This turning away from claiming humanity is a risky endeavor for people of color, perhaps one that we can ill afford given the steady infringement and erasure of legal and social protection for those of us who are deemed less than human. I remain convinced, however, of the importance of residing in the fraught, hybrid spaces between racialization, animalization, and humanization in order to choreograph what Hortense Spillers describes as "a radically different text" of being (72). Returning to Williams, what happens if we broaden the definition of rights and recognition to those things that have traditionally been seen as objects of use, such as slaves, trees, rocks, cows, and rivers—those things that traditionally have no voice? "Allowing this sort of empowering opens up the *egoisme á deux* of traditional contract and increases the limited bipolarity of relationship that characterizes so much of western civilization" (Williams, *Alchemy* 160). I wish to place this expanded notion of life (beyond limited notions of human) in need of protection alongside the insights of disability scholars such as Rosemarie Garland-Thomson. The flickering between the human and animal reveals the jagged edges of human ontology. This allows for the recentering of bodies, epistemologies, and choreographies that arise out of hybrid bodies (polar bear/law professor) that are normally rendered invisible, excluded, and deemed as freaks and always in need of a cure.

In order to consider the oscillation between racialization, humanization, and animalization, I would like to begin with Nandipha Mntambo's ghostly sculpture *Umfanekiso wesibuko*, in which two cowhide-draped women appear to be on all fours (fig. 3.1). Only there are no hands or knees. The long sleeves of the dresses end a hand's distance away from the ground; the mind's eye fills in the empty space. The cattle/female forms are wearing long dresses that pool around where the knees and feet would be. The sculptures are formed around multiple absences: the missing body of the women *and*, if we push against our tendencies to anthropomorphize, also the missing body of the cattle. The flat-backed position of the women on all fours evokes the standing of cattle. In addition, one cannot view the two sculptures as separate from each other. They acquire meaning through the interplay between their hybrid forms. Four limbs become eight, hooves change into feet, the fall of fabric becomes a tail and vice versa.

The figures in *Umfanekiso wesibuko* signify on the material reality of black women in South Africa. Despite sore knees or aching backs, many poor black women get on all fours to scrub and polish. There are also disabled women who cannot stand on their two feet, who sit or roll or crawl or lean on one another. All these women are dehumanized abject bodies that are subsumed into what Achille Mbembe describes

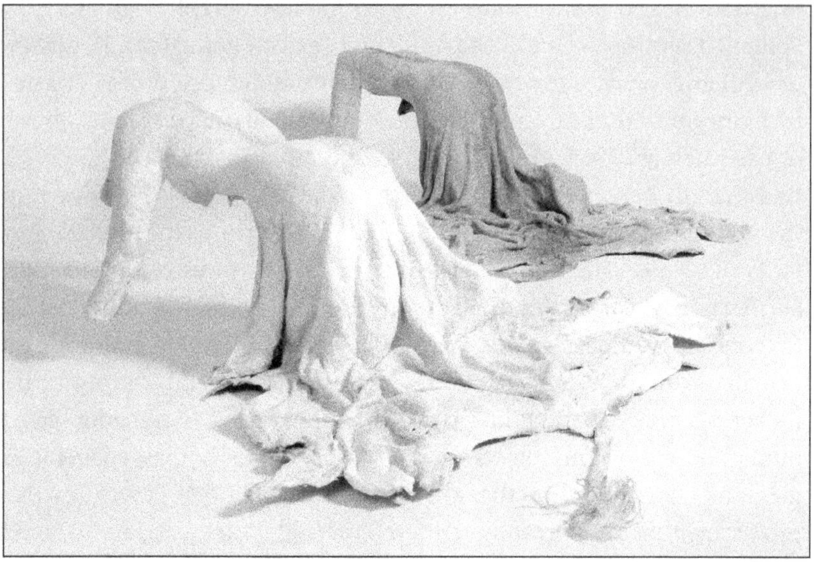

Figure 3.1. Nandipha Mntambo, *Umfanekiso wesibuko* (2013) (© Nandipha Mntambo; photograph by Jean-Baptiste Beranger)

as the colonial "meta-text" of the animal: "In this meta-text, the life of Africans unfolds under two signs. First is the sign of the strange and the monstrous. . . . The other sign . . . is that of intimacy. It is assumed that, although the African has a self-referring structure that makes him or her close to being 'human,' he or she belongs, up to a point, to a world we cannot penetrate" (*On the Postcolony* 1–2). Mntambo's sculptural comparison between human and animal is not simply one of resemblance—that is, women kneeling on all fours and cattle grazing look the same, so they must be related. Instead, she writes that she is interested in "how we understand . . . animal/human and how we determine the separation," because "sometimes human beings forget that we actually are animals" (Kriel 47). Or as Ruth Lipschitz puts it, Mntambo's sculptures "restage race, gender, and animality 'otherly' and thus open onto another nonanthropocentric reimagining of the notion of the (postapartheid) subject" (550).

The violent conversion of animal into human, hide into torn-apart flesh, can never be complete. Rather, it moves back and forth. Small pieces of animal hair cling to the hide; the resin molds of her body that

Mntambo dries the hide over traces the outline of her shape. The smell of animal flesh lingers. The stench and maggots emanating from her process forced her to move her studio after a studio-mate complained. The process of making the sculptures allows Mntambo to engage with material memory, both cellular and physical, as she scrapes away layers of fat that need to be removed (Buikema 289). Mntambo's fingerprints, her skin cells, and her hair settle like dust all over the work as she scrapes, dyes, dries, and molds hide to create sculptures that seduce even as they repel, make us breathe deep even as we want to hold our nose.[2] The sculptures are thus always in the process of shifting and resettling, never only one thing. The sculptures toggle between human and animal, attraction and repulsion, presence and absence, male and female. Thus, the "indivisibility of humanity and animality in Mntambo's work is not an effacement of boundaries but a critical intervention that multiples differences across limits presumed to be stable. In this folding complexity, it retraces what Haraway elsewhere calls an 'eccentric' subjectivity of 'inappropriate/d' others" (Lipschitz 562).

Lipschitz points out the disturbing absence of the head and the hands, which she claims support human embodied exceptionalism. After all, it is supposedly humans' ability to reason that distinguishes us from our fellow creatures and our opposable thumb that cements the species's superiority. However, what is also missing is the bull's flared nostrils, the cow's jaws and soft eyes. Perhaps, then, the missing heads, hands, and hooves put on display the shared somatic vulnerability of human/animal as the terrible forces of violence produce these distinctions in the first place. In the sculptures' performative citation of dead cattle, they emphasize the fleshy substrate of the black body. Spillers distinguishes between "body" and "flesh," which she famously terms "that zero degree of social conceptualization" that ideology cannot and/or refuses to recognize (67). Mntambo, directly influenced by her work with a taxidermist, links the flesh of human and animal through its implied presence under the skin. Her work forces us to think about wounded, lacerated, and torn "flesh." Through an emphasis on both women and cattle being captive to exploitative forms of labor and consumption, the sculptures perform the torn-apartness of the flesh as women/cows struggle to remake themselves into shapes that gesture toward freedom. Nirmala Erevelles takes up Spillers's notion of "flesh," insisting on injured flesh as being the substrate that allows us to theorize the material reality of disabled bodies. The Middle Passage, she claims, and the forces of colonialization produced not just black not-quite-humans but disabled black captive subjects (Erevelles 26). The sculptures' monstrous embodiment, then, not only links (certain) humans and animals by violence but also recognizes disability not as an identity but as a mode of becoming that is essential to practices of freedom.

It is important to consider the fact that the sculptures are paired. The folding in of fleshy human and animal, individual and group, challenges the possessive individualism of the liberal humanist subject, whose "ethical standing and civic inclusion are predicated upon rationality, autonomy, and agency" (Wolfe 110). Traditionally "rights-bearing" subjects have control over their autonomous bodies, with which they enter into what Cynthia Wu describes as "social relations informed by labor, accumulation, competition, and consumption" (17).[3] People of color have had a tenuous affiliation to such social relations, as instead of being thought of as individuated laborers and consumers, our social experiences are marked by the historical theft of our labor and bodies and our continued fungibility. Our inclusion as individual subjects who are rational, autonomous, and agential with "rights" has been uneven at best.

However, rather than insisting on being individuated subjects in order to be recognized, what happens if we embrace the messy indeterminacy of the flesh. Despite its link to captivity, Mntambo claims the flesh as an opportunity to rethink raced, class, and gendered human and animal subjectivity and embodiment. Instead of normative models of subjectivity predicated on a "politics of recognition" (N. Fraser 107) and on the insistence of bodies as "neatly bounded powerhouses of capacity" (Belser 6), what happens, Mntambo asks, if we claim different kinds of relationality that insist on the fractures, difficulties, and heterogeneities between variously embodied beings that move across animal-human binaries? What happens when we consider all sorts of embodied variations as underpinning new forms of relationality that occur between different nonhierarchical beings?

As I discuss throughout this book, choreography is not limited to the composition of dance. If we extend the notion of choreography to include techniques whereby the self is recomposed and refigured, then this chapter is about alternate embodied choreographies that challenge our understandings of normally embodied humans and animals. As Rachel C. Lee argues, "the language of the kinesthetic . . . might help in construing . . . the nonsovereignty and nonautonomy of biological life processes and species-being" (160). This choreography puts together the body in different ways, surprising us as we arrive at "unexpected innovation and embodied understanding, . . . demonstrating the inexhaustible capacities of . . . bodies" as they move and lie still (DeFrantz, "*This Is America*"). (Embodied) intellectual practice, as Fred Moten insists, is "irreducibly chor(e)ographic" (*Stolen Life* 230).

Racialization, or, "Serena Williams Looks like an Ape"

There is a long history of denying black people their humanity by equating them with animals. One need only read Twitter comments about one of the greatest athletes in the world, Serena Williams, to be reminded of this: "I'm sorry. But Serena Williams Looks Like An Ape" or "Can the monkey be gone tonight?" (Hannigan). We see how the trope of "animal" animates racist biopolitics. In the first tweet, Serena is likened to an ape as she is relegated to a status below the human but still above the animal (not-quite-human). The second tweet goes further in denying Serena any semblance of humanity as she becomes the ape who is morally, socially, and politically inferior to the human. This bestialization, in which Serena becomes an ape, has its roots in the nineteenth century, when, as Cristin Ellis argues in *Antebellum Posthuman*, the definition of the "human" was increasingly destabilized by "the clash between liberal humanist and biological discourses of the human" and "also between pro- and antislavery strains of biological thought that vied to define the political ethics of this new empirical episteme" (5). Humanism was thus *not* the progressive alternative to biological discourses, as many liberal whites/abolitionists believed. Not all biological discourse can simply be dismissed as being invested in scientific racism. Nor can humanism be simply seen as an alternative to the racism of biology. Instead as Sylvia Wynter, Alexander Weheliye, and Zakiyyah Jackson write, the hierarchies of the human established by Western Christianity were reinforced by certain types of biological discourses, resulting in a conservative Western humanism that hid its racism behind the kinder, gentler mask of universalism.[4] "Humanization," as Jackson reminds us, "is not an antidote to slavery's violence; rather slavery is a technology for producing a *kind* of human" (*Becoming Human* 46). This kind of human is marked by their fleshiness, by the burden of an inescapable animal-like embodiment that does not attach itself to the universal, white subject who can easily access the transcendental. Black bodies mired in the sensory have little access to the universal or transcendent due to their animalistic, always-alien forms of being.

As mentioned earlier, Denise Ferreira da Silva calls the transcendental, universal subjectivity characterized by its rational, ethical superiority and associated with white normativity the "transparent I." This transparent I exists alongside the animalistic embodied affectable I, "those others of Europe . . . [who are] always already vanishing [from the unlivable spaces they have been relegated to] either [due to] the weakness of their affectable minds or when confronting the 'active power' of the transparent I" (Ferreira da Silva, "No-Bodies" 224). In other words, race produces the transparent I, protected by law and the state and the affectable I, embodied homeless racialized subjects who are constrained and regulated as nonsubjects by the forces of law and order. By virtue of their differential embodiment, these "others of Europe," or what Mntambo calls the "children of Europa," pose an omnipresent threat to the universal subject even as they come to stand in for the border, for the edges of universal humanity.[5] The "heart, the mind, the soul, and the body" of the affectable I are "manipulated and prefigured as animal, whereby black(ened) humanity is understood, paradigmatically, as a state of *human* animality, or 'the animal within the human'" (Z. Jackson, "Losing Manhood" 97).

The equation between blackness and animalistic embodiment has been deployed in various ways. The most obvious use is the relegation of black peoples to a kind of fungible, exploitable human, such that the term "animal," rather than being a description, is understood as "a license to harm," in which inhumane treatment and being treated like an animal are collapsed (Pergadia 290).[6] In "Like an Animal," Samantha Pergadia exposes how claiming that black peoples are treated like animals does not comment on the ethical behavior toward animals. Instead, such a claim rests on the assumption that black people should be treated better than animals, as they are human. One sees this illustrated in Jacob Zuma's response to the furor generated by his tenuous claim that pet ownership is part of "white culture." Zuma writes, "This is not to say that animals should not be loved or cared for. The message merely emphasised the need not to elevate our love for our animals above our love for other human beings" (Woodward 179). Zuma does not link the treatment of animals to the historical treatment of black peoples; rather, he is only interested in black peoples being treated better than the ontologically inferior animal.

Animal-rights groups, in their attempt to advocate for the better treatment of animals, have also relied on the connection between the historically violent treatment of black peoples and animals, though in a different way. As Pergadia notes, "Since Peter Singer's 1975 landmark case for animal rights proposed that the present-day tyranny over animals 'can only be compared with that which resulted from the centuries of tyranny by white humans over black humans,' . . . this analogy has been enthusiastically adopted in animal rights campaigns" (289). In order for groups like PETA to generate empathy for their cause, they juxtapose visually and rhetorically similar images of black people and animals, constructing a teleological narrative in which animals should be freed, just like slaves were freed in the past. While analogies can be useful, they often flatten out complexity by focusing on superficial, often aesthetic or discursive similarities. A block of tofu might look like a block of cheese, but how each is made, their ingredients, their cultural and social histories, and how they taste are very different. It is not physical resemblance so much as material histories that determine how beings and objects are related.

The problematic use of analogy can be seen in the PETA activist Robbyne Kaamil's award-winning video titled *Animal Captivity Is Slavery* (2015).[7] The video compares African American chattel slavery to the plight of animals in zoos by juxtaposing black people and animals. The video begins with a Kara Walker–like silhouette of an enslaved African American woman with a head wrap. A voice-over in a stereotypically black southern accent (Kaamil herself) narrates a story of chattel slavery that begins with "My great great grandmother was a slave on a North Carolina plantation" and ends with an animated drawing of a putatively free black woman with short afro and V-neck dress that accentuates her curves ("And today I can stand here a free woman without chains and shackles on my hands and feet"). Drawings of the woman's wrists bursting free of shackles and her chained feet give way to line drawings of elephants with shackles on their feet ("Unfortunately slavery is still a reality for some"). These elephants are sympathetically drawn, with trembling feet and kind eyes, in white with black lines. This reverses the earlier color scheme of black silhouettes against sepia backgrounds, rendering the animals more lifelike and more "human" than their slave counterparts, who are rendered as flat outlines. The narrator ends the film by stating, "As many stood up for me, let us all stand up and fight for the freedom of animals in captivity."

Kaamil uses slavery as a reductive analogy for the treatment of animals in zoos in order to generate empathy for animals. The video fails to theorize that the treatment of animals and the subjugation of black bodies is part of the same hierarchical ideology that determines moral and social value, what Pergadia describes as the "human entanglement with the animal [that] produced both racial . . . and species knowledge" (290). According to the video, racist regimes of slavery against humans who happen to be black are over and done with, not because of the struggles of black peoples themselves but rather because "many stood up" for us. Black people have been freed by the mythic "many," and now it is the turn for this "many" to end the enslavement of animals. Given that PETA's membership tends to be white and that several black activists have reacted negatively to comparisons between black people and animals, this "many" who are being called to action might safely be assumed to consist mainly of white humanists. The video strips away the agency of enslaved peoples themselves, suggesting that benevolent white people freed them from their shackles. There is no acknowledgment of the dehumanization and animalization of black peoples that continues today or of how the treatment of animals maintains the hierarchy of full and less than humans. Slavery is reduced to an analogy for the treatment of animals, used for shock value as it defamiliarizes the treatment of animals by depicting the black silhouettes of shackled and beaten black men and women side by side with caged and shackled elephants. The video also fails to consider how many animals, even those in zoos, are treated far better than people of color are. As Mel Chen writes in *Animacies*, "the statement that someone 'treated me like a dog' is one of liberal humanism's fictions: some dogs are treated quite well, and many humans suffer in conditions of profound indignity" (89). Kaamil's video for PETA fails to theorize the afterlife of slavery with its criminalization and incarceration of (shackled) black bodies. It ignores the constitutive role of black embodiment in establishing a hierarchy of value, thereby further exploiting the black body, this time in the name of animal rights.

Mntambo's video performance *Ukungenisa* (2009) provides a useful counterpoint to Kaamil's *Animal Captivity Is Slavery.* The performance refuses the flattening of nuance that analogy effects, instead focusing on multiple, shifting choreographies of human and animal. It also allows us not to collapse blackness into the experience of transnational slavery but instead to also pay attention to (post)colonial subjects and Africanity as it relates to animality.

Shot in an abandoned bullfighting arena in the former Portuguese colony of Mozambique, *Ukungenisa* performs a bullfight, an activity that no animal-rights activist would condone. Mntambo's performance begins with her dressing before her fight. In traditional bullfighting, a squire helps the matador into his *traje de luces* (suit of lights), an ornate suit with sequins and gold and silver threads.[8] This private ritual, before the very public spectacle of the fight, constitutes a quiet moment of reflection before the fighter performs his bloody role as *toredor.* The bull similarly has his quiet moments—he is sedated and left alone the entire night before the fight. When the time comes, an electric jolt forces him out of the dark into the blinding glare of the arena. *Ukungenisa* begins with this private ritual of "before" for both bullfighter and bull.

Mntambo's suit is not shot through with gold or silver threads. Rather, she wears a cowhide coat, with a bustle made from cow ears, faces, and tails in resin and polyester mesh. Her pants, tight, high waisted, and knee length, are worn over white stockings and ballet-like slippers that tie around the ankle. Black hands belonging to a person we never see help Mntambo insert her arms into the armholes so that the heavy coat rests on her shoulders; there is a tight snap and an exhale as those same hands pull the laces tight from the back, tying the coat to her body. There is a delicacy to their touch, a gentleness that also speaks about a community of black men and women and their role in ritual as they dress and prepare Mntambo as a female bullfighter/female bull for her entrance.

In an interview with Mntambo, Ruth Simbao asks about the meaning of the performance's title. Mntambo replies, "[*Ukungenisa*] means to allow passage, to allow something to happen, to allow space. Not in the way that you just let the thing happen on its own; you are guiding it, you are allowing the passage for it to happen" (Simbao 15). We follow a fully dressed Mntambo as she walks through the dark, narrow entryway into the wide-open arena. This moment of walking into the arena is a communal send-off, a rite of passage in which the bullfighter and the bull pass through a temporal, sensory, and spatial tunnel into the open to confront their fears and to survive each other. The deserted space of the stadium, with its dirt floor and crumbling bleachers, dominates *Ukungenisa*. We are standing in the wreck of colonial power—what Mntambo calls the "remnants or the crumbs of [the space]" (Simbao 11). There is no live audience, only us far away on our screens. For a moment, the camera moves from the intimate shot behind Mntambo to a wide shot of the entire stadium as Mntambo walks to the center of the ring, small and insignificant. Up close again, we hear the sound of her feet in the dirt, the coat bumping against her body, and we are struck by a deep sense of loneliness.

Mntambo worked with the choreographer Mpho Masila for her movements in the ring. Mntambo and Masila studied footage of bullfights and watched over and over Pedro Almodóvar's *Hable con Ella* (2002), in which one of the female characters is a bullfighter. Most bullfighters are men, and Mntambo was struck by the androgynous nature of the female bullfighter's movements in the film. Mntambo's treatment of gender cannot be reduced to representations of black women as victimized, wounded, bartered. Time and time again, Mntambo has refused readings of her work as "comparing women to cows or making an overt comment on femininity" (Moret). Instead, by dwelling on those fraught moments when "male folds into female" (Simbao 11), she challenges and subverts preconceptions of women "as victim, damaged, abused or abject" (Buikema 289). Instead, women are corporeal material beings who reside in that zone of attraction and repulsion where male becomes female and animal becomes human. Mntambo's aesthetic is therefore one of multiple, flickering identities that oscillate between attracting and repelling the viewer.

As the bullfighter stands in the empty arena, there is a creaking sound, almost as if a gate has opened or a horn has been blown and the bull has entered the arena. Mntambo appears to be afraid as she looks carefully around, waiting for the bull. When she sees the imaginary animal charge into the ring, she waves her short red cape, elegantly pivoting so that her body turns, cape behind her back. Her movements around the space of the bull conjure up the animal in his absence. She outlines his shape through her movement. Suddenly, Mntambo's nostrils flare, her slipper-clad feet paw at the ground as she moves backward, and the dust rises. The viewer is now watching a terrified bull, provoked, angry, and confused. The performance moves between bull and bullfighter, and often we don't know which is which. Mntambo says, "Performing as an animal has been an eye-opener. There are elements of myself that I don't really understand, don't necessarily like, don't know how to handle at the moment, so being able to draw from that experience was interesting" (Simbao 9). There is a vulnerability to both bull and bullfighter, a shared fear and animosity that has different consequences based on hierarchical systems of value. *Ukungenisa* details the painful occupation of another's vulnerable positionality. The performance is not a facile stepping into another's shoes but rather reveals the mutual imbrication of animal and human embedded in the wreckage of colonialism as it litters the African landscape.

Animal Tales from Fulham Road: The neighbor's backyard is crowded with animals, loosely tied to each other or to our shared fence with fraying rope. Everyone is visiting. There is no parking on the street. It is Eid ul Adha. I watch from under the paw paw tree as head-scarfed women blow out cigarette smoke when the men are not looking and wave their hennaed hands about to disperse the smell. They giggle. They keep cooking. All the girls have to help. I hate cooking, so I am glad that I am not Muslim and stuck in a hot smelly kitchen. The men sharpen knives and spit in the heat. The boys throw rocks at the fat sheep and at the black goats that bleat slit-eyed, silently promising vengeance. The old lady shoos them away. "Ayye, ushiye," she says, taking off her slipper as she threatens to throw it at them. When they insist on returning each time, she turns her back; she gets serious. Both slippers on her rough-soled feet, she warns them. Allah might have saved Abraham's son by replacing him with a goat, but you boys might not be so lucky. The monkeys sitting on the red tile roof of our house pause, watching.

Conjoining: On All Fours

> Where do we draw the line between one creature and another? Where does one organism stop and another begin? Is there even a boundary between you and the non-living world, or will the atoms on this page be a part of your body tomorrow? How, in short, can you make any sense out of the concept of man as a discrete entity?
> —Neil Evernden, "Beyond Ecology"

Alexander Weheliye in *Habeas Viscus* thinks through the possibilities of performing new modalities of the human that are not predicated on liberal humanist Man as master-subject. I wish to imagine one such modality—*conjoining*—by focusing on bodies that are held together and inextricable from one another in several literary and performative texts. In Chris Abani's *The Secret History of Las Vegas*, for example, conjoined twin Water is six feet tall, while his twin, Fire, is "little more than a head with two arms projecting out of the Water's chest" (13). Throughout the novel, various doctors agonize, plot, and scheme to separate Fire and Water, even though such a separation would result in the death of one of them. One head apparently is always better than two—what Rosemarie Garland-Thomson calls the "will-to-normalize the nonstandard body" ("Integrating Disability" 12). The problem lies in deciding whether to sacrifice Fire or Water as doctors struggle to determine who is capable of being an individual. Is Fire the brains and Water "merely" the body? Which one is less "able"? The end of the novel reveals that one brother hides his other brother's incapacities. He does this in order to refuse the logic of individualism, in which value lies in individual parts. Instead, he insists on their conjoined value as a multiple differentially embodied being with various capacities and incapacities.

In Nalo Hopkinson's *Sister Mine*, sisters Makeda and Abby are separated at birth: "We'd had to be cut free of our mother's womb. . . . Abby and I were fused, you see. Conjoined twins. Abby's head, torso and left arm protruded from my chest. We shared a liver and three and three-quarters legs between us. We had two stomachs, two hearts and four lungs, and enough colon for us each to have a viable section. . . . Abby and I could have lived as we were, conjoined. Between us, we had what we needed" (29). Even though they could have lived conjoined, the will to normalize resulted in their being surgically separated. The separation results in Abby having a permanent limp, skin-graft keloid scars, and an indentation on the left side of her skull, while Makeda has supposedly lost her mojo, the magic that connects her to her celestial relatives. Makeda's anger and jealousy at having lost her mojo, at the beginning of the novel, lead her to further separate herself from her sister by finding her own apartment. Her own apartment, she thinks, will complete the trajectory begun by the surgical procedure that made her a singular, separate entity. The novel, however, shows the impossibility of either sister thriving without the other. Being self-contained individuals not only proves impossible but also leads to the sisters being less than they are. The novel ends not with them separated but rather being intertwined. "I wrapped my arms and legs around my precious sister-burden. I couldn't let go, I couldn't" (300). Unconscious on a hospital bed, Makeda realizes with the help of spirit that her kin—an African pantheon of deities or Orisha—each "govern a range of tensions between a particular set of related dualities" (302). These related dualities (salt and sweet, joie de vivre and fear, life and death) are poles between which the gods oscillate. Similarly, Makeda and Abby are related dualities, amplifying and dampening each other's sounds in an intricate dance of connection. Hopkinson reconnects the twins, insisting not only on the value of their conjoined nature but also on the impossibility of fully individuated humans.

Instead of conjoined twins, the South African popular novelist and journalist Lauren Beukes's *Zoo City* rests on the premise of inseparable humans and animals. Written in 2010, *Zoo City* won the Arthur C. Clarke Award for best science fiction novel. Billed as a "*muti* noir" novel, the main character, Zinzi Lelethu December, lives in the inner-city Johannesburg ghetto called Zoo City, populated by "zoos," or "aposymbiots." These "zoos," as a punishment for their crimes, are afflicted with a disease known as "Acquired Aposymbiotic Familiarism" (APF), in which they are forcibly emotionally, physically, and telepathically bonded with an animal who becomes a kind of scarlet letter, openly marking their criminality. Separation from their animal results in the death of the "zoos" as they are overtaken by the Undertow, a mysterious force that sweeps them into a painful and terrible darkness. Along with an animal, aposymbiots inherit unusual abilities, called "mashavi" or "shavi." Zinzi's inadvertent killing of her brother results in the acquisition, along with an animal, Sloth, of the ability to find lost objects. Death for one results in the Undertow coming to claim the other; neither can exist without the other. In fact, the central plot point is the music producer Odi Huron's hatred of not being a single subject and the lengths he will go to sever his connection with his white crocodile. His anxiety over his nonnormative, nonindividuated body is directly linked to his position as a capitalist who exploits the differentially embodied. He cannot exploit others if he is entangled with them, if he is them. The very act of exploitation necessitates liberal Enlightenment subjects who see themselves as sovereign, able to extract value from something that is not connected to them.

Zoo City dwells on the immense societal pressure and desire to separate alternatively embodied characters into individuated subjects. However, like in *Sister Mine* and *The Secret Life of Las Vegas*, the radical nature of the text lies in its insistence on leaving the conjoined and "animaled" intact. The novel, through its portrayal of differential embodied characters who thrive not in spite of but because of their conjoined nature, refuses the ideology of a "cure" as a way of eliminating difference. Like Mntambo's sculptures that refuse any separation of individual animal and human (her sculptures utilize the parts of more than one cow), diverse beings are fused, glued, and stitched together in ways that leave the seams exposed, refusing notions of singularity. Beukes and Mntambo reimagine the human as a series of choreographies that are relational, uneven, interdependent, and alternatively embodied, what Cristin Ellis describes as "a 'biological continuum' of material flows" that "exists as and through a vast ecology of interdependencies" (12). Cynthia Wu, also stressing the conjoined nature of certain beings, connects this biological continuum to the "combined frictions of spanning-across and splitting-from-within" of body variation (104). The embodied intimacies of fragmentedly relational nonnormative bodies exposes as chimera the fantasies of whole, singular, independent actors freely entering the marketplace. This ecology of interdependencies undercuts the individualized notion of subjectivity as agency, instead insisting on a subject whose agency arises from its ethical relations with others as it flickers between the human and the animal.

Different bodies move differently. When Zinzi in *Zoo City* leaves her apartment at the beginning of the novel, she has to fetch Sloth. "Sloth gives a sharp sneeze of disapproval and extends his long downy arms. He clambers onto my back, fussing and shifting before he finally settles. I used to get impatient. But this has become an old routine for the pair of us" (Beukes 5). Sloth changes the speed with which Zinzi moves. She has to curb her impatience; carry him on her back, which changes her gait; and blow her cigarette smoke away from his face if she insists on smoking despite his disapproval. In *Sister Mine*, the novel juxtaposes the way both Makeda and Abby climb down to a strip of shore, for example. Makeda scoots over the side of the incline and scrambles down over the rocks and concrete. She stumbles over a rock and slides down but straightens herself when she reaches the bottom. Abby knows that if she stumbles, she might break her leg. Instead, she hands her cane down to Makeda, then sits on the ground and makes her way forward with her legs hanging over the edge. "She half pushed herself, half slid over the edge, her fingers splayed out in front of her with a childlike, graceless grace. Her foot thudded onto and then slid off the first rock. Her other leg didn't quite hold her . . . and over she went" (Hopkinson 220). Makeda catches her and falls backward under Abby's weight. They both thump down onto the sand, Makeda's body below and Abby's above. These are two different ways of movement, two different ways of interacting with the uneven and shifting landscape. Both sisters, even though one girl needs crutches or a cane to walk, stumble and fall. Their movements, scoot/scramble/stumble versus sit/push/slide, form a complex repertoire that shows how differential embodiment requires different choreographies.

Kalpana Seshadri writes about how often disabled bodies are recognized as exceptionally accomplished when they defy expectations and display acrobatic movement. Abby's navigation of difficult terrain with crutch, limp, and shaking ankle, for example, is remarkable. However, Seshadri reminds us that the body is not inert flesh capable of moving through space. Instead, she theorizes the disabled or abled body "*as* movement" (197). Abby's body, even when still, is movement itself. Seshadri discusses the embodied potentiality of the tightrope walker Philippe Petit as he steps out onto the rope suspended between earth from sky: "Let us not mistake the threshold for the tightrope, a place that is physically entered. The threshold here is not a demarcated place into which the autonomous body enters, in which it has a determinable experience. Rather, the *threshold is itself what the body can be*" (198). Body as threshold reworks the relationship between the material environment and the human/not-quite-human body so as to move away from understandings of discrete individuals existing in neutral space and time. The body does not move through space; rather, it is ever-changing, fluid movement that creates the environment around it. Heather Houser in *Ecosickness in Contemporary U.S. Fiction* insists on recognizing texts that "eschew causal models for representing human bodies enmeshed in their environments and instead posit the interdependence of earth and soma through affect" (2–3). Environmental and somatic vulnerabilities intertwine—Makeda and Abby and the shore are part of a collective energy that flickers between one person and another, that wraps around the space they create. They are not single beings, as their movement, in Fred Moten's words, "is, at once, collective and in concert, but also disruptive or deconstructive of the idea of a certain coherence or integrity of the single body/being" (*Stolen Life* 230).

Zoo City: The Lost Sparrow

Zoo City is fundamentally a performative text. Even though, as Phoenix Alexander notes, it masquerades as a "kind of textual, South African indigene"—a *muti* noir—it "veers continuously into virtual domains" (160). In some ways, it is a novel meant to be read on a screen, images and threads flickering in the dark. Emails, comment threads, film reviews, and interviews continuously disrupt the narrative, causing the novel to jump off the page into digital time. The text performs the onslaught of digital information and the unraveling of genre as promiscuous hypercapitalism reaches into homes all over the world in an "activat[ion of] the dreams and the nightmares that concern the ways in which groups of people arrange their lives" (Sargent 3). Performative, postcolonial, and hybrid, *Zoo City* is a speculative vision that centers itself not in the "old world" of Europe but rather in those "new worlds" (Beukes 309) that are traditionally deemed the "third world"—those places from which one escapes, the "home" one leaves behind.

The novel begins in Elysium Heights, a run-down "apartment" complex in Zoo City. As Zinzi wryly tells us, calling her "dank room with its precariously canted floor and intermittent plumbing an apartment is optimistic" (Beukes 4). Following Zinzi as she leaves the building, the reader is immediately alerted to the abject conditions that characterize the lives of most zoos. Navigating a stairwell that smells of the Undertow and that is "mummified" with yellow police tape, Zinzi drops through a hole in the floor in number 526, steps over a junkie passed out in the doorway with his dirty animal on his chest, and crunches over the remains of broken lightbulbs used as *tik* pipes. When she gets to the street, she passes a sex worker with a "scruffy sparrow" hopping around her heels who "pulls her denim jacket closed over her naked breasts, too quickly for [Zinzi] to figure out if they are hormone-induced or magic" (8). Zinzi then buys a cigarette from a Zimbabwean vendor's pavement stall as his wife unpacks cheap clothes and electronics to sell. The picture Beukes paints is both achingly familiar in its portrayal of a reality that characterizes the lives of many people in South Africa and also speculative, with departures from realism such as "zoos" or "magic" breasts.[9] Phoenix Alexander writes that *Zoo City* is not so much a "counterhistory" that departs from South Africa's history in a global context but instead a "dystopian counter-locality" (162)—a world with a familiar cluster of historical forces but this time projected into a hypercapitalist, unlivable space where the logic of our current ontologies plays out, with devastating consequences.

The failed approximation of Zoo City and its inhabitants to the "homes" of white, normal subjects with their "perfect green lawns and chorus lines of hissing sprinklers" (Beukes 86) focuses our attention on the notion of uninhabitable spaces. Sara Ahmed asks, "How is it that some bodies are recognized as stranger than others and come to be liveable as unliveable, as the impossible object that both establishes and confounds the border? . . . How can bodies populate zones which are uninhabitable" (*Strange Encounters* 52)? A fully human subjectivity relies on the xenophobic expulsion of "strange bodies" from the "domain of the livable" (52) and also on the deliberate forgetting of "the histories of labour and production that allow such a [strange] body to appear in the present" (52–53). The transgender sex worker with her scruffy sparrow in *Zoo City* is a case in point. Hers is an "unimportant" strange conjoined body, a "transgression" (Beukes 8) expelled from the domain of the livable, relegated to the street, where her labor is erased, only surfacing as deviant criminality. When Zinzi and Sloth first encounter the nameless sex worker, Sloth tenses in concern at the tendrils of lost things that surround her. Zinzi, however, immediately dismisses these concerns, calling Sloth too "sensitive" and asserting that the sex worker and her sparrow are none of their business (9). The novel begins by demonstrating how postapartheid nationalism has come increasingly to rely on a xenophobic ghettoization and expulsion of difference, where the affectable I marks the limits of Western humanist ontologies that determine value.

I wish to focus on this unnamed transgender sex worker, for she is key to approaching and perceiving difference in what C. Riley Snorton calls its "transitive form . . . expressed in shifting modalities of time and meaning from within the abyss" (10). Blackness and trans identities are capacious strategies of identity that are always in relation with one another and to their reduction to fungible objects. The novel dwells on Mandlakazi Mabuso's transphobic newspaper article "Hate Crime Hack Job," which, buried on page 6, reports, "The body of an *oulike* young boy-*nooi* was found yesterday afternoon on one of the Crown Mine dumps in the deep dark south of the city. After a hot tip-off, our photographer was first to discover the hacked-up body. The victim, said to be ladyboy of the night, had apparently had magical and surgical alterations done before the madman killer did a little altering of his own, cutting he/she/it to bloody ribbons with a panga. Was it a hate crime—a dissatisfied customer complaint taken to the extreme? The Gauteng police say no comment" (Beukes 302). The compound words used to describe her, "boy-*nooi*" and "ladyboy" disrupt binary notions of fixed gender, casting gender as a "territory of cultural and political maneuver, not at all gender-related, gender-specific" (Spillers 67). As Snorton develops, the undoing of gender precipitated by slavery and colonialism meant that "the dichotomized and collapsed designations of male-man-masculine and female-woman-feminine remained open—that is fungible—and the black's figurative capacity to change form as a commoditized being engendered flow" (59). This flow in *Zoo City* is not just an embrace of transness but also an insistence on an oscillation between animal and the human, flesh and the ground, in its reworking of black sociality.

The newspaper report about the sex worker with the sparrow is actually her second appearance in the novel. Readers often fail to identify her as the woman whom we fleetingly glimpse and who are told is none of our business in the beginning pages. This multiple resurfacing speaks to the constitutive nature of transness to blackness, to the ways that transness works both above and below the surface of the text, saturating the meaning of blackness itself. Let's imagine this trans-woman's name is Danai in order to establish a sociality of mourning, though it could just as easily be Tandiwe or Nate. Danai's reappearance is heart-wrenching—her body has been mutilated, brutally separated from her sparrow, and discarded on the last of the sulfur-colored mine dumps on the outskirts of the city. The bloody gashes all over her body are what Spillers calls the "anatomical specifications of rupture, of altered human tissue, a . . . hieroglyphics of the flesh" (67). The woman becomes inhuman flesh, the fungible object, the nonbeing that remains after her value is extracted.

Danai's corpse illustrates the intertwining of environmental and somatic vulnerabilities that results in expelled bodies living unlivable lives. Mbembe writes in *Critique of Black Reason*, "As a human whose name is disdained, whose power of descent and generation has been foiled, whose face is disfigured, and whose work is stolen, [s]he bears witness to a mutilated humanity, one deeply scarred by iron and alienation. . . . [S]he represents a kind of silt of the earth, a silt deposited at the confluence of half-worlds produced by the dual violence of race and capital" (36–37). Danai with her missing sparrow literalizes this mineralogical silt, insisting on a material configuration of race as a "geologic proposition" (Yusoff 6). She is sprawled across the sand, and there "is dust embedded in every hollow and fold of her body, in the scooped palm of her hand, banked up against her lower eyelids like unshed tears, encrusted in the bloody gashes over her arms and legs and stomach and head" (Beukes 297). This "human whose name is disdained" is created through a geologic alchemy in which the materiality of mining/extraction reinforces the "biopolitical category of nonbeing" (Yusoff 5). As Yusoff goes on to say, "Slavery was a geologic axiom of the inhuman in which nonbeing was made, reproduced, and circulated as flesh. . . . Gold shows up as bodies and bodies are the surplus of mineralogical extraction" (5). Danai is black gold, her value extracted, her body dumped like all the other slag.

Beukes describes the sulfur-colored mine dumps where Danai was found in detail. The dumps are made even more unsightly by erosion and the deep gouges in the hill where slag was carried away for reprocessing. Reprocessing—a repurposing that Zinzi calls "the way of the slums" (Beukes 8)—entails going back through the slag heaps in the hopes of finding any gold that the mining companies previously missed. It is strangely appropriate, Zinzi remarks that, "*eGoli*, a place of gold, should be self-cannibalizing" (296). Danai's value has been reprocessed. No longer sex worker, "transgression," woman, or sister, her body has been stripped of any remaining value, like the mine dumps. However, even as she is discarded, Danai's body becomes part of the earth as dust covers her. Her blood and skin soak into the sand as she becomes what Yusoff refers to as an "earth archive," an earthy deposit that testifies to "conjoined violences of extraction practices and their ongoing legacies of toxicity" (49). As earth archive, Danai's body testifies to the lie of the liberal human that continues its regime of inhumanity by establishing itself as the master-subject. Her blackness, her transness, takes on the shape of what Dionne Brand's calls a "tear in the world" (4–5), a moment of shifting modalities in which one can begin to glimpse ways of being that exceed reductions to fungible objects caught with self-cannibalizing imperial economies.

The difference in the treatment between the human corpse and the animal carcass is one of the key ways that certain humans are distinguished from animals. As Deborah Posel and Pamila Gupta write, "If we are in a perpetual and never-ending search to separate ourselves from animals, then it is clearly productive to think about death practices as about restoring and reclaiming our humanity as distinct from animals" (303). One need only think about the furor generated by the German anatomist Gunther von Hagens's *Body World* exhibit and public performance of an autopsy in 2007. In "Dead Body Porn: The Grotesqueries of the 'Body World' Exhibit," Thomas S. Hibbs writes in response, "The problem is one of desensitization to violence in general and to the violation of the human body in particular. It is awfully easy in our culture to forget that the bodies depicted are *human* bodies" (129–30). So much of the anger and disdain evoked by von Hagen's work revolves around his violation of one of the markers of the human, the treatment of the corpse. As Posel and Gupta remind us, the "control of corpses is always simultaneously about the social production of life" (308). How we treat the dead is just as important to the exercise of sovereignty as is the determination about who lives and who dies. But as is evidenced by the treatment of black and brown bodies washing up on Europe's shores as they fail to cross the Mediterranean Sea alive or the disposal of black South African paupers, many of them miners, into unmarked graves between 1886 and 1960, this distinction is provisional at best.[10] It is therefore crucial to consider that Zinzi cannot find Danai's little bird with matchstick legs. The "human" is discarded unceremoniously, brutally, while the animal is saved from the mining dump. Also, the fact that bird and its person have been separated demonstrates how the severing of relationality, of the conjoined, is essential to the extraction of value from black bodies that become "living ore from which metal is extracted" (Mbembe, *Critique* 40) and to the reinforcement of dominant modes of liberal individualism. The less-than-human status of blackness is shown to be less valuable than a sparrow in capitalism's obscene discourse of equivalencies. Blackness, as Yusoff develops, is a "historically constituted and intentionally enacted deformation in the formation of subjectivity, a deformation that presses an inhuman categorization, [the animal,] and the inhuman earth into intimacy" (203).

Animal Tales from the Sloth: o o. o. green mOss. A thickness. GhOst trees. Amashangaan pOuch crOuch. She is sinking under. time mOves rOll ripple wave. Nails click clack. Blink slow o o o over turning need to be clOser. COming click clack. O. stOp that shit can't breathe lOst tendrils wrapping arOund and arOund thrOat green mOss scraped OOffff raw pelt underneath O o lOst and fOund

Being Towed Under

Mel Chen reminds us, "Animality can shift, attaching itself to different kinds of groups. That the domain of the animal is treated as a zone of deferral means that animality subtends a great deal below the white human man at the top, who in spite of his own superior position, can be dragged down by his own queer association" (*Animacies* 115). Through the use of aposymbiots, whose affectable Is are symbiotically conjoined with the bodies of animals, *Zoo City* shows how the stigma of nonhuman animality accrues mainly onto black and brown bodies. White universal subjects, though less likely, do not escape this plight. One sees this in the descriptions of Odi Huron, the rich white producer who is revealed to be a "zoo" at the end of the novel. Unlike most other zoos, who struggle to eke out a living, Huron lives in a Sir Herbert Baker stone house on a multimillion-rand estate. However, the property is "practically derelict" (Beukes 84), the lapis-lazuli blue of the pool "faded to a dull glaucoma" (88), and hanging over Huron's head is "a black tumor of lost things . . . thrashing with severed stumps, like an amputated octopus" (90). While amputation itself is not about lack, the simile of an amputated octopus foregrounds Huron's castrated masculinity. Huron is dragged down from his superior position by his metaphoric and literal attachment to octopus and crocodile, respectively, both of which pull him under.

But whereas Huron's racial and gendered privilege protects him for most of the novel (he is able to hide his crocodile), black and brown bodies cannot even pretend at an abstract universalism. Instead, for zoos like Zinzi and her lover, Benoit, their animals literalize the regulatory forces of the law. As in Samuel Taylor Coleridge's *The Rime of the Ancient Mariner*, in which an albatross carcass is hung around the neck of a sailor who makes the mistake of shooting it, Sloth is Zinzi's punishment for her involvement in her brother's murder. Sloth and Mongoose (attached to Benoit) mark their humans' subjectivity as criminal, exposing how neither is protected by the law but instead are both subject to its controlling violence. As Zinzi sarcastically tells one of her customers, "nothing says guilty like a spirit critter at your side" (Beukes 12). It is not clear what Sloth did to deserve being symbiotically bonded to Zinzi. Law, as Seshadri reminds us, "denies those it deems 'inhuman' access to speech and law, thereby producing the inhumanity it excludes" (34). Ethics lies beyond the scope of the law, which functions to performatively suture the affective I of liberal humanism to the criminal.

How the animals attach themselves to people is left unclear. In an excerpt from a fictional set of prison diaries titled "Caged: Animalled Behind Bars: Photographs and Interviews by Steve Deacon. HarperCollins, 2008," Caleb Carter describes shanking a fellow prisoner, only to find a tapir covered in jungle mud scratching outside his solitary-confinement cell. Carter wonders about his tapir's arrival: "I mean, there's cameras everywhere. And this thing's from a different continent. How come no one saw her arrive? How did she get here? If she can walk through walls or fly or something, why can't she carry me out of here?" (Beukes 97). Beukes's animals are just as displaced and relocated as their zoos are. Tapirs, like sloths, are indigenous to Central and South America and have a complex history of (in)voluntary migration. Sloths supposedly cannot exist outside their jungle habitat, yet here Sloth is living in the unlivable space of Zoo City. The novel depicts refugees and immigrants from Angola, Cameroon, Congo, Côte d'Ivoire, Rwanda, and Zimbabwe. The South African 2011 census estimated 2.2 million (irregular and legal) migrants in a country of 52 million (Haleta). Of course, these massive relocations of animal and not-quite-human result from the ever-increasing reach of global capital and the free-market system, but equally important in these upheavals is the not-so-slow global ecological crisis that increases the wealth of the First World even as the rest of us get poorer, thirstier, and hungrier. Gesturing toward this point, Zinzi suggests that one explanation for the sudden appearance of zoos could be "toxic reincarnation": "Global warming, pollution, toxins, BPA from plastics leaching into the environment has disrupted the spiritual realm or whatever you want to call it, so, if you're Hindu, and you go through some terrible traumas, part of your spirit breaks away and returns as the animal you were going to be reincarnated as" (Beukes 154).

Does the fact that Zinzi earns a sloth and not a bear, for example, say something about Zinzi or the sloth? Some critics such as Lara Buxbaum might argue that Beukes's zoos indigenize Philip Pullman's animal daemons from his *His Dark Materials* trilogy (78–93).[11] For Pullman, the human's inner self manifests itself as an animal-shaped creature. The animal comes to stand in for certain aspects of the human's character, only existing to reflect and epitomize their inner essence—quick like a fox or lazy like a sloth. There is little to suggest in *Zoo City* that specific animals are related to the moral shortcomings of their zoos. Who gets attached to which animal appears random—a vicious murderer is just as likely to be attached to a butterfly as he is to a panther. To assume that the animals are a manifestation of the human's inner self is profoundly anthropomorphic, as it implies that the animal exists only to provide us with greater insight into human subjectivity.[12] As Chen reminds us, "Actual animals often bear little if any resemblance to the signifiers and discourses used to reference them. . . . Amid the fluctuations of animals' lives, 'the animal' *as* animal sustains, while humans project the vexed peculiarities that are the consequences of interested human's psychic fibrillations onto the specters and accomplices of animal representations"

(*Animacies* 101). Consider the symbolism attached to a sloth. Synonyms for the word "sloth" include "idleness," "slackness," and "indolence." Jocelyn Fryer writes that since "slothfulness is one of the Seven Deadly Sins, [Zinzi's acquiring Sloth] can also be read as Zinzi coming to terms with her own *sinfulness*, her very humanness as it were" (122; emphasis added). Another critic, Cheryl Stobie, writes that though the sloth hangs off Zinzi's neck, her sin is not one of *laziness* but of the destructive behavior of addiction that leads to the death of her brother (377). In other words, the punishment of a sloth fits Zinzi's crime—her supposed "sin" of laziness and addiction that reveals her flawed "humanness." There is nothing, however, to suggest that sloths are lazy or slothful. For example, the tremendous amounts of energy required for them to digest a meal mean that they usually move very slowly. While they inch forward slowly when on the ground, they move rapidly through the trees. The way they move is physiologically and environmentally determined. Their slowness has nothing to do with the "sin" of laziness, which is less a descriptor and more of a moral evaluation. Moral evaluations have everything to do with the power invested in a universal subjectivity.

Zinzi and Sloth affect each other, as they ultimately are each responsible for the other's well-being. Zinzi is careful not to get drunk, as it affects Sloth; Sloth guides them through underground tunnels, as Zinzi cannot see in the dark. But while their survival obviously depends on each other, the ways that they learn to interact transform both of them into a conjoined being, greater than the sum of its parts. For example, Sloth drives Zinzi like a motorbike (Beukes 12), squeezing her shoulders like handlebars (212). The monstrous animal/machine/not-quite-human hybrid of Sloth and Zinzi—in its oscillating movement between affiliation, dependency, intimacy, and desire—creates and changes the world around them. This is "ontological choreography" at its finest (Thompson, *Making Parents* 8).

In many ways, *Zoo City* is about Zinzi's continual attempt to escape this relationality. Consider, for example, her participation in what she calls "the current affairs sympathy scam," in which, in order to pay off her debt, she feeds foreigners "plausible constructs" in order to take their money (Beukes 35). Cheryl and Jerry Barber are depicted as well-meaning Americans whose benevolent racism enables Zinzi and her unscrupulous boss and creditor, Vuyo, to scam them out of their entire pension. Zinzi expresses no remorse for her participation in the scam as the orphaned refugee, instead noticing that "some perverse part" of her was getting off on cheating them in the "same way [she] ticked off points on a scoreboard when [her] parents actually believed the bullshit [she] spun them" (45). Exploitation of others is a game of wits—their loss is her gain. It is only later in the novel, when Benoit discovers her participation in the scams, that she starts to question whether other people's suffering is really "none of her business." Benoit is furious, devastated that Zinzi would involve herself in these schemes, no matter what the reason. When she insists that she didn't mean to hurt Benoit and defensively asks him, "Why do you care about these idiots giving away their money?" (266), Benoit tells her the harrowing details of his life as a child soldier in the Lord's Resistance Army and then the attack on him and his family by the Forces Démocratiques de Libération du Rwanda (FDLR), which severely burned him.[13] Zinzi's scams callously appropriate the tragedy of real-life people, of him and his family, and he is hard-pressed to forgive her. Zinzi says nothing after he tells her his story: "In my chest, the poison flower bursts open, an explosion of burning seeds. I imagine Mr. and Mrs. Barber experienced something similar whenever they finally realized that the bearer bonds were forged. It is the death of hope" (268).

Ironically, it is precisely this recognition of social entanglement that leads to the novel's departure from heterosexual romantic conventions. Benoit's wife and three children were missing, presumed dead after the attack on them by the FDLR. Benoit spends more than five years trying to find them again, only to receive a phone call, early in the novel, indicating that his wife is alive. Benoit immediately makes plans to leave Zinzi for his wife. In a dirty, grimy, and depressing world, Benoit and Zinzi's relationship is incredibly poignant. A rooftop picnic, kisses on the fingertips, jokes about polygamy and adultery, putting a wastebasket next to the bed for ease of puking after Benoit comes home drunk—the desire and love between Benoit and Zinzi is just as vibrant and real as Benoit's love for his wife and children is. This heterosexual romance is never depicted as the solution for the brutal realities of racialized animaled existence. Benoit and Zinzi's relationship shifts and changes when he learns that his wife is alive, though the mutual responsibility they feel toward each other does not. At the end of the novel, in order to help Zinzi prevent the death of targeted zoos, Benoit risks "his asylum status, his family's chance of a future here" (Beukes 324). The gamble does not pay off. After being resuscitated, he ends up in the hospital in critical condition, "sway[ing] between fevered moments of wakefulness and unconsciousness that's borderline coma, but with more erratic brain activity, like he's still fighting monsters in there. The Mongoose paces the corridors, looking thin and miserable" (357). It is at this moment that Zinzi surrenders what Jennifer Schmidt calls "her attachment to the possibility of romance" (140). I would argue that Zinzi broadens out the notion of romance by her insistence on a queer sociality. "Celvie. Armand. Ginelle. Celestin. It's going to be awkward. It's going to be the best thing I've done with my miserable life" (Beukes 358). Zinzi, in direct contrast to the Zinzi who began the narrative, recognizes her conjoined status with the community and environment around her. Celvie's plight as mother, Benoit's wife, and refugee is intertwined with Zinzi's own situation as recovering addict, zoo, lover, sister, and daughter. This is not a competition between two women but rather an insistence on queer kinship that foregrounds ethical relationality and that recognizes desire as a social force that shapes the landscape. To love Benoit means not just finding his "lost" family but re-creating it in a queer image.

This relationality is materially rendered by the Undertow that haunts the novel. Whenever an animal or its human dies, the Undertow opens like a portal, dragging the remaining animal or person into it. The Undertow is not exceptional; the text is riddled with examples of the conjoined fate of animal and zoo. However, the dramatic nature of the Undertow forces people to stop and listen and feel. In a powerful evocation of the haptic, shadows descend, darkness pools, and tendrils lick skin in an anticipation of nonbeing. Neither animal nor not-quite-human are supposed to be able to survive this Undertow as one drags the other behind them. This is not a visualization of death so much as a deathly performance of the concatenation of somatic and environmental vulnerabilities. The Undertow is the moving, breathing quantum field of relationality, an ontological "mutuality of being" or a "complexly conjoint becoming" (Ellis 150). Like Sloth riding his Zinzi bike, the Undertow represents what Jasbir Puar calls the "perpetual motion of assemblages" (213), in which a myriad of hapticities, energies, and forms of being (human and nonhuman) intersect. The flows, currents, and undertows of these forces continuously unsettle what it means to be a discrete human body in space and time. To wit, Cristin Ellis writes, "The complexity and unpredictability of material entanglement means that the 'bedrock' of empirical reality is, in the long view, oceanic. . . . In light of this incalculable restlessness, every future is uncertain; every order is provisional; every life is a life lived at sea" (165). The illusion of separate, discrete lives is swept away as organic and inorganic matter join, creating "a black hole, cold and impersonal as space" where we might "become stars" (Beukes 208–9). These stars can actually be seen as "bright cracks—interstices of possibility opening up in the unpredictable encounter of myriad forces: the skill of the captain's navigational science intersecting with the power of Atlantic winds, the iron fastness of the chains that hold human cargo countered by the force of that cargo's memory of her name" (Ellis 162).

Crocodile Tears

I would like to turn to the six-meter-long crocodile concealed in a grotto beneath Huron's swimming pool in *Zoo City*. Crocodile surfaces from its depths to reveal that Huron is, in fact, a zoo who has ordered the murder of other aposymbiots and the sacrifice of their animals in order to create *muti*, or medicine, to cure his animaled status. Crocodile's consumption of Huron's victims ironically assists Huron in getting rid of Crocodile. At the end of the narrative, Zinzi has just managed to rescue Benoit from a rotting stash of bodies under the water when she turns to find herself face-to-face with the crocodile: "Its mouth gapes, a clear sign of aggression. I hold up one hand, all I can manage, in surrender. They're planning to kill you. Chop you up for muti. They've got all the tools waiting." It studies me impassively with slit gold eyes. I persevere. 'Monster like you? You're probably worth a fortune. I can help you. I can try to help you. I have to get out.' It jerks its head at me. I flinch, but it's not attacking, it's motioning towards the stairs. For me to go" (Beukes 340).

Cheryl Stobie sees a connection between Beukes's crocodile and the former prime minister of South Africa P. W. Botha, who was nicknamed "Die Groot Krokodil." Botha's time in office was characterized by what Kevin Hopkins calls "the systematic killings and clearly orchestrated elimination of people who opposed apartheid" (290). It would be oh-so-tempting to read Crocodile as a metaphor for the white nationalist state, especially given Botha's nickname. Crocodile's human, Huron, after all is one of the very few characters recognizable as white in the novel, and Crocodile is described as an "albino" (Beukes 288). As Louise Bethlehem observes, "Hidden beneath a Westcliff swimming pool, Huron's albino crocodile reworks *complicity* from within the abyss. It is not time, not yet, to relinquish our knowledge of the 'ghost dances and the slave spectacles' at the dark heart of the metropolis'" (14). Crocodile can be seen as the legacy of apartheid that is not yet over, as it lurks below the surface of official nonracialism, influencing the present and the future with its continued relegation of certain bodies as disposable and in need of "elimination."[14] Crocodile's stash of bodies, his powerful jaws and tail that sweeps through the "thick black" (Beukes 339), can be seen as a material rendering of what Saidiya Hartman has called a "matrix of dispossession." She writes, "The matrix of our dispossession encompasses the fungible and disposable life of the captive/slave; the uneven distribution of death and harm that produces a caesura in human populations and yields a huge pile of corpses; the accumulation, expropriated capacity, and extracted surplus constitutive of racial capitalism and modernity; and the premature death, social precarity, and incarceration that characterize the present. Our dispossession is ongoing" ("Dead Book" 208). Crocodile as a "matrix of dispossession" conjoins the organic and inorganic as myriad "unpredictable forces" bump into one another.

However, to reduce Crocodile to metaphor or matrix does what Mel Chen warns us against: it reduces animals "not [to] the class of creatures that includes humans but quite the converse, the class against which the (often rational) human with inviolate and full subjectivity is defined" (*Animacies* 95). As Suzanne Ericson observes in her insightful article "Thinking with Crocodiles, Thinking through Humans," this narcissistic anthropocentric thinking that both Beukes (and I) engage in "has become a hugely contested practice . . . in the burgeoning field of animal studies," as the projection of humans and their concerns onto animals reinforces human/animal hierarchies (24). Throughout *Zoo City*, animal imagery personifies feelings and actions, adding depth and nuance through metaphor and simile. Yellow light "feels like a mole digging its way into [Zinzi's] skull through [her] right eyeball" (Beukes 233), the sound of gunfire is likened to cicadas (49), and car horns honk like mechanical ducks (118). Beukes writing from the perspective of Crocodile or Sloth and I writing as critic, interpreting the various animals' head shakes and hisses, continue this anthropomorphism. However, despite the dangers, critics such as Kari Weil argue that what she calls "critical anthropomorphism" (20) can function "as a potentially productive, critical tool" (19) to reveal a shared corporeal vulnerability that forms the basis of relationality. Something passes between Zinzi and Crocodile when she asks it for help and when it snaps its deadly jaws and stares at her with its gold slit eyes. The shared precarity of their entangled lives is revealed in this moment of confrontation.

Using this critical anthropomorphism, Ericson writes that "both characters become aware of their mutual vulnerability" but not because, I would argue, "fleetingly, the binaries of human and nonhuman, predator and prey, cease to matter" (23). Instead Zinzi's need for Crocodile's help unsettles the presumed hierarchy of not-quite-human and animal—Crocodile has to save the day. In a hierarchical landscape where the power of life and death is grounded in an ontology of the universal I and the liberal human subject's superiority, as well as human dominance over animal, Zinzi lets go of the reins. Of course, the not-quite-human moving aside for the animal is more theoretical than actual. The novel doesn't write itself. Giving Crocodile the power, however, constitutes a powerful ontologic gesture that recalibrates different materialities that exist in different kinds of time, requiring us to imagine new types of bodies and modes of being. Equality is not sameness, nor is it a careful portioning out of power so that neither side has more than the other. Rather, equality is oceanic, restless, a constant back-and-forth—giving Crocodile power requires surrendering to the relationality that should characterize "a highly complex timescape of entangled and bifurcating layers" (Nuttall 156).

Let us imagine, for an instance, what is commonly referred to as the crocodile's "death roll." In the article "Death Roll of the Alligator: Mechanics of Twist Feeding in Water," Frank E. Fish et al. research how crocodilians accomplish this roll. Keeping their legs close to their body, crocodilians centralize their mass and axis of rotation, much in the same way divers keep their arms and legs close to their body when they leap off a diving board or skaters spin on the ice. Tail and legs tucked in, the

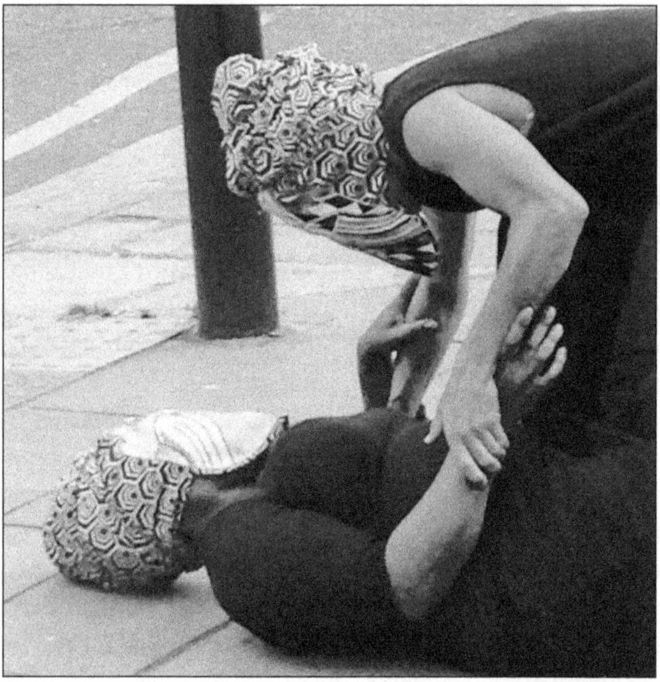

Figure 3.2. Wura-Natasha Ogunji and Mary Okon Ononokpono, *And Fight* (2015) (© Wura-Natasha Ogunji and Mary Okon Ononokpono; photograph by Yvette Greslé)

alligator produces torque through the axial components of its body. The alligator only attempts rotational feeding when the prey is more powerful. "Spinning," as Fish et al. tell us, "does not work with small prey animals, because as the crocodile spins, the prey will also rotate" (2815). If we were to choreograph Zinzi and Crocodile's relationality, theirs is not a death roll but rather an embrace of two equivalent beings. Clasped tightly together, they spiral through the water, one on top of the other, now this one below that one. They alternate being in control, struggling to remain conjoined, desperately trying not to drown. Not a death roll but a twisting embrace of power flows between human and nonhuman, between animal and animal, between you and me.

This embrace is not unlike the embrace photographed by the blogger Yvette Greslé, who documented Wura-Natasha Ogunji and Mary Okon Ononokpono's performance titled *And Fight*, which occurred in

June 2015. In the photograph, two masked women struggle as one hovers above the other as she attempts to pin the other to the ground in a twisting embrace (fig. 3.2). Representing human and spirit, ancestor and animal, at times their "fight" resembles being in love, as they hold hands, appear to kiss, embrace, and grapple for power. This lovemaking/battle blurs the boundaries between who is who—dressed and masked alike, Ogunji becomes Ononokpono, and Ononokpono becomes Ogunji. Animal and human twist and turn in their morphology, blurring their ontology until what we are left with is an "exquisitely timed" flickering that is the complex relationality of (not-quite) human and animal.[15]

Epilogue

And Fight, Ogunji tells Erin Gilbert, was inspired by a drawing by fellow artist Ruby Oyinyechi Amanze, titled *That low hanging kind of sun, the one that lingers two feet above your head, (never dying) house plants in exchange for your freedom . . . orchids in exchange for your love, who are you kissing, when you kiss a mask?* (2015; fig. 3.3). The question of whom one is kissing when you kiss a mask disturbs simple distinctions between mask and the person behind the mask, between inner essence and outer surface. Instead, one is always engaging with both, and it is difficult to tell where one ends and the other begins. The self, both Ogunji and Amanze suggest, is multiple with changing faces. Ogunji tells Gilbert that the mask "is the space of the Atlantic in a way. It is a space that is solid and historical, and physical. But it's also metaphysical. . . . In Nigeria the mask is used to invoke something or allow something to enter a space that isn't always there." In the oceanic restlessness between mask and self, hybridity emerges.

Born in Nigeria, Ruby Amanze has spent significant time both in the United Kingdom and the United States, and much of her work focuses on what it means to reside in multiple spaces, inhabiting what she terms a "post-colonial non-nationalism as a mundane norm" (Visiting Artist Program). She tells the interviewer Oliver Enwonwu that she does not "fit neatly into any single identity": "I'm not any one of them, I'm all of them and it is just what it is." Instead of the multiplicity of belongings and heritages being a source of loss and despair or evidence of her lack of African "authenticity" or "oyibo shame," Amanze's "post-colonial

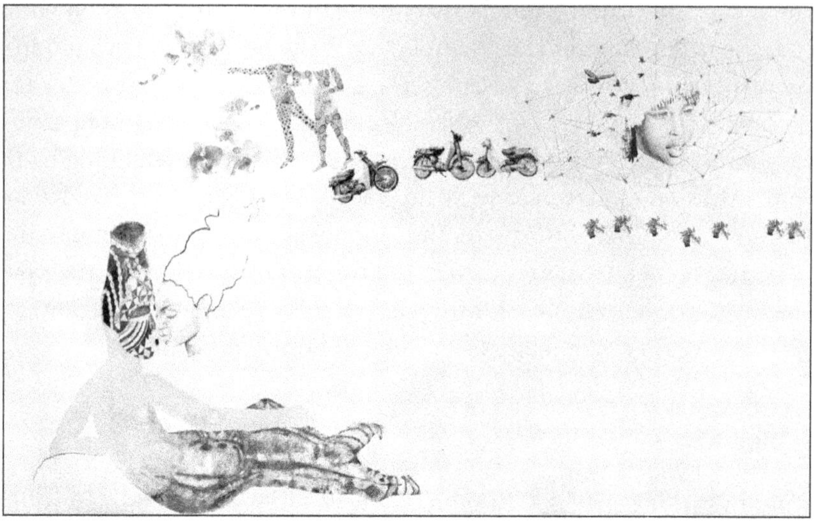

Figure 3.3. Ruby Onyinyechi Amanze, *That low hanging kind of sun . . .* (2015) (© Ruby Onyinyechi Amanze; photograph by Thibaut Voisin)

non-nationalism" requires a constant engagement with a multivalent present.[16] Thus, a kiss could mean the pressing of our lips against a shifting array of selves.

Amanze's mixed-media drawings are populated with a strange menagerie of recurring characters who are alien, hybrid, or ghost, such as the conjoined figure of Twin, ada the Alien (alien/human), audre the Leopard (leopard head/human body), and Pidgin the bird (pigeon/human). In *That low hanging kind of sun . . .* , the conjoined figure of Twin appears in the top left of the piece. Twin never appears with a head/heads. Instead, Amanze emphasizes their physicality, in particular through the use of photo transfers in which the skin of the characters consists of Dutch wax print or Ankara cloth. While wax print is thought to be traditionally African, colonial Dutch merchants originally encountered wax-resistant dying technique in Indonesia. Using machine printing processes, the merchants imitated the look of Indonesian batik without the labor, and the fabric was then eventually sold along the coast of Africa by Dutch and Scottish merchants. This simulation of Indonesian batik thus became an essential part of West African aesthetic and commercial systems. Twin, whose Ankara skin, conjuring the look of this batik, might seem authentically African, instead speaks to this multiplicity of origins and aesthetic forms. Indonesian, Dutch, African, drawing, photo transfer—like Abani's Fire and Water, Twin is a conjoined body that cannot be separated out into different entities. Nor can Twin be described as two bodies missing their heads. Instead, Twin is a hybrid that pushes at the limits of normative embodiment.

Another character that walks through many of Amanze's drawings, such as in *Either way, you'll be in a pool of something* (2015), is audre the Leopard (fig. 3.4). Like Twin, she is a nonsingular new being. Drawing from a genealogy of mythological creatures such as the sphinx, Amanze creates audre the Leopard's head using a realistic photo transfer atop a not-quite-human drawn body. Amanze explains, "It's less that Audre is a human figure with a leopard head. . . . It's a new thing, it's not a human and it's not a leopard. . . . [Hybrids] exist as they are, they're not two things anymore" (Greslé).

That low hanging kind of sun . . . also features what appears to be a merman or mermaid in the bottom left-hand corner. Anne Cheng writes that the obsession with mermaids reminded nineteenth-century viewers of the "contingent nature of the human" (67). Mermaids revealed the

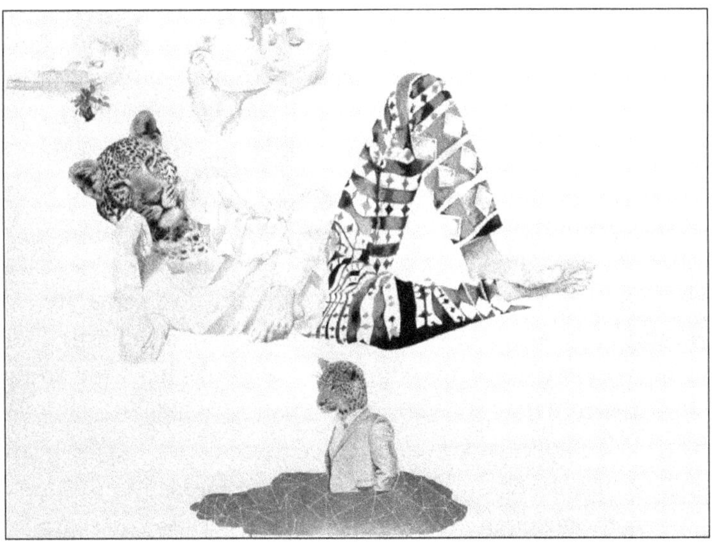

Figure 3.4. Ruby Onyinyechi Amanze, *Either way, you'll be in a pool of something* (2015) (© Ruby Onyinyechi Amanze, Goodman Gallery)

nineteenth century's "deep-seated anxieties about interspecial encounters, worries that survive in modern-day eugenics and antimiscegenation sentiments" (80). These nineteenth-century mermaids were grotesque, ontological perversions of the human, with their fish tails and human "halves" that often resembled stereotyped African, Asian, or simian torsos and heads. The monstrosity of these creatures was bound up in their interspecial melding and their materialization of the monstrosity of miscegenation. Contemporary viewers, brought up on a steady diet of sexy mermaids and Disney's animated red-haired, clam-shell-bra-wearing Ariel with big baby-blue eyes, would have a difficult time recognizing these early depictions. It was Hans Christian Andersen, Cheng writes, who domesticated and feminized the monstrous mermaid, recasting her as a painfully beautiful creature who sacrifices herself for the prince in order to preserve "'proper' and 'pure' human kinship" (80). For Andersen, her beauty, instead of being strange, wild, and queer, becomes sympathetic, aspirational, and honed on the sharp edges of sacrifice.

In Andersen's *The Little Mermaid*, the little mermaid must give up her beautiful singing voice in order to obtain the potion that changes her tail into legs and feet. To gain a mortal soul, she must make the prince fall in love with and marry her. Though he treats her kindly, calling her his "foundling" and giving her a pillow to sleep on by his door, the prince eventually sails away to marry a human princess. Given the option to murder the prince in order to return to her family in the sea, the little mermaid chooses death. What has been lost in most retellings of Andersen's fairy tale are the slaves who haunt the little mermaid's time in the prince's kingdom. Her painful attempts to win his love revolve around competing with these slaves for his attention.

Andersen's description of a dance scene crystallizes what is at stake for both mermaid and slave: "The slaves next performed some pretty fairy-like dances, to the sound of beautiful music. Then the little mermaid raised her lovely white arms, stood on the tips of her toes, and glided over the floor, and danced as no one yet had been able to dance. At each moment . . . her expressive eyes appealed more directly to the heart *than the songs of the slaves*. . . . She danced . . . to please him, though each time her foot touched the floor it seemed as if she trod on sharp knives." As the little mermaid raises her "white" arms, she attempts to transcend the status of slave and to be seen as fully "human." Each of her actions only serves to reinforce how human ontology rests not only on severing the animal from the human but also on racial hierarchies of free and unfree. The concatenation of species and racial difference forces us to confront their mutually imbricated epistemologies that create the universal white subject. Consider the following: Because the mermaid is in love, she "voluntarily" gives up her family, the ocean, her voice, and her tail to compete with slaves who were forced to surrender their families, voices, names, and bodies for the sake of capital. The chains of her tail that bind her to the sea as animal and the chains of "love" that shackle her to the prince are entangled with the literal manacles and chains of the slave trade. The mermaid's sexual vulnerability, suggested by her two legs, is inherently part of the condition of being a slave. Marriage to the prince would make her mortal and capable of dying; however, the prince's "love" for his slaves results in their literal and social death. I am not saying that being an animal-human hybrid is similar to being a slave. Rather, the technology of slavery produces both racial and species difference that consolidates the hierarchy of the universal, fully human, white subject embodied in the prince. The monstrous hybridity of the mermaid as animal/human and the slave who is not-quite-human/not-quite-property creates the prince before whom both must dance.

European and African cultures have their own respective traditions of hybrid human/water animal/spirit creatures such as Mami Wata or Simbi or Oshun. As Ras Michael Brown states, "The fact that a number of people in Africa and the Atlantic diaspora have employed the word 'mermaid' to describe certain entities should not mislead us to assume that they perceived these beings in ways bound by European-Atlantic views of mermaids. Indeed, it appears the term 'mermaid' has served primarily as a lexical and cultural point of contact to open dialogue between [various] people[s]" (124). However, tracing various authentic lineages onto Amanze's light-skinned, masked merman/mermaid would run counter to Amanze's constant engagement with hybridity. The figure in Amanze's *That low hanging kind of sun . . .* is fundamentally Other in their differential embodiment, in their wearing of a mask that refuses simplistic distinctions between outer surface and inner essence, in their kissing of a ghost. Amanze visually asks the question that Cheng posits in her writing: Can "kinship . . . be formed in the face of . . . alienness" (80)? How do we make family without domesticating and eliding difference? Can we embrace the wildly and uncomfortably ontological Other without pretending at sameness?

Amanze's visual art and ultimately this chapter are about recognizing ontological differences without resolving them. They are about living with the restless and nauseating discomfort of being grasped in a crocodile's death roll, smelling its rotting meat breath, and feeling the power of its tail as we struggle to breathe and recognize a relationality that just might kill us.

4

Spasming and Passing Out

My son gets off a Zoom session with his talented speech therapist, Lauren Henchey. He is irritated and goes immediately to his room, where he retreats into the world of his smartphone. Later on, I discover that Lauren had asked him to stutter on purpose, a practice called "voluntary stuttering." For an hour, he had to communicate by deliberately placing blocks, ellipses, and easy prolongations and repetitions (known as "sliding" and "bouncing") in places where he normally would not. Lauren tells him that research points toward how voluntary stuttering reroutes cognitive, behavioral, and embodied pathways, increasing self-mastery and minimizing her patients' fear of stuttering (Byrd et al.). My son is not buying it. He complains.

D: "What is the purpose of asking someone with one leg to stand on one leg? It's degrading. What's next, she gonna ask me to talk like a nigga?"

I wince. I talk to him about how the goal of speech is not smoothness but rather being able to say what he needs in various ways. Also sliding and bouncing are supposed to increase fluency in his normal speech. He is not convinced.

D: "Stuttering is exhausting, especially for a whole hour. It makes me vulnerable on purpose. The fake stuttering starts to turn into real stuttering too towards the end. And I feel like I am mocking myself. [*Belligerent tone*] If someone else stuttered around me on purpose, I would cuss them out or swing."

I ask him whether it would matter that the person was not trying to make fun of him but instead trying to rethink the ways we all speak.

D: "Nah."

I ask about two of his favorite hip-hop artists, genuinely curious. Doesn't Yung Thug have prolongations and repetition of words—skrrrritttt, skrrrittt, skrrrittt? And Playboi Carti in "Uh Uh" by Chief Keef says "uh" over and over as if he can't stop.

D: "Not the same thing, Ma. . . . I don't think so. [*Pause*] Yung Thug says words that people don't recognize. He sounds like he has a, stutter but he is not making fun of people like me. [*Another pause*] But Shad Levi, who actually has a stutter, doesn't stutter when he performs. The beat helps him. Kind of like me in the car rapping along to Pop Smoke. 'I need that money, power, respect, huh.'"

We both laugh. My son doesn't stutter when he is pretending to be the now deceased Pop Smoke, whose voice is about two octaves lower than my son's. But the question is raised. How does one perform racialized disability without essentializing the performance by insisting that only disabled people have access to particular somatic vocabularies? Can one perform a disability that is not one's own without reinforcing ableism? Can deliberate stuttering and other differential embodiments be an aesthetic practice that creates black sociality out of difference?

To answer these questions, I turn to South African popular culture, in particular the Afro-futurist Spoek Mathambo's cover and video for "Control" from his album titled *Mshini Wam* and the controversial performances of Die Antwoord, fronted by Ninja and Yo-Landi Vi$$er. These artists collaborate with "high art" filmmakers and photographers such as Pieter Hugo, in order to create hybrid performative moments that engage with the cacophonous materialities of race and disability in postapartheid South Africa. Spoek Mathambo and Die Antwoord's work causes me to struggle with the differences between what Angela Smith calls "ableist scripts for disenfranchised bodies and disabled reimaginings of [collective] self and motion" (431). These artists anchor my attempt to parse out the differences between often static reinscriptions of ableism and moments of differential movement as insurgent practice.

The underlying question of this chapter is whether there can be aesthetic performances of disability that do not end in the pageantry of self-mastery. Can one perform a spasm or stutter or stare into the camera from a wheelchair one doesn't "need" without reinforcing the normativity of able-bodiedness? I do not want to resort to a strategic essentialist positioning that concludes that an aesthetic of disability must be performed only by people who identify as disabled. Instead, I am attempting to distinguish between performances of disability that shore up investments in certain kinds of legitimizing ableism and those that open up, through differential movement, a different way of being black and embodied in the world. This capacity for openness is *not* the capacity of the self to try on different costumes—what I develop later as the "fungibility" of difference as a market commodity. Instead, this chapter discusses how the contemporary fungibility of difference deployed by privileged Enlightenment subjects works to obscure the fungibility that forms the ontological core of blackness. As an alternative, I gesture toward the liberatory potential of lacerated, wounded flesh through a conjoined choreography of differential movement. I argue that Die Antwoord, in an attempt to "transcend" their whiteness through the fungibility of difference, reinscribe ableism, while Spoek Mathambo's use of the spasm demonstrates the desirability of "disabled" movements that allow for reimaginings of black sociality.

For those who are not familiar with Die Antwoord or Spoek Mathambo, a brief overview might be useful, with the caveat that, as with all popular culture, it will be out of date by the time you read this. Die Antwoord, who describe themselves as a "zef rap rave crew," consist of Ninja (Watkins Tudor Jones), Yo-Landi Vi$$er (Anri du Toit), and DJ Hi-Tek (who takes on various personas but is called Justin De Nobrega on MaxNormal TV). They have been described as "one of the most socially, politically, and culturally divisive and problematic music groups of the 21st century" and "exceptionally racially disturbing" (Burning Memories). Their music is an in-your-face, foul-mouthed mix of crunk and hip-hop in English, Afrikaans, and Cape Coloured patois. They have been described, like Spoek, as blurring musical boundaries, stressing hybridity of genre, and promoting a transnational music culture that speaks specifically to the realities of South Africa. Describing the group as "the love child of diverse cultures—black, white, coloured and alien" (Eggington), Ninja states, "I represent South African culture . . . Blacks. Whites. Coloureds. English. Afrikaans. Xhosa. Zulu. [Freak] Watookal. I'm like all these different people, fucked into one person" (Die Antwoord, "Enter the Ninja").

As part of this bricolage aesthetic, Die Antwoord appropriate a visual iconography of disability in order to exaggerate their "lack" of normativity. In the rapid cuts for "Enter the Ninja" (2010), directed by the photographer Roger Ballen, we see close-ups of the face of the late hip-hop and visual artist Leon Botha, who suffered from progeria, while Ninja leads into his verse. At the end of the series of jump cuts, Ninja's gaunt face and

Botha's prematurely aging visage alternate: Ninja–Botha–Ninja. Another important example of their use of disability aesthetics is Die Antwoord's short film/video directed by Harmony Korine for "Umshini Wam" (2011). Scored by DJ Hi-Tek, with Yo-Landi only occasionally chanting in a breathy singsong voice and Ninja rhyming a couple of verses here and there, the short film is less a promotion of a single track and more a vehicle for the celebrity of Yo-Landi and Ninja as they reimagine themselves as the Bonnie and Clyde of wheelchairs. A review praises DJ Hi-Tek's lush and complex score as it "vacillates from grimy and dirty Die Antwoord techno-rap beats to plaintive and beautiful piano pieces illustrating the pulchritude and vulgarness that's always inherent in Korine's work" (Perez). Each clad in a pink and yellow bunny suit, respectively, Yo-Landi and Ninja roll around a largely deserted suburban landscape, playing wheelchair basketball, stealing "better" wheelchairs, and tricking them out with rims, all the while carelessly murdering people with machine guns and smoking oversized joints. Ninja's character occasionally passes out (perhaps from narcolepsy), his wheels spinning in the air as his chair capsizes. Yo-Landi responds by berating and beating him with various objects. Ninja's continued unresponsiveness results in Yo-Landi eventually plaintively begging him to wake up. The violent surrealism of "Enter the Ninja" and "Umshini Wam," as well as of several other of Die Antwoord's videos, clearly marks contemporary South African music's move away from the political protest art of apartheid and the buoyant upbeats of newly democratic South Africa to something more tired, cynical, and increasingly savvy about playing to an international audience.

Spoek Mathambo's album *Tales from the Lost Cities* was released on February 26, 2020. Hailed as his best album yet, it is a masterfully mixed, scathing critique of contemporary South Africa, featuring songs like "Anatomy of a Campus Rape Riot" and "The Greedy Always Want More." I focus on an older album, *Mshini Wam*, released in August 2010, which Percy Zvomuya has described as a "unique take on electronic music that infuses futurism with a strong sense of pride in where he comes from. This is clearly African music, but not what you might expect from that title." Born in Soweto in 1985 as Nthato Mokgata, Spoek grew up relatively privileged socioeconomically in Sandown. His stage name comes from a popular television show called *Emzini Wezinsizwa* (House of Young Men) that Spoek watched as a child.[1] Roughly translated, *Spoek* means "ghost" in Afrikaans, and *Mathambo* in isiZulu signifies "bones" or a skeleton. The name Spoek Mathambo thus conjures up an image of a ghostly skeleton or skeleton-like ghost. As such, the name plays with themes of presence, absence, and embodiment. Haunting black presences that signify on the marginality of the black laboring body (consider the migrant workers depicted in *Emzini Wezinsizwa*) overlay the bare-bones structures of inequality. Spoek lives in Malmo, Sweden, in between sojourns to South Africa. During a 2011 TEDxSoweto titled "The Scare Tactics of Spoek Mathambo," Spoek recalls looking overseas for artistic influence until he realized that he needed to encounter South Africa not as a place of nostalgia but as a vibrant contemporary scene characterized by "dread" and "elation" (Mathambo, "Scare Tactics"). These two seemingly antithetical emotions are key to understanding Spoek's performances. The dread, he argues, stems from the historical terror of black and white antagonisms that continue after apartheid as well as the catastrophic AIDS pandemic. The threat of illness and the omnipresence of death permeate his performative sphere. Couple that dread with the elation, euphoria, and Bash culture that marked the end of apartheid, and one is left with a "dark electronic sound that relates to music all around the world but . . . is specifically African and the themes are kind of mind blowing" (Mathambo, "Scare Tactics"). Insisting on Africa's being a generative site for the production of contemporary music, Spoek states, "Being a kid from here, you grow up always looking up to foreign music. I never really respected what was happening in South Africa . . . until realising how . . . track for track [South African house and kwaito is] badass" (Bradshaw, "How Kwaito Became a Global Force").[2]

Directed by the white photographers Pieter Hugo and Michael Cleary, Spoek's video for "Control," the fourth single released off *Mshini Wam*, "established him as the heir apparent of Afro-futurists such as Sun Ra, Bootsy Collins, George Clinton, . . . Andre 3000, DJ Spooky and Kool Keith" (Leonard). Most viewers would be hard-pressed to locate the video both spatially and temporally—the characters appear to reside in a sonic Afro-gothic and/or Afro-futuristic landscape that pulses with electro-funk, electro-wave hip-house, and township-house vibrations. "It is not until you hear a familiar riff hidden in the layers of the song that you realize that this is a cover of 'She's Lost Control' by that whitest of groups Joy Division. And that makes it even eerier" (R. Smith).

Located in Langa, Cape Town, with a cast made up mainly of kids from the local dance troupe Happy Feet, "Control" begins in a graveyard. Shot in a crisp black and white, it features Spoek in a well-tailored white suit, chanting through a megaphone. Children chase each other through empty buildings; characters are doused in white and black viscous substances and powders; dancers spasm, and their eyes roll back into their heads; Spoek convulses on the ground while the dancers beat him with rubber hoses. The numerous seizing bodies, while convulsing rhythmically, convey a pain that ruptures the smooth surface of the video. The seizures and violence intensify until the final scene, in which Spoek curls into a fetal position on the ground, apparently spent. Coiled at the heart of the video, then, is the dread inspired by illness and the rhythmic elation of living with it through differential embodiment and movement.

In order to analyze Die Antwoord and Spoek Mathambo, we have to consider the way that music videos have become part of a larger media ecology that includes photography, film, documentary, and social media. Given how quickly the boundaries between digital platforms and genres are crossed and blurred as information flows accelerate, popular culture can best be described as what Carol Vernallis terms "a nexus of evolving audiovisual relations" (232). In her book *Unruly Media: YouTube, Music Video, and the New Digital Cinema*, Vernallis demonstrates the impossibility of dividing media along strict genre lines as similar technologies and socioeconomic pressures reconfigure the media we consume. The blurring of genres—including that Spoek Mathambo's "Control" premiered on *Dazed* magazine's online platform, called dazeddigital.com, "where pop culture meets the underground," and the crossover work of film directors such as Harmony Korine into music video and vice versa—points to what Vernallis calls a "'mixing-board' aesthetic" informed by "genealogies" produced by the music video's suturing of music and image (4). The kind of censorship and vetting done by MTV in the 1980s and '90s has largely gone by the wayside due to the proliferation of commercial websites, YouTube, and our increasing dexterity with digital technologies such as downloadable editing software and computer-generated imagery. It is in this global mediascape that we must place Spoek and Die Antwoord, knowing that their music videos reflect a transnational South Africa, thoroughly caught up in global media swirls of capital. Thus, claims to an African authenticity on either of their parts are necessarily undercut by how media is produced and consumed today.

At the center of this global mediascape, even as it has evolved today, is still often the exceptionality of the iconic individualized artist, be it Kanye, Beyoncé, or Lady Gaga. The genre continues to establish the superabilities of these larger-than-life celebrity figures. As Krystal Cleary states, the "machinery of celebrity is designed to produce iconic figures, not provide transparent access to personhood, even when it tries to convince us otherwise" (179). Die Antwoord, in particular, is obsessed with this aspect of the music video, insisting on thumbing their nose at it even while using this function of the genre to reestablish themselves as the ultimate anticelebrity celebrities. Ninja's and Yo-Landi's personas are so carefully constructed as exceptional individuals and so meticulously performed that it is impossible to distinguish between the fictions of their anticelebrity celebrity status and their racialized gendering as postapartheid white citizen-subjects. It is when we get to Spoek Mathambo's "Control" that we see a push against the horizon of singular, autonomous, exceptional bodies. The complicated genealogy of the song originally performed by Joy Division, alongside performances by the South African dance troupe Happy Feet, in particular provides us with a media experience of reimagining black sociality as we read against the grain of exceptionality, moving instead toward a conjoined "we" slowly losing control.

Both Die Antwoord and Spoek Mathambo have produced hybrid-genre sonic and visual texts around postapartheid identity that link race, class, and gender to disability through performances of the spasm, narcolepsy, and riding wheelchairs. This investment in disability comes as no surprise if we consider the growing disillusionment of many white South Africans who feel "crippled" by current sociopolitical conditions as well as a nation struggling to come to grips with the influx of other African nationals, often stereotyped as the bearers of contagion. This particular political moment in South Africa has some performers reaching for false equivalencies that erase nonnormative bodies by making (dis)ability stand *in* for gendered, racial, or sexual "Otherness." Others pay close attention to the conditions that give rise to disability, thinking about disability as a welcome opportunity to imagine new forms of black sociality. This chapter dwells on whether Spoek and Die Antwoord's marketing discourse, as Mitzi Waltz and Martin James develop, "use . . . the attraction/repulsion of difference to sell tickets and products" (367–68) while marginalizing the material consequences of illness and disability. Are they using "the disabled body [to serve] as the raw material out of which other socially disempowered communities make themselves visible" (Mitchell and Snyder 6)? Is their differential movement a problematic appropriation, a means to distance themselves from apartheid's racial legacies, or is it a liberatory gesture that constructs black sociality from flesh? Is this too simplistic a binary?

"It's a Zombie Stopper": Zef and the "Crisis" of Whiteness

Something is definitely different in the photographs of the white Afrikaner photographer Pieter Hugo, whose color image of a white Afrikaner heterosexual couple holding a black baby across their laps is the first image one sees in the *Figures and Fictions* exhibit at the Victoria and Albert Museum (fig. 4.1). The bare-chested white man has his arms around the shoulders of his partner, whose pretty but cheap blouse hangs loosely around her breasts. Her face is sun-damaged; there is what appears to be a sore or a scab on the side of her nose. Her eyes are a brilliant blue, her hands long and elegant. The man's shorts reveal his prosthetic loosely fitted onto his residual limb, one hand on the connecting sleeve or cuff. The couple sit on a makeshift couch, covered with a dirty white sheet, awkwardly holding a well-dressed black baby between them. The plump health of the baby highlights the dented prosthetic leg of the man and the scabbed face of his female partner. The photograph is a story of three sets of feet: the woman's tan-lined feet face inward, big toes touching, like a chastened child's; the man's feet are stuffed into black sandals presumably for the sake of his prosthetic; one of the baby's pudgy feet is held loosely in the woman's hands, while the other rests against the man's knee. Hugo tells us that this image of the white couple who rent a room from the black child's father is the "New South Africa, warts and all" (O'Hagan, "Figures"). We are supposed to be shocked by the photograph, not by the poverty per se, which is exhaustingly familiar, but rather because this is *white* poverty and black wealth. The photograph disrupts notions of the nuclear family as the primary vehicle of white primogeniture, the black baby a sullen impossibility in the fiction

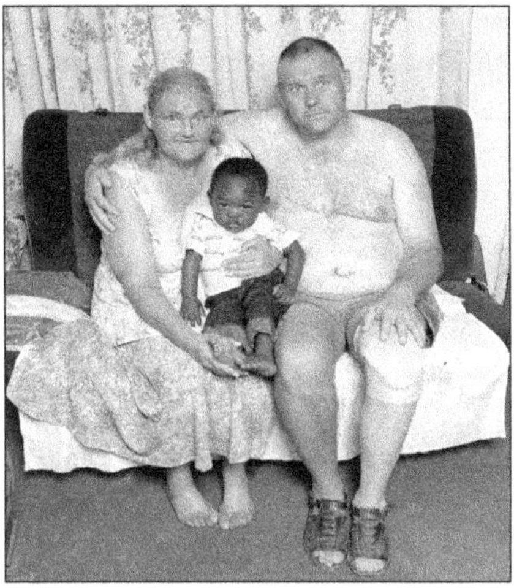

Figure 4.1. Pieter Hugo, *Pieter and Maryna Vermeulen with Timana Phosiwa* (2006) (© Pieter Hugo)

of racial sameness and kinship. The naked prosthetic and sleeve further the demasculinization of the white man, who has supposedly failed to produce a white heir, to fulfill the rigorously protected coupling between whiteness and socioeconomic privilege. This demasculinization can also be seen in the man's body, particularly his bare torso, being open and vulnerable to the gaze of the camera, which looks down on him. His legs are held close together, in a position associated with femininity. This is "a world turned upside down," Sean O'Hagan writes, where the racialized optic regime that constructs whites as those with the ability to look and blacks as those forced to appear is inverted ("Figures").[3]

South Africa is not a world turned upside down. In 2015, four years after the release of Die Antwoord's "Umshini Wam," whites only constituted 1 percent of all people officially living in poverty; 93 percent of the nation's poor were black (Wilkinson). The photograph, then, indexes not a changing society so much as a deep anxiety about shifting axes of privilege. As certain scholars have argued, "white South Africans are suffering a crisis of delegitimacy and, despite the social and economic privileges they might have retained in a postapartheid context, many claim they no longer have a legitimate space from which to enter the national conversation and their voices are not heard" (C. Scott 746). Hugo himself says, "My homeland is Africa, but I'm white. I feel African, whatever that means, but if you ask anyone in South Africa if I'm African, they will almost certainly say no" (O'Hagan, "Africa"). Hugo's photograph in which poor, disabled whites rent rooms from well-off and healthy blacks captures the anxiety that arises from this crisis. The cramped space of the photograph, the forced smile of the woman, the baby awkwardly held between the couple—the discomfort emanating from the image is palpable.

The 2016 article "Skin Salvaged" by Kiera Obbard and Stephanie Cork on Die Antwoord reflects this anxiety. Consider the following language used by the authors to describe a postapartheid landscape of exceptional white suffering characterized by an *increase* in race and class tensions rather than a continuous renegotiation: "White Afrikaners experienced a great sense of shame and disgrace 'inculcated by the accusations from the international community' of the mistreatment of ethnic bodies during segregation. . . . In contrast to the idealistic vision of a united nation in which all are created equal, . . . South Africans, particularly white ones, must negotiate a new identity within postapartheid South Africa—leading to an increase in race and class tensions within the nation" (418). This increase in race and class tension can only apply to those people whom apartheid benefited. For the rest of us, removed from our homes when areas were rezoned racially, made to carry pass books, forced to enter through back doors, given subpar education, imprisoned, beaten, drowned, and thrown out of windows—the postapartheid era, though not without its challenges, cannot honestly be seen as an escalation in tension but rather as a continuation in different forms.

Henke Pistorius, father of the famous six-time Paralympic gold medalist and convicted murderer Oscar Pistorius, explains why the men of his family own upward of fifty guns among them: "Some of the guns are for hunting and some are for protection, the hand guns. It speaks to the ANC government, look at white crime levels, why protection is so poor in this country, it's an aspect of our society" (Swartz 1158). As Leslie Swartz develops, Pistorius is convinced that whites are more vulnerable to attack by the "swaart gevaar" (black threat) and that the ANC is not only failing to protect whites but actively encouraging violence against them (1158–59). While Henke Pistorius does not mention disability, Oscar Pistorius's deep interest in guns "for protection" is necessarily related to converting his marginalized male status as disabled into the hegemonic masculinity of his father, grandfather, and uncles.[4] A video clip of Oscar Pistorius shows him shooting at a watermelon as he remarks,

"It's not as soft as brains, . . . but it's a zombie stopper" (Nkosi). It is no accident that Die Antwoord's "Umshini Wam" is centered around guns (as well as wheelchairs and weed) as they shoot at everything indiscriminately. Even as the group insist that they are not white but "zef" and that their being armed in the video references the ANC's armed struggle for liberation during apartheid, their exaggerated, almost farcical gunplay borrows from the iconography of besieged whiteness for legitimacy. Even as they attempt to distance themselves from their whiteness, they reinscribe it.

Obbard and Cork analyze Die Antwoord's notion of "zef" (all these different people "fucked into one person") that the group claim is central to understanding their project. To be zef, then, is to transcend the boundaries into which you were born in favor of the adoption of identities that better reflect the inner self. In this sense, the body becomes "the original prosthesis we all learn to manipulate"; race, class, and sexuality all become prosthetics that can be taken on and off at will (Obbard and Clark 424–25).

Even though "zef" means to "transcend the boundaries into which you were born," the term is deeply rooted in a history of whiteness in South Africa. It was once a term for the "commonness" and lack of sophistication of working-class, Afrikaans-speaking whites who lived in caravan parks. The term originated from the tricked-out Ford Zephyrs that these poor whites drove from the 1950s to 1970s. Today, thanks not only to stage and television shows like *The Most Amazing Show* but also Die Antwoord, the term signals a trendy aesthetic of vulgar kitsch. This aesthetic borrows freely from other races, aligning what Bryan Schmidt describes as "Afrikaans-speaking working class . . . with certain aspects of coloured gangster culture" (136). For example, Ninja's gold caps are part of his "zef" persona. Gold caps were popular in the 1960s among Coloured and black communities, but through a sleight of hand, "zef" folds this practice into a poor white culture reimagined as authentic. Zef, as Claire Scott writes, is a "deliberate re-framing and embrace of the perceived marginalization and negativity associated with a lower-class, white South African identity" (751). It reimagines the culture of poor whites by borrowing notions of authenticity from the very communities that poor whites took great pains to define themselves against during apartheid. As Anton Krueger writes, "a new designation of *Zef* also implies an attitude of resilience . . . linked to notions of authenticity" (402). Krueger goes to explain that this white resilience is "linked to a kind of rudeness which implies a sign of health—as in the idiomatic expression, 'to be in rude health'" (402). What does it mean to be in rude health? While the British idiom simply means to be strong and healthy, the word "rude" in the context of "zef" implies vulgarity, an in-your-face confrontational quality that links health to what Ninja and Yo-Landi would call "not giving a fuck," to being everyone and anything.

In an interview, Ninja famously remarks, "God made a mistake with me. I'm actually black, trapped in a white body. South Africa has 11 languages, different cultures, I don't feel we're separate. Die Antwoord is like South Africa, all these cultures in one fucking person" (Stone, "Ninja"). In "Never le Nkemise," a track off the *Ten$ion* album, the group express similar sentiments: "Ninja, die wit kaffir / Ja, julle naaiers / Skrik Wakker" (Ninja, the white kaffir / Yes, you fuckers / Wake up). In "Umshini Wam," the white Afrikaner who tells Ninja and Yo-Landi that they can't afford his wheelchairs calls them "white kaffirs" who are a "waste of white skin." In "Enter the Ninja," Ninja's face is repeatedly juxtaposed with the face of the late Leon Botha, who suffered from progeria. In a sleight of hand, Ninja borrows Botha's face, using Botha's disability as an aesthetic strategy to reinforce his own legitimacy as outsider. Looking closely at these interviews, lyrics, and videos, it becomes apparent that Die Antwoord are obsessed with their own bodies' ability to absorb racial diversity and stand in for the differentially embodied Other due to the "prosthetic" nature of their whiteness and their ability to suture other identities, sometimes literally, onto their bodies. Zef, then, is not just about racial but also about disabled identity.

Die Antwoord thus often rely on prosthetics to alter their bodies and the bodies of others in their quest to encompass any (racial/differentially embodied) identity that they choose. In "Evil Boy," featuring the amaXhosa rapper Wanga, for example, Ninja has a prosthetic arm that ends in a lobster claw. Through the use of makeup, blackout contact lenses, and hair dye, Yo-Landi presents herself as albino in numerous videos. Contorted rubber mouths, plastic breasts with no nipples, a blue prosthetic penis that juts up and out like a monkey's tail—theirs is a world of bodies that are grotesquely disabled and supplemented. Die Antwoord's emphasis on artificiality can be attributed to postmodern play, to an understanding of the body as plastic and malleable. Their use of the spectacle of difference, I feel, points toward their continual appropriation of differential embodiment. The assumption that their whiteness is a prosthetic that can be removed when necessary is only matched by their careless borrowing of the often pained, historical embodiment of others as they master racialized performances of disability.

Nowhere is Die Antwoord's appropriation of race, class, and disability more obvious than in Ninja's and Yo-Landi's presentation of themselves as belonging to communities that are "indigenous" to the Cape Flats. In the YouTube clip "Zef Side," shot on the border of the Cape Flats in a poor suburb, Ninja tells us, "DJ Hi-Tech lives with his granny, and then I live with my mom and dad down the road and Yo-Landi's the next-door neighbor." Neither Ninja nor Yo-Landi is from anywhere close. The Cape Flats is an area of Cape Town plagued by desperate poverty, high murder rates (almost one thousand deaths in the first six months of 2019), violent gangs (the Americans, Hard Livings, Fancy Boys, Clever Kids, Dixie Boys, and others), and a booming drug trade in cannabis, *tik* (crystal meth), and opiates.[5] Die Antwoord's depiction of the Cape Flats does not include its community gardens or schoolchildren or even, for the most part, any women of color. Instead, we watch young men drink and smoke weed as they awkwardly listen to Ninja rap. A random amputee, leg stumps bared as he sits in a wheelchair at the side of the road, stares into the camera. "House of Zef—MegaMix9000" features clips from Die Antwoord's latest album, *House of Zef*. A minute and half into the video, we see a group of young men, several of them shirtless, holding a gun to a man's head as they rob him. The rest of the clip shows this "gang" robbing and beating passersby in a street surrounded by shacks.

Ninja is enamored with the aesthetics of gang culture, in particular prison gangs. The Number, according to Fareed Kaviani, is one of the world's oldest gangs, with a sophisticated hierarchical system of three factions: the 26s, 27s, and 28s.[6] The bodies of members of The Number are covered with tattoos that mark them as belonging to a particular faction as well as have specific meanings based on the complex historical lore of a group dating back hundreds of years. These tattoos are almost always done by hand, using a sharpened guitar string and burned rubber ash and water paste. Ninja started going by the tattoo studio of Tyler B. Murphy and tattooing himself. This self-tattooing further suggests

Ninja's capacity to literally write himself as an autonomous subject with mastery over his own body, unlike black, disabled bodies that are subject to being marked. He later asked Murphy to do hand-poked tattoos based on images of ex-prisoners he brought in. Ninja's body has slowly morphed as he attempts to resemble gang members. One of Die Antwoord's latest videos, "Baita Jou Sabela," featuring Slagysta, depicts Ninja as one of several orange-jumpsuit-clad, tattooed prisoners in Pollsmoor (actually Castle of Good Hope), and aesthetically, he is almost indistinguishable. Adam Haupt argues that the tattoos work "connotatively without actually making denotative connections. The band does not refer directly but alludes to the numbers gang . . . via tattoos and graffiti that [often] appear[] in the background of their set" ("Part IV" 420). Ninja literally rewrites his white body as he attempts *not to be* but to look like the (incarcerated) men of the Cape Flats.

As Die Antwoord supposedly distance themselves from the normative white, bourgeois subject, they embrace all those who they think are either countercultural or have been rejected from mainstream society: the gangbanger and prisoner, the easily identifiable disabled person, the homophobe, the trash and detritus of South African society—all that is strange and "freeky."[7] As they rap in "I Fink U Freeky": "I fink you freeky and I like you a lot. . . . It's nice and different, yo fuck the system / My system pumps off its fucking face."

A Market Economy of Fungible Diversity

Cork and Obbard's celebratory use of "prosthetic whiteness" (also developed by John Preston) needs to be unpacked. I would argue that it is in the ability to imagine oneself as an unmarked, normatively embodied "human being" with a meaningful "inner self"/intrinsic value that the privilege of whiteness is deployed. In other words, only the transcendent, able-bodied, independent subject can "discard" whiteness "at the door" (Preston 332) and freely adopt "identities that better reflect the inner self" (Obbard and Cork 424). Ninja and Yo-Landi's deployment of white privilege necessitates that DJ Hi-Tek, who is black and queer, is largely absent visually from Die Antwoord's performances. When he does appear, either he is being played by someone else (often white) or his body is masked and augmented with prosthetics; Obbard and Cork describe him as "dwarf-like, horribly disfigured" (427). Very few consumers of Die Antwoord's performances know what he actually looks like. It is precisely when we confront DJ Hi-Tek's absent, substituted for, and "monstrous" body that the limits of theorizing whiteness as a prosthetic as well as Die Antwoord's entire project is revealed. His displaced, nonnormative body speaks to what Hortense Spillers, Saidiya Hartman, and others suggest is the mechanism of fungibility and its formative relationship to blackness as an undesirable social category. Fungibility, in its legal, economic, and ontological sense, entails the abstraction of certain bodies into units of exchange, stripped of the Enlightenment's notion of individuality and interiority. As Hartman writes, "The fungibility of the commodity makes the captive body an abstract and empty vessel vulnerable to the projection of others' feelings, ideas, desires, and values" (*Scenes of Subjection* 21). Hartman goes on to argue that the "fungibility of the commodity, specifically its abstractness and immateriality, enabled the black body . . . to serve as the vehicle of white self-exploration, renunciation, and enjoyment" (26). In other words, the fungibility of blackness enables the pleasurable self-fashioning of whiteness. Elaborating on Hartman, Tiffany Lethabo King argues that the fungible black body functions as an "open-ended commodity form that can stand in for the other commodity forms and other meanings," in particular "the 'raw material' of the human" (104). As abstracted raw material, the black body is precluded from the attendant normative categories of gender, kinship, and able-bodiedness.

While I argue in my introduction, à la Spillers, C. Riley Snorton, and others, for the powerful potentialities that black fungibility allows in unmaking prescriptive essentialized identities, I am more interested here in what Shannon Winnubst calls "fresh itineraries of fungibility" (109). The contemporary consumption of diversity or difference is one such pathway. Winnubst writes, "'Diversity' becomes the direct aim of the neoliberal social rationality, externalized and internalized as prudent market practices" (109). Taking up "diversity" means rendering opaque fungibility's essential role in the ontology of antiblackness. Ninja and Yo-Landi's neoliberal reworking of fungibility, as they consume difference as a market practice, therefore necessitates DJ Hi-Tek's visual erasure and distortion. To have him center stage would force them to acknowledge how

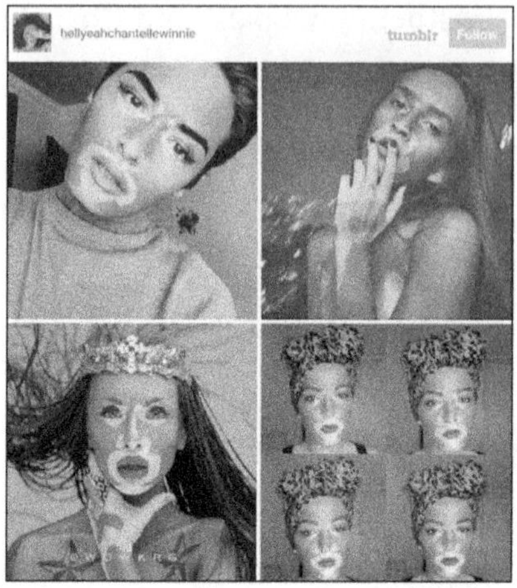

Figure 4.2. Four images of white women on Tumblr using makeup to resemble Winnie Harlow (© Chantelle Brown-Young, known as Winnie Harlow; HellYeahChantelleWinnie on Tumblr)

their neoliberal "mode of subjectification frees white persons, communities, populations and institutions from struggling with anti-blackness as a grounding ontology of . . . whiteness" (Winnubst 111). DJ Hi-Tek's body indexes the historical fungibility of abstracted black bodies whom colonialism and slavery converted into replaceable objects, an indistinguishable zombie horde. The "fresher itineraries of fungibility" practiced by Ninja and Yo-Landi refuse to recognize how differences between social bodies and communities form the historical basis of abstraction, subjugation, and death. Their structural enjoyment of black flesh enables them to conceive of difference as nothing more than a market commodity, a fungible unit stripped of its historical gravitas.

Let us consider for a moment the model Winnie Harlow, whose supposed difference helps sell products and brands—she is the "face" of the Spanish fashion label Desigual, for example. Harlow was so relentlessly bullied for her nonsegmental vitiligo during her childhood that she was homeschooled. It was only after she was chosen as a finalist on *America's Next Top Model* that her career as a model took off and people (especially white women) began emulating her look. On the one hand, the fact that the women in the Tumblr pics in figure 4.2 can replace Harlow's body with theirs speaks to the ontological fungibility of blackness. But it is also Harlow's differential embodiment that has become fungible. Like Ninja and prison tattoos, these white women replicate the very specific markings on Harlow's face and body to demonstrate their mastery over their own bodies and also their ability to consume her difference rendered fungible. Thus, "vitiligo" is about an alternate aesthetic that does not come with the painful history of being called a "cow" and "zebra" and being unable to attend school. It has no history of race and disability. Nor does it acknowledge that access to market economies and what is fungible or not is deeply shaped by antiblackness. This is difference that is detachable, emptied out, enacted, and discarded once the new, trendier form of difference comes along. It is static and fixed, whereas for many people, patches of vitiligo can spread at different rates to different parts of the body. Making difference fungible is to construct a circuit of simulation that slides over the epistemic violence of racism, pretending that it was never there.

Control

While at first glance Spoek Mathambo and Die Antwoord both utilize a similar aesthetic of racialized disability, there is something very different going on in Spoek Mathambo's work. I am not arguing that because Spoek Mathambo is black, his aesthetic practice has greater authenticity. A close reading of his sonic and visual performance in "Control" demonstrates that he does not rely on stereotypical images of race or disability. There are no floating images of sufferers of progeria, random shots of amputees, or grotesque prosthetic limbs. Nor does he get into a wheelchair and roll around a deserted suburb. Instead, his deliberate cover of a song with a particular resonance for disabled peoples allows him to think through the traditional exploitation of nonnormative "outsiders" that has characterized the popular music industry. Spoek Mathambo's referencing of disability that operates on various registers includes a discussion of the material conditions of (disabled) artists themselves. He utilizes the somatic vocabulary of the spasm even as he insists on a socio-material history of the spasm in both popular music and South African culture. His contextualization of the spasm refuses to reduce differential embodiment and movement to a fungible commodity. Instead, he reveals how difference has been commodified, gesturing to the possibilities of spiritual practice and spiritual elsewheres where differential embodiment and movement are not obstacles to be overcome but instead a conjoined way of being in the world.

Despite Spoek's living in Sweden and traveling to South Africa, his work does not revolve around nostalgia for the country he grew up in. Nor is he obsessed with legitimizing his music as an "authentic" South African. Rather, he is interested in black aesthetic practices and the forms of sociality that can be constructed through the cocreation of music and video. His vision includes exploring the production of other African artists, both black and white, as he works through histories of exploitation and the problem of artistic control. Ghanaian and Nigerian horror movies and posters influence his visual aesthetic, particularly the concepts behind his video performances. As Spoek Mathambo posits, lacking the slick production value of Hollywood, Nollywood and Ghanaian cinema creates images using whatever technology is available, shooting "video with cell phone light and [being] pretty happy with it, . . . making Africa a lot smaller place [by] sharing aesthetics and sharing moods" (Mathambo, "Scare Tactics"). These shared and reinterpreted, stripped down and evocative (rather than representational), aesthetics permeate his videos. The spaces in the video are dark and moody. Empty concrete rooms are juxtaposed with scenes from shadowy graveyards. Black and white viscous substances are poured over bodies, and gothic stone figures lurk behind Spoek Mathambo as he holds a megaphone tightly in hand. The apparent lack of lighting makes the images difficult to discern. The overall visual impression establishes "Control's" place in a genealogy of popular African film.

Spoek Mathambo's interest in Ghanaian and Nigerian film is not just aesthetic: he has repeatedly stated that he is concerned with issues around self-representation and how Africans find themselves represented by others. "As South Africans we are always represented by other people whether it is marketing firms trying to sell you this by showing you yourself or foreigners coming in and getting their actors to play your heroes. I wanted South African youth to write the South African youth story without selling them anything" (Mathambo, "Scare Tactics"). It is no accident that Spoek Mathambo asked fellow South African Pieter Hugo, whose photograph of the poor white couple and black baby we peered intently at earlier, to codirect his video "Control." His choice to work with Hugo insists that we move beyond racial essentialist notions of Africanity as only black. At the same time, Hugo's whiteness is not

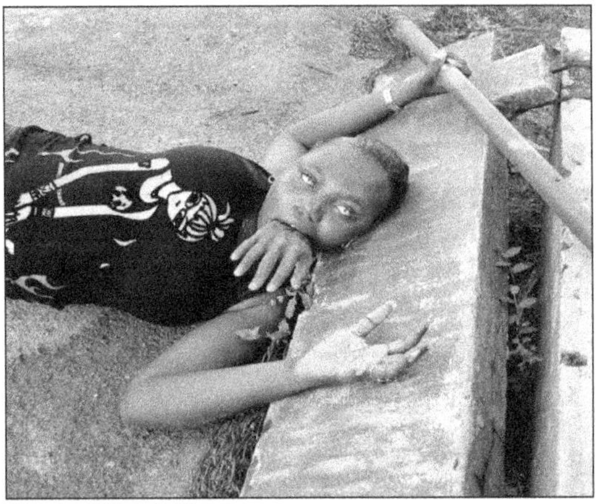

Figure 4.3. Pieter Hugo, *Princess Adaobi* (2008) (© Pieter Hugo)

something that Spoek ignores. Rather, he explores specifically the relationship between control over one's representation and racial privilege.

Let us consider another of Hugo's photographic horror series, called *Nollywood* (2008–9), a series that led to Spoek hiring him as one of the directors of "Control." Masked, bloody, and horned, the frightening fictional monsters of Nollywood gaze out at the camera in staged tableaus in Hugo's "Nollywood" series. In Nomusa Makhubu's nuanced reading of the photographs, she describes the characters in the series as "the living dead" or necromantic zombies ("Politics" 55).[8] Many of these characters appear blind and mute. In *Princess Adaobi* (2008), for example, a young woman with "zombie" contact lenses (similar to the ones worn by Yo-Landi) lies awkwardly across the visual plane, a protruding ashy hand stuffed into her mouth (fig. 4.3). Another of the images, titled *Omo Omeoni* (2008), depicts a muscular, bare-chested Omeoni holding a long sword that emphasizes his diminutive stature. His skin is mottled with black, tar-like substance, and the tall grass obscures his lower limbs, exaggerating his status as a little person.[9] Even though the title of each photograph bears the name of the actors, there is no contextualization of where these various characters are from, leaving viewers confused as to what they are actually looking at. This confusion leads to viewers accepting these images as less fictional and more anthropological. The photographs thus contribute to general perceptions of both primitive African bodies and the deviance of blackness; as Makhubu writes, the photographs in their "hyperventilating realism . . . celebrat[e] . . . the image while affirming stereotypes at the same time" (60). Makhubu concludes, "Accepting this imagery as mere fiction necessitates recognizing the tinge of pathological precarious misapprehension that lies deep in the crevices of reality and threatens to coagulate divisive fear" (60).

About the Nollywood series, Spoek insists that Hugo "made an intervention, he is an artist. That's the stuff he came up with. *Not to say that this is interesting or amazing* but to say . . . the more we don't represent ourselves, the more people like Pieter with the clout and the connections will make entire careers out of misrepresenting us or representing us the way they want to represent us" (Mathambo, "Scare Tactics"; emphasis added). Spoek, instead of arguing for "authentic" racial representation based on his blackness, focuses his comments on which artists and performances are privileged. Whose speculative fiction is given a hearing, and whose is overlooked and subsumed into reductive notions of the authentic? Instead of insisting, like Die Antwoord, that his is an authentic South African voice, he raises questions about the politics that undergird the making, distribution, and consumption of artistic representations. Given these concerns, as well as his lukewarm description of Hugo's work, we must ask why Spoek asked Hugo to work with him on the video for "Control" in the first place. By collaborating with Hugo, Spoek makes clear that he is not attempting to retrieve an authentic form of black artistic expression. He goes out of his way to show himself as a contemporary young South African, equally at home in Sweden as he is in Johannesburg, comfortable with metal and kwaito, articulate in English, isiZulu, and Sesotho, and able to use technology in all its various media to convey his artistic genius. Rather than a reductive (though sometimes strategic) black nationalism, Spoek is more interested in controlling representation. As such, he tackles head-on the legacy of privilege that makes black bodies the object of the gaze and the white artist the producer of the image. Collaboration, cultural play, and a polyglot voraciousness are what make postapartheid South Africa, not a return to "authenticity" or cultural purity or a simple inversion of racial dichotomies, he insists. Spoek focuses on dismantling the legacy of artistic "control" over representation. Spoek's "Control" asks how one collaborates across racialized lines of privilege in this in-between space "where political power may have shifted but old codes and structures of authority and deference remain in place" (O'Hagan, "Figures"). The resulting performance isn't a warm fusion or a cheery hybridity where blacks and whites hold hands in the "rainbow nation" claiming that they are one ("Simunye").[10] Instead it is colder, uncomfortable, replete with violence and the push and pull of "control" over oneself and over others. This notion of control is also about mastery over one's physical body, one of the attendant myths of able-bodiedness.

Ian Curtis and the Spasm

Given the history of imperialism, Mark Priestly warns that it is "important to retain some caution about the ease or desirability of transferring Northern solutions to Southern problems. . . . To further an agenda for disability and social change in South African we need to ensure that Disability Studies programmes are informed by developments in an international context, but that they remain rooted in knowledge and action for change in South Africa (and more broadly for the southern African region)" (20). Spoek Mathambo does exactly this. In "Control," his cover of a song that is so central to the history of disability and British popular music, he explores whether and how a Western aesthetic practice of disability can apply to the South African context. Specifically, Spoek intervenes in the notion of "enfreakment," asking us to consider how race and Africanity shift the concept. But first, let us consider how "enfreakment" works in Western popular music as it pivots around the idea of "outsider" music and artists.

"Enfreakment," a term coined by David Hevey in 1992, describes the way that people with disabilities become the "voyeuristic property of the non-disabled gaze," which recasts their differential embodiment as cultural and racial otherness (377). Rosemarie Garland-Thomson similarly defines "enfreakment" as "emerg[ing] from cultural rituals that stylize, silence, differentiate, and distance the persons whose bodies the freak-hunters or showmen colonize and commercialize" ("Introduction" 10). She goes on to develop how even while enfreakment focuses our attention on "specific bodily eccentricities," these differences are subsumed into one large "amorphous category of corporeal otherness" (10). Thus, often the actual disabilities of artists are obscured by a generalized, pseudoscientific discourse of disability that does not name specific conditions so much as exploit the notion of difference itself.

Mitzi Waltz and Martin James in "The (Re)marketing of Disability in Pop" point out how music marketing has linked the commodifying process of enfreakment to Romantic ideas of musicians as outsiders. These outsider musicians are perceived as rare "authentic" individuals whose failure to conform to conventional society, due to their differential embodiment and movement, enables them to feel more than the rest of us, to overcome their challenges with superhuman or not-quite-human strength, and to make art differently. While these individuals are seen as having greater access to an authentic truth that adds pathos to their songs, their appeal also lies in their putative failure to sound "normal." Our feelings for musicians oscillate between admiration for their ability to overcome their disability and a profound pity for their failure to approximate normalcy.

Kathleen McDougall in her analysis of the narratives of respondents in a Human Sciences Research Council study of disability and the mass media in the South African context describes this oscillation as shifting between an "ag shame" narrative and the myth of the supercrip. The respondents in her study struggle with being thought of as unfortunate, in need of the "gift" of support from society and the state. One respondent states, "if you read a disability story, it's 'ag shame,' 'ag fooi tog,' or 'this poor person has managed eventually to get somewhere' kind of slant, . . . and it's horrible" (392). This "ag shame" narrative is accompanied by the myth of "supercrip," in which the disabled person ekes out a life that resembles normalcy "in spite of" their differential embodiment. Thus, the disabled performer, while pitiable, is also admirable as they transcend their limitations and expose their vulnerabilities for all of us to see. Enfreakment thus trades in an economy of pathos, repulsion, and desire that sells music performances to those who are eager to consume differences while leaving able-bodied racial hierarchies intact (Waltz and James 367–68).

These dynamics of enfreakment that characterize "outsider music" can be seen in the way consumers digest the work of disabled musicians such as the late Wesley Willis, an African American who suffered from schizophrenia. The market economy's rendering fungible his schizophrenia obfuscates the fungibility that historically has defined ontological blackness. Consider, for example, the following description of Willis on a fan website: "When you're listening to the radio, do you ever stop to think about how few songs are played by obese schizophrenic black musicians from the streets of Chicago? . . . The airwaves are cluttered by alternative rock, rap, and R&B; meanwhile, the 'obese schizophrenic' musical genre is underrepresented. That's why everyone should start calling their local radio station and requesting songs by Wesley Willis" (Aminzade). While tongue in cheek, Dan Aminzade's praise for Willis's music stems simultaneously from its ability to represent an abject, fungible blackness ("obese" here connotes the excess of black flesh) and disability as a fungible difference (schizophrenia), as well as its status as outside conventional genre categories. These dynamics can also be seen in "Remembering Wesley Willis, Ten Years Later," in which Daniel Stuckey writes, "I cracked up whenever I heard his music, but usually found myself meditating on Wesley's inner demons and enemies when I sang along to lines like 'Put some tartar sauce on a horse's cock and suck it.'" Stuckey goes on to portray Willis as *unable* rather than *unwilling* to perform conventionally. Willis's inability, which supposedly stems from his blackness and his schizophrenia, provides other artists with a painless, even funny (at Willis's expense) way out of the maze of convention. The outsider musician here, instead of displaying skill or talent, becomes reduced to his performance of authentic suffering and disability that is worthy both of pity and of admiration as he has heroically overcome his limitations to the best of his ability—the "ag shame" superhero. This, in turn, establishes a template for other accomplished artists to emulate if they want to be "authentically" different.

We see some of the same dynamics operating with regard to Ian Curtis and Joy Division. "Control" is one of Joy Division's most famous songs. It was written while Curtis worked with disabled people at the Job Centre in Macclesfield, Cheshire. One of his clients had epilepsy, and when he learned that she had died as a result of a fit when she was sleeping in 1978, he wrote a song about her: "Confusion in her eyes that says it all / She's lost control / And she's clinging to the nearest passerby." He wrote this song before he began to have the same epileptic symptoms. He was diagnosed in early 1979 after bandmates were forced to take him to hospital. The difficulty of being a musician living with epilepsy supposedly led to his suicide in 1980. Our familiarity with this narrative of his epilepsy is relatively recent. Joy Division's label, Factory Records, suppressed all information in its press releases regarding Curtis's epilepsy during his lifetime and initially posthumously, as the company regarded it as negative publicity. Perhaps it also was attempting to avoid any kind of culpability, as the grueling schedule of touring and performances of dancing out of control led to increasingly frequent and more intense epileptic seizures. Instead, Curtis's emotionally sensitive, dark, and brooding lyrics, which foreshadowed his suicide, were used to authenticate his "outsiderness." His frenzied performances were cast as him "losing himself" in the music. Factory Records portrayed him not as a supercrip but as normal, just overly sensitive. He was the master of his own body, even as his emotional depth resulted in his losing control.

However, given "fresh itineraries of fungibility," more recent marketing has exploited Curtis's disability as a newer, hipper way to signal his "otherness." Publicity material such as the films *Control*, *24 Hour Party People*, and Grant Gee's documentary on Joy Division have explicitly marketed Curtis's epilepsy as the ultimate physical manifestation of his alienation, as well as a heroic narrative of an artist attempting to overcome the odds against him. Curtis's illness has been used to define him in ways that are out of his control—heroically tragic, misunderstood, attractive, and a "freak." Little attention, if any, has been paid to the difference between his performances of epileptic seizures onstage, such as the "crazy dancing" he did when performing "She's Lost Control," and his own epileptic fits, which often forced him offstage and/or into hospitals. Audiences often assumed that a seizure was actually "only" a performance of one. By covering this song with its complicated history around disability and popular music and staging it in an entirely different, southern African context, Spoek Mathambo enters into a conversation about disability, swirls of media and race. He asks us to think about performances of losing control over one's body and the ways that have been marketed and sold to us. Can he create another narrative about losing control? Can this narrative move away from sentimentalized supercrips to foregrounding the spasm as central to how the black body can exceed the limited ways in which it has traditionally been represented?

Vibrating

Franco Berardi in *Heroes: Mass Murder and Suicide* defines the spasm as "sudden, abnormal, involuntary muscular contractions and relaxations, . . . a sudden, brief spell of energy and . . . painful intensification of the bodily nervous vibration" (217). Medical sources such as the US National Library of Medicine and Healthgrades define it similarly as caused by "uncontrolled, repetitive contractions of a muscle" (Healthgrades). The related movement of twitching results from minor muscle contractions, or the twitching of a muscle group or small area of muscle serviced by a single motor nerve fiber (US National Library of Medicine). These muscular contractions and releases can range from pleasurable to uncomfortable to extremely painful.

Berardi in "Chaosmic Spasm and the Educational Chaoide" and *Heroes* and Félix Guattari in *Chaosmosis* have written extensively on the spasm, which both authors see as stemming from the alienation and hyperrationality of a violent global capitalism. Guattari develops that profitability as the raison d'être for every transaction refigures the global economy as one driven by competition over supposedly scarce resources. These unevenly distributed resources result in individuals becoming "zombies," ensnared in a haunted state between the living and the dead as they lurch through "un-world[s]" that are "ecologically unsustainable and unliveable" (Featherstone 252). The zombie's lurch and drag struggle and fail to keep up with what Berardi calls finance capital's exploitative and ever-accelerating "spasmogenic rhythm." Capitalism's "zombies" find their cognitive work taken over, he writes, by "the abstract acceleration of the info-machine" that "destroy[s] the singularity of language, transforming language into a chain of automatic techno-linguistic interfaces" (Berardi, "Chaosmic" 188). The chaosmic spasm, then, is a symptom of the unsustainability of capital's relentless, ever-increasing speed as it takes over the individual's body, their mind, and the way they move. The unsustainability of capital, according to Berardi, has contaminated "the psychosphere and provok[ed] disharmony in the psychic breathing: fear, anxiety, panic, and depression are the symptoms of the illness provoked by this kind of pollution (*And* 132). As we are inundated by an avalanche of meaningless quantitative data, it becomes increasingly difficult to imagine a tenable future or to comprehend the past. The spasm makes evident the toll that capital has on the body; the body twitches and shakes as it fails to keep up with an unsustainable ordering of time and labor. For Berardi, the unrelenting spasmogenic rhythm of capital leads to the destruction of individualism, the fall of an agential hero who has the capacity to act on the world. What is needed instead, Berardi goes on to say, is a "new rhythm" that "relaxes the spasm and heals the spastic sensible organism" ("Chaosmic" 188).

This disappearance of the agential hero obviously refers to the white, Western subject who is the victim of the abstraction of finance capital with its language of quantitative value. This is not the black body, created out of the crucible of slavery, colonialism, and the aftermath, whose torn and lacerated flesh renders it outside of formulations of volitional, individual subjects. Berardi's and Guattari's crisis of fungibility, faced by presumably white, universal subjects like Die Antwoord, whose autonomous, independent subjectivities were supposedly a fait accompli, highlights the spasms of black, differential bodies that tremble when faced with racism and ableism. These universal subjects, alienated by capital, are in need of "the language of embodiment" (Featherstone 248), whereas for the black, disabled person, there has never been an escape from the weight (or potential) of embodiment, the fleshy substrate of property. Fanon's *Black Skins, White Masks* reanalyzes seven narratives of the Malagasy that evidence a different chronology than Berardi's and Guattari's contemporary formulation of capital's ever-accelerating transformation of language into technological interfaces with its emphasis on rapidity. Fanon writes, "Six children and an adult tell us their dreams, and we see them trembling, seeking flight, unhappy" (*Black Skin* 101). The terror and pain of ontological blackness is expressed in muscles as they spasm and twitch.

How does one fold Berardi's and Guattari's analysis of the spasm as a symptom of semio-capitalism into understandings of blackness as embodied, spasming flesh and into disability's centering of differential embodiment and movement? How can we theorize this movement so that we are not working on curing the symptomatic spasm but rather recognizing its beauty and value as what Melissa Blanco Borelli calls "a choreographic strategy" (59)? How does one embrace the body as it slips in and out of control? Eli Clare in *Brilliant Imperfection* recollects how they imagined their spasming body, first at twelve and then later as an adult: "I imagined electrical storms, collapsing bridges, a twelve-year-old turning my body-mind into a metaphor, *out-of-control* and broken. I didn't liken my tremors to sunlight stuttering through wind-tossed trees, my slurs to an earthworm curling over itself, my stumbles to the erratic rhythm of a pileated woodpecker drumming a tree" (37; emphasis added). Not broken but something beautiful like stuttering sunlight. Simi Linton in "Cultural Territories of Disability" writes about her friend who is a painter. Her friend "has a tremor in her hand and other *uncontrolled* movement. . . . Might her brush strokes, unmediated, render something on the canvas worth viewing? Not only because the resulting painting comments, in color and form, on the way her body functions, but because her work might display rhythm and pattern that are exciting" (45; emphasis added). Note the repetition of the notion of being out of control, which is necessary to unpack in light of this book's emphasis on conjoined differential embodiment and movement.

Gabrielle Brandstetter in "Choreography as a Cenotaph" discusses what she calls "playing with the disturbance of balance, with the loss of control" (124), in improvisation and falling. If we apply this to spasming and twitching, something else rises to the surface. She writes that it is precisely in the body's "loss of control" that it "slips out of itself": "Not a point zero of knowledge or a complete forgetting, but a virtual limbo between bodily knowledge and lack of knowledge, between control and the failure of the controlling factor. This interval holds the potential of 'another movement,' in which the known and the repeatable simultaneously contain the turning point of unlearning—a feature which opens the possibility for unknown, 'foreign' movement" (126). In other words, differential movement emerges from the gap between bodily knowledge and lack of knowledge. It emerges from the moment when our body moves in unexpected ways, in ways that astonish even us. This moment represents an opportunity for new ways of being and moving in bodies. It is a partial forgetting and a surprising remembering, both a voluntary and involuntary surrender to a disturbance of normalized patterns of movement and something else that can emerge.

Curiously, Brandstetter begins her essay by bracketing off people with disabilities. In a parenthesis, she excludes people with "disturbances of the brain and of the nervous system" (118) from her theorization of the unlearning of normative movement. Thus, departing from normative movement can only be achieved by those who are capable of meeting its expectations. Perhaps for Brandstetter, the potential of unlearning acquired movements can only be actualized by people with a certain degree of mastery over their body. In order to occupy the gap between somatic knowledge and lack of knowledge, one needs to always already have control over one's body. But such a caveat assumes that differentially abled people don't have complicated and nuanced awarenesses of our bodies. A drop into the unfamiliar, into disorientation, and a subsequent resurfacing into unexpected movement can occur even for the epileptic like Ian Curtis. Curtis, like most disabled persons, probably had acquired a variety of collective strategies that allowed him to navigate the world in specific ways because of his expectation of seizures. Likewise, my son expects to stutter and he communicates knowing this. But he can also deliberately stutter. He can push himself until voluntary stuttering becomes another kind of stuttering; he can unlearn how his body moves until words erupt from the gap between control and failure of the controlling factor. Similarly, something emerges in the spaces between Curtis's epileptic seizures, his "spasming" onstage, his knowledge of himself, and his disorientation. This is spasming as a "productive corporeal interruption" as it oscillates between being in and out of control (Borelli 58).

Spirit Possession: "And Finally There Is Movement"

The aesthetic similarities between spasming, spirit possession, and mediumship in Spoek Mathambo's "Control" might provide us a way to bring together Berardi and Guattari, Fanon and Eli Clare, Ian Curtis and my son. Through various kinds of choreographed spasms, Spoek Mathambo raises questions about what kinds of political, social, and spiritual openings might emerge from the fleshiness of black bodies. His video, through its insistence of conjoinment and "contagious" movement, refuses the Western dichotomy between body and spirit, instead asking us to imagine what potentialities might emerge from differential movements that name and work through the disposability of black populations and lacerated flesh.

Spoek's video directly alludes to the disposability of certain people. "Control" is shot almost entirely on location in a squatted train boarding house in Langa, Cape Town, and in a graveyard. The black-and-white video manages to capture the desolation and griminess of roughhewn rooms with broken windows, marked with graffiti ("Out of order Aziz and Ben"), and later flames leaping out a window as the building catches fire. Cell-like, the rooms, like the desolate urban landscape, help convey the sense of a people bearing the brunt of capitalism's violence. The scenes shot in the graveyard only reinforce the sense of a community, dead to the state, ignored and left to their own devices. The stark black and white of the surroundings invoke the creeping dread that Spoek describes as part of living in contemporary South Africa, where one waits with bated breath for the "Inkatha" to "hack [one] to pieces" (or to die of AIDS and other diseases) (Zvomuya). This is the atmosphere that permeates postapartheid South Africa: great promise that has given way to great despair as what appeared initially to be a victory sinks into the morass of capitalist exploitation and violence. These children born after apartheid are ill, painfully convulsing while the house/state burns.

"Control" crucially also holds out the promise of healing, embodied in the collaborative act of making this music/dance/video performance, as well as in the transreligious rituals of healing that the video evokes. "Control" conjures up various healing traditions with different understandings of illness. The video *does not* contain accurate anthropological information—rather, the images are suggestive, aesthetically evocative. Rozanne Rocha-Gray also notes the religious symbolism in the video, which she describes as follows: "Spoek's pious control-freak character, with megaphone in hand, is reflected in his stiff colonial wardrobe and stiff dance moves, and this is beautifully contrasted by the kids' crazy loss of control. The kids' movements have these undertones of . . . [religiosity] (exorcism, baptism, fervor, speaking in tongues). . . . I love how their rebellion eventually overcomes the religious institutionalism represented by Spoek." The kids' "crazy loss of control," given the overt contextualization of various African spiritual practices in the video, remembers Ian Curtis's epilepsy even while gesturing toward the language of spirit possession. The aesthetics of "Control" exploit the confusion and ambivalence between ritual possession and spasming as a symptom of illness, blurring lines for viewer as they watch bodies drop into spaces of disorientation and differential movement, spaces that are created between control and failure of the controlling factor.

terms, notions of spirit and the sacred are key. This is not to say that the sacred only works psychologically—it is not a placebo that supplements Western medicine's treatment of individual symptoms. Instead as Thomas Csordas writes, "A complete account of religious healing . . . must not only examine the construction of clinical reality with respect to medical motives, but also the construction of sacred reality with respect to religious motives (334). In order to understand either religious or health issues, one needs to look at both the sacred and the medical. I would go a step further and argue that health and ill health also encompass communities; individuals get sick within a larger cultural and political context. HIV/AIDS or COVID-19 or cancer or even war doesn't affect isolated individuals, but rather, its effects demonstrate the tangled webs of history, culture, and health that make up conjoined individuals. Thus, Victor Igreja et al. note that exposure to wartime violence results in an increase of what they call "spirit possession afflictions . . . and possession by war-related spirits . . . as an idiom of distress" (593). These war-related spirits remind us that spirit possession or trance is not always a benign or healing experience. Harmful spirits can wreak havoc on bodies, causing great pain and suffering. In central Mozambique, for example, Igreja et al. show us that entranced individuals "experience the incursions of spirits as a continuation of violence and injustices being perpetrated against them. . . . Spirit shakes their bodies" (598). In "The Ancestors Are Beating Us," Vendula Řezáčová describes how among TshiVenda speakers in South Africa, the ancestors are violent and coercive as they reprimand immoral humans, correct improper conduct, or demand reverence: "'the ancestors are beating us' (*whadzimu wha lwa rine*)" (115). The spasming children beat Spoek Mathambo to the ground to the rhythm of the beat.

"Control" evokes this complex matrix of health, spirit, violence, and community without purporting to be anthropological. Rather, "Control" evokes and mediates the gestural lexicon of seizure, illness, spirit possession, somatic knowledge, and the surprise that arises when our bodies move in ways we do not expect. This is what Paul Connerton in *How Societies Remember* describes as the "past . . . sedimented in the body" through inscription (written texts and photographs, for example) but crucially also through what he terms "incorporating practices"—taste, sound, smell, posture, gestures, and differential movement" (72). The body as wounded, spasming flesh opens out the possibility for something else to emerge. Keeping Connerton as well as Victor Turner in mind, Paul Stoller describes a ritual of Songhay possession:

> *And finally there is movement.* In a blur of movement, the various dance steps of Songhay possession recount the journey of the spirits from water to heavens and back to earth. But there is more still, for spectators also see the faces of old women dancing, faces creased and folded by sun and hard work. The frail old women dance, their movements in time with the quickening pace of the music. Closer they come until one sees smiles so radiant that they wash from those old faces years of sun and hard work. Those smiles speak to pride and power, for these women know—as do members of the audience—that without their bodies, which they lend to the spirits, there would be no possession in Songhay. (*Embodying Colonial Memories* 35; emphasis added)

Differential embodiment and movement provide us with a way of thinking beyond body-mind dualities, insisting rather on conjoined body, mind, and spirit. The dancers lend their body to the spasm, trance and shake. Their embodied enactments of possession create temporary instantiations of community across difference. The children become one when they start to vibrate and spasm on the same frequencies, giving rise to shifting networks of alliance forged out of movement. Theirs is a performance of differential movement that emerges when one lends one's body to movement and is surprised by the unexpected.

But lest we romanticize community, the video insists that any kind of alliance forged out of shared practices can quickly become a group predicated on identitarian sameness and the violent exclusion of the Other. As I described previously, toward the end of the video, the children turn on Spoek Mathambo, beating him to the ground with black rubber hoses. On the one hand, this beating operates metaphorically to invoke an idea of ancestors who beat us to make us pay attention. It also is a commentary on community as potentially disabling. The very people who suffered together from seizures and who facilitated healing rites over one another turn into a frightening mob that attacks the only adult figure dressed in white. They beat him until he falls to the ground. In this way, "Control" draws attention to the growing distinctions and exclusions that result from suspicion and fear of the Other and the desire for an impossible security. The video shows how fluidity between various religions such as Islam and Apostolic Christianity, between the state and faith, and notions of illness and health ends in the diverse children closing ranks and beating Spoek to the ground.

This is not a death knell for the community. Instead, Spoek Mathambo's performances enable us to think about differential movement not as an essential, biological state of being but rather as a temporary, strategic practice of black sociality. This practice foregrounds the black body as variously abled, neither free nor bound (Wong). Instead of the autonomous individual subject in perfect control of their limbs, black conjoined flesh spams, jerks, and quivers in time to each other's vulnerabilities.

Conclusion: Umshini Wami or Zuma's Penis

Umshini wami, umshini wami	My machine gun, my machine gun
We Baba	Oh Father
Aweuleth' umshini wami	Please bring me my machine gun

In a 2017 interview with South African performance artist and drag queen Steven Cohen, she describes walking past a homeless man lying on the pavement. Looking up at her, the homeless person remarks, "Madam, I can see your penis." (Boulle 78)

Spoek Mathambo's album on which "Control" appears is named *Mshini Wam*. Die Antwoord's fifteen-minute video directed by Harmony Korine is also called "Umshini Wam." Both Spoek Mathambo and Die Antwoord are referring directly to the Zulu freedom song "Umshini Wami," first sung by exiled members of the Umkhonto WeSizwe. In it, the cadres insisted that someone bring them their machine gun so they could "return" to fight the pre-1994 apartheid regime that led to their exile. For the cadres, the song articulated a painful dispossession that crossed ethnic lines and the collective need to bring about change through armed struggle. More than a gun, the AK-47 also began to stand in for a masculinist agency, a call by those who were regarded as less than human to be recognized as citizen-subjects in the as-yet-unrealized just society that they were hoping to bring about. Liz Gunner argues in her brilliant article "Jacob Zuma, the Social Body and the Unruly Power of Song" that "at the heart of the song is the verb '*-letha*' ('bring') suggesting a movement of process, of moving towards something yet to be made; suggesting too that the action is sanctioned by a giver or bringer. The instrument of the machine gun, *umshini wami*, suggests not so much the brute power of war but that of agency, and the ability of the individual sanctioned by the group to bring about change" (43). Sung at marches and rallies, at mass funerals and camps in the bush, the song belonged to a time when enemies were putatively clearly defined, when right and wrong were supposedly as simple as black and white.

The resurfacing of the song in early 2005 in South Africa, where the perpetrators of injustice were difficult to identify and the ground was littered with broken promises of revolution and black enfranchisement, is both surprising and depressingly predictable. Jacob Zuma, then still deputy president of South Africa, performed the song at the trial of the Durban businessman and ANC activist Shabir Shaik, where he was summoned to give evidence. It resulted (along with other behaviors) in President Mbeki firing him from national office. Despite this, the performance became an essential part of Zuma's political repertoire as president. I have watched it over and over on YouTube ("Jacob Zuma Sings Umshini Wam"). As Zuma holds his fists in the air as if holding an assegai and shield, his performance is palimpsestic, overlaying the figure of a president clad in suit jacket and pants with nostalgic images of a freedom fighter and nationalist evocations of a Zulu warrior. Starting off his performance almost casually, Zuma skillfully elicits the response to his call. His hand gestures get more pronounced, he gets louder, and his body starts to lean and fall back as if he is about to raise his legs and stomp his feet into the ground. The crowd responds to his performance by responding more passionately, and the air is filled with ululations as the painful memories of a not-yet-distant past rise like dust. Zuma's performance foregrounds the relationship between what Gunner describes as the "sonic and the somatic," in which "the presence of the song and the dancing body" become "powerful, unstable signs at work in the making and operation of the public sphere" (28). Spreading with a speed and ease made possible by electronic media, Zuma's continually remembered performance of "Umshini Wami" brings together a vast array of political constituencies, uniting them temporarily through a performative genealogy in which the able-bodied, virile Zulu warrior becomes the heroic freedom fighter and eventually the suave president standing before them. The assegai morphs into the AK-47, which in turn comes to represent the masculinist power of the phallus.

Zuma himself began to cement the links between "Umshini Wami" and his phallus. During his 2006 sexual assault trial for the alleged rape of "Khwezi," the HIV-positive daughter of a fellow activist whose clothes supposedly signaled her sexual availability, Zuma would often emerge from court performing the song "Umshini Wami" to rally his supporters. His problematic performance of the song at a trial for rape insisted on centering a hyperaggressive, ethnic masculinity in which rape becomes an essential part of a freedom fighter's repertoire as well as integral to political leadership in a fractured South Africa. The association between "Umshini Wami" and the phallus has become so widespread that in certain parts of South Africa, "umshini" has become a euphemism for the penis (Haupt, *Static* 58). My family members insist that it is not just any penis but the circumcised one. Among the Zulu, the circumcised penis evidences the virility of the man who was able to survive the cut of circumcision, the pain of the wounding. Thus, to perform the song "Umshini Wami," to evoke it through movement and sound, is to conjure up the authentic, ethnic man whose able-bodied virility can conquer not just any woman but also the oppressor.

It therefore should have come as no surprise when in 2012 two paintings were independently exhibited that exposed Zuma's penis—Ayanda Mabulu's *Umshini Wam (Weapon of Mass Destruction)* and Brett Murray's *The Spear*. The two artists, one black, the other white, created two very different works that exposed Zuma's flaccid penis to their audiences. Murray's painting evoked a storm of conflict: the painting was defaced not once but twice; there was a furor around censorship and free speech; vague threats against the artist were issued. Mabulu's painting was met with a formulaic statement by the ANC condemning it and then an eerie silence. Rebecca Davis in the *Daily Maverick* writes that this silence evidenced "a severe bout of Spear fatigue." Andy Mason argues that while depicting Zuma as a victim of Murray's racism served the government's political agenda, there was little to be gained from attacking a black artist. I would argue that the difference in response revolves around the fraught but differing relationship between fungibility and sexuality in the two paintings.

The acrylic on canvas was part of Murray's Goodman Gallery exhibit *Hail to the Thief II*, which featured extensive use of Russian typography and Soviet iconography. The gold and red stylistic ornateness of Soviet revolutionary propaganda was used to rework antiapartheid posters to demonstrate what Alexis Okeowo calls Murray's "irritatingly obvious . . . disappointment with what he views as the A.N.C.'s greed, cronyism, and abuse of power." In *The Spear*, Zuma is Vladimir Lenin, a man of the people boldly striding forward.[12] The grandeur of Lenin's pose, typical of Soviet propaganda, is undercut by Zuma's naked penis, hanging between his legs. Murray is defensive about his painting. He tells us he is not a racist. He writes,

> Details of . . . [Zuma's] sex life have been well documented in the public domain. Notwithstanding the fact that he has four wives, he has engaged in extra-marital sex on at least two occasions. For me, satire is critical entertainment. While I might be attacking and ridiculing specific targets, what I am actually doing is articulating my vision of an ideal world in which I want to live. In this instance, that preferred ideal in the South African context is the Freedom Charter. . . . For me, The Spear . . . is a metaphor for power, greed and patriarchy. (Stone, "Artist Brett Murray")

Mabulu's *Umshini Wam* went on display at the AVA Gallery in Cape Town in August 2012 as part of an exhibit titled *Our Fathers* ("Mixed Reviews"). As far as Mabulu's paintings go, this one is relatively tame.[13] *Umshini Wam* is painted in vibrant oranges, reds, and golds and depicts Zuma in the middle of a Zulu dance, right leg raised as if he is about to stomp the ground. Zuma is dressed in traditional Zulu warrior attire: a leopard-skin shawl and headband (a sign of royalty), *amaShoba* (cow tails worn on upper arms and below the knee), his calf-skin *ibeshu* (rear apron) trailing behind him. Rays emanating from the emblem on the ANC flag in the background suggest the figure's forward motion. A red question mark is painted over the emblem. To the right of this point is a fragment of a newspaper with the heading "Uprising" and dated 2012. Zuma's flapping *isinene* (front apron) in the center of the canvas exposes his genitalia and some of his buttocks. The fleshiness of Zuma's body is exaggerated, grotesque. The image is not flattering; Zuma's exposed penis and bare buttock are less a deft portrayal of the vulnerability of the body and more a ridiculing of the supposed propriety of a figurehead and statesman. This is an emperor with his pants down.

Writing in response to Murray's *The Spear*, Achille Mbembe describes the contemporary South African political and cultural moment as characterized by a "carnivalization of politics, the increasing tendency to settle political matters through the courts, the proliferation of forms of lumpen radicalism that privilege a politics of expediency in lieu of a disciplined politics of principle" ("Spear That Divided"). He argues that the ensuing emotional torrents of racial rage, anxiety, and despair precipitated by this state of affairs also express "a deep longing for a community worthy of that name" ("Spear That Divided"). Recall here Murray's statement that his painting articulates his vision of the ideal world in which he wishes to live. These frustrated longings, Mbembe goes on to write, have resulted in artists resorting to "defacement, desecration and profanation," hence Zuma's penis as object of ridicule ("Spear That Divided"). *The Spear*, Mbembe suggests, arises from colonial imaginings of the black profane body as a container for white anxieties and uncertainties, specifically in this instance about postapartheid identity. This is the violent rendering of black bodies into sexualized, fungible objects—what Hortense Spillers has famously called the "pornotrope." Black flesh is (un)made through a violence that operates in the register of the sexual. Thus, Murray's justification of his painting foregrounds Zuma's sex life: the number of his wives and his extramarital affairs. Murray's articulation of his ideal community is predicated on the pornotroping of the black body. Mbembe writes, "What has irked many is not the desecration of President Zuma's genitals as such, . . . [but] once again, the black body (of which Zuma's has become in this instance the cipher) is the repository of the anxieties . . . and sense of estrangement of white South Africa. What has irked many is the realization that, after almost 20 years of freedom, the black body is still a profane body . . . [that] does not enjoy the kind of immunity accorded to properly human bodies" ("Spear That Divided"). It is Murray's use of the pornotrope that strikes Rory Bester when he notes that *The Spear* reminds him "less of the reference to Lenin and more of Robert Mapplethorpe's photograph, *Man in a Polyester Suit* (1980), the in-your-face opening image in the

1982 book, *Black Males*" ("Brett Murray"). *The Spear* undoes the black male body, reducing it to wounded flesh through the concatenation of objectification, commodification, and desire.

Mabulu's *Umshini Wam* overtly questions the ANC with the red question mark over the ANC emblem. The painting is dedicated to the victims of the Marikana Massacre, further conjured up by the fragment of newspaper with the word "uprising." The Marikana Massacre occurred on August 12, 2012, at the Lonmin PLC mine when some three thousand workers walked off the job in what was called an "illegal strike" for better wages and working conditions. The massacre was one of the deadliest uses of police forces against civilians postapartheid. The South African Police shot 112 protesting miners, killing 34 of them. Some of the victims were shot at close range and appear to have been crushed by police vehicles. On full display were the technologies of apartheid, reconfigured around xenophobia, specifically targeting migrant workers and informal settlement dwellers. The incident functioned as a stark reminder of the consequences of the ANC's neoliberal policies and its move away from progressive labor politics toward conservative global capitalism.[14] Julius Malema, a former youth leader of the ANC, states about the Marikana Massacre, "A responsible president says to the police you must keep order, but please act with restraint. He says to use maximum force. He has presided over the killing of our people, and therefore he must step down. Not even apartheid government killed so many people" ("Anger Mounts"). Mabulu's painting works side by side with Malema's criticism of Zuma. According to Mabulu, the painting was meant to ask Zuma, "as an elder and a traditionally circumcised man," the following question: "I respectfully, as one of his children, ask my father why he is starving us" (Knoetze). This is a calling of Zuma to task.

Why, then, as one of Zuma's "children," does Mabulu expose Zuma's penis? The painting, according to Mabulu, does not depict Zuma as "naked." He states, "I did not paint him with an uncircumcised penis. This is a metaphor that shows he is not a boy; he is a man, an elder, a father, a leader" (Conway-Smith). I can't help but take these statements with a grain of salt. They are perfect performances of the culturally required respect toward an elder. Other statements and the painting itself are a little more biting. In particular, I am interested in Mabulu's description of Zuma in an article from *Cape Argus* as "a shell with a colonial master dancing inside" (Knoetze). This is Zuma as a puppet, controlled not by strings manipulating him on the outside but instead by an internalized master that jerks his body around. This is a stark commentary on Zuma's repeated embodied sonic performances of *Umshini Wami* outside courthouses and at political events. Mabulu exposes Zuma's performances as a performative reiteration not of a communal identity but rather of colonialism's pornotroping of the native. Rather than the painting itself being an example of a pornotrope, Mabulu is exposing how Zuma's linking of "Umshini Wami" and his penis is, in and of itself, a pornotrope. Thus, Murray's painting reinforces the pornotrope, while Mabulu's grotesque, exaggerated body and penis demonstrate how Zuma's misuse of power reinforces the pornotroping of the black body. The colonial master dancing inside our bodies. We've lost control again.

The streets outside my door are deserted as the coronavirus drifts like smoke and cars smolder downtown in the wake of protests. In the rain, the deathly quiet streets look like stills from any number of zombie movies. Wheezing, I try to straighten stiff joints in order to get something to drink. I have been ill with COVID-19 for almost two weeks now, and I am finally able to leave my bed. Sweat beads my forehead as I lurch zombie-like to the kitchen and into the next chapter.

5

Shaking the World

Imaginatively Exceeding

The African postcolony is experiencing a veritable pandemic of zombies: ranging from examples in popular culture, such as Howard Fyvie's film *Last Ones Out* (2015) and Lily Herne's *Mall Rats*, to young-adult novels to accusations with serious consequences of zombie-keeping by "witches" in numerous communities throughout the African continent. Isak Niehaus's ethnographic research in Bushbuckridge (a Native Reserve under apartheid), for instance, details how prevalent the notion of witches keeping zombies has become in postapartheid South Africa. This belief in zombies as real shape not only the social imaginary but also the material relations between communities and their members. As zombies lurch and reach for me, they allow an imaginative retracing of the relationship between disability, bodies, and movement in the necropolitical postcolony in what Mel Chen describes as their "rehearsal of cognitive and physical disability in their specific movements" ("Lurching" 27). Something uncontainable emerges out of Jean and John Comaroff's description of the zombie's "disoriented wanderings, the loss of speech, sense and will, the perverted practices that erase all ties to kith and kin" (799).

Using Chris Abani's novella *Song for Night* and kuduro, an Angolan dance form, I attempt to trace what Comaroff and Comaroff call the "symbolic excess and expressive exuberance" (797) of lurching zombies and other dead-eyed creatures.[1] Instead of only privileging functional understandings of zombies as symptoms and metaphors for the ravages of neoliberal capital or as a means to shore up notions of "normal" agential subjects who move effortlessly, this chapter explores the relationship between liminal transnational bodies, (un)death, and differential movement. It asks if and how southern Africans' use of the movement vocabulary of "deformed" monsters might enable an articulation of a postcolonial black sociality. Or to quote Marissa Moorman, how can a politicized "imagination fill[] the spaces . . . of disenfranchisement" (*Intonations* 14)? This chapter explores the thickets of our imaginative excesses that use the lurch, the raised shoulder, the severed vocal chord, and the limp to say something more. This is disidentification at its core, a twisted embrace of a spectral creature so that a radical potential emerges when we open our arms. Performances of atypical movement, as I developed previously, can be instances of ahistorical "enfreakment" that reproduce self-aggrandizing ableism centered around whiteness. But they can *also* provide us with a way of affectively interacting with what Comaroff and Comaroff call the "visceral implications of the factory, the plantation, the market, the mine" (796). Shared moments of nonnormative motion that gesture toward imaginative excess can give rise to powerful modes of black sociality.

Examples of (dis)identifying with the lurching, drooling, disoriented zombie can be found in the writing of disabled writers who compare themselves to zombies in order to narrate their own experiences of differential embodiment. For instance, in "Zombies Are Loose," Hal Sirowitz, writes, "Having Parkinson's in a marriage is equivalent to the old Hollywood B Movie, *I Married a Zombie*. I got to like being a zombie. It was ultimate bliss" (238). While the sarcasm of the phrase "ultimate bliss" draws attention to his isolation and anger at the ways he is treated, Sirowitz finds the zombie useful in order to articulate how he moves through the world. The figure of the zombie describes both the way the world treats him *and* also his creative disidentification with a term that devalues the way he moves. In another example, Mark Mossman in "Acts of Becoming" describes his differential movement that results from sixteen major surgeries including the amputation of his left leg and four of his fingers on one hand. When he walks, he tells us, he limps with his left shoulder falling below the right, giving him "an awkward, seemingly uncertain gait." Reading *Frankenstein* for the first time at age eighteen enabled him to make sense of his body in the world:

> I read myself as the creature, as a body that has no place in the world. . . . I felt all of the resentment of the creature, the anger, the isolation, the loneliness. . . . Being constructed in postmodern discourse, being the person

> I was and am, I read the creature as "powerful" in its resistance: the creature gained power through its disempowered body; it took the imposition of "abnormality" and used it as an articulation of strength and purpose. When I read the narrative, I read these terms into my own body; I used them to explain my own life. (Mossman)

The Creature's walk is not simply a metaphor for his pain and isolation. Rather, he uses the zombie walk as a way to link his movement to those of other "abnormal" creatures and to formulate his pleasure in the embodied reality of moving differently. As in the case of Mossman, the zombie enables him to describe the social difficulties of living in an ableist society and also to value the way he is embodied and the way he moves. Neither Sirowitz nor Mossman, however, considers the impact that their race plays in their identification with the figure of the zombie as it appears in the West, a figure fundamentally haunted by slavery.[2] What would it mean for African bodies to disidentify with the walking dead given that Africa, as Mbembe writes, is a "strange and monstrous" site characterized by the "meta-text about the beast" (*On the Postcolony* 1)? How do African spiritual and material histories allow for alternate conceptualizations of necropolitics and the politics of embodiment? In order to discuss this topic, I would like to look at the character My Luck, the narrator of Chris Abani's *Song for Night*, a child soldier whose vocal cords have been cut. My Luck wanders through an irrational, "anti-economy" deathworld (Mbembe, *On the Postcolony* 15), trying to remember the song his grandfather taught him so that he can return to the world of the ancestors. He does not realize that he is dead.

A tsunami of occult-related killings in South Africa, some three hundred cases between 1985 and 1995, led to the establishment of the Commission of Inquiry into Witchcraft, Violence, and Ritual Murders in 1995. Chaired by the anthropology and ethnomusicology professor N. V. Ralushai, the commission reported with alarm an increased traffic in body parts, witch burnings, and everyday violent encounters with the occult. Of particular interest is their definition of the figure of the zombie (*dithotsela/diphoko*), who was reported to be terrorizing local communities. The *dithotsela*, they elaborate, "is a person who is believed to have died, but because of the power of a witch, he is resurrected . . . [and] works for the person who has turned him into a zombie. . . .

Whenever he meets people he knows, he vanishes" (Ralushai et al. 142). Or as Niehaus writes, "Sometimes witches are said to change their victims into diminutive *ditlotlwane* (singular *sctlothvane*). To do so they first capture the victim's shadow or aura (*seriti*) and then gradually take hold of different parts of his or her body until they possess the entire person. However, witches deceive the victim's kin by leaving behind an 'image' (*seswantoo*) of him or her. The kin, believing that the victim is dead, bury what they assume to be his or her body, but which is instead the stem of a fern tree that has merely been given the victim's image" (192). In one version, the *dithotsela* vanishes when they encounter anyone familiar. In the other, a profound instance of nonrecognition results in burying a factotum.

What does it mean to vanish when you encounter someone you are familiar with? The instance of recognition that flares up during an encounter is an acknowledgment of several things: familiarity, mutual vulnerability, and interconnectedness. During an encounter with the *dithotsela*, the sense of estrangement produced by the way one has forcibly been changed results not in stoic indifference but in a vanishing. The physical disappearance of the *dithotsela*, its flickering—here one moment, gone the next—is an embodied language that acknowledges not only the pull of familiarity but also painful temporal and geographic estrangement. I am no longer here with you as I once was, it says. Who I have become scares you. Be careful, the same fate awaits all of us in the postcolony permeated by the technologies of war.

What characterizes most of these southern African zombies is that the front part of their tongue is cut off, which prevents them from speaking. Thus, the *dithotsela* is, as Comaroff and Comaroff summarize, "speechless and unspeakable, . . . fad[ing] away as soon as it becomes visible and knowable. It is a mutation of humanity made mute" (787). The *dithotsela* is unable to speak of their condition, and the mutilated tongue means that only the witch can speak for the zombie. The zombie's will is entirely subsumed by their master. Even when the witch no longer keeps the zombie, the zombie is unable to return to their community. Niehaus records one such story when a *dithotsela* or zombified young boy attempts to return to his mother after the death of the witch. Catching sight of him, the mother begs police to kill him. Instead, the police sequester the boy in the local mental hospital (Niehaus 199). This relegation of mute zombie boy to an asylum reinforces the zombie's restaging of disability. The boy's differential movement, his muteness, and the way he carries himself are dismissed as deviant and quickly folded into the category of the (mentally) disabled.

This story of a dead boy who cannot speak, released from his master and seeking his lost mother, resonates in startling ways with Abani's *Song for Night.* A mute character named My Luck, who has been blown apart by a land mine before the novella begins, wanders a war-torn landscape in search of his lost platoon. Neither My Luck nor the reader initially realizes that he is dead, despite Abani's insistence that "death is always the expectation here" (*Song* 31). This misreading of him as a living character is exemplified in the novella by Allison Mackey, who describes My Luck as "concussed and adrift in an eerie memory-landscape" at the beginning of the novella (111). As I discuss in the next section, such critical missteps stem in part from the precarious status of life in the postcolony. Within this "deathworld" that zombifies the wounded soldiers and civilians reeling from the aftermath of independence and brutal civil wars, it is extremely difficult to recognize a character who is actually dead. *Song for Night* demonstrates that while exposing the postcolony's oversaturation with death can critique the necropolitical forces of transnational capital, it can also facilitate certain racist Western narratives that relegate Africa and its inhabitants to suffering, dying, and diseased victims in need of rescuing. By beginning with a character who is already dead, Abani forecloses on the possibility of sentimental, humanitarian gestures of rescue and redemption by offering us no one to save. He also refuses to privilege Western Enlightenment thinking, instead exploring what arises if we take seriously indigenous African belief systems that are seeing a resurgence throughout the continent today. These belief systems resituate bodies, assigning alternate meanings to the way both the living and the dead move. A palm pulled down over the face to suggest nightfall, a young amputee who jumps into a circle of dancers without her supporting cane, small crosses cut into My Luck's arms that are his personal cemetery, or a bundle of herbs burned in front of ghost soldiers—Abani foregrounds the imaginative excesses of Africans as they forge a tenuous black sociality out of differential embodiment and movement.

Being a Wounded Soldier

The country in which *Song for Night* occurs is left unnamed. Abani notes in an interview on NPR, "It's meant to be not nation-specific. It is region-specific. It's West Africa. I was born just as the Nigeria Biafran Civil War was beginning. And there'd been countless wars in that one little region. . . . I sort of thought it was a sad commentary on the region of the world where I come from that you could throw a war literally anywhere in West Africa, and it can stick." (Martin). There are no front lines, as entire regions become battlegrounds with shifting and indeterminate allegiances. David Gerber summarizes that anticolonial and postcolony guerrilla fighting occurs "across no fixed frontiers, in which territory fails to change hands except very briefly and for short periods of time, and which fighting is waged continuously. Civilians are continually vulnerable to the fighting, which forms unpredictably everywhere, whether in the countryside, small villages and towns, or cities" (xvi). The indeterminacy of the location of the war in the novella is accompanied by a temporal conflation. While many of the details in the novella resonate with the Biafran War of 1967–70, references to satellite phones or Lexuses, for example, suggest a more contemporary moment. Thus, to paraphrase Abani, one can throw a war anywhere *and* anytime in West Africa, and it would stick. While this could be read as a stereotypical depiction of postcolonial African countries as always in crisis, Abani instead is commenting on the regime of necropolitics in the postcolony with its proliferation of spaces of violence that exceed the boundaries of any one nation-state. Populations are divided not into traditional identities but rather, as Mbembe writes, "into rebels, child soldiers, victims or refugees, or civilians incapacitated by mutilation or simply massacred, . . . while the 'survivors,' after a horrific exodus, are confined in camps and zones of exception" ("Necropolitics" 34). The national, tribal, or party allegiances of these combatants takes a backseat to the business of war, as privately employed "peacekeepers," mercenaries, armed civilians, and child soldiers flood the market.

If, as Mbembe insists, colonialization was a "writing on the ground of a new set of social and spatial relations" ("Necropolitics" 26), few things reinforce these social/spatial relations as well as land mines. In addition to plantation, mine, market, and factory, technologies of war have forever altered the geographic terrain of the postcolony. Mines have become the "metal undercarpet" (Abani, *Song* 47) of everyday living, and the simple act of foot connecting with ground has devastating consequences.[3] If you are lucky, My Luck tells us, mines will kill you, scattering your body parts so that there is "an arm here, a leg over there in the foliage" (50). If you are unlucky, you live with painful injuries. My Luck describes how those who survive the blasts have their "arms and legs and parts of faces" torn off by shrapnel (48).

Combatants returning to civilian life with serious injuries have foregrounded issues of disability in connection to the military, particularly in First World countries. The value placed on the differential embodiment of veterans, heroic and willing to sacrifice themselves for the country, differs starkly from the way disabled civilians are perceived. My dear friend tells me about an incident in an airport when a fellow traveler struck up a lively conversation with her. When the stranger thanked her for her military service, assuming her differential embodiment was the result of war injuries, my friend corrected her. The stranger's attitude toward my friend's body shifted dramatically upon the realization that her morphology was not evidence of her sacrifice for country and kin. Now there was something embarrassing about my friend; her embodiment pointed to weakness, inadequacy, and deviancy rather than heroic nationalism. The stranger withdrew. Such incidents reveal a great deal about the nation-state's concatenation of militarism, masculinity, and the rhetoric of sacrifice. Gerber identifies how "remasculinization narrative[s]" (xiv) enable disabled veterans to reclaim the masculinity stripped from them by their disability. They accomplish this reclamation via discipline, physical and emotional stamina, and sheer determination. These "wounded warriors" overcome all adversity to live "normal" lives, even returning to battle. Hollywood does a lot to instantiate this narrative with characters such as Kovic in *Born on the Fourth of July*, played by Tom Cruise, or Gary Sinise's Lieutenant Dan Taylor in *Forrest Gump*. Rather than advocating for differential movement and embodiment, disabled veterans fight the odds in order to reembody and reinvest in normative notions of the body and gender. Another narrative identified by Gerber concerning disability and war posits disability as "a medal for service" (xiv), such that disability is instrumentalized as evidence of and reward for military valor. The third narrative, according to Gerber, is the use of the soldier's suffering as testimony against waging war. The suffering, I would also argue, can also be used to justify war, as governments exact revenge on the "foreign" forces that did this to "our" soldiers or to prevent future disability. For the most part, women soldiers are largely absent from this discussion, with their disability providing further evidence of a gendered vulnerability that they seemingly can never escape, no matter how good of a soldier they are.

Such discourses around disability and war are largely absent from the postcolony, due in no small part to the increasing blurriness of lines between civilians, civilian soldiers, professional military, private mercenaries, and forcibly conscripted child soldiers. State-supported tropes of heroic, masculinized sacrifice can't really be applied to acts of violence and their consequences, which do not conform to national borders. Consider, for example, the case of Angola, which the second part of this chapter focuses on. The MPLA (People's Movement for the Liberation of Angola), supported by Cuba and the Soviet Union, engaged in prolonged battles against UNITA forces (National Union for the Total Independence of Angola), which were backed by South Africa and the United States. While MPLA soldiers tended to be urban and more ethnically diverse, UNITA largely drew its supporters from the ethnic group of Ovimbundu in the central highlands and eastern provinces. Thus, the Angolan Civil War (1975–2002) was simultaneously a proxy war as US and Soviet forces attempted to establish a foothold in southern Africa, a battle between ethnic and regional identities, and a continuation of the vicious fighting for Angolan independence (1961–74). Given this confusing tangle of allegiances, veterans have become the men and women that the contemporary state needs to forget in order to consolidate its shiny new global identity.

I am particularly struck by a series of photographs by the AFP photographer Rodger Bosch that accompanies an article titled "Long after Angola's Civil War, Its Veterans Are Destitute," by Maryke Vermaak and Daniel Pensador. One of the photographs depicts Domingo Seiala, a veteran of the MPLA armed wing (fig. 5.1). Wearing a faded military camouflage cap, Seiala stands in front of the partially collapsed and bullet-hole-ridden abandoned school that he calls home. "There is no support. We are waiting for God to do something," he tells Vermaak and Pensador in 2019 as he leans back, elbow on crutch. He has ex-

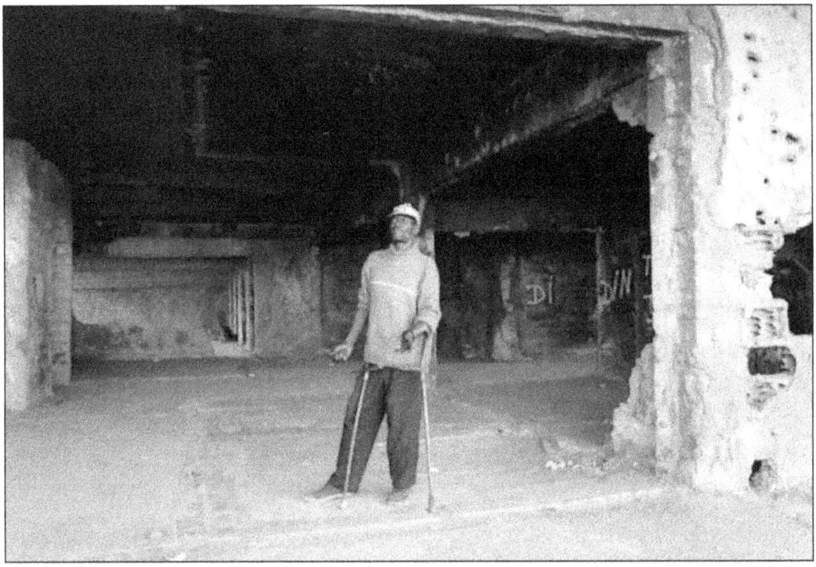

Figure 5.1. Rodger Bosch's photograph of Domingo Seiala in front of the partially collapsed school (© Rodger Bosch, AFP)

tensive foot and leg injuries from stepping on a land mine. Another MPLA veteran, Domingo Tomas, lives with Seiala and others in what remains of the school. Tomas lost his entire family during the war. Both men, Seiala and Tomas, still reside in the city of Kuito, which was once UNITA headquarters, the area they defended during the war. They linger among the ruins of their former battleground, haunting the edges of the nation-state, both dead and alive. They have become what Abani calls the "presumed dead," who, when the war is over, "will stream back to their families only to be rejected as ghosts or zombies" (*Song* 50). If they have families to go back to. Their injuries are not medals for serving their country through heroic sacrifice or testaments to their status as soldiers. Instead, both men's experiences are disturbing commonplace in the postcolony, where some twenty civilians are hospitalized each day for injuries caused by land mines, where entire families have been lost to decades of war and poverty.[4]

The destitute Seiala and Tomas, like My Luck, resemble the young *dithotsela* with a cut tongue who returns home to be rejected by his mother. They are examples of what Mbembe describes as daily "spectacles of pain" that spin off from colonialism's "spiral of terror" ("Variations" 81). At peak moments of this spiral, Mbembe tells us, "the human body . . . become[s] a site of violent confusion: distinctions between what is 'flesh' and what is 'meat' . . . fall[] away. So too, distinctions between what is true and what is false, that which is to be believed and that which is 'beyond belief.' Power has been shown to break bones and strip subjects of their flesh, disfiguring them, forcing them into a demonic dance" ("Variations" 81). The human body as a site of confusion where distinctions between "flesh" and "meat" fall away is graphically illustrated in a scene from *Song for Night* when My Luck's platoon comes across a group of women cooking over a fire. "We are brave warriors fighting for your freedom," My Luck reminds them when he asks to share their meal (Abani, *Song* 28). The "meal" turns out to be the head, arm, and hand of a newborn. My Luck empties the clip of his AK-47 into the women. This incident, in which a newborn baby is wrenched out of her mother's arms and then cooked while the mother lies dazed and bleeding on the ground, draws attention to the category of the "human," showing it to be embedded in racist hierarchies of value that deny relationality. The women's survival, which they assume is worth any cost, reiterates the cannibalistic logic of colonialism, which converts black bodies into the fleshy raw material of capital.

Lest we assume that this story is only a tragedy, Abani reminds us over and over about the powerful performances of survival that "half-people holding onto life" (*Song* 50) enact. Even though there is no moral high ground in the demonic dance of violence where bones snap and flesh cooks, I discuss later the radical potential inherent in differential embodiment and movement that reworks autonomous bodies into conjoined flesh and spirit.

Imagining Other Worlds

I struggle to consider what My Luck's story might mean specifically for me as an African in the United States. I have often been on the receiving end of humanitarian empathy despite my enormous privilege. Two images keep coming to mind. The first is from Abani's "Ethics and Narrative," in which he describes sobbing as he pulls his knife across a goat's throat, holding its head so that its blood drains into the ritual pot. As a girl, I was never called on to kill a goat, but there were plenty of chickens. Grab a chicken's head, break the neck with the circular motion of my wrist, pluck feathers with dry hands. It wasn't hard for me to kill, but I hated the sensory onslaught of the taste of feathers in my mouth, the sight of pale plucked skin, having to scrub at blood stains on the concrete with Vim. I grew to hate chickens with a passion: playing in the backyard, I would throw stones and rotting fruit at them, but they were undeterred by my cruelty, accepting the hail of debris as if it were rain. The second image is of my grandmother lying strangled on the floor, her neck at an awkward angle, her normally neat braids fuzzy. The wailing, the grief all around me, recedes so that I can no longer hear. All I wanted to do was to twist oil around strands of hair, smooth and tuck stray fuzz, rebraid so that her scalp stretches tight. What both these images point to is the arbitrary line we draw between valuable life and not, who and what is disposable, who is worthy of our grief. And our love. The connection between chickens, grandmothers, and the reading of *Song for Night* that follows has to do with remembering the dead (both not-quite-human and creature), the business of killing, and the ways that embodied performances of braiding, smoothing, and loving can imagine other worlds.

Song for Night stages a confrontation with and an embrace of African cosmologies by positing alternate notions of life, death, and the passage of spirits between realms. A *dithotsela* with cut tongue, a mud-eater stuck in mines deep under the surface of the Earth, a boy who knows the "terrible intimacy" (Abani, "Ethics and Narrative") not just of killing but of being killed: these are real beings who cast long shadows over the landscape of the novella and over us as readers. As Sam Durrant argues, "Spirits too, in Africa, are material, and the worlds of the living and the dead, matter and spirit, interpenetrate one another. . . . Keeping that passage between the living and the dead . . . makes it possible for culture to inherit itself" (184). My Luck represents the forces of capital that render black bodies into fleshy, fungible substrates. But he is also a spirit, a dead person wandering through the landscape of the postcolony as certain spirits want to do. Several characters throughout the novella recognize My Luck as real, implicitly suggesting that we as readers also see him for who and what he is. Peter, the catechist with a sheaf of smoldering green herbs, shares a cigarette with My Luck; an old woman shouts

"Tufia" at him, "Tufia" being the "old word for banishing spirits or bad things" (Abani, *Song* 84); another woman, carrying a coffin, gives him water to drink; a man listening to records on a gramophone he received for fighting the Nazis feeds him bananas. These characters encounter and react to My Luck according to their various belief structures. Each interaction demonstrates Durrant's notion that Igbo cosmology "is not a closed system but a mode of apprehension that remains 'open to the world,' capable of accommodating modernity within its sense of the sacred" (199). The belief in the actual, spiritual presence of the dead is not a vestige of primitivism but rather demonstrates the entanglement of Enlightenment thinking with continuously reimagined indigenous belief systems. And while these cosmologies, as the Ralushai Commission of Inquiry remind us, should never be romanticized as benevolent or liberatory, they are essential to understanding black sociality.

Openly embracing My Luck in all his contradictions as killer and the killed, as *dithosela* or zombie, as not-quite-human and spirit is about recognizing what Durrant calls the "*spiritual* . . . [and] also the *creaturely* dimensions of biopolitical thought" (186). To recognize a biopolitics inculcated with the spiritual (including the dead) and the creaturely is to move beyond notions of relationality formed only through a sentimental, shared corporeal vulnerability that characterizes the "human condition" and that is defined around suffering bodies. Instead, Abani binds the not-quite-human, the creature, and spirit to one another to create a monstrous conjoined being that stretches across time and space.[5] This is best illustrated in a scene in *Song for Night* when My Luck describes a cobweb between the arm and empty chest of a skeleton that he encounters floating down the river in a canoe: "[The cobweb] is beautiful and shimmers in the fading light. . . . It reminds me of another time. . . . Before I take the skeleton out of the canoe, I reach in and pull the cobweb free. I drape it over my head like a cap and then lift the skeleton with ease, careful not to shake any bones loose" (Abani, *Song* 76–77). He then lays the body in the shallow grave he had dug. By wearing the cobweb, My Luck honors his dead father, who was a Muslim Iman. He also pays his respect to the spider, perhaps Kwaku Anansi, the consummate trickster god who spins out stories. He claims spiritual relations to the dead, both recent and long gone, to the spider as creature and also to African cosmologies that are continually reimagined anew.

Thus, the conjoinment figured in the novella encompasses a myriad of life forms. It would be easy to focus on the injured and dead people in the novella, given the West's humanitarian rhetoric around child soldiers. Indeed, My Luck converts his body into a "cemetery," with tattooed crosses for grave markers: on his left arm, these crosses represent lost loved ones, and on his right arm, they represent everyone he has enjoyed killing. By rubbing the raised bumps on his arm, My Luck remembers death through a corporealized braille. But the novel also lingers on and refuses to let us forget those deaths that we traditionally might regard as insignificant and not worth marking, such as the catching and killing of a lazily floating catfish: "My hand snakes out with the speed of a cobra and catches the fat catfish behind its head" (Abani, *Song* 67). After slamming the catfish on the bank hard, My Luck laconically ends the chapter with "It dies" (67). This too is an important death, Abani is saying. In the next chapter, My Luck recollects fishing on Cross River with his grandfather, who tells an Igbo story about "a lake in the middle of the world, . . . a lake of fire and water, . . . invisible, hidden in a fold in time, but there" (69). His grandfather goes on to explain that this lake "is the repository of human souls who are yet to gain access into the world. . . . Legend says that the fish in the lake guard the souls, swallowed deep in their bellies" (73). To find the lake, his grandfather teaches My Luck to sing a song, and they sing it until their voices blend into one and it is impossible to tell where the river ends and My Luck's and his grandfather's blood begins. In other words, My Luck must blur the distinctions between himself and his grandfather, between his body and that of a fish, between his blood and the water of the river. Rather than striving to be an autonomous Enlightenment subject, he must come to the realization that his body, his spirit, and the creatures around him are conjoined. This monstrous conjoined being, while a product of necropolitics, also crucially resists the postcolony's management of the living, the dying, and the dead.

It is through differential embodiment and movement that *Song for Night* embraces modes of apprehension based on contemporary indigenous notions of spirit. Such gestural modes allow for an "imaginative excess" that exceeds closed systems of violence. This powerful potentiality or "language of life," as Mbembe observes, allows "particular African [embodied] cultural practices" to act as "as resources for fashioning a new African subjectivity" and to "continually resist the necropolitical drive towards annihilation" (*On the Postcolony* 15). Nowhere is this potential more poignantly illustrated that when My Luck remembers encountering a ragtag group of "half-people holding onto life [and hope], . . . children without arms or legs or both, men with only half a face, women with shrapnel-chewed scars for breasts" (Abani, *Song* 50). All of them have a "fire that burned feverishly in their eyes" (50). A group of disabled children begin dancing in a circle. I quote the scene at length:

> A young girl with one leg standing off to the side leaning on a stick made fun of the dancers. Challenged to do better, she laughed, threw the stick away, and jumped into the circle. She stood still for a moment as through she was getting her bearings, and then she began to move. Still balanced on one leg, her waist began a fierce gyration and her upper body moved the opposite way. Then like a crazy heron, she began to hop around, her waist and torso still shaking. She was an elemental force of nature. I couldn't take my eyes off her. I have never seen anything like it before or since—a small fire sprite shaking the world and reducing grown war-hardened onlookers to tears. (51)

In this dance, the power of differential embodiment and movement embedded in African cosmologies offers us a way of creating black sociality. The girl's performance centers and celebrates her corporeality, demonstrating, as Mbembe writes in a different context, that the "body is not so much 'harmed' as it becomes a site of transgression, the locus of blurring—between the transcendental and the empirical, the material and the psychic" ("Variations" 85). The girl's brokenness is not transcended but rather becomes the vibrant force that completes the circle between not-quite-human and heron, between performer and audience. Her fiercely gyrating torso forms the substrate of black sociality that enables us to survive the blast of land mines, the sigh of bullets as they sink into flesh, and the devaluation and theft of black life. The girl's dance thus is at the core of this chapter, as she uses differential movement to transform into a figure bursting with the fierceness of life.

My Luck is mute, his vocal cords severed, like the others in his platoon. The platoon leader, Essien, also known as John Wayne, orders these swift cuts of a scalpel to silence the supposedly distracting and demoralizing death screams of his platoon members. One suspects that this severing of vocal cords is but one tool in Essien's arsenal of cruelty meant to break down a group of young men and women and remake them into the living dead, with him as their master. In "Variations on the Beautiful," Mbembe describes a similar process of making soldiers in which "power has taken to producing carcasses, penetrating the bodies of its subjects with nervous energy. This has become its *raison d'etre*. Its *modus operandi*, tried and true, is to thrust them into extremely dangerous and vulnerable situations which arouse in them different orders of sensations" (80–81). After Essien orders My Luck to either "rape or die" (Abani, *Song* 85), My Luck finds his senses reordered in order for him to develop "the taste for rape" (86). But Abani insists, even while the platoon of carcasses embraces and surrenders to the lust of killing and raping, they are always something more. Their "different order of sensations" means that they learn to hear each other and speak in different ways, which, to evoke Mbembe, "blur distinctions between sound and noise and, in the process, . . . join art to the world of screams" ("Variations" 81). My Luck narrates that "in the silence of [their] heads, the screams of those dying around [them] were louder than if they still had their voices" (Abani, *Song* 55). The children are able to hear what we cannot. They develop a system of signs to communicate based on imaginative reuses of the body and ways of making sense of war around them. "Our form of speech is nothing like the kind of sign language my deaf cousin studied in a special school before the war. . . . But it serves us well. Our job is too intense for idle chatter," My Luck insists (20).

Each chapter of *Song for Night* is organized around a sign or gesture from this lexicon born out of, but exceeding, the necropolitics of the postcolony. Chapter 1 thus is called "Silence Is a Steady Hand, Palm Flat" and is about the gesture for silence. We might initially mistake these signs as functional and obvious ("A Hand Held like a Pistol" is a gun), but we are quickly disabused of these misconceptions. The signs alternate between the prosaic and the lyrical: "Dreaming Is Hands Held in Prayer over the Nose" and "Music Becomes Any Dance You Can Pull Off" and "Imagination Is a Forefinger between the Eyes." Rather than directives that facilitate military operations and basic communication, the signs point to the way My Luck and the others utilize their invented language of the body to imagine other worlds. As Durrant writes, "While

My Luck denies that the wiggling fingers [for the sign for *silencio*] are a '*playful* touch' . . . : on the one hand, each sign testifies to their muteness, their violent subjugation to necropower, while, on the other, they are irrepressible affirmations of the creativity" (195; emphasis added). The signs that stem from the differential embodiment of the children enables not a clumsy approximation of the spoken word but instead a sensuous interaction that ties the members of the platoon to one another by a language that arises from the world they inhabit and who they are. These signs are merely one aspect of My Luck and his platoon members' choreography.

Abani shows how the platoon must learn new ways of moving that are not just about communication. Though these ways of moving resemble the ways animals move, they are not "natural" but rather painfully practiced and developed. If the one-legged fire sprite moves like a crazy heron, the members of the platoon resemble "flamingoes on drugs" as they "learned to balance on one leg for hours at a time, forty-pound packs on our backs" (Abani, *Song* 33). Barefoot, they use their toes like fingers: "feeling for the carefully scattered lumps in the ground, being careful not to step on them, clearing the earth around the buried mines with our toes. . . . We balanced on one foot, reached down, and disabled the mine" (34).[6] This is differential movement that is part "creaturely mimesis" (Durrant 192), part grueling survival strategy, part creative genius.

Throughout the novella, My Luck recounts stories of Ijeoma, a fellow platoon member and the person he loves. Ijeoma was blown to pieces by a land mine before the novella begins, and My Luck's recollections of her provide a crucial counterpoint to the cruelty and devastation around him. Not only do My Luck and Ijeoma protect each other on the front lines, but their love enables their spiritual survival. Ijeoma "saves" My Luck's soul by reminding him that he is more than a zombie created by the machines of war. She keeps him grounded by looking at him with a "mocking smile" instead of adulation or praise when he is made platoon leader (Abani, *Song* 42). While other members of the platoon rape women and men after raiding a town, Ijeoma and My Luck have sex to ensure that amid "all that horror, there was still love" (86). It is Ijeoma whom My Luck sees in his dreams, rising out of a lake with claws of fire and star-bright laughter as she turns, dancing: "*What a thing of beauty she is, what a thing*" (87).

I would argue that key to understanding the love between My Luck and Ijeoma is the concept of play. Play is the secret at the heart of their relationship, a "veiled thing, . . . a private language within a private language, sweeter for being secret" (Abani, *Song* 105). Given that the chapter "Child's Play" is only a page long, it might be easy to overlook the importance of this private language, the sign for which is "a forefinger pointing to the sky while the whole body gyrates" (104). As the sign suggests, play is a spiritual connection even as it is anchored in moving, conjoined bodies. Play undergirds My Luck's relationship with other members of the platoon as well. The group wiggle fingers *playfully* when making the sign for *silencio*; Hannibal jokingly ties an arm or leg behind him, pretending to have lost a limb (130); the soldiers play cards and soccer and challenge each other to dance. The idea of play counters humanitarian arguments that child soldiers have been denied their childhood. Their lost childhood, such thinking insists, means that while "real" children play games, these boys and girls work as soldiers. Abani undercuts this rhetoric of restoring the stolen childhood by rejecting the opposition between childhood play and soldiering brutality.

I would like to spend a little time with "Rock Paper Scissors," a game between Ijeoma and My Luck that cements their relationship as they move across land-mined terrain, hoping not to be killed by enemy forces. "Rock, paper, scissors: one tap on our gun's stock, two taps, three . . . One tap. One / One tap. Two. A loss. / Two taps. One. A win. / Two taps. Two. A draw. / Endlessly we play, never looking at each other but smiling into the distance, hearts racing with anticipation. Then a steady hand, palm flat. Silence. Still we smile as we scan for the danger, our hearts beating: One. One. Two. / Two. Two. Two. / Three. Three. Three" (Abani, *Song* 105). One character taps out a sign; they both pause, waiting for the effects of that movement; then another person countermoves. As Hector Rodriguez writes, such "play is seldom radically subjective [as] the player must respond to some event, in the context of a structured situation. Playing consists in a trans-individual process of action and reaction, which often takes on a to-and-fro quality reminiscent of dance." The back-and-forth of move and countermove is not just the interplay between rock, paper, and scissors. It is also about the war in which they find themselves. They pause when they think the enemy might be near; they tap the stock of their guns; they translate the visual language of rock, paper, and scissors into taps in environs where a single click means possible detonation, mutilation, and death. Theirs is a joint evocation or playful ritual that conjures up a different reality with different cultural scripts. Play, as André Droogers writes, "is constructed with a certain degree of pleasure. The ritual occasion creates the opportunity for enjoyment" (118). Play, pleasure, and enjoyment wrap around each other in the creative remaking of worlds. Ijeoma and My Luck smile; their hearts beat faster until they match each other's rhythm ("Three. Three. Three"); they speak out loud without vocal cords.

Due to play's supposed lack of productivity, it has typically been contrasted with the capitalist ethos of work, efficiency, and linear progress. Even when play is regarded as psychologically and physically useful, its utility is centered on the mental and physical health of workers. We play in order to become more efficient laborers. A great deal has been written on this subject by scholars such as Johan Huizinga in his famous *Homo Ludens*, first published in 1938. For the purposes of this chapter, I would like to think about play not as specific activities or games per se but instead as embodied sets of relational modalities. These modalities supplement the ruthless efficiency and productivity of capital with an embrace of differential abilities, contingency, and improvisation. Every Sunday during quarantine, cousin Nate comes over, and we play Uno as it accommodates the differences in our age and ability. No matter how well the cards are shuffled or how determined my son is to beat us all, there is no strategy that results in winning being a sure thing. Besides, if only one of us won all the time, no one would want to play. There would be none of the unpredictability, the surprise at a run of bad luck, the victory dances, the squabbling mess of family that rolls eyes and sucks teeth around the beat-up dining-room table. This is the relationality of embodied play. When we play Uno, there is also an unstable balance between feelings of agency (if I play well, I will win) and a confrontation with the limitations of individual agency (chance determines much of the outcome). Thomas Malaby writes that play is an attitude "that reflects an acknowledgement of how events, however seemingly patterned or routinized, can never be cordoned off from contingency entirely" (211). Thus, no matter how prepared, "unpredictabilities and constraints saturate experience" (208). Play as relational modality allows for more open and contingent ways of encountering the indeterminacy of the differentially embodied world around us. Rock—a fire sprite laughing as she jumps into the circle to dance; paper—encountering a dead boy looking for his mother; scissors—speaking through signs after one's vocal cords have been cut. This is a relational choreography of contingency, of play, that I would argue lies at the heart of kuduro.

The remainder of this chapter look at the Angolan dance form of kuduro, in particular the style known as Milindro.[7] As Marissa Moorman writes in *Intonations: A Social History of Music and Nation in Luanda, Angola*, "it is in and through popular urban music [and its accompanying social relations] . . . that Angolan men and women forged the nation and developed expectations about nationalism and political, economic and cultural sovereignty" (2). Thinking specifically about the dance form kuduro, I develop the themes of differential embodiment and movement on a "metal undercarpet" of land mines begun in *Song for Night*. With almost 50 percent of the country still heavily mined, any understanding of movement must deal with the necropolitics of the postcolony and with creative reimaginings of life and death (ICRC 10). Kuduro is simultaneously a musical form, a playful dance practice, and means of social mobility for Angolans. As António Tómas writes, it is "a kind of assemblage that comprises a number of cultural practices, namely music, performance, and particularly a certain disciplined refashioning of the body, through dance" (262). Roughly translated, "kuduro" means "hard ass" or "in a tough place." A driving electronic beat produced by the mixing of sounds from keyboards, cell phones, samples, and everyday noises, kuduro plays with themes of surviving hard times by being "hard" or "tough." Surviving hard times provides the context for the production and dissemination of the music and dancing as well as its subject matter.

In "Becoming Famous," Tómas writes that like house or techno music, "there is nothing transgressive or subversive about *kuduro*. The main asset of *kuduro* . . . lies in its capacity to mobilize agents and infrastructure outside of the purview of centralized power" (272). Tómas argues that kuduro, with its "poor lyrics" and bad singing, is easily appropriated, as its main function lies in providing social visibility for its practitioners and in advancing the values of a particular kind of global capitalist consumption. Cringing while watching a local Austin Zumba class gyrating to Don Omar's ubiquitous *Danza Kuduro*, one might be inclined to agree. However, what Tómas neglects to see is how radically kuduro intervenes in notions of normative movement and embodiment. Kuduristas, acutely aware of the six to twenty million land mines still waiting to be detonated as well as the fact that one out of every 334 Angolans has lost a limb as a result of land-mine detonation, emulate to various degrees the movements of the land-mine victims around them and of themselves who are victims.[8] In addition to hip-hop-inspired movements, carnival and traditional Angolan dance steps, both able-bodied Kuduristas and amputees dance on their knees as if their lower legs were amputated or crawl across the floor in a performance of differential embodiment and movement. Kuduro incorporates disability as part of its movement repertoire even as it also includes able bodies in its performances. The virtuosity of these performers does not rely on their ability to "pass" as normative. Rather, dance itself and what it means to be able-bodied are reconceptualized so that depending on the context, nonnormative embodiment can function advantageously. I focus not only on the inclusion of disabled performers but also on what I call "Afro-alienated" performances of impaired movement—the use of a dance vocabulary of disability to imaginatively disidentify with the normative landscape of the black body.[9] Kuduro as what Jayna Brown calls "a specific celebration of the broken body, . . . a lexicon of twisted limbs" (141), belies its reduction to an easily appropriated, vacuous form.

While this chapter focuses on dancing kuduro, it is impossible to understand movement without sound. Central to kuduro's mythology is the unusual belief that the dance form developed before the music. The notion that music precedes dance is part of an ideological common sense: the dancer responds to the beats, rhythms, flows, and lyrics of sound. Indeed, part of kuduro's lack of legitimacy as a musical form for critics like Tómas derives from this fact. However, as Tony Amado, the supposed originator of kuduro, repeatedly insists, the dance gave birth to the music. Watching *Kickboxer*, a 1989 Jean-Claude Van Damme movie in which the actor dances with a "stiff bottom" and clumsy movements, Amado claims to have been inspired to create kuduro. Creating music to accompany the drunken movements of Van Damme's character's dance, Amado put together a driving electronic beat and some pared-down lyrics over the track (Amado). While no cultural form has a single origin and an insistence on the veracity of Amado's story would be to underestimate how important fictional narratives are to cultural production, Amado's account arrests my attention for two reasons in particular: his claim that an Angolan dance was inspired by a Belgian actor and practitioner of karate who lives in the United States, and the claim that the dance preceded the music. Van Damme's influence reveals the engagement of kuduristas with a transnational politics that refuses discourses of (Angolan) authenticity. Amado's second claim, that the dance and not the music came first, insists that kuduro dancing cannot simply be seen as a response to the music. Rather, it constitutes a simultaneous aesthetic moment that interacts with the historical urban landscape of Angola. The movement of bodies elicits a punctuating and accentuating auditory response. This is a *sonic listening to the body and of the body*, a careful attention of sound to the contours of space, movement, and a history of physical violence.

No matter which came first, it is important to understand kuduro as a musical, cultural form that engages with and remaps the war-torn landscape of Angola. Borrowing from house, techno, soca, and electronic music genres from the Global South such as kwaito, different generations of kuduro musicians have used innovative performance practices to create an adaptable musical form that responds to the aesthetic and political climate. The musicologist Garth Sheridan describes the various generations of kuduro and how the beats and music were produced. The first generation of producers were largely middle-class youth such as Tony Amado. They made beats at around 128–135 beats per minute (bpm) using sampler keyboards with limited memory. The loops were thus short, and due to the lack of equipment and studio capacity, opportunity for overdubbing or vocals was limited. The second generation saw the center of production shifting from middle-class neighborhoods to large, underserviced informal settlements called *musseques*, with producers like Os Lambas preferring a lo-fi, gritty aesthetic.[10] By the 2000s, Fruity Loops (a pattern-based musical sequencer now known as FL Studio) had revolutionized home studios, in particular the Roland TR drum machines. Pirated copies of Fruity Loops and producers' ability to copy their tracks onto disks and drives democratized kuduro, Sheridan writes (88). This sound was also more layered with choruses, delays, sound distortions, and more complex beats produced at 140 bpm.

The third generation of kuduristas operated on two fronts: while many middle-class producers like Hochi Fu insisted on the importance of global markets, a significant section made up of artists such as Titica was also interested in kuduro providing a voice not just for Angolans but also for impoverished and marginalized neighborhood communities. The popularity of kuduro exploded in Angola, with live shows occurring in venues ranging in size from tiny clubs in the *musseque* to massive stadiums. It also spread internationally, clinging specifically to the contours of the Lusophone and socialist diasporas, demonstrating Angolans' skillful negotiation of the transnational economies that produce their inherited legacies of inequality. Transnational kuduro does not so much mark an equitable engagement with a utopic Atlantic world of exchange but rather manipulates diasporic sociopolitical forces that perpetuate imperial power and the growth of African poverty. For example, Angolan kuduristas have transformed the inability to afford and access instruments into an electronic postcolonial sound that borrows from a racialized urban repertoire that includes US hip-hop. When M.I.A. states in an interview, "It initially came from kids not having anything to make music on other than cellphones, using samples from their PCs and mobiles' sound buttons" (McDonnell), this is both an example of ingenious creativity and a response to the lack of access. These sounds are then picked up by DJs and MCs who can afford instruments and more sophisticated technology (predominantly in Europe) and who transform kuduro in production via better editing, more polished beats, and the incorporation of recorded instruments such as the guitar, which was previously largely absent from Angolan music. This in turn becomes part of the repertoire of sounds available for incorporation through sampling by Angolan kuduristas.

This diasporic reach of contemporary kuduro music is complemented by the insistence of various artists like Cabo Snoop on the importance of the *musseques* both as sites of production and as the source of aesthetic influences that center the life of the poor and disenfranchised. The spreading popularity of producing, recording, and emceeing kuduro (which could only come about due to more accessible technology) has a profound impact on community formations and organization. Acts develop their own unique style, meant to be consumed by the neighborhoods from which they originated. Sheridan thus writes, "Emerging technology . . . strengthen[ed] community bonds . . . [and] challenged economic structures by strengthening local cultural participation and building creative communities that served as support networks in a country with negligible social services and disrupted family networks. The studio as a site of social cohesion and support was common amongst musically active Luandans, with one producer suggesting that the construction of their studio was 'a synonym of humanity, an act of revolution'" (91).

The studio as a site of social cohesion is accompanied by local ways in which the music is marketed, distributed, and advertised within Angolan neighborhoods. The large number of rural Angolans displaced to urban areas (particularly to the *musseques*) mostly can only find work within Angola's informal economy. Sex work, the sale of food, street vending, drivers, and money collectors on *candongueiros* (privately owned and run taxis) are some of the options for migrants eking out a living. The drivers and money collectors on *candongueiros* play a key role in the production and dissemination of kuduro. The production of kuduro on shoestring budgets in makeshift home studios, with their own informal circuits of distribution and consumption, shows how (poor) Angolans manipulate systems of global capital to enable alternate forms of cultural production. They are not simply its victims, but also, according to Tómas, through kuduro they "reconfigur[e] Angolan society, positing . . . alternative infrastructure[s]" (267) that challenge the hegemony of the state. These alternate pathways are temporary: studios don't have the necessary equipment from day to day; artists rise and fall into obscurity with great regularity; and informal markets are forcibly shut down. But the challenge posed by a dynamic aesthetic practice to the necropolitics of the postcolony remains.

These themes are developed in Alfredo D'Amato's beautiful series of photographs called *The Sound of Kuduro* (2010). The first photograph of the series is an exquisite aerial view of a Luandan *musseque*, with the flat roofs of crowded-together shacks stretching almost to the horizon (fig. 5.2). Far in the distance, the hazy blue verticality of the city center, or *baixa*, closes in on the shacks, exaggerating the ramshackle quality of the homes in the *musseques*. Almost as if to emphasize the origins of the word *musseque* (the sandy place where the asphalt ends), the foreground of the image is dominated by a dirt road with randomly parked cars and a few pedestrians. A bright-blue *candongueiro* parked in front of a two-story building that looks to be a storefront arrests our attention.

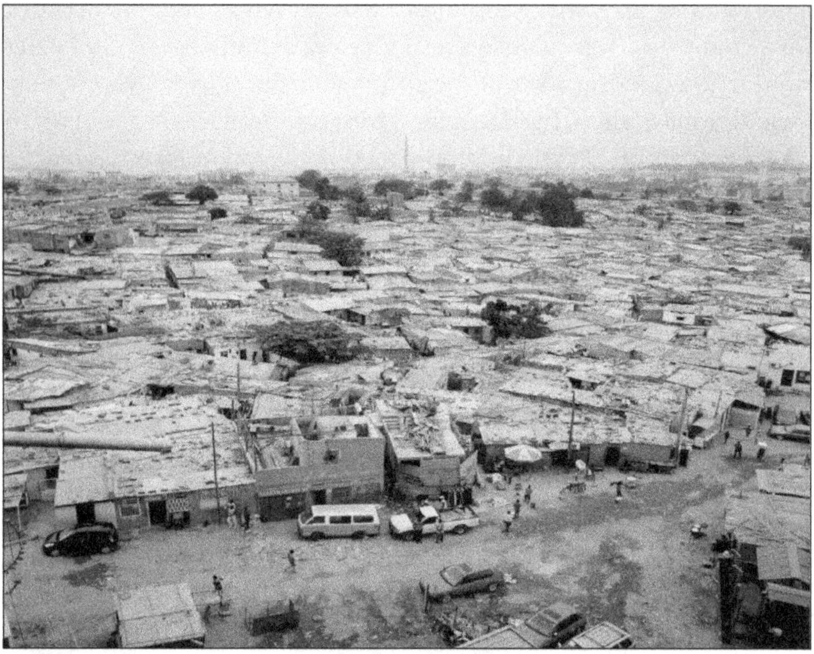

Figure 5.2. Alfredo D'Amato, "a slum, known in Angola as a musseque, in Luanda"; from photography series *The Sound of Kuduro* (2010) (© Alfredo D'Amato)

Later in the series, we get a shot of the rear of what is perhaps the same *candongueiro*, with pasted white letters in the back window that read, "DOBIESY PRODOÇOES." Like the other passengers in the *candongueiro*, we travel through the *musseque*, listening to the booming beat of kuduro. The other photographs are various stops along a kuduro journey. For example, from the inside of a tiny homemade studio, behind a small computer screen with a rudimentary keyboard, we watch a local artist recording his work. Other images include a table of CDs for sale, graffitied walls advertising particular kuduro acts, a pretty woman glancing coyly up at the camera from within a small club, her body under red night lights. Yet another photograph depicts two kuduro musicians climbing a ladder up the side of a house in a *musseque*. The ladder, squeezed between two walls in an alley littered with an abandoned tire and broken cinder blocks, leads to a rooftop recording studio where the kuduristas who work as *candongueiro* drivers live and record music. Such self-built studios, precariously attached to the roofs and sides of houses, have started to proliferate, like hardy corrugated-iron vines, changing the meaning of space through architectures of performance.

D'Amato also carefully details kuduro's presence in different areas of the city, not just the *musseque*. Four beautiful, scantily clad women stand in front of an expensive villa. There is another image of two musicians posed in front of a blue-screen backdrop and yet another of a group in front of a pool. All the images of kuduristas outside the *musseque* depict artists, their dancers, and/or their fans posing for the camera. D'Amato's insistence on including images of cameras in most of these shots draws attention to the ways that wealthy and middle-class kuduristas are being marketed to international audiences by advertising glamorous lifestyles far out of reach for the average Angolan. This layer of mediation is absent from the images taken in the *musseque*, perhaps revealing D'Amato's perception of a rawer, more honest aesthetic practice springing from the ghetto.

The inclusion of cameras could also provide subtle commentary on the state's attempt to appropriate kuduro for its own ends. During the struggle for independence and the subsequent civil wars, Angolans used music as an independent cultural practice that operated on a different register than formal politics. Much like the kongonya, a vernacular dance developed by guerrillas and the poor during the fight for independence in Zimbabwe, kuduro "facilitated political mobilization, morale boosting, psychological anchoring, and above all, a comforting sense of the ordinary in an otherwise traumatic context" (Gonye 66). As Moorman puts it, through music, "urban men and women . . . created an angolanidade, a sense of identity both rooted and cosmopolitan, and . . . secured it in the beat of a song, the lilt of a dance step, or the fold of a head-scarf—and in the shuffle of bills and the ring of coins in the club's cashbox" (*Intonations* 7). Unfortunately, also like the kongonya, politicians attempted to subvert the revolutionary potential of vernacular aesthetic performances to demand that citizens support national projects.[11] The Angolan Ministry of Culture sought to appropriate kuduro for its own uses, first by attempting to censor the "violent" messages of kuduro. Later it began sponsoring and supporting the production of aspirational, nonthreatening forms of kuduro in order to defang the radical potential of a politics embedded in vernacular aesthetic and cultural performances. As Roderick Ferguson argues in another context, "One of the staple features of liberal capitalism is the way in which it enlists culture as the moral agent of capital. As such, liberal capitalism gives culture the task of regulating citizens and noncitizens for the good of capitalist relations of production" (38). Rather than kuduro voicing the rage and despair of people like the war veteran Domingo Seiala at the lack of substantive change, the state attempts to convert kuduro into an advertisement for the commodity as it centers the quest for fame, big houses, and fancy clothes. D'Amato conveys this idea of the state always watching and manipulating kuduro for its own ends by foregrounding the conspicuous consumption, glossy production, and self-conscious artificiality of (upper)-middle-class kuduristas, who are always under the omnipresent eyes of the camera.

But what these photographs further demonstrate is that even while kuduro as performance reimagines what the body means, it also resists the classed antiblack geography of the postcolony. By utilizing what Katherine McKittrick calls "different practices of spatial manipulation," kuduristas disidentify with and "manipulate the categories and sites that constrain them" (*Demonic Grounds* xvii). Acts of political and social oppression are ultimately always spatial practices of subjugation, changing the way we perceive and utilize the landscape. Subjugation necessitates the ordering of space, for example, into formally and informally segregated neighborhoods, safe and dangerous pathways, *musseque* and *baixa*, and "Third World" and "First World" geographic couplings of exploitation and control. Building studios on rooftops, using transportation routes as circuits of sound, dancing on the roofs of cars, and stomping one's feet into the dirt are performative acts that resignify on the hierarchical structures of domination that play out in the architecture of the city and its informal settlements.[12] As Joseph Roach reminds us, performances "activate the spatial logic of . . . cit[ies] built to make certain powers and privileges . . . perpetually reproducible" (14). Kuduro's continual repurposing of space, achieved via the production and consumption of its beats in vans, in makeshift studios, and in narrow alleyways and the innovativeness of its movement repertoires, results in new engagements with the material landscape and architecture of the postcolony.[13]

Stefanie Alisch and Nadine Siegert argue in their article on kuduro as a dance form that "trauma is . . . situated within the biographies of the victims and perpetrators, not inscribed into the topography of the Luandan cityscape. . . . Luanda might be understood as . . . an open space in which to perform embodied traces of the past and imagine concepts of the future" (54). Such a reading illustrates what Katherine McKittrick calls "the ideological weight of transparent space, the idea that space 'just is'" (*Demonic Grounds* xv). Instead, McKittrick goes on to argue, "*who* we see is tied up with *where* we see," so that racial and class identities are inextricable from the hierarchy of space and place and vice versa (xv). Thus, manipulating space differently requires engaging not only with what haunts the landscape but with current hierarchies of human and not-quite-human that render certain people valuable only as necropolitical labor. Kuduristas work against geographies of domination via a repurposing and respatialization of their bodies and the terrain of the postcolony. Imagine in the middle of a dusty street a young kudurista, clad only in dusty shorts and flip-flops. He is a counterpoint to our fire sprite. This unnamed boy's rapid footwork and repeated fall, face first onto the ground, reclaims the terrain he inhabits. To fall so carelessly instead of gingerly walking imaginary tightropes between land mines, to insist on the *musseque* as a site of creativity and production rather than a repository for zombie labor, reveals the vibrancy of a performative black sociality that cannot be contained. This is a geographic language set to a driving beat that remaps the historically produced terrains of disenfranchisement and injury and that claims an embodied space that refuses the displacement, impoverishment, and criminalized unruliness of our boy in shorts.[14]

The Crazy Ones: Afro-Alienated Vocabularies of Debility

Ah, eu aqui, sempre cuduro! (Ah, I am here, moving forward despite the obstacles, always tough)
—Albano Cardosa, multimedia artist

One of the most well-known kuduro-influenced bands is Buraka Som Sistema featuring DJ Znobia, Saborosa, and Puto Prata. Named after Buraka, a neighborhood in Lisbon heavily populated by Angolan immigrants, the group has helped popularize kuduro with the help of M.I.A., who devastatingly chants on the song "Sound of Kuduro," "One job, two job, three job, four. Sound of kuduro knocking at your door" (Buraka Som Sistema). The video begins with an aerial view of a busy street along the coastline with the caption, "Angola 2007." The camera then cuts to the inside of a car, where we see the members of the group proclaiming in English and Portuguese that this is their first time in Angola and that it was a long journey there. Various shots of Luandan streets are interspersed with close-up depictions of a man whose face is horizontally oriented. The camera pans back, and we see him with several other men crawling across the floor, surrounded by an audience. We see another man's bare torso as he painfully walks across the floor with one hip much higher than the other, his arms held at rigid angles as he moves. The beat gets faster; we watch a man fall flat to the ground, bounce a little, then shoot back up. We start to realize that we are watching dance, a dance that does not just use but also comments on and remakes the black body in the postcolony. Shots of the group recording on-site are interspersed with some of the most interesting, breathtaking, and creative dance sequences that I have seen. Young kids whose feet whirl in the dust, one young man pretending that rigor mortis has set in and another lifting the rigid body of his partner, a woman walking with a load on her head that causes her hips to sway in time to the beat: the video is replete with some of the best examples of what it means to dance kuduro. Examples of dancing kuduro abound on YouTube and other internet platforms, ranging in quality from professional videos such "Sound of Kuduro" to digital phone snippets. This ease of accessibility has resulted in the rapid spread, adoption, and reinvention of dance movements from region to region and country to country.

The various choreographic elements of kuduro are called *toques*. According to Alisch and Siegert, most of these *toques* are borrowed from three different movement traditions. The first tradition is hip-hop, with popping and locking, breakdancing, head spinning, and the call and response of dance battles. Kuduro also draws its inspiration from traditional and carnival Angolan dance steps. Alisch and Siegert identify "graphic theatrical movements" as another source of inspiration, citing choreography as evidence, such as "crawling on the ground as if in battle, dancing on the thighs as if the legs were amputated, dancing with legs turned inwards as if on crutches, dancing on crutches with missing limbs, slapping themselves in the face and falling flat on the ground as if shot, or mimicking media images of 'starved Africans'" (56). This enactment of injury, they go on to argue, "makes trauma bearable [symptoms of trauma include 'hyper-vigilance' and 'short tempers'], as it offers a possibility to perform the unutterable in all its controversies" (63). Rather than an aestheticization of trauma, I would argue that these *toques* are acts of what Daphne Brooks in *Bodies in Dissent* calls "Afro-alienation," an imaginative excess that remakes bodies in new ways. Thinking through Bertolt Brecht's insistence on the inclusion of socially critical performative techniques that "generate 'alienation effects' and . . . 'awaken' audiences to history," Brooks argues that certain performers like Aida Overton Walker "critically defamiliariz[e] their own bodies by way of performance in order to yield alternative racial and gender epistemologies" (5). In other words, through disidentifying with certain racist, sexist, and classed tropes and practices, the body is refashioned. Thus, kuduro's embrace of differential embodiment and movement is less about trauma and more about somatically reimagining a black sociality that departs from notions of discrete individual bodies toward a collective remapping of the postcolony and a reanimation of the living dead.

In an article in *Vida Online*, Agre-G says of kuduro,

> If the dancer . . . lifts his body acrobatically to the sound of music that is, in form, arhythmic and uncoordinated, to a music that basically challenges gravity and physical pain, then we are speaking of the dance called kuduro. It is a genre of dance that appears to invoke a trance characteristic of the ancestral dances of young guerrilla fighters and at the same time a dance that draws on the marginalized cultures of the American ghetto (breakdance and rap). First you disconnect/leave yourself, and then you enter into the unusual techno beat with the traditional rhythms of Angola, into the dignity of difference, into improvisation, into the ongoing story of everyday *mangolê*. (Guimaraes and Oliveira)

Agre-G made popular a style of kuduro called Milindro or Melindro that originated with a group of men in Bairro Militar.[15] According to dancers in the five-part YouTube video "A Origem do Milindro-Angola," the adjective *milindrosa*, after which the style Milindro is named, signifies that which is offensive, precarious, and dangerous but overlooked.

It is the dance of crazy people, of the insane, of those to whom nobody assigns any importance. Through imaginative acts of Afro-alienation, kuduro dancers claim their differential embodiment and movement not as a sign of deviancy but instead as important sources of creative ability. Danced by famous kuduristas such as Costuleta, the style centers awkward movements with rigid limbs at various angles, plank-like falls to the ground, acting "crazy" and with a seeming lack of coordination. Agre-G goes on to describe Milindro as "characterized by a way of walking/moving as if you have a physical deficiency, as one who lives with a deformity" (Guimaraes and Oliveira). Dancers strut unevenly down the hallway with faces raised as if they are blind, with one arm bent behind the back as if it was amputated, limbs held stiffly as if they cannot bend. One could argue that able-bodied dancers of Milindro are passing as amputees. The conversion of what some people see as the inability to move into a complex dance step that signals a mastery of movement moves the performance away from parody. Rather, the lines between various differential embodiments are blurred: virtuosity of movement and overcoming the difficulty of navigating a physical and social environment designed around able-bodiedness look the same. This is not to underemphasize the difficulty that disabled people have negotiating a world that is not designed to accommodate them. Rather, kuduro incorporates disabled perspectives via a broadening out of an urban dance vocabulary around differential embodiment. Able bodies and dance itself are reconceptualized around a disability aesthetic coupled with a praxis of disability.

Milindro is not the only style of kuduro that foregrounds disability. Differential movements that characterize Milindro play a large role in all styles of kuduro dancing, so much so that there is now a dance step called "Do Milindro," in which dancers are unsteady on their feet, falling over only to spring upward. The various styles of dancing are more similar than dissimilar in their sharing of a basic movement vocabulary, with differences arising predominantly from different genealogies and circuits of production and consumption. Returning to Agre-G's description, kuduro is acrobatic yet uncoordinated, traditional and improvised, trance-like and choreographed, a challenge to gravity even as one falls to the ground, a means by which to leave oneself and enter someplace else characterized by the "dignity of difference." Despite one's initial impressions, Agre-G's description is not contradictory. Instead, he draws attention to the contrapuntal nature of kuduro's movements. The various *toques* call and respond to each other in ways that dramatize, contextualize, and exaggerate each other. The moments of stillness or death accentuate the frenetic movement of life and the living dead. Instances in which dancers appear to transcend the confines of their body speak to the violence and pain of embodiment. A boneless fluidity alternates with popping, locking, and breaking to suggest the ways that bodies have been broken, injured, and made anew, altering their flow.

I would like to take a closer look at some of the characteristic movements of kuduro, many of which integrate embodied alterity and movement. In rehearsing certain movements and qualities of kuduro dancing, the complex relationship between kuduro and differential embodiment and movement becomes clearer. As Alisch and Siegert write, "According to Diamondog, the practice of mirroring movements of handicapped people has a long tradition in Angolan vernacular dancing" (56–57). While disabled bodies perform a "surprising" dexterity, able-bodied kuduristas play with awkwardness and falling, catching and releasing. The *toques*, found across styles of kuduro that stress differential embodiment and movement, include popping, locking, and breaking; the total cessation of movement when dancers lie still on the ground as if they are dead; the Tio Guerra *toque*, in which the dancer simulates dancing with one biological and one prosthetic leg; a limping *toque* made famous by Ti Nogueira, "where dancers jump on one leg while the other lags behind, slightly rotating in the air" (Alisch and Siegert 57); and *cara podre* (foul face) or *cara feia* (ugly face), in which the face is contorted with mouth twisted, lower lip protruding, and eyes rolled back. There are others in which dancers walk on their knees as if their legs were stumps; or move as though they are on crutches, with feet rotated inward; or spasm on the ground, as though they are either in death throes or in the middle of a seizure. As Lesley Braun, or Drop Legs, notes on her blog, "Dancers integrate their prosthetics as a part of the physical discussion with their world of war. It is a lexicon of twisted limbs, distinguished by sudden drops to the ground, bended feet to the face; in one move, a prosthetic foot becomes a cell phone, lifted to the ear." Kuduro shifts and alters the vocabulary of dance by including embodied disabled perspectives in which "difference is exciting and interesting, not swallowed up in the certainties of social meaning, with its distinction between normal and other" (Kuppers, "Bodies" 159).

Popping, locking, and breaking. Part of kuduro's dance vocabulary are the alternations between staccato muscular isolations and fluidity that make up popping, locking, and breaking. Borrowed from hip-hop, popping, locking, and breaking conjures up the violence against the black body that results in the physical breaking of limbs. This is a language of rhythmic breaks where the isolation of muscles and the emphasis on the body's capacity to break down into smaller and smaller parts stresses the fungibility of the black body and also a resistance to this fungibility. As Moorman writes, "Just as goods and services in Luanda and other African cities are broken down into their smallest saleable units—a plastic bag of clean water; a cigarette; one stick of gum; a ketchup packet of whiskey; a tomato paste tin filled with peanuts . . .—so too do kuduro dancers subdivide the body" ("Anatomy" 30). Kuduro abstracts the body into tiny units, making overt the link with an economy of poverty in which Angolans need to break down market goods into the smallest units of exchange in order to afford them. In the postcolony, where bodies are made into mechanisms of labor, kuduristas' alternating fluid motion with tightly focused snapshots of rigid stillness draws attention to the necropolitical alienation of their labor, to the breaking down of the body into parts, some of which are more valuable than others. Bodies are not the sum of their parts, kuduro insists. Instead, they are an embodied Frankenstein-like collection of conjoined limbs that move to an animated, vivacious beat.

Popping, locking, and breaking comment on what it means to confront the brutality of contemporary life. The backbreaking labor of making ends meet, kuduristas are saying, necessitates the acquisition of new movements and different modes of muscular control. The imperial violence that forces joints, muscles, and limbs to go rigid with fear, hunger, overwork, and anger and to break under the strain of daily survival also remembers the "broken" body of a war or land-mine victim. My Luck reminds us, "It is rare to die intact in a war. Bullets and shrapnel from mines and mortars and shells can tear a body to pieces. An arm here, a leg over there in the foliage—all of which have to be retrieved and assembled into the semblance of a complete body before there can be a count. The worst thing about this job may be the irreconcilable math of it: Many of the parts don't add up" (Abani, *Song* 50). Popping, locking, and breaking revalue the black body by insisting on the importance of every tiny, twitching muscle. No matter how small the movement, it is an animated sign of survival, of living life to the fullest despite the odds. As Drop Legs writes, it "is a celebration of the broken body" (Braun).

Lying dead. Over and over, kuduristas drop to the ground, sometimes face first. Dancers mimic being shot, slapping themselves in the face, stiffening their body before falling board-like to the ground. There is a brief moment when they lie still, as though dead. I am struck by those moments of stillness that often are accompanied by another dancer gyrating above the "dead" body. What does it mean to fall to the ground and "play dead," a strategy my son was encouraged by his teachers to choose, should a gunman enter his school? I argued previously that horizontality functions crucially as a ritually embodied position of subjugation and death. The power of lying on the ground does not stem from the body's resurrection but rather in that still moment of zombification, when one feels kinship with the dead and a renewed fellowship with the living. Those seconds on the ground pretending to be dead after an imaginary gunshot, for example, can seem eternal in their discomfort, in their thick silences, in the involuntary spasm of muscle and the tremendous effort required to hold muscles as still as possible.

In *Embodying Black Experience: Stillness, Critical Memory, and the Black Body*, Harvey Young examines how stillness and critical memory embody a historical black experience that repeats across time and genre. Looking, for example, at James Zealy's daguerreotypes taken in 1850, he sees in the stillness of Ophelia, Alfred, and others a restaging of the coerced stillness of their captivity that refuses their violent objectification. This is not the stillness of decontextualized flesh but rather a "physically taxing" performance that foregrounds the history of black people reduced to captive flesh. The kuduristas' performance of stillness belongs in this tradition of black captivity. Dropping to the ground as if dead signifies on the awful danger that black bodies face when they move as well as on black refusals to move. Kuduristas insist that stillness is a matter of life and death: the moment when one hears the click of a detonating land mine necessitates a sudden and absolute stillness, as one's life hangs in the balance. Fighting guerrilla wars involved long stretches of time when citizen-soldiers lay concealed in the brush, still as if dead. A slight movement when one has been asked to stand motionless, with one's hands up before a gun, can result in death. As Young writes, "Motion is stillness. . . . It collapses the past with the present with the promise of extending into the future. [The kudurista] stands still and still stands" (44).

Making ugly faces. By making "ugly" faces, kuduristas insist that ugliness is not an aesthetic category. Instead, the *toque cara feia/cara podre* suggests that ugliness is a political performance that allows dancers to disidentify with systems of oppression that relegate them to the realm of the ugly, poor, and disabled. In "The Politics of Ugliness," Ela Przybylo argues that ugliness is political in the following ways: "It denotes and bookmarks inequalities and hierarchies, serving as a repository for all that is 'other.' . . . Ugliness is necessarily contingent and relational, . . . exist[ing] because bodies are compared to one another, and because they are evaluated in accordance to the 'norm'" (3). Ugliness cannot be defined around a specific set of descriptors, as beauty standards are constantly changing. Despite this mercuriality, categories of beauty and ugliness always reassemble around hierarchies of race, gender, and able-bodiedness. And while ugly bodies don't have any single characteristic that they all share across space and time, what they do share is a relegation to spatiotemporal zones where the "unsightly" are supposed to remain out of sight due to their filth, their deformity, and their monstrosity. As Susan Schweik develops in *The Ugly Laws*, part of ugliness lies in the belief that one can easily visually identify it because it is writ large on the body. The self-evidence of inferiority lies in the dirtiness of black skin, the monstrosity of the primitive savage, and the grotesquery of the cripple with their eyes rolled back in their head. Schweik thus writes that "unsightliness . . . [lies] in or on skin, skin 'exposed,' skin 'disfigured,' skin that disgust[s]" (187). Ugliness is part and parcel of the scopic regimes of race, gender, and disability. The unsightly body becomes a source of shame, something that should be hidden away, corrected, and discarded. Ugliness, thus, works to sequester certain peoples into uninhabitable death worlds.

In "We Are Ugly, but We Are Here," Edwidge Danticat builds her essay around a Haitian saying, "Nou led, nou la," which translates as "We are ugly, but we are here." This saying, she writes, "might upset the aesthetic images of most women. . . . Like the modesty that is somewhat common in Haitian culture, this saying makes a deeper claim for poor

Haitian women than maintaining beauty, be it skin deep or otherwise. For most of us, what is worth celebrating is the fact that we are here, that we against all the odds exist." Danticat suggests that ugly bodies can be what Przybylo calls "politically transgressive" (10) simply by existing and demanding to be seen. Like kuduristas, these Haitian women's Afro-alienated demands that we look at them in all their putative ugliness are a profound challenge to gendered, racialized, and able-bodied expectations built around Western imperial patterns of commodification and consumption. By performing ugliness, the women reveal the hierarchical systems of value that render them monstrous, zombie-like creatures. Greeting each other as they navigate neighborhoods or dance on street corners, both kuduristas and Haitian women are what Schweik in another context names "spatial dissidents . . . [who] insist[] not only on exposing themselves to public view but also on occupying and radically reconfiguring public space" (6). Through the claiming of ugliness, not only are beauty standards disrupted, but space is reclaimed. Rather than hiding from view, "ugliness" on display denounces capitalistic aesthetic practices of beauty and makes space for itself out of the shadows.

This shared ugliness is one of the ways that kuduro enacts a ritualistic black sociality. The ugly contorted face elicits a shout from fellow dancers. It is both an inquiry into their own state of being and an assertion of survival. The ugly face functions as a call and a response, a krik to another's krak as the Luandan dancer revels in the ugliness of a conjoined survival. Rather than a reversal, such as when children participating in the Black Panthers' Breakfast Program chanted "black is beautiful," the *cara feia toque* seizes hold of the very binary of beauty/ugliness and rips it apart in an act of Afro-alienation. The bodies and faces of kuduristas signify on regimes of power that circumscribe their existence by isolating them and etching meaning onto their skin. Their ugliness binds together postcolonial communities through gestural enactments. Thus, we look at you in all our ugliness, and you look back at us with familiar faces.

Catching and falling. Unlike kizomba or semba, kuduro is not a couple's dance. When more than one dancer performs simultaneously, one usually witnesses the reenactment of heterosexual coupling—the female kudurista pops her booty and grinds her hips, while the male dancer signals his sexual prowess. If both dancers are male, in addition to an aggressive heterosexuality, we see explorations of fall and recovery using contact and release techniques. Dancers throw each other across the performance space into a plastic chair located at the other end of the courtyard; one lifts another and drops him; a dancer uses another's weight to flip over, and yet another dances through the portal-like space between another's legs. Not only do different parts of the body come into contact with the space and the other dancers, but also the assumed symmetry of the normate body is undercut and the notion of balance shifts. By supporting the weight of another dancer, by carrying and dropping, by yielding and pushing off against, balance becomes located in multiple bodies. The illusion of individually bound bodies that can do everything themselves shatters under the rhythm of release and hold, catch and fall. This emphasis on falling and multiple sources of support locates the dancers in a continuum of nonhierarchical strengths and capacities that they creatively explore through dance.

The dance can be described as a complex interaction between the geographic terrain, dancers who challenge each other, and their audiences. A successful performance, according to Alisch, is one with *carga*. Alisch writes that *carga* is a word that generates a set of meanings that constellate around the idea of "force" or "power." A performance with *carga* carries a weight or electric spiritual charge that moves through space, dancer, and audience, loosely binding them into one conjoined being. *Carga*, I would further argue, can also be thought of as the ability to elicit a historical and culturally conditioned kinesthetic empathy from viewers across difference. As the energy flows back and forth between performer and viewers, the performer becomes reanimated and their performance more vibrant. If the performance is successful, something in excess of intentionality or technique springs up between all the participants, binding them together through acts of critical imagination. Bodies are made and unmade through movement. The performances of various kuduristas are not isolated instances of contemporary music and dance, but rather they invent clandestine, tactical, and elastic moments of possibility tied to a cultural and material history. Kuduristas form part of an African diasporic genealogy of gendered, raced performances that embody the past's and present's claims on each other. This genealogy becomes the site of the emergence of possibilities forged via a critical imagining of modes of sociality that bend and mold space to constitute new black geographies.

Dancing with a Hundred Legs

Kuduro is crucially an example of a physically integrated performance that includes both disabled and nondisabled performers, along with their various prosthetics such as canes, crutches, and wheelchairs. It does not just incorporate disability into its movement repertoire but also includes differently abled bodies without insisting that they move as if able-bodied. Kuduro thus is an artistic and political practice that allows for the possibilities of "truly collaborative performances with people who embody a spectrum of physical and cognitive variety" (Solga 698). As Owen Smith argues, it "reconfigure[s] the codes that inscribe and privilege a particular representation of corporeality, . . . countering the tyrannical trajectory that fetishes a particular type of body within prevailing aspects of cultural life and representational practice" (77). Performance remakes space and the body so that human variation is not incidental or deviant but rather constitutes an essential part of performance. Thus, as Jennifer Parker-Starbuck writes, kuduro "rehearses a new paradigm of bodily practices that makes visible—in an attempt to make understandable—the differing strengths bodies can possess" (101). In order to explore what it would mean for someone with differential embodiment to perform kuduro, I turn to a kudurista who is particularly well known for his dancing ability, Costuleta. While the themes that play out in his life are specific to his biographical narrative, his presence (alongside the presence of others like him) allows us to think about the role of differential embodiment in a dance form that uses the somatic vocabulary of disability as part of its repertoire. One of Costuleta's legs has been amputated. What does it mean that one of the most famous kuduro dancers is differentially embodied, that his one-leggedness is not something for him to overcome but rather elevates his performance? Like Abani's one-legged fire sprite who shakes the universe, how do Costuleta's performances allow us to reimagine a world where differential embodiment and movement are its heartbeat?

An early grainy video shows Costuleta on the top of a car roof, popping, locking, and grinding his pelvis to an ear-thumping upbeat tempo of 130–40 bpm before jumping to the ground with an incredible acrobatic athleticism. Sexy and visually exciting or full of *carga*, his performance elicits corresponding booty popping and oohs and aahhs from spectators who transform from passersby to enthralled audience. A boy off to the side awaits an opening so that he too can perform and complement as well as compete with Costuleta's dancing. Costuleta's street performances have gradually been replaced with videos with high production values, international tours, and well-marketed albums. In "Mama Kudi," Costuleta begins the video dancing with another young amputee at his side. He later goes on to use his crutch as a prosthetic to ride a bicycle and roller-skate. At a certain point, he dramatically throws the crutch away and jumps up, touching his leg to his hand before landing, in perfect time to the beat, on his one leg. Costuleta has cemented his reputation as a dancer, so much so that he is known colloquially as the "man with one leg who in truth has a hundred legs." Rather than being seen as an exceptional amputee who can dance kuduro as well as an able-bodied person with two legs can, Costuleta is something more. Kuduro, for him and other dancers like him, does not constitute a form of rehabilitation or uplift in which disabled bodies obfuscate their differences via their exceptional performances of able-bodiedness. There is no attempt to transcend disability. Nor is it an attempt to minimize or overcome differential embodiment by passing as an able-bodied dancer. Rather, Costuleta's hundred legs enable him to perform both as an able-bodied dancer incorporating nonnormate movements and as a disabled dancer capable of performing many of the same movements as an able-bodied kudurista.

Costuleta's performances allow us to think about kuduro not only as including differential movement but also as a mixed-ability dance form. Despite having access to a prosthetic leg, Costuleta often performs with his pants' leg pinned under his stump and a metal crutch. Rather than his amputated leg and metal crutch being a deterrent to dancing kuduro, the stump and the crutch force a rethinking of hierarchical binaries of disabled/largely immobile and able-bodied/athletic. Costuleta's skill with his crutch, as Telory Davies argues, "presupposes a new model of self-sufficiency that incorporates . . . technology. [His dancing] . . . therefore revises both cultural assumptions about dancing bodies as non-assisted entities and disabled bodies as entities incapable of self-sufficient movement" (53). Costuleta does not use the crutch to disguise himself as nondisabled or to triumph over his putative lack of dexterity. Instead, the crutch becomes a body appendage, a dance partner, and a way to imagine new bodily configurations. The materiality of the prosthetic or mobility aid becomes part of his body schema, challenging our very ideas of what constitutes a body in the first place. Wanda Strukus in "Mining the Gap" writes that mobility aids such as wheelchairs can become part of one's body schema, which she defines as "a representation of the body that is produced by proprioceptive, vestibular, somatosensory and visual information and is used by the brain to control bodily movements" (93). One's body schema continually adapts and changes so that a wheelchair or a crutch or prosthetic "becomes part of the lived-body experience of the world" (94). Thus, the dancer Alice Sheppard insists about her chair, "It's not so much a thing as a real body part. . . . It's not like dancing with a chair. . . . It's like dancing" (Weber). The plasticity of one's body redefines the borders of flesh, deemphasizing discourses of loss and limitation. What dancers like Costuleta foreground through exceptional somatic movement with and without prosthetics is what Michelle R. Nario-Redmond et al. identify as the "liberation associated with [differential] mobility, the creativity involved in navigating [various environments]" (325). The emergence of a plastic body, conjoined to others and to certain devices, affirms the joyfulness of movement. Costuleta dances because he wants to and he can. He thereby "stakes claim to a radical space, an unruly location [of Afro-alienation] where disparate assumptions about representation, subjectivity, and visual pleasure collide with one another" (Cooper Albright, "Strategic Abilities" 478).

The Politics of Sex and Differential Embodiment

In an online interview, Costuleta writes about why a white Italian family in Luanda adopted him as a child (and not his able-bodied brother) from his mother's home: "[They] thought I was cute as a handicapped dancer" (Bonneville). The racism of the family who found Costuleta's ability not as a dancer but as a *handicapped* dancer "cute" results in Costuleta's bitterness and "bad feeling" toward the Portuguese and white settlers because of what he terms "a continuation of the colonial relationship" (Bonneville). His adoptive family's racism and ableism generate liberal narratives of uplift in which both as a tragic African and as a tragic amputee, Costuleta, unlike his able-bodied brother, needed rescuing. As a nonthreatening, dependent black boy with one leg, he was praised by the family for his dancing, even encouraged for it. However, as he got older, his dancing transformed from "cute" to an active performance of his black masculinity and sexuality, from an endearing hobby to a professional career choice that was not in keeping with the family's bourgeois expectations. His adoptive family encouraged him to give up dancing to attend school and to settle down with a black African.[16] Costuleta's resentment toward the family is obvious when he boldly states, "I am no longer in touch with them" (Bonneville). Instead of gratitude for their supposed benevolence, Costuleta's anger at being asked to abandon his mother, brother, and then later his dancing is palpable. He chose to leave his adoptive family and move to a violent and deeply fractured South Africa in order to further develop as a dancer and to wait for a chance to go to Portugal. The Italian family later moved to Brazil.

The resistance of Costuleta's adoptive family to kuduro is located at the fraught crossroads where sexuality, class, and disability come together. Despite the international attention kuduro has garnered and the inroads it has made into upper-middle-class communities, the association between the savage, almost uncontrolled beat of kuduro and the primitivism and lack of morality of the lower classes still prevails. The segregated neighborhoods of Luanda are not just about a racialized class ghettoization but also about policing sexual desire. The potential transgression of Costuleta marrying a white woman threatened the enforced boundaries between *musseque* and *baixa*, between poor black and wealthier communities with white settlers. But the transgression was also fundamentally about policing the desire of differentially embodied persons. Key to understanding the attempt by Costuleta's adoptive family to distance him from kuduro is his differential embodiment. As Robert McRuer and Anna Mollow develop in another context, the conjunction of sex and disability "is most often the occasion for marginalization or marveling: the sexuality of disabled people is typically depicted in terms of either tragic deficiency or freakish excess. Pity or fear, in other words, are the sensations most often associated with disabilities" (1). But Costuleta's sexuality, which is at times aggressive and at other times playful, refuses the deeroticization of disabled bodies as well as the relegation of the sexual/disabled to the private realm. Rather, in his very public performances, Costuleta claims space as a sexual being with complex desires. Costuleta's powerful deployment of the erotic combined with a virtuosity that refuses the category of "disabled" exceeds not only his deeroticization as an amputee but also the commodification of his sexuality as a "thug" and/or player—the "primitive" urban masculinity that his adoptive family was so afraid of.[17]

Disability, Tobin Siebers insists, "defamiliarize[s] how we think currently about sex" (38). Costuleta's sexualized performances expose how racialized ideologies of ability value some sexual practices over others. Instead of his amputated leg being a hindrance to acts of intimacy that are typically predicated on sex as a "privileged domain of ability" (Siebers 40), his performances open out our very definitions of sexual behavior, asking us to consider sexuality as an eroticized field of possibility. Disability is not an obstacle or limitation to be overcome to enable sex, nor does blackness signal hypersexual, primitive heterosexuality that has to be "controlled"; rather, performances of blackness as they intersect with disability interrogate normativity to result in pleasurable acts that arouse audiences in their evocation of new epistemologies. Put another way, Costuleta's sexuality, which his adoptive family wished to control through marriage to a respectable black girl, does not stem from his blackness, nor does it exist despite his disability. Rather, it arises from the fact that through his performances as a differentially embodied black man with a public sexual identity, he represents exciting new ways of being in the world, a "complex embodiment that enhances sexual activities and pleasure" (Siebers 47).

Many of the battles Costuleta fought over sexuality also played out in the 2011–12 emergence of the kuduro dance queen Titica. Titica, born in Luanda, is Africa's first public "transsexual" artist, according to *Masalacism.*[18] Teca Miguel Garcia became Titica after breast-enhancement surgery in Brazil. While audiences love her kuduro performances, reception of her gendered identity is difficult to gauge. Some people seem either oblivious to or ignore her complex gendering; a few argue that no matter her intentions, she is an ambassador for the LGBT community, while still others derogatively call her "one of the weirder combos [they] . . . have seen lately" and reduce her identity to "the transvestite gimmick" (Virtual Crack Distribution Services). In an interview with the BBC in April 2012, Titica explained that her success had been hard won: "I've been stoned, I've been beaten, and there is a lot of prejudice against me, a lot of people show that. There is a lot of taboo" (Redvers). Titica refuses to make any recorded statements about whether she considers herself transsexual, a transvestite, and/or homosexual. This is not surprising given that homosexuality is illegal in Angola.[19] However, rather than only a result of absolutely appropriate caution, perhaps Titica's refusal to fix her identity allows her performances to set gender, race, and body into fluid play. This play, always anchored in the material violence of a hegemonically gendered society, catalyzes critical inquiry and forces her viewers to examine their own expectations around embodiment, dance, and gender. Titica is trained in ballet, a field with particular symbolic resonance for girls and young women. Traditionally, ballet dancers hold themselves upright, conveying power through a verticality that ends in a pointe, even while emphasizing a feminized vulnerability through fluid lyrical movement. Hips are turned out, poses are elongated, and movement and balance are centered in the small of the back. This is very different from the female kudurista who performs her gender through a display of sexual prowess located in the flaunting of breasts, the rotation of hips, and the popping of the booty. The already-very-tall Titica emphasizes her height by holding herself erect and posing like a ballet dancer and then dropping low to the floor. Using lyrical hand gestures, she cups her breasts to emphasize them and slaps her ass. Her performances are a bricolage of various somatic repertoires of racialized gender, thereby perhaps gesturing to a space beyond them.

Essential to Titica's performance is the name she chose to represent herself to the world: Titica. An informal word, *titica* translates as "chicken shit"—small bits of feces or droppings. It can also mean a worthless or useless person or thing. Why would an artist choose to name herself with the very epithets that are derogatively applied to marginal members of society? Darieck Scott in *Extravagant Abjection* insists that sexualized blackness cannot be reduced to its constitutive elements of traumatizing domination or the violence of (post)colonial abjection. However, he also doesn't want to simply overcome or overturn this "inescapable aspect of blackness—lying coiled at its historical heart, repeated, echoed . . .—which can be described by terms such as defeat, violation, and humiliation" (5). Rather than follow the path of lionizing the transcendence of historical violation, Scott asks whether there might not be something politically productive in embracing certain injuries and their outcomes. He suggests that the experience of injury in its creation of abject blackness can also map a path toward potential practices of freedom. Titica, by naming herself as worthless and as a piece of shit, embraces her abjection as a practice of freedom.[20] Her name, along with her performances of racialized femaleness, cuts across naturalized identitarian positions. Given the often-sanctioned violence against Africans who identify as members of the LGBT community, Titica's presence in popular music requires tremendous courage. However, instead of simply overcoming the failed interpellation of certain nonnormative identities, she disidentifies with certain experiences of humiliation, shame, and defeat. Using performative techniques of Afro-alienation, Titica defamiliarizes the naturalized gendered body, taking damaging stereotypes and, in José Esteban Muñoz's words, "recycling them as powerful and seductive sites of self-creation" (*Disidentifications* 4). Titica's disidentification reveals how socially constructed identities universalize, naturalize, and exclude minoritarian positions and how those very same stereotypes in turn can be deployed as a strategy of resistance, survival, and self-making. While it might seem that Titica performs stereotypical female identity with fetishized breasts and ass, she remakes what it means to be male and female, worthless detritus and sexual citizen, ballet dancer and reigning kuduro dance queen.

6

Unhinging

Experimenting in Black Feminist Cripistemologies at the Edge of the World

"Aster, you are without a doubt completely and utterly unhinged," said Mabel, her tears dried but her bronchial distress evident. Clutching her chest, she wheezed. . . . Mabel needed oxygen.
—Rivers Solomon, *An Unkindness of Ghosts*

Saidiya Hartman in *Wayward Lives* writes of an upheaval in December 1919 at Lowell Cottage, Bedford, where women sentenced to reform school and exhausted by the abuse they had to endure staged a "vocal outbreak," a "sonic revolt, a 'noise strike,' the 'din of an infernal chorus . . . [seeking] retribution in noise and destruction" (279). Laughing, screaming, cursing, banging on walls with their fists, they tapped into a genealogy of the improvisational "collective utterance" (285). This collective utterance that springs from conjoined black bodies does not synthesize together harmoniously. This is no choir but a din, an unhinging, a babbling of voices that overlap, contradict, and talk over one another. This is a cascade of dissenting sounds, emerging cacophonously from our black, queer conjoined bodies as we insist on the power of our presence. This chapter, then, is a staging of a noise strike, an insistence on our various forms of cognition and expression emerging noisily from the page. A neurocacophony.

COVID-19 and its wake have left me increasingly isolated. Unable to sleep, I find my brain stuttering, lurching, crawling, and twitching. I find myself straining to triumph over my "limitations." I *can* teach even though I can't sit up straight without pain, and yes, even partially blind, I will make the faculty meeting. Reaching out to various friends and colleagues, we started to wonder out loud if it was possible to imagine different ways, times, and places for doing intellectual work, broadly defined. What would scholarship look like if we folded into our writing the ways that our brains and bodies misfire, fog up, and lose time? Instead of conquering individual shortcomings, can we produce work situated in and expanded by our neurodiversity? Can we produce work as conjoined beings across our differences? The answer is "not very easily" and sometimes "not at all."

Academic institutions play a key role in producing what Mel Chen in "Brain Fog: The Race for Cripistemology" calls "disciplined cognators" (178). Disciplined cognators, with their sophisticated cognitive tool kits, transcend the body and privilege a certain kind of individual productivity—best symbolized by end-of-year faculty progress reports, comprehensive exams, and reader reports. When I tried to work with various scholars of color to cowrite this conclusion, the first person grew overwhelmed by the pressure to finish her own book. Another had health issues and found herself with no time for "nonessential" work. We talked, we began to spin stories together, we faltered. Other friends drifted in and out. The traces of these other women as writers and readers remain embedded in this conclusion, standing as testimony both to the power of disciplinarity to isolate cognition and to our stuttering attempts to produce noise riots that bridge our coerced aloneness.

Act 1: An Experiment in Thinking Performatively

Scene: Five girls in different rooms in front of a computer screen. In each room there is loud background noise—a television blaring, a child demanding to be picked up, a wife making beats in another room, a roofer hammering, skin itching. Five voices repeat the following line over and over. They are not in sync, and it is difficult to make out what they are saying.

Look at us, the daughters of Ntozake Shange's colored girls.

(One voice starts to separate from the chorus)

Girl in Red (*lying on the floor as her back hurts*): My mother, a behavioral psychologist, thought I was retarded, as I didn't meet any of the developmental benchmarks. Then autistic. Then, as diagnostic categories shifted, gifted and on the autistic spectrum. Then difficult. Then a pain in the ass. "Why don't you write something that people can understand? You don't have to make things so complicated all the time."

GIRL IN ORANGE (*lifting child onto her hip as she apologizes profusely*): I have two deadlines coming up, and I've found that these days, it's best for me to focus on one project at a time. . . . For my mental health, I'll need to take a real break from work. . . . With all that I am managing, I . . . can't take on the pressure you're under.

GIRL IN YELLOW (*as she recovers from surgery*): How's my godbaby doing? Girl, my calves are screaming at me cuz for some reason we went on a damn six-mile walk. I just don't have anything left in me after this year to write anything but a poem about thinking creatively:

> Like catching lightning in a bottle
> Sometimes I capture you on a Post-it
> Sometimes I wake up and write it all down
> But when I read it back, I hear you whisper, "Is that what you thought I said?"
> Thought
> I don't do it right
> I don't do it fast
> And when I do it the way they say I should
> It feels like trying to hold sand in my hands
> Slipping through my fingers
> So instead, I dance
> And you show up to sway to the beat.

GIRL IN GREEN (*as she moves to another city*): I don't have time, but some of my most productive thinking and working out my own tributaries of thought have emerged from misreadings. I laugh at all of the ways that I have been confused by Spillers and Da Silva as of late. A good "fuck it, I don't get it, I think this is it, and I will go with it for now" is a helpful surrender. Surrender to the murky and uncertain. Ain't nothing gospel. So I allow my thoughts to be available to revision.

GIRL IN PURPLE: Chanda.[1] No response. As seen on Zoom. Elegant fingers and even more elegant writing. The crisp edges of mathematical thinking softened by bright eyes and cosmos imaginings.

We are all our ancestors' deepest fears come to life, a chorus of riot girls, pained and vivid, vibrating as we attempt and sometimes fail to produce embodied and environmentally responsive cripistemologies.

Using similar vocabulary to Chen, Katherine McKittrick in *Dear Science* recalls growing weary under the weight of our current self-referential systems of knowledge "that profit[] from recursive normalization" (43). She writes, "Disciplines are coded and presented as disconnected from experiential knowledge; experiential knowledge is an expression of data. . . . Disciplines stack and bifurcate seemingly disconnected categories and geographies; disciplines differentiate, split, and create fictive distances between us. Discipline is empire" (36). Discipline, as a function of empire, is therefore also a continually reinscribed neurotypicality. Or as Therí A. Pickens in *Black Madness: Mad Blackness* puts it, the "professoriate *hinges* on our ability to pass as sane, or rather the right type of sane" (15; emphasis added). What happens if, using diverse black creative strategies or what Chen calls a "decolonizing cripistemology" ("Brain Fog" 182), we reconsider not just what knowledge is but also how we organize and produce it?

A decolonizing cripistemology insists that we "unhinge" ourselves (McKittrick, *Dear Science* 16). To become unhinged, according to *Miriam-Webster's Dictionary*, is to become "highly disturbed, unstable, distraught." It is a process of disorientation in which connected parts are no longer stable or fixed but instead thrown into disorder. Even though to be unhinged can mean literal separation (train cars separated from one another), it is a word marked by relationality (even when separate, the train cars bear the trace of their conjoinment). Rather than learning requiring processes of orientation, of organizing knowledge into genealogical, progressive staircases such that "the demonstrated knowledge of Jurgen Habermas' texts requires the refusal of W. E. B. Du Bois and can in no way imagine—even in refusal—Ida B. Wells" (McKittrick, *Dear Science* 36), perhaps to become unhinged is to claim the madness of blackness as our own. Or as La Marr Bruce puts it, if "reason is the benefactor of white supremacy . . . and patron of patriarchal dominion, a black . . . woman might fare better going insane instead" (305).[2] This is the sanity of becoming unhinged, unfixed, of veering off the narrow constraints of disciplined, imperial epistemes into fraught, contradictory, and fragile black space.

Kafui Attoh, when confronted with the rights claims to a city of various populations such as the homeless or bus riders, insists on what he calls "*strategically* fuzzy" navigation of these claims (678). The differences between various rights claims to a city "shape not only the nature of political conflict, but also the kind . . . of cities that are created" (Staeheli and Mitchell 106). Attoh's use of "strategic fuzziness" suggests at certain moments in his argument a more "capacious" understanding of the rights to a city (678). At other times, the fuzziness describes a certain kind of an "incoherence" of thought around rights (679). In other words, his strategic fuzziness allows for disparate narratives and claims of rights to the city to exist alongside each other without resolution. As a *capacious incoherence*, Attoh's "strategic fuzziness" renegotiates meaning through a juxtaposing of different "registers of intelligibility" that allows a black sense of place to flicker between various meanings (Adeyemi 550). A black sense of space thus is palimpsestic, outlines bleeding through one another. This strategic fuzziness is not unlike what Chen describes as "brain fog," a practice of undisciplined cognition, replete with detours, undercurrents, haunted spaces, and slow drifts. Brain fog, she argues, enables not only haptic, embodied knowledge production but also the survival of the unhinged thinker and the collaborative spaces it creates.

Thinking and writing is not the product of an isolated individual brain whose firing synapses snappily deduce, synthesize, identify, and retrieve. Rather than corralling knowledge and producing individual products attributed only to us as single brains, what opportunities does it afford us to imagine a cripistemology that is affective, embodied, and emergent in the interactions of collaborators? Can we value "seriously twisted ways of knowing" (McRuer) that escape like water through my fingers only to fall like sugar into your bowl? Can you hold my breath? Is there value in cripistemologies that are not-quite-human, not sharp but fuzzy and blurred, not straight but crooked, not able but crippled? Cripistemology insists that cognition cannot be collapsed into "unit[s] of analysis" that are part of an abstract "symbol system . . . protected from the world somewhere far below the skin" (Hutchins 289). Instead, thinking is collectively embodied in affective, cultural performative rehearsals of knowing. Put simply, we think with our entire bodies, which are always relational. As Kara Keeling writes in *Queer Times, Black Futures*, thinking does not mean a retreat into a "dimensionless place in which the idea of thought alone persists" (15). Instead, thinking moves through the work of other scholars, other worlds, other cosmologies; it "recruit[s] matter(s) that perhaps have not participated in previous knowledge projects, or that have not been recognizable as ways of knowing" (15).

Anting

I would like to apologize to ants everywhere, as rather than recognizing what Zakiyyah Jackson calls the "biopolitical entanglement of discourses on animals, environment, and African diasporic peoples" (*Becoming Human* 15), neuroscientists have utilized ants and ant movement as a rudimentary template for a putatively more sophisticated template of (liberal) human cognition. The intricate navigation of ants across sand has provided neuroscientists with a way of thinking about "human" cognition, first developed in Herbert Simon's *The Sciences of the Artificial*. Simon, in an anthropocentric dismissal of the ant's seeming intelligence, writes that the "apparent complexity of its behavior over time is largely a reflection of the complexity of the environment in which it finds itself" (64). Mapping the ant's behavior onto human cognition, Simon argues that human cognition, distinguished from the ant by the increased amount and complexity of knowledge, similarly reflects its environment. A person is only as intelligent as their immediate environment, and this intelligence is located in the brain.

Edwin Hutchins in *Cognition in the Wild* critiques the past thirty years of cognitive science, pointing out that a refusal to look past the "disembodied cognition [of singular entities] . . . has created systematic distortions in our understandings of the nature of cognition" (132). He insists not only on a history of cognitive movement but also on studying a collective of ants over a longer period of time as they wander across the beach. He shifts the loci of cognition from individual ants to communities. The beach becomes a historical cultural environment, created by generations of ants as they comb the beach looking for food sources—moving sand, leaving behind chemical trails, taking wrong turns, creating well-worn ant paths. Hutchins concludes that after we have watched this community, following a single ant that now moves more efficiently across the sand might lead us to conclude that this is a smart ant. "No," he insists, "generations of ants have left their marks on the beach, and now a dumb ant has been made to appear smart through its simple interaction with the residua of the history of its ancestor's actions" (169). I am not convinced about the dumbness or smartness of the ant or even about the logic behind creating binary categories of intelligence in the first place. But I am struck by the image of the ant interacting in tandem with its fellow ants, with the ancestral residua that makes up their environs, with what Édouard Glissant calls "an accumulation of sediments" (33). Cognition and ancestral (epistemic) movement are inseparable—ants only know what they know because of each other and the lingering ancestral presence that saturates the landscape. This is what Hutchins calls "an ecology of thinking in which human cognition interacts with an environment rich in organizing resources" (viv). Furthermore, bodies remember what previous bodies learned. They rehearse choreography over and over until the body moves *not without thinking* but using a conjoined cognition that saturates cell, skin, exoskeleton, and space.

It might seem obvious, but perhaps it bears repeating: how we know is just as important as what we know. The ants live in the shadow of the neuroscientist. His alien presence gradually becomes incorporated into their daily routines; they navigate the shape of his glass, the smell of his breath. This is an example of what Kriti Sharma calls "contingentism," in which "one's existence is dependent on other contingently existing things" (15). The ants do not have an inherent existence that interacts with the existence of other ants and things. Instead, recognizing "the full interdependence of perceivers and perceived phenomena" (Sharma 17), between ants and the scientists following them across the sand, between this ant and the ones that came before, as well as the ones that come after, allows us to reconsider cognition as fundamentally interactive, dependent, and queer. Or as Keeling puts it, this kind of thinking, forged from bodies situated in historical context, demands "a mobile, fugitive perception of the interconnectedness of all things, which does not insist upon a universal system of commensuration, but instead allows for every thing's right to opacity" (196).

Underlying the ant parable is an assumption that the "smartest" way to progress from point A to point B is the most direct. Meandering, wandering, a "wrong" turn provide the scientist with evidence of inefficient cognition, with an inability for the self-directed, self-motivated cognition/movement that characterizes the ideal Enlightenment subject. Glissant in *Poetics of Relation* writes about three stages of movement in his formulation of a poetics of relation. The first two stages are arrow-like trajectories, from center to periphery and then from periphery to center. In the third stage, arrows curve, dismantling the notion of center and periphery and refusing journeying from end point to beginning point, origin to telos. "The time came, then, in which Relation was no longer a prophecy made by a series of trajectories, itineraries that followed or thwarted one another. By itself and in itself Relation exploded like a network inscribed within the sufficient totality of the world" (Glissant 29). Consider the lost ant, the one that doesn't make her way back, the one who keeps turning to the right instead of left. Her errancy, traditionally dismissed as a lack of intelligence, thus models an important mode of cosmic imagination that is part of cripistemology. Cripistemology, with its embodied cognition that can seem errant, illegible, and seemingly meaningless, offers us radical possibilities for new types of conjoined cognition and movement. In these wanderings, as Sarah Cervenak states, "the world-making potential of spirit, the erotic, desire, and the private, simultaneously disrupts illusions of bodily readability and discursive availability at the heart of hegemonically sanctioned, post-Enlightenment constructions of black . . . subjectivity" (13). We are obviously not talking only about ants anymore.

This kind of cripistemology refutes the notion of progressive linear time. Departing from normative time demonstrates what Michelle Wright calls "epiphenomenal time," "a time frame in which return is a matter of not simply backtracking along the progress narrative but recognizing that one is manifesting the past in the present moment" (74). Epiphenomenal time "empower[s] the exploration of a spacetime *horizontally* . . . because instead of simply interpellating the plot . . . through the eyes of one character alone, the views and experiences of many others are presented as all equally valid, . . . render[ing] the moment under interpellation as multivalent with no one truth that dominates" (42). Time opens up, it caves in, it dives, and it stutters.

The notion of "epiphenomenal time" is what I describe in the introduction as "stuttering time" or what disability scholars have called "crip time."[3] Alison Kafer describes "crip time" as "a challenge to normative and normalizing expectations of pace and scheduling. Rather than bending disabled bodies and minds to meet the clock, crip time bends the clock to meeting disabled bodies and minds" (27). Bending the clock is necessary to prevent the "endless deferral" of promises of justice or a cure through a future that never arrives. Cervenak reminds us that "people move in ways that are invisible, along the grooves of their own mind, in the motion of a rambling tongue, outside the range of an administrative and purportedly enlightened gaze" (6). As Christopher-Rasheem McMillan holds his recently injured muscles tightly during a workshop at the Black Performance Theory Colloquium, he emulates a ticking clock. Head moving from twelve to one to shoulder in staccato, he tells the audience, "I was not late for the bus. The bus left me." McMillan's insistence becomes more urgent as the performance progresses. He bends the clock to fit his embodied way of thinking. His pain, the memories of those dancers and spirits that came before him, and the spacetime he occupies rupture normative time. McMillan is at the right space at the right time; the bus wasn't.

What is it for us to be in crip time, to write and think together, to imagine blackness as the desirable ground of fecund possibility that folds in the sedimented residue of violent past deaths? What does it mean to be in and of a bodied existence in a world of networked communicators consolidating power in both fictitious modalities, like the twenty-first-century tech dystopias of torrented bit markets, and hyperreal excavations of earth matter at the scale of biomes? Let us imagine a sudden gust of wind over the terranean canvas of sedimentary accumulations that blows salt and sand into our eyes, redirecting two or three wayward ants into uncharted but not unimagined galactic space. This is aspirational travel, a speculative quest for queer ghostly insights in which noisy, differentially embodied rioters with neurocacophonous cognition rework linear spacetime.

Diagnosing the *Matilda*

In order to move toward a riotous, unhinged way of thinking, I would like to turn briefly to *An Unkindness of Ghosts* by Rivers Solomon, one of the few African diasporic speculative novels whose central character is marked as neuroatypical.[4] Using the way the novel theorizes embodied thinking, differential embodiment, and movement, a quick journey through space might help us better understand how to construct a conjoined cripistemology. *An Unkindness* takes place on board the *Matilda*, a spaceship of former Earth inhabitants traveling for almost three centuries, whose organization resembles that of a plantation. Dark-skinned people known as Tarlanders inhabit the neglected and crowded lower decks and serve as the primary source of (agricultural) labor, while their lighter-skinned counterparts live in luxury on the upper decks. An entire disciplinary system of guards, overseers, cameras, and legal statutes makes passage between the decks almost impossible, trapping large numbers on the lower decks, where conditions deteriorate as timespace passes and labor requirements become more stringent. Each lower deck develops its own sociality with dialect/language differences, varied conventions around gender, and disparate access to technological and medical information. A despotic but ailing Sovereign rules the ship with the help of the Surgeon Theo Smith, a figure who melds the spiritual and medical to wield considerable power on board the ship. This is a radically queer ship whose decks and corridors suggest the noisiness of black radical thinking.

The *Matilda* functions as a messy analogy for the afterlife of slavery writ large. It centers a form of plantation slavery to think through the way power and subjugation change shape to fill the contours of various spaces and times even while keeping intact hierarchies of fungibility and the human. Illustrated is what Kathryn Yusoff calls the "geologic determinism established in genocide and the master-slave relation, . . . where the geologic praxis of extraction that required both slavery . . . and its continuance as a mode of labor and psychic extraction of pleasure and sadism . . . codified Blackness in proximity to the qualities and properties of the inhuman" (57). The novel forces us to see again, as if for the first time, black men and women working in the fields and the mines, restricted to certain decks, deprived of the very materials for survival that their labor enables upper deckers to enjoy. This is a world where a painful disposability and interchangeability are inscribed on racialized bodies day in and day out. What do we make of a child's foot being amputated due to frostbite while upper deckers swim in heated pools? How does one live with the knowledge of Giselle's inherent vulnerability, as guards frequently rape her and then send her back to work? How do we watch women ensure the smooth running of Baby Sun even as they are poisoned for the "greater good"?

But the *Matilda* is not merely an homage to the untenability of anti-black life. It is also a technological beacon, an anguished howling into the darkness of space about the necessity of cacophonous ways of imagining other worlds. This call to imagine new worlds is wrapped around the novel's central narrative conceit: there is something wrong with the *Matilda* and its power source. The *Matilda* is gradually slowing down and veering off course; the ship is both directionless as it heads for an unknown "home" and going in the wrong direction as it returns to the home it left behind. Its trajectory, like Glissant's third stage, is curved: the ship uses the relative immobility of planet after planet to gather momentum—a swimmer kicking off the pool wall to shoot through water. The *Matilda* as a system of racialized and gendered exploitation is fundamentally broken, but it is not the everyday suffering of lower deckers that brings this permanent crisis to the fore. Instead, it is the inability of the ship to maintain the illusion of a progressive forward trajectory and the vulnerability and death of the Sovereign, who is supposed to be immune to the violence of exploitative capital, that exposes the failure of the *Matilda* as a "new" world. As Yusoff writes, "a sudden concern with the exposures of environmental harm to white liberal communities . . . [occurs] in the wake of histories in which these harms have been knowingly exported to black and brown communities under the rubric of civilization, progress, modernization, and capitalism" (xiii).

The novel begins with Aster attempting to "fix" the ship. To do so, she must "diagnose" the mysterious illness that eventually leads to the Sovereign's death as well as understand her mother's apparent suicide by deciphering a series of notebooks that she left behind. Central, then, to the novel are diagnostic systems as objects of analysis, in and of themselves. As Annemarie Goldstein Jutel reminds us, "Diagnoses do not exist ontologically. They are concepts that bind the biological, technological, the social, the political, and the lived" (13). Thus, despite certain factors being empirically observed and clinically reasoned, the grouping of various symptoms into one illness reveals diagnosis to be a classification or framing device that establishes the authority not only of particular ways of organizing information but also of the organizer themselves.

In other words, people have to agree not only to grouping a certain set of similar symptoms together but also with the way to recognize similarity and with what grouping together these putatively similar symptoms means. Peter Kinderman writes, "It is entirely possible to make reliable diagnoses of entirely invalid diagnoses—the mere fact that there is agreement between diagnosticians is no guarantee that the diagnoses about which they agree actually correspond to meaningful clusters of symptoms. . . . We have seen many potentially reliable but nevertheless invalid 'diagnoses' in the past" (155). Samuel Cartwright's infamous diagnosis of "drapetomania," the disease that caused slaves to run away, or the *Diagnostic and Statistical Manual*'s classification of homosexuality as a mental illness until 1973 are cases in point.

Critics continually "diagnose" Aster as neuroatypical. Thomas Wagner, for example, in a review of the novel states, "Aster is intellectually gifted, intersex, and, to put it mildly, *not neurotypical.* Nonverbal until eight years old, she doesn't grasp emotional cues very well but understands human connection in a detached way. She makes to-do lists that include reminders of normal stuff, like eating. She excels at botany, a science she more or less taught herself, and prefers the company of her plants in her botanarium to most people" (emphasis added). Similarly, M. Milks writes that "Aster's character is [Solomon's] real masterwork. Aster is black, intersex, genderqueer, neuroatypical, and multilingual: righteous, bold, tender, abrupt, stubborn as hell. Through Aster's worldview, Solomon centers blackness alongside gender-variance and neuroatypicality, and they do so deftly, through characterization that eschews familiar identity categories." Aster's "neuroatypicality," diagnosed by many readers as autism, foregrounds the timespace of cognition. The ease with which readers, including my students, diagnose Aster as suffering from autism spectrum disorder (ASD), even though the word "autism" never appears in the text, speaks volumes about how certain behaviors are explained by labels that are then in turn evidence of that behavior.[5] As Kinderman develops, "It is presumed that people are behaving as they are, or experiencing unusual perceptions, because of the illness. But, in the absence of valid underlying pathological processes, this argument is logically circular—the behaviour is explained by a label which consists of nothing more than a shorthand for that behaviour" (155). This commonsensical misrecognition of Aster as autistic prevails despite the fact that the cluster of symptoms that is autism has changed considerably from what Berend Verhoeff describes as "a rare disorder characterized by a pervasive lack of responsiveness and gross deficits in language development" to "first and foremost a disorder of sociality" (452).[6] Despite these changes, autism, like other systems of classification, as Jutel reminds us, "bears the indelible imprint of its antecedents" (97). In other words, the diagnosis carries with it the continued ableism of previous periods, the unethical research practices, the sexism that temporarily linked autism to inadequate mothering, the racism that modeled social norms on Western middle-class modes of interaction, and the deep insistence on there being only one way of being and thinking in the world.

Solomon continues their critique of traditional diagnostic thinking through their discussion of gender binaries. Tarlanders do not always present as male or female due to a broad range of hormone levels. Reviled as having "demon forms" that do not "conform to the Holy Order set forth by the Heavens," Tarlanders have been diagnosed with "hereditary suprarenal dysregula" by upper-deck doctors. The diagnosis then justifies the violent reanimation of the Tarlanders' "defective" bodies through electric currents into "perfect, obedient workers" (Solomon 19–20). First, Tarlanders have to be seen as similar to one another and dissimilar to the occupants of the upper decks. The expression of gender as a binary has to be valued in order for Tarlanders' gender expressions to be pathologized, which in turn further reinforces the social hierarchy that marginalizes them. Put another way, diagnoses are historical systems of classification that establish social structures of power and powerlessness.

An Unkindness of Ghosts, even as it ontologically unpacks categories of diagnosis, refuses to contrast neuroatypicality with "normal" ways of thinking. Instead, it dismantles categories of normal/mentally healthy by insisting that no single form of embodied cognition is, in and of itself, saner or more deficient than any other. Andrea Nicki writes,

> Just as we need to discard a paradigm of humanity as young and healthy against which physically disabled people will be seen as lacking, . . . we need to overcome a paradigm of humanity as mentally healthy so that those with mental illnesses will not be judged deficient. Further . . . we need to reject a paradigm of humanity as rigidly self-controlled, moderate, dispassionate, pleasant, and conformist, with strict adherence to

> norms of one's gender. . . . People suffering from mental illness may be irrational, disordered, cognitively impaired, or frightening, but no more so that those not suffering from mental illness. (82, 87)

The novel goes a step further by arguing that various forms of cognition must work noisily, all at once, in order for a community of ants and other creatures to journey across the stars. Aster's literalism, her nonbinary gender, her status as an "insiwa" (her supposed intellectual disability) palimpsestically overlay her best friend Giselle's pained and volatile responses to repeated trauma (her psychiatric disability), which in turn add noisily to the Surgeon's intellectual "giftedness."[7] When Aster confronts Giselle about her "psychotic" behavior—the setting of fire to her nightgown and the cupping of the burning fabric in her hands, Giselle replies, "You think something's wrong with me. With my mind. . . . But I'm the one who understood what your meema was trying to say. I'm the one who gets her" (Solomon 63). It is Giselle's "psychosis" (63) that enables her to read Lune's notebooks and to understand the codes in which it has been written. She understands, unlike Aster, that the drawing of a dissected fish in Lune's notebooks is actually a representation of the *Matilda*'s power grid (62). While Aster has been unable to read the code for years, repeatedly running into cognitive roadblocks, her dead ends alongside the information that Giselle has deciphered enable her to approach an understanding of her mother's death. Aster makes the correlation between electric blackouts suggested by the drawing of the dissected fish and the onset of Sovereign Nicolaeus's and Lune's illness. To fully expound on this correlation, she consults several other people on board the ship, some of whom work to prevent her from figuring out the "truth." There are numerous impasses, as well as considerable friction and noise, that emerge from these various types of thinking being sounded at once. Giselle's "voices and visions" in which she cuts and burns her body, Aster's nightmares, episodes of mutism and bouts of the "endless raving" (63), the Surgeon's self-flagellation and constant pain—these are the unreconcilable effects of conjoined thinking. To describe this cognitive noise, I would like to deploy the neologism *neurocacophony* (and not "neuroatypicality" or "cognitive disability") as a capaciously incoherent category that includes what has traditionally been called "intellectual disability," "developmental disability," and "psychiatric disability."[8] It is neurocacophony, the unhinging din of a noise riot, I would argue, that allows for multiple cognitive pathways that are not always productive but that are essential to black sociality.

In Audre Lorde's classic essay "The Uses of Anger," she writes, "Women of Color in America have grown up within a symphony of anguish at being silenced, at being unchosen, at knowing that when we survive, it is in spite of a whole world out there that takes for granted our lack of humanness, that hates our very existence, outside of its service. And I say 'symphony' rather than 'cacophony' because we have had to learn to orchestrate those furies so that they do not tear us apart" (282). This fear of becoming unhinged by the pressure of antiblack violence causes Lorde to insist on the symphony as a mode of cognition. Lorde is referring less to symphony here as an extended musical composition in Western classical music and more to an "agreement or concord of sound" (*OED*), something harmonious emerging from multiple, different noises. The alternative to this agreement of sound, Lorde writes, can break and unhinge us, resulting in our demise, in the failure of our anger to become the sharp-honed tool that enables our survival. But what if we value our coming together and falling apart in ways that are discordant, abrasive, and difficult to listen to?[9] What if instead of symphony, the eardrum-splitting noise riot that exceeds meaning can help constitute an embodied black praxis of "unhinging"? What if we as black women need to break apart, shatter under the weight of our anger and anguish, fall silent, and go "crazy" before becoming something new? *An Unkindness* demonstrates neurocacophony as multiple, overlapping modes of thinking that never form a concordance but that lead various characters in the novel to be unhinged or torn apart, sometimes literally. McKittrick writes in *Dear Science*, "Black method is precise, detailed, coded, long, and forever. The practice of bringing together multiple texts, stories, songs, and places involves the difficult work of thinking and learning across many sites, and thus coming to know, generously, varying and shifting worlds and ideas" (6).

The novel begins with an amputation and a friendly argument between Flick, whose leg is about to be amputated, and Aster, about to perform the surgery. The two people think differently, and all of their difference does not resolve into shared symphonic meaning. Rather, there are moments of absolute opacity, when the neural pathways of one completely bypass the other. But it is in this ensuing neurocacophony that intimacy across difference can emerge.

Act 2: Another Experiment in Thinking Performatively

Scene: Imagine a small, dark room with a slanted ceiling. It is cold. There is a door at the back of the stage through which characters enter and exist. The audience hears them arguing before the lights come on. The stage is dimly lit so that the characters' shadows loom large. Aster stands over Flick, whose foot lies propped up on two trunks. Beside them on the floor is a star jar that sends out weak tendrils of light. Aster rubs her hands together, trying to warm them. The smell of Flick's rotting foot permeates the air.

FLICK: It's like a star, see? [*Flick grabs and shakes the lantern next to them, setting off its chemical show*]

ASTER (*looking at Flick, the jar, and then Flick again*): I'm afraid I don't.

FLICK (*exasperated*): A star's a bunch of little things coming together to make light, yeah? Chemicals and all that. And our little special jar here is a bunch of little things coming together to make light too. Also chemicals. . . . So they the same. Chemicals plus more chemicals makes magic. [*Flick glares stubbornly at Aster*]

ASTER (*unable to modulate the harshness of her response, as she is tired*): Your model lacks specificity and is therefore useless. . . . According to such a theory, a suitcase would be no different than a bomb. Sugars and synthase react to make the cotton of the luggage. Oxygen oxidizes gunpower to make an explosion. *Chemicals plus more chemicals makes magic* describes both scenarios really well, but, of course, we know a suitcase is nothing like a bomb . . . [*Aster searches for an analogy as she gently palpates Flick's calf. Flick's mother comes through the door holding a basin. They ignore her*] You're arguing that a person is identical to a dog because they've both got bones and blood.

FLICK (*hands clenched into fists*): Guards be calling Tarlanders dogs all the time.

[*Aster, startled by the statement, lets go of Flick's leg, straightens her body, and blinks. Her breath glides like exorcised ghosts.*]

End Scene (10–11)

Here is another example of neurocacophony, the irreconcilable interplay between multiple forms of cognition. Flick and Aster's embodied thought resembles the many different paths that the ants take across the beach, paths that are informed by the ants foraging for food before them and the changing material environment. Flick's thinking demonstrates how many of us have been taught to create categories or filing systems that group similar objects and instructions together so that we can respond to them in the same way when we encounter them in the future. Take a dog, for example. It has four legs and fur; it barks and wags its tail. When we encounter a dog or a picture of a dog, even if it has no tail or curly hair instead of fur, we assume that we know how to react based on the category of dog that we have already created. This category of dog is informed by the categories formed by the people around us—a black community's fear of police dogs shapes the category of dog for its members. If we are afraid of dogs and our cognitive map includes vicious teeth, for instance, our body responds to the category of dog by tensing or getting ready for flight. Or if our notion of a dog is one of cute, cuddly pet, our bodies melt, and pleasurable endorphins flood our body. Flick demonstrates this kind of synthesized thinking. The light of the jar resembles the light of stars—a connection made by Flick crucially because it was *already made* by their community, which named the jar a "star jar." While such communal thinking is childlike in its insistence on the magic of star light captured in a jar, it is also strategically poetic; in order to counter the bleakness, poverty, and deprivation of the inhabitants' deck, they find magic in little things. Often dismissed as unscientific or childlike, theirs is a devastatingly appropriate response to social conditions of oppression and violence.

Aster's insistence on specificity makes groupings difficult. A star is an astronomical object that emits light due to the thermonuclear fusion in its core; it has nothing in common with the star jar. She wields language precisely, and "the precisionist in her hated oral history and memory and that flimsy, haphazard way people spoke about the past. . . . They offered summary and conclusion where there were none, by grouping data that should not necessarily be grouped" (Solomon 49). Aster tells us that for the twenty thousand lower deckers, they are at least ten thousand different ways of living and thinking (16). Aster doesn't automatically group diverse bodies into simplified gender categories. She regrets calling Flick "she," as such a generalization fails to account for Flick's location, their social histories, and the different meanings that can be assigned to physical characteristics. Aster "was used to the style of her own deck where all children were referred to with feminine pronouns. Here, it was *they*" (10). Aster's neurophysiological ability thus enables her to enact a radical politics of gender that is gestured toward by Hortense Spillers when she writes, "At a time when current critical discourses appear to compel us more and more decidedly towards gender 'undecidability,' it might appear reactionary . . . to insist on the integrity of female/male gender" (66).

Solomon's discussion of Aster's cognitive specificity and her difficulty generalizing encapsulate many of the dilemmas around diagnosis as a classificatory system that can reproduce traditional power dynamics. Early in the novel, the Surgeon takes Aster to see a blond upper-deck girl whose nose wouldn't stop bleeding and who has bruises everywhere. Aster diagnoses her immediately as suffering from hemophilia, with the "bruises . . . the logical result of the life of play and pleasure allowed upper deck children" (Solomon 49). Aster's dislike of the little girl due to her privilege and the girl's racist dismissal of Aster as one of those lower deckers who smells all contribute to Aster connecting the nosebleed and bruises into a single diagnostic classificatory system. But as Aster learns, the girl's bruises were a result of abuse, and the nosebleed the result of hereditary disease. Aster extrapolates the lessons she learns from her incorrect diagnosis to her mother's journals, concluding that with "history . . . people often settled for the most obvious answer. Aster wondered if that was what she'd done with her mother's journals: written Lune off as mad instead of investigating obvious clues. Or maybe . . . any random assortment of dots could be connected into a picture, whether there was an actual picture or not" (50). Aster must move across the ways she thinks into other realms if she wants to find her mother and solve the mystery of the ship's power outages. Her thinking cannot remain singular.

Doing research aboard a naval ship, Hutchins writes that a "visitor quickly learns to search out alternative pathways, because corridors are frequently closed for cleaning or maintenance" (18). In other words, knowing the correct way to navigate the ship, the most efficient way to get from point A to point B, is not sufficient to move about the ship successfully. Instead, one must develop palimpsestic ways of moving through space, multiple "alternate pathways" that arise from cumulative engagements with others who navigate the ship, embodied choreographic rememberings of the ship and the ever-changing materiality of the environment. Instead of pathologizing or privileging any one type of thinking, the novel insists on the generative possibilities of neurocacophony by showing how the time and space of the ship, with its various decks, require different kinds of embodied cognition. Returning to Sharma's theorization of contingentism, all forms of cognition on board the ship are necessary to another's creation. Similarly, *An Unkindness* points us toward the necessity of different ways of thinking, no matter how seemingly unproductive or deviant, to perform a generative black sociality.

As Aster realizes that she must include various types of cognition if she wants to solve the mystery of her mother, she is "always memorizing new ways of being with people" (Solomon 12). She places her literalism alongside various other forms of cognition that she learns from the people around her. The novel shows her experimenting with different kinds of thinking, shows her stacking and jumbling various cognitive approaches palimpsestically to arrive not at the truth but at a version of redress that allows her to love, mourn, and grow. Thus, the last paragraph of the novel is crucial. It sees Aster feeling "sentimental, . . . superstitious" (349). She is too dehydrated to make tears, but she wants to cry. She would resurrect Giselle with magic tears, but she knows that the water would only "wet Giselle's dead, indifferent face, then evaporate" (349). She hopes to whisper "sorry" into Giselle's or perhaps her mother's ear, knowing both that the dead animate the living and that they can no longer hear. A creature of the stars, she anchors herself in soft, damp earth. She buries herself alongside her mother's bones and Giselle's corpse in order to live. This is a neurocacophony of literalism and magic, poetry and geology, science and stardust, what Chanda Prescod-Weinstein calls "black feminist physics at the End of the World" (253). Memory, retellings, symbolic codes, the short circuits of trauma all become essential to Aster's survival as embodied cognitive pathways that in their strategic fuzziness help her move closer to new world imaginings and multiple, conjoined cripistemologies of "*smells, stains, scars. . . . Everything is a clue. It wants you to know its story. Ancestors are everywhere if you are looking*" (Solomon 59).

The interaction between Flick and Aster not only theorizes different neural pathways but also represents the characters' resistance to capital's language of equivalency. The exchange between Aster, Flick, and Flick's mother represents an instance of the possibility of exchange that exists outside of capital. Flick's great Meema tells us, "Materials are meaningless without knowledge" (Solomon 21). Here is an informal system of barter and gifts through which Aster receives a warm cloak, not only for performing the operation without expectation of pay but also for her teaching the women on the deck how to make a heat lamp. Thus, relationality becomes a barter of energy resources in a gift economy, an autonomous politics of surviving the violence of this world that "proved a distraction against resolving the matter of the cold" (12). The interaction between the various women departs from what Yusoff describes as the neocolonial "grammar of materiality that privileges equivalents above relation" (50). Rather than our extracting knowledge from one another, neurocacophony privileges not the correct or most efficient answer but instead our conjoinment, which emphasizes alternate (neural) pathways.

Returning to the scene between Flick and Aster, both of their cognition falters at the same point: when confronted with the violent policing of the decks by the guards. "Guards be calling Tarlanders dogs all the time" (Solomon 11). Without resorting to hierarchies of humans over animals, Aster insists on the specificity of dog and human morphology, despite shared blood and bones, while Flick shows that dogs and some humans can easily be subsumed into one category. Flick's statement that Tarlanders are called dogs by the guards accomplishes several things: it exposes the limitations of Aster's insistence on rational specificity, and it reveals to Flick how too-general categorizations can be manipulated to perpetuate devastating violence on subjugated populations. This is not to say that the violence of the guards is irrational. On the contrary, it is a skillfully honed strategy that reduces the body of those who are marked as Other to a fleshy substrate, penetrable and always vulnerable. There might be various types of cognition, various ways that one can understand star light and magic and suitcases, but these cognitive pathways must maneuver around people with the power to police and enforce their ways of thinking. Thus, the belief in the valuelessness of Tarlanders suggested by comparing them to dogs (not as a species but as a signifier of something less than human) results in the power being cut to the lower deck, which leads to Flick's frostbite and the eventual amputation of their foot. *An Unkindness* thus insists that the embodied cognition of Aster, Giselle, and others like them is not evidence of mental disability but rather a valid, complex response to violent oppression. Such an insistence does not diminish or dismiss the tremendous amounts of pain and disorientation and social difficulty the characters face. *Sometimes in the face of violence that tears our bodies apart, we fall silent. We cannot write together.*

Thermodynamic and Astromatic Thinking

An Unkindness is divided into four parts, each ostensibly about a separate field of science: part 1, "Thermodynamics"; part 2, "Metallurgy"; part 3, "Phylogeny"; and part 4, "Astromatics." While these branches of science function metaphorically, the novel also incorporates various principles that are foundational to each branch of science. Science is therefore not just a metaphor but also a methodology. Part 1 thus posits the *Matilda* as an isolated thermodynamic system, detailing how large-scale, observable thermal energy is converted to and from other forms of energy. In isolated systems, entropy is constantly increasing. As entropy increases, events occur more sporadically and closer together. At the same time, this section is a social commentary on the distribution of resources, specifically thermal energy. *An Unkindness* begins with heat being cut off to the lower decks, which results in Flick's frostbite. This is as a result of energy inequality, such that the upper deckers heat their woods, lakes, and game fields, while the lower deckers huddle together to try to keep warm. This is relationality gone awry, a morbid theft of the life and limb of lower deckers to sustain the privilege of the wealthy elite. Part 2 on metallurgy deals with Aster's discovery of a mysterious metal that cannot be broken down into smaller parts and the mechanism used to separate metals, the centrifuge. Aster compares this mysterious metal, siluminium (Solomon 157), to "eidolon," the spirit image of a living or dead person or a ghostly look-alike of the human form: "This is the stuff ghosts are made of" (142). Part 3 thinks through questions of phylogeny as it concerns itself with questions of kinship genealogies. Rather than racist notions of evolutionary development, with its creation of various groups of organisms with genetic or anatomical similarities, the novel shows relationality to be constructed along vastly different, queer axes.

While one could read these various parts as a progression toward the undefined "astromatics" of the last section, I argue that this is cognition that noisily *accumulates* like environmental matter. In other words, rather than Aster attempting to use various fields of science to find the "truth" and then abandoning them for their limitations, all these ways of thinking come together to create astromatics, a neurocacophonous critique of disciplined knowledge that offers us something akin to a cripistemology. As such, astromatics is not relegated to the last section of the book but appears throughout as various fields of science bow under the weight of black fungibility and differential embodiment.

I would like to use the first part of the novel, titled "Thermodynamics," to illustrate how Solomon exposes the limits of science, pointing instead to the neurocacophonous astromatics as a new way of understanding the world. Growing out of the practical application of the steam engine, traditional thermodynamics, as Sebastian Deffner and Steve Campbell explain, can be seen as one of the most intuitive, easily defined, and "universal" fields of knowledge, with its five axioms commonly called the "laws of thermodynamics." Revolving around the notion of equilibrium and the transformations of systems from one state of equilibrium to another, thermodynamics is the perfect science with which to begin a section about heat distribution and growing changes such as increased power outages that disrupt the grotesque equilibrium of antiblack life on board the ship. The *Matilda* is a thermodynamic system and, as such, governed by its ordinal set of laws. Thermodynamic laws state that if two systems are in a state of equilibrium, then they are in equilibrium with each other. The increase of total energy in an idealized subsystem equals the increase in thermal energy plus the work done on the system. An addition of energy is necessary to transfer energy from a body at the lower temperature to a higher temperature; otherwise, heat flows from warm to cold bodies. The entropy of a pure crystal at absolute zero is zero.

The novel starts by illustrating, through the work of a fictional scientist, Frederick Hauser, the scientific "truth" that the transfer of heat from matter at a lower temperature to matter at a higher temperature requires energy. Hauser suggests reanimating the bodies of Tarlanders with an electric current so that their "spiritless cadavers" could continue to work to fuel the upper decks (Solomon 19). For him, the ship is a closed thermodynamic system in which black corpses generate the increased energy that allows the transfer of heat from cold to warm matter. The resulting "work" allows the ship to move forward. Hauser later "compromises," suggesting instead that body parts might work in lieu of entire corpses. The work accomplished via a harvesting of black beings appears to have been a macabre historical suggestion until one realizes that the novel begins in the present day with Flick's limb being amputated due to frostbite. Their limb represents the addition of energy to a closed system that allows the ship to maintain its equilibrium that is anything but equal. Heat, traditionally seen as a by-product of work in steam engines, for example, becomes central. Equilibrium means that the heated upper decks see no change in temperature, while the lower-deck inhabitants begin freezing to death. Thus, if we overlay metaphor and science, the (il)logic of race, with its alternate notions of time, insists that energy moves from cold matter to warm matter in a closed system of white oppression. Race, like rape, is always part of any scientific story (Prescod-Weinstein 199).

Working through Solomon's critique of thermodynamics and trying to figure out just what astromatics is, I eventually find myself staring at a copy of Deffner and Campbell's textbook on quantum thermodynamics in the college bookstore. The authors recommend that students take graduate statistical physics and quantum mechanics before enrolling in a class that uses their textbook (3). Their recommendations are the correct stairway to mastery, one step at a time. The colleague whom I call for help laughingly backs away, shaking her head at my hubris. I am stubborn, instead shaking the book between my jaws like a dog. Of course, I don't understand it, but my fingers trace the patterns of equation after equation, a kid's face pressed against the glass of a candy store. Like Aster staring at her mother's indecipherable notebooks written in a language she doesn't understand.

As I read through page after page of various materials on quantum thermodynamics, there appear to be many conflicting theoretical claims. It is the clashing of these multiple claims, their open-endedness, the way they unmake previous commonsensical notions so that the laws of thermodynamics, for example, "no longer perfectly predict the thermal behaviour of quantum systems" (Merali), that leads me to posit astromatics as a yet-to-be-defined quantum field of neurocacophonous possibilities. These possibilities are always anchored in the social: what we know, how we think, and who we are within social systems of inequity are inextricable.

Crystals, diamonds as quantum heat engines, hot "baths" that get hotter, and I am suddenly arrested by an image of a mug full of dark liquid—the physics of coffee. The quantum physicist Sandu Popescu and his colleagues at Bristol University insist that the laws of thermodynamics need reinventing if we take into account microscopic systems, context, time, and the subjective nature of thermodynamic laws in the first place, which divided energy reductively into useless heat and useful work (Wolchover, "Quantum"). Popescu and his colleagues demonstrate that energy can appear to move from cold objects to hot ones "because of the way information spreads between particles":

> According to quantum theory, the physical properties of particles are probabilistic; instead of being representable as 1 or 0, they can have some probability of being 1 and some probability of being 0 at the same time. When particles interact, they can also become entangled, joining together the probability distributions that describe both of their states. . . . (The present state of the universe preserves all information about the past.) Over time, however, as particles interact and become increasingly entangled, information about their individual states spreads and becomes shuffled and shared among more and more particles. . . . The arrow of increasing quantum entanglement underlies the expected rise in entropy—the *thermodynamic arrow of time*. (Wolchover, "Quantum")

If the present state of the universe preserves all information about the past, what we see on board the ship is a system of what can be described as entangled particles. Knowledge is now located in the correlations, not in individual particles. As the physicist Seth Lloyd argues about matter reaching a state of equilibrium, "What's really going on is things are becoming more correlated with each other. . . . The arrow of time is an arrow of increasing correlations" (Wolchover, "Time's Arrow"). Using the example of a cup of coffee, physicists postulate that over time the "black" coffee particles become entangled with the "blue" air particles of the room, creating "black/blue" entangled correlates that house information about the room, the coffee, and the cup. These entangled particles with their set of information "leak . . . out and become . . . smeared over the entire environment" (Popescu, qtd. in Wolchover, "New Physics"). While the cup of coffee might have reached equilibrium, the entire room continues to change under the impact of passed-on knowledge. Similarly, a group of physicists based in Barcelona using "baths" of particles discovered that the hot bath looked like it was getting hotter, while the cold bath got colder. Manabendra Nath Bera realized that this was not a violation of thermodynamics but instead a demonstration of the entanglement of particles in which the making and breaking of correlates stored and released energy (Merali).

Thus, we return to "crip time," which is a time of increasing correlation, not of a forward progression. The *Matilda*, after all, is boomeranging itself backward. Plantation systems of the past and present resonate with one another, atoms spinning in each other's embrace. Aster says repeatedly that she needs to chase down information that has "leaked" across the entire ship. It is entangled in Giselle's hair, Lune's notebooks, power outages, the poison leaking into the Sovereign's body that kills him and that links his death to her mother's. Heat moves from the shivering bodies of the lower deckers, from their icy corpses and frozen amputated limbs, to the warm upper deck. The result at the end of the novel is an uprising, a blistering conflagration as old correlates are broken, new ones are formed. The ship burns noisily.

Looking at strings of magnesium ions in a crystal, the researchers Tobias Schaetz and his colleagues discovered that such microscopic levels behave differently from larger systems. Whereas standard oscillations will die down as they interact with the surrounding atoms in the crystal, the coffee in my cup getting colder as it sits undrunk next to my computer, something strange happened when the ions cooled and stopped oscillating. After a few milliseconds, there was a sudden resurgence, and the ions began oscillating again. Schaetz explains that "rather than dissipating away entirely, the phonons [quantized vibrations in a lattice] rebounded at the edges of the crystal and returned, in phase, to their source ions, reinstating the original spin oscillations" (Merali).

This moment, a cessation of movement, a stillness that simulates death, is almost as if the universe is holding its breath. Wait. Reanimation. Neural pathways regenerating. Spinning. Flickering. Crawling. Falling. Breathing. The resistance of enlivened black bodies is "smeared" across the universe in what Chen calls "a cripistemological context of collective devising" ("Brain Fog" 178). This is the noise revolution of black sociality.

ACKNOWLEDGMENTS

The sea change has dumped me on this shore, more than a little bedraggled. But I am still moving, thanks to all the people who continue to share their precious breath with me. As always, my work is deeply informed by Barbara Christian, VèVè Clark, and Saidiya Hartman. VèVè's sudden, fierce choreographic movements as she insisted on a "deformation of mastery" and Barbara's generous laugh echo in my head as I write. I am driven both to follow in Saidiya's footsteps and to pave my own way. I do neither successfully, but the result is a love story that never ends.

The Black Performance Theory Workshop continues to guide me every step of the way. Tommy De Frantz, E. Patrick Johnson, Tavia Nyong'o, Jennifer DeVere Brody, Uri McMillan, Melissa Blanco Borelli (thanks for the COVID care package), and Fadeke Castor, as well as all the wonderful and talented artists/scholars I have been fortunate enough to meet over the years, have shaped both who I am and who I am becoming. Stephanie Batiste inspires me to think and play big, especially when I feel small. Jeffrey McCune always is right on time—he knows when the dark starts to encroach. Omi Osun Jones's kindness and deep spirituality radiate out around her, and I am grateful to be in her orbit. Eric Zinner and his assistant, Furqan Sayeed, at NYU Press have been enthusiastic, clear, and generous editors; I can't thank them enough. Also thank you to Andrew Katz, who copyedited the book. I promise I will never write the words "qtd. in" again.

My colleagues at UT-Austin have been incredibly welcoming and warm. Thank you to the handsome and charming Ted Gordon, who helped me with everything from contract negotiations to a lift during a snowstorm. Cherise Smith is someone with whom I can be myself, a rare gift. Lyndon Gill dazzles and feeds me. Neville Hoad, Lisa Thompson, Ashley Coleman-Taylor, and Xavier Livermon have all helped me understand what it feels like to be in a supportive environment. Minkah Makalani opened his home to us when we had no water, heat, or electricity. Pavithra Vasudevan, Tiffany Lethabo King, and Chamara Kwakye began cowriting chapter 6 with me. Their ghostly hands continue to shape my words. The Arthur M. Blank Center for Stuttering and Research (formerly the Michael and Tami Lang Stuttering Institute) was an incredible resource. Watching them teach my son and other people who stutter to claim the way they speak convinced me that I was on the right track with this book.

The best thing about moving to Texas has been meeting Alison Kafer. Her gentleness, coupled with a razor-sharp intelligence and a depth of knowledge about Disability Studies that I can only hope to emulate, has made her an incredible interlocuter. In addition, she has been the person with whom I drink coffee in empty parking lots. We will always walk/roll together alongside the railroad tracks when the train derails. She has modeled for me the true meaning of feminist care.

Not much has changed when it comes to my (queer) family. You all keep waiting for me at the shore and riverbank, no matter how close I get to drowning. Thanks to the Bhanas—Hemant, Angie, Kiri, Aiden, and Palvih—for more things than I can count. I am especially grateful for standby flights, visits during snowstorms, band concerts, Libby pictures, and Zoom birthday calls. Chamara, I only know that we begin and end the same circle. Patrick Walter continues to be the steady eye to my hurricane, the grain to my sand. Nathan Moore dug holes in the garden for my mother and is there for Drees and me at every turn. Her warmth and poetry fuel my soul. This book would never have been completed without Aleksandra Szaniawska. She hunted down obscure references, corrected mistakes, and constructed bibliographies from nonsensical fragments. She understands me and forgets to take me to the river. Sincere thanks to Jason Young, LaKisha Simmons, and the vivacious Layla Bell. Susan Cahn, Tandy Hamilton, and Dana and John Rigney keep me sane and show me what true friendship looks like in all its forms. You keep me breathing, though your pets are another story.

My father's love weathers every paragraph of this book—the edges of the pages curl in the damp sea air. I can never find the words to thank my mother, Kala Bhana, for her courage to live even after my father passed, for being the best example of what it means to survive even when people constantly underestimate and overlook you, and for her unrelenting love. Finally, this book is for my son, Idris—I have never heard me like I hear you.

NOTES

INTRODUCTION

1. Johanna Bruckner is a poet and performance artist whose work deals with ecologies of care and intimacy that expand traditional notions of the human body. In "How Will I Remember Your Embrace: Episode 2, *Phylum Lava*," she writes, "In a redistributed sensorium— / suggesting a dizzying sense of vivifying / potentiality."
2. As Kara Keeling writes in *Queer Times, Black Futures*, "Instead of reinforcing a political stance and rhetoric that insist upon recuperating the historical situation of Black women's boundarylessness into the logics of enclosure, ownership, and privatization, . . . [what is needed is a politics of] enfleshment . . . [that] demand[s] a society which is bound together through a shared stewardship of all matter" (155).
3. The video provides the perfect vehicle of Solange's stardom in its depiction of her as strikingly beautiful, her body as eminently capable with its choreographed set of gestures, her more experimental sensibilities different from her sister Beyoncé Knowles-Carter's popularism.
4. Porco's discussion on disability also needs to consider how disability and hip hop might reinforce certain perceptions of blackness. Run DMC's Darryl McDaniels's spasmodic dysphonia, caused by excessive drinking and smoking while on tour, rather than changing how we think about disability, might reinforce myths of black male excess and pleasure-seeking tendencies. Such a reinforcement rests on assumptions of what are legitimate or "positive" causes of disability. Thus, being injured by a drunk driver or a thief elicits a different array of responses than being injured by *being* the drunk driver or robber. It is always easier in the popular imaginary to imagine blackness as criminally culpable and therefore deserving of disability.
5. In the novel, "claypicken" refers to humans without mojo, those who are unable to communicate and participate in the spirit world. To use an analogy from another speculative world that is primarily rooted in the Western imaginative tradition, claypickens are similar to J. K. Rowlings's muggles.
6. Fleming writes that traditional time "has operated as a historical weapon of anti-black violence and a charged arena of necropolitical maneuver. . . . Time is a key variable in the 'racial calculus' and 'political arithmetic' that generate the afterlives of slavery" (587–88).

7. My choice of a word that is not part of my indigenous South African culture deliberately interrogates the idea of "native informant."
8. Chandler and Johnson rely on Carrie Sandahl's famous essay "The Tyranny of the Neutral" to develop their argument.
9. Touretteshero is a collaborative space founded by Jessica Thom and Matthew Pountney that creatively engages with Tourette's syndrome. Using humor, blog posts, and various other popular media such as illustrated comics, the site not only archives various "tics" or obsessional impulses but also stresses the creativity of people with Tourette's as they conquer the world, one tic at a time. See the Touretteshero website: www.touretteshero.com.
10. The disability scholar Nirmala Erevelles similarly argues that Deleuze and Guattari's "discursive flourish" with its dismissal of embodied hierarchical relations through the idea of the "'horizontal rhizomatic proliferation' . . . is rendered inadequate in the historical context of transnational capitalism, where bodies encounter each other often in violent collision such that captivity and mutilation are no longer metaphors, but instead inform a brutal materiality" (29, 28).
11. In many ways, this flickering can be seen as similar to what Zakiyyah Iman Jackson calls an "ontological plasticity," a kind of "coerced formlessness as a mode of domination and the *Unheimlich* existence that is its result" (*Becoming Human* 71). She writes that as a praxis, plasticity "seeks to define the essence of a black(ened) thing as infinitely mutable, in antiblack, often paradoxical, sexuating terms as a means of hierarchically delineating sex/gender, reproduction, and states of being more generally" (11). I find this useful, though my emphasis in the chapter lies in the *embodied movement* between states and how conjoined bodies, even as momentarily captured into certain forms, flicker between states, like candles next to open windows as they cast shadows and illuminate dark rooms. "Flickering" foregrounds not the blackened inert flesh so much as *how* that flesh moves into and out of categories. In addition, while I do not have the space here, it might be useful to parse the differences between plasticity and fungibility. As I elaborate in chapter 4, I remain attached to the concept of fungibility. Even as we think of the black body as a "vessel" of coerced formlessness, fungibility foregrounds the hierarchical relations of capital exploitation that evacuate/refill the black body with shifting meanings and desires to continue ontological systems of the human, and also to use those ontological systems to control and exploit black bodies within global regimes of colonialism and slavery.

CHAPTER 1. FALLING AND CRAWLING

1. Ideally, given that I focus on polio sufferers in Sierra Leone, I would be able to discuss creative performances in Sierra Leone. However, I was unable to find such performances. Ogunji's work in Nigeria allows me to continue the discussion, especially as the country has an even larger number of polio-disabled who support themselves through public performances of begging.

2. Not all squats are illegally occupied, as groups sometimes negotiate with the building's owner to occupy the space. Diana Szántó chooses to use the word "squat"' in her study of them in her brilliant book, to emphasize two things. The first is the terrible neglect that results in buildings that are more often than not unsafe for "human" habitation (a category from which the poor are often excluded). She also uses the word "squat" to mean "to take initiative, to reclaim closed urban spaces for life, to transform the meaning of public and private by creating collective life forms" (50).
3. Many of these images come from Diana Szántó's descriptions of various polio-squats in Sierra Leone. The squat on Walpole Street was disbanded in 2009.
4. *Zakat* is a required 2.5 percent of one's income donated to charity, while *sadaqah* is charity offered to anyone at any time.
5. In *Escaping Stigma and Neglect: People with Disabilities in Sierra Leone*, Mirey Ovadiya and Giuseppe Zampaglione note that the number of beggars "has grown significantly since the end of the conflict [in 2002], or at least they are more visible than before in what seems to be a growing industry" (13).
6. Mbugua Wa-Mungai writes about how the following sayings are commonly used in the Kakuma Refugee Camp in northern Kenya, where they do research. In Gikuyu, "Urahooya ñi kwonja wonjete?—Why beg as if you are crippled?" In Kiswahili, the phrase is "mbona unaomba kama wewe ni kileme?—Why are you begging as if you are a cripple?" This shows the ubiquity of the link between disability and begging in various countries in Africa.
7. There were increases in efficiency when it came to treating injured combatants, as this population was the focus of governments, the UN, and NGOs.
8. Trani et al. write that sexual and gender-based violence was prevalent during the civil war and continued into the immediate postwar period.
9. In *The Wretched of the Earth*, Fanon argues that the native/colonized "is dominated but not domesticated. He is made to feel inferior, but by no means convinced of his inferiority. He patiently waits for the colonist to let his guard down and then jumps on him. The muscles of the colonized are always tensed" (16).
10. In *Black Skin, White Masks*, Fanon writes, "I move slowly in the world, accustomed now to seek no longer of upheaval. I progress by crawling" (116).
11. This performance elaborates on an earlier video installation, titled *Belongings* (2007), in which Ogunji similarly drags herself across a dirt path, with empty jugs tied to her ankles. The video emphasizes the slow pull of her body as it passes the camera. Ogunji is alone in this performance, except for the camera. The isolation of the piece is a marked difference from later pieces in which onlookers' responses to her body movement form a crucial aspect of the performance.
12. She repeated a version of this performance most recently on September 6, 2014, in South Africa, titled *Can't I just decide to fly?* This performance, according to her website, raises a different set of additional questions: "Can we develop philosophies for embodying both joy and justice through performance? What is the significance of enacting physical labor in the service of beauty and poetry [rather

than as a demonstration of struggle and injustice]?" Ogunji, "*Can't I just decide to fly?*"

13. He borrows the idea of the "still-act" from the anthropologist Nadia Seremetakis (Lepecki, *Exhausting Dance* 15).
14. For example, in a 1931 letter, the Reverend John Dudley of Mount Morris, Michigan, describes a recent runaway slave, forced to work in the fields with a fetter on his ankles: "To prevent it from wearing his ankles, a string was tied to the centre, by which the victim suspended it when he walked, with one hand, and with the other carried his burden. Whenever he lifted, the fetter rested on his bare ankles. If he lost his balance and made a misstep, which must very often occur, . . . the torture of his fetter was severe" (Weld 156–57).
15. Judy Richardson, who witnessed the incident, insists that Carmichael was making a joke. She writes, "His ribald comment was uproarious and wild. It drew us all closer together because even at that moment he was poking fun at his own attitudes. Casey and I felt, and continue to feel, that Stokely was one of the most responsive men at the time that our anonymous paper appeared in SNCC" (186).
16. Note that because Pope.L is already on the ground, the resident cannot threaten to knock him out or knock him down. He resorts instead to the grammatically awkward "knock him off."
17. The discovery of oil in Nigeria allowed for the development of a modern industrial petrocapitalism riddled with corruption and exploitation. An estimated $300 billion in oil revenues over the past fifty years has flowed mainly into the federal exchequer, with significant amounts disappearing overseas (Douglas et al.). With little of Nigeria's wealth being invested back into the country, it is no surprise that the average Nigerian's living standards resemble those at the start of independence in 1960.
18. Akiyode also talks about how the disproportionate use of women and girls to procure water has led to higher absenteeism of girls in schools and lower work productivity of women.
19. Despite the seeming ease of movement, there are several health implications for water portage. Recent studies suggest eliminating the need for water carrying, as water portage often results in musculoskeletal disorders and physical injury. Poor women and children, precisely the population carrying water as well as the group disproportionately suffering from chronic poor health, are more vulnerable to injury (Geere et al.).
20. In the original Afrikaans: "In die kantoor op die tiende verdieping was die mees ontspanne atmosfeer wat 'n mens jou in sulke omstandighede kan voorstel. Ahmed Timol het rustig op 'n stoel gesit. Daar was veiligheidsmanne by hom. Twee van hulle het in 'n stadium uit die kamer gestap. Toe vlieg Timol skielik op en mik na die deur. Die een veiligheidsman het opgespring en na die deur gehardloop om hom te keer. Maar die Indier storm toe op die venster af en spring deur. Niemand het hom bang geraak nie. Die lykskouing sal did wys." See Myburgh.
21. George Miller's tavern on F Street was so thoroughly involved in the slave trade that it was known locally as "the Negro Bastille."

CHAPTER 2. FLOATING

1. At its narrowest, the Strait is only eight miles wide.
2. Denise Ferreira da Silva writes that the "racial and the global . . . are mutually constitutive, as the global institutes the ontoepistemological conditions for raciality, white raciality serves to maintain (and is maintained by) spatial boundaries and control" (*Toward a Global* 23). Thus, the affectable, racial body in its association with the global, no matter where that body is located, is always seen as a threat to whiteness even while simultaneously being vulnerable to being colonized/ killed because of that very affectability.
3. Tahar Ben Jelloun in *Leaving Tangier* describes the sensory overload of his characters as they wait on the beach before crossing the Mediterranean: "You can smell it, you can see Europe and its lights, you can touch it, it smells good, it's waiting for you" (179). This hapticity provides a stark contrast to the ways migrants are imagined by Eurosur.
4. Rizvana Bradley in "Poethics of the Open Boat. In Response to Denise Ferreira da Silva's 'Fractal Thinking'" argues that "Ian Baucom and others have insisted that slavery's particularly brutal and exceptional event does not belong to a distant and concluded past, but is indeed a fundamental and paradigmatic event in the historical formation of our own present and its dominant cultural logic."
5. This system was scaffolded around the monetarization and anatomization of the slave body as a commodity.
6. Katherine McKittrick in "Diachronic Loops" describes how the "seemingly scientific underpinnings of modernity—acts that weigh, measure and differentiate—are insinuated into and push up again, the knowledge systems" of affective bodies (12). Speaking specifically about the postslavery term "deadweight tonnage," a measure of weight that indicates how much weight a ship can carry, i.e., its fuel, cargo (human and otherwise), provisions, crew, etc., she wishes to talk not about the violent abstraction of the black body but rather about how antiblack violence "lends a voice to black life" (12). I would argue that the ways that the black body is violently abstracted remain important. This historical detritus, the maritime mathematics of iron and flesh, is the substrate from which performance is born.
7. The *São José*'s fame lies in that it is the first archaeologically excavated wreck that was lost while carrying a full cargo of slaves. It is even more significant, as Lonnie Bunch III (founding member of NMAAHC) tells us, "because it represents one of the earliest attempts to bring East Africans into the trans-Atlantic slave trade—a shift that played a major role in prolonging that tragic trade for decades" (National Museum of African American History and Culture). As such, this shipwreck speaks directly to the saltwater journeys of Searle's ancestors as they landed at the Cape through voyages that included but were not limited to the Atlantic Ocean.
8. Nirmala Erevelles writes about transforming her and her husband Robert's "somber cancer narrative into a *sensuous* exposition of the limits and possibilities of

living with terminal illness" in order to create different kinds of narratives around bodies, illness, death, and living (9; emphasis added).

9. In physics, a "plenum" is a space completely filled with matter.
10. One of the firefighters sent to bring up bodies from the shipwreck off the Libyan coast writes that the bodies were cramped into small spaces "like a slave ship." To collect them and not to walk on them, the firefighters had to lie across them to pull them up (Amade and Casartelli 747).
11. There is considerable confusion over the use of the term "Cape Malay." As Gabeba Baderoon writes, the term applies to Muslims from the Indonesian archipelago who, as early as the 1660s, were enslaved, exiled, and banished to the Cape. It could refer to the lingua franca, Bahasa Melayu, used by slaves at the Cape brought from Mozambique, Madagascar, Indian, and Southeast Asia (Baderoon 13). Under the apartheid government, it was used interchangeably with the racial category of "Coloured" and/or to designate Muslims even though many "Coloureds" are Christian.
12. The North African vernacular word for Mediterranean migrants is *harraga*, deriving from the Maghrebi Arabic root cluster *hrg*, meaning "to burn." Many migrants burn their documents on African shores so that if they are captured, it becomes difficult to deport them to their country of origin. *Harraga* has come to mean those who burn their past lives for the hope of a better future elsewhere.
13. One sees how difficult it is to float in the iconic scene from Barry Jenkins's film *Moonlight* (2016) in which Juan (Mahershala Ali) teaches the young Terrance (Shariff Earp) how to float. "That right there, you are in the middle of the world." The waves keep coming up over the camera to create a feeling similar to Searle's piece. When the characters "progress" from floating to learning how to swim, Juan tells Terrance, as he simulates the arm movements for free style, to be "more athletic."
14. The emphasis on slowness is the underlying principle of the Slow Movement, a growing social protest against the high speed of globalization. Beginning with Carlo Petrini's protest against the first McDonald's fast-food restaurant in Rome, the Slow Food movement has spread in several directions: Cittaslow, slow academia, slow reading, slow religion, slow money, and others. "Slow Food at once insists on the pleasures to be derived from slow living and demonstrates the critical democratic potential of such a lifestyle" (Schneider 394).
15. Scarlet describes the slave girl Prissy as "slower than molasses on a January day." January in South Africa is the dead of summer, reinforcing the fact that racism is not only about when but also where.

CHAPTER 3. FLICKERING

1. I am thinking here of Teenage Mutant Ninja Turtles or werewolf films such as *Teen Wolf*.
2. Mntambo states, "I have a very hands-on approach to working—hence the traces of my hand or process in the finished product" (Moret).

3. This rights-bearing subject has been the cornerstone of the disability rights movement, especially in its early focus on accessibility and independent living, even as "access to liberal rights . . . function as/at the 'horizon of death'" (Gorman 251).
4. In particular, see Weheliye; Wynter, "On Disenchanting Discourse" and "Unsettling the Coloniality"; Z. Jackson, *Becoming Human*.
5. Mntambo's artwork is titled *Child of Europa*.
6. When John Merrick in David Lynch's film *The Elephant Man* cries out, "I am not an animal," he is begging for the kind of treatment reserved for able-bodied humans.
7. Lauren Beukes satirizes this discourse when she writes that "Huron screams like a slaughterhouse pig in a PETA video" (342).
8. The suit was introduced in the mid-eighteenth century by a famous torero named Costillares, a butcher's son who wanted to cement his rise into the upper classes by dressing like them. The over-the-top ornateness and bespoke fit make these suits very difficult to produce and extremely expensive to purchase.
9. Beukes claims that *Zoo City* draws from her experience of visiting the Central Methodist Church in Johannesburg and being overwhelmed when confronted by the conditions in which refugees were living. "People were sick, desperate, there were babies—conceived through rape at the border—being washed in buckets, sleeping on bits of cardboard if they were lucky—all the horror of a refugee camp condensed into one building" (Low).
10. Garrey Dennie, in "The Standard of Dying: Race, Indigence, and the Disposal of the Dead Body in Johannesburg, 1886–1960," points out that Johannesburg's cemeteries were racially segregated before the segregation of living spaces, showing how the treatment of the dead "human" body is a major site for the production of hierarchical racial regimes (312).
11. Beukes herself draws attention to this connection to Pullman in *Zoo City* by following a film review of "The Warlord and the Penguin: The Untold Story of Dehqan Baiyat (2003)" with a list of recommendations for further viewing and reading that includes "Steering by the Golden Compass: Pullman's fantasy in the context of the ontological shift" (79).
12. It would be an interesting thought experiment to ask whether the human attached to the animal tells us something about the animal's interiority. Instead of the sloth suggesting something about Zinzi's nature, could Zinzi's impatience, her self-loathing, her desperation describe who the sloth is.
13. Benoit has a "mapwork of scars over his shoulders, the plasticky burnt skin that runs down his throat and his chest" (Beukes 3). This map of scars, like Mongoose, evidence his history that is at once intensely personal but also shared by many others.
14. P. W. Botha's State Security Council "enjoyed a mandate that authorised them to 'eliminate' belligerents" (Hopkins 290).
15. "Hungry and patient, impassive and exquisitely timed . . . A complexity of messages implied in our being" (Williams, "On Being" 24).

16. By "oyibo shame," Oyibo refers either to a white person or to a Nigerian who ostensibly performs an uppity whiteness.

CHAPTER 4. SPASMING AND PASSING OUT

1. The television show takes place in a single-sex hostel, built by the apartheid government to house those whose temporary labor was considered disposable, such as men working in and around the mining industry as well as cleaners and factory workers, for example. Insightful and funny, the show explores black masculinity, mobility, labor, and sexuality.
2. Kwaito supposedly originated when two house DJs in Johannesburg, Oskido and Christos, slowed down house and other records to around 110 beats per minute (bpm), putting their own lyrics to it, using *tsotsitaal* initially to articulate their new freedoms. Today, some people argue that kwaito is in decline, as producers revamp it to produce a clipped sound at 125 bpm that house DJs can use in their sets. Recent successes, however, that include the underground hit by Okmalumkoolkat with a London act, LV, and the occurrence of "morning bangs" ("banging" means being high on ecstasy) argue that kwaito, while changing, is still relevant. For more about kwaito, see Bradshaw, "Speaking the Kwaito Language."
3. As some embittered citizens believe, to "be white in South Africa is . . . to face a choice between, on the one hand, flight and embittered nostalgia for the sun-drenched homeland and, on the other, abject consent to violation/[black rage]" (Toit).
4. Eddie Ndopu in "Oscar Pistorius: Salvaging the Super Crip Narrative" has argued that such a reading of Oscar Pistorius's murder of Reeva Steenkamp constitutes a "psychosocial strategy" that "deflect[s] attention away from Oscar as a crip with agency and direct[s] blame to external factors." These external factors compensate for Pistorius's previous status as "super-crip" and "absolve[] him of responsibility in relation to violent conduct." The idea of agency as an idealized "free will" located in the individual body is one of the myths of liberal humanism, as I have argued in previous chapters. Pistorius's agency is necessarily entangled with socioeconomic forces, and violence is always a language that requires an audience, imagined or otherwise, as it communicates value and valuelessness in a social order.
5. The various neighborhoods that make up the Cape Flats, such as Manenberg, Khayelitsha, and Mitchell Plains, originated either as the Nationalist Party's dumping ground for Coloureds forced out of central and western Cape Town when these areas were rezoned as white-only or as vast informal settlements of (Xhosa) migrant workers and their children. The Cape Flats evidences this legacy in its continued lack of resources and amenities, housing shortages, and a dismal infrastructure. Given the forcible removal of people of color to the Cape Flats to make room for whites, Ninja and Yo-Landi's reoccupation of and spectacularization of life in the Cape Flats are an astonishing act of hubris.
6. The 26s traffic money, tobacco, and drugs into prison; the 27s enforce the law; and the 28s "defend prisoners' rights" (Kaviani).

7. "Fok Julle Naaiers" and a later track, "Faggot/Simunye," contain numerous references to "niggers" and "faggots." DJ Hi-Tek, wearing a prosthetic over his face in "Fok Julle Naaiers," raps, "You can't touch me, faggot. . . . I'll fuck you till you love me, faggot." According to Ninja, South Africans don't mind being called "niggers," as the epithet historically applied only to African Americans. Feeling policed by "intellectuals" and "some people from America" who are "heavy sensitive" or politically correct about the word "faggot," he refused to stop using it. Ninja insisted that since DJ Hi-Tek is black and gay, the songs were parodic. He thereby made an appeal to Die Antwoord's putative insider status with regard to South Africa as a nation as well as to South African minoritized communities, suggesting fallaciously that symbolic membership in a group makes reactionary politics against group members impossible. Obbard and Cork write that the Die Antwoord "both represents and satirizes homophobic violence in South Africa, and causes the listener to question the rhetoric of acceptance that stems from the [failure of] Rainbow Nation ideology" (425). I remain unconvinced that "playing" the homophobe doesn't replicate the violence of homophobia itself. Also see the disturbing 2012 video depicting an altercation between Ninja, Yo-Landi, and the gay musician Andy Butler, in which Ninja hits Butler and says to him, "Run, faggot, run."
8. Makhubu herself is an artist whose work also revolves around the need to create art that speaks to colonial representations of African women. She writes, "Colonial photography is the documentation of violation and the terror of dispossession. Re-enacting colonial photography is to come close to this terror and to realize its present manifestations. For me, post-memory is lived memory—it is a way of coming to terms with the persistence of the same repressive structures" (*Intertwined* 30).
9. Die Antwoord's visual landscape bears an uncanny resemblance to Hugo's "Nollywood" series, particularly in its adherence to aspects of the horror genre.
10. The now outdated catchphrase "Simunye" means "we are one." First used by politicians, it was later used by advertising companies to promote a TV channel in the 1990s. Ninja repeated this line in his defense of "Fok Julle Naaiers." See Jacobs.
11. This scene could also be reference to water torture. While there are similarities, I see the dunking of the head more as religious, on the basis of how quickly the boy's head is raised out the bucket. He is not held under the water for more than a few seconds, and his face appears calm and focused, as do the faces of the boys watching. He does not appear to be distressed.
12. *The Spear* is based on a commemorative poster by Victor Ivanov titled *Lenin Lived, Lenin Is Alive, Lenin Will Live*. Produced in the year of Lenin's death, the 1924 poster in reds, golds, and blacks represents a defiant Lenin surviving a failed assassination attempt. Each part of the poster's title stands in for a bullet that didn't kill Lenin. Considerable irony can be found in the fact that while the assassination attempt did not kill Lenin, it weakened him considerably, leading to his ultimate demise. Lenin will not live.

13. Some of his other paintings include *Spear Down My Throat (The Pornography of Power)* (2015), in which Zuma has his penis down the throat of a woman being penetrated by a hyena in Victorian dress. The woman represents South Africa. Another infamous painting depicts Zuma licking the ass of Atul Gupta. The Gupta/Zuma piece is called *Ingwe ayizidli ngamabala isakuluma ikaka okwesihlumi senyama, ayidliwa ikaka nokuba ungalamba ungagabha (Prostitutes)* (2016). Roughly translated from Zulu, the title reads, "A leopard cannot be proud if it eats shit as if it were a piece of meat. Shit cannot be eaten as the act causes one to vomit."
14. Like Mbembe, Patrick Walter notices how "the state has tried to replace a political struggle with a legal dispute and thus recast itself as a legal arbitrator of citizens' 'rights' rather than an opponent of the workers' socioeconomic empowerment" (9). Zuma acknowledged that living and working conditions for the miners needed to change. However, instead of supporting the miners' push for nationalizing the mines, Zuma insisted that South Africa was a "constitutional democracy": "We must deal with things properly within the framework of the law and then the constitution" (Walter 11).

CHAPTER 5. SHAKING THE WORLD

1. Consider the mud-eater. Patrick Harries's study of Mozambiquan migrant workers in South Africa details the notion that witches (*baloyi*) capture the "life essence" of workers so that they become automatons, toiling endlessly under the ground for days, subsisting on a diet of mud (221).
2. In Wade Davis's key text *Passage of Darkness*, he develops connections between the processes of zombification and Kongolese/Haitian Vodun Bizango secret societies, whose role includes the poisoning of certain individuals so that they become zombies. Wade's ethnobiology thus insightfully situates zombies as the result of historical and cultural indigenous juridical communal ordering. These historical links have largely been dismissed or ignored, Wade goes to write, in favor of spectacularized zombies that reinforce racist understandings of African diasporic religions and peoples.
3. Oppong and Kalipeni write that most land mines are laid on paths used by civilians on route to fields, schools, hospitals, and markets. The second major site of land mines is at the side of roads (17).
4. Eight of Angola's eighteen provinces, making up almost 50 percent of the country, are still heavily mined, with the Moxico province accounting for a particularly high number of the country's injuries (Oppong and Kalipeni 11).
5. Alyson Cole describes this state as being characterized by "changing temporalities and enduring interdependence" (269).
6. These movements directly echo those of the famous Luandan Joana Pernambuco, dancing in the 1950s and 1960s. Pernambuco's name comes from the words *perna mbuka*, which mean "limping leg" in Portuguese and Kimbundu. Pernambuco balanced on one leg and could write her name in the sand with her toes as she danced (Moorman, *Intonations* 118).

7. Marissa Moorman and Garth Sheridan very kindly shared their work in various stages with me, and I am tremendously grateful.
8. According to Unicef reports, children represent one in five of all land-mine casualties. Even though the conflict that utilized land mines may be receding historically, the effects of that conflict are increasing.
9. Daphne Brooks in her key text *Bodies in Dissent* defines "Afro-alienation" as "a trope that reflects and characterizes marginal cultural positions as well as a tactic that the marginalized seized on and reordered in the self-making process" (4). I elaborate on this concept later in the chapter.
10. In *Intonations*, Marissa Moorman writes that the Portuguese word *musseque* comes from the Kimbundu *mu-seke*, which translates into "sandy place." She writes that *musseque* "originally referred to areas of the city where the asphalt did not reach" (32).
11. Gonye details how the Zimbabwean state used the kongonya to gather support for the 2000 *jambanja* (the violent repossession and supposed redistribution of white-owned farms) (67).
12. Moorman calls this "'sonorous capitalism' . . . the motor that circulated this new sound and sensibility throughout the territory, . . . unmoored from the strictures of literacy," and "the pedagogical narratives of the nation-state" (*Intonations* 7).
13. Tómas also writes about the importance of informal marketplaces such as the now defunct Roque Santiero, which "radically reorganized the flow of the city, . . . reconfiguring Angolan society, . . . positing . . . alternative infrastructure[s]" (267).
14. As Jayna Brown notes, in early "video clips from Luanda, physical spaces are repurposed by the dancers: vacant lots, streets, empty bathrooms, hallways, bedrooms, the ruinous structures of poor cities—perhaps demanding that we consider occupation from an alternate view" (142).
15. Many of the men in Bairro Militar claim that Agre-G stole Milindro from them.
16. Costuleta claims that the family explicitly forbade him to marry a "white girl," insisting that his proper role was as a husband to a black African. One sees in this a further attempt to manage the frightening specter of miscegenation.
17. One could read Costuleta's performances as heterosexual posturing that is par for the course in popular culture. Kuduro can be downright misogynist given the scarcity of female artists, the objectification and demeaning of women through lyrical content, and the presence of scantily dressed female dancers who perform raunchy routines behind the male lead. While one could argue that kuduro privileges a compensatory heterosexist display of phallic power typically thought to be the province of white masculinity, I would say that it does this and more.
18. Titica's album *Chåo*, made with DJ D-Victor, already had three huge singles: "Chåo," "Olha o Boneco," and "Kusse de Pole." Titica has a show on Angolan television on which she gives dance lessons. She has performed with other respected female kuduristas such as Ary, and her album was ranked in the top ten of Angolan albums of 2011.
19. Louise Redvers writes in her article "Transsexual Artist Titica Takes Angola by Storm" that there are no recorded convictions for homosexuality in Angola.

20. Titica's self-naming enacts a similar politics suggested by the dance style Milindro, discussed earlier.

CHAPTER 6. UNHINGING

1. Much of this chapter is inspired by listening to Chanda Prescod-Weinstein talk about her book *The Disordered Cosmos: A Journey into Dark Matter, Spacetime, and Dreams Deferred.*
2. Moya Bailey and Izetta Autumn Mobley write that "anti-Black racism is crazy-making for both white and black people alike" (31). Being called crazy, they also insist, "has been weaponized against Black women," in particular when tropes of the crazy black woman have been collapsed into stereotypes of the "rebellious black b[itch]" (31).
3. Later in this conclusion, I also mention physicists' notion of the thermodynamic arrow of time.
4. Solomon is following in the footsteps of Octavia Butler, whose main character in *Parable of the Sower*, for example, has been described as neuroatypical. In many ways, Solomon's work can also be seen as part of an African diasporic lineage that includes the South African writer Bessie Head's *A Question of Power*, in which Head reimagines gender in order to consider how a painfully embodied blackness travels across borders.
5. The Neurodevelopmental Disorders (ND) Work Group, which is "responsible to the formation of criteria and diagnostic categories of autism and related disorders," has defined Asperger's disorder, pervasive developmental disorder not otherwise specified (PDD-NOS), and autistic disorder into the extant category of autism spectrum disorder (Verhoeff 442). Autism has a fascinating and rich history as a diagnosis that I only gesture at here, since Solomon refuses the diagnosis of autism in the novel.
6. The irony of positing a theory of black sociality based on a "disorder of sociality" is not lost on me.
7. Flick's great-meema says of Aster, "You're one of those who has to tune the world out and focus on one thing at a time. We have a word for that down here, women like you. *Insiwa.* Inside one. It means you live inside your head and to step out of it hurts like a caning" (Solomon 23).
8. Benjamin Fraser points out that historically the distinctions between intellectual disabilities, developmental disabilities, and psychiatric disabilities have been fuzzy at best. The distinctions have often rested on racialized and gendered systems of oppression. Thus, Anna Stubblefield, for example, shows how the concept of "feeblemindedness" in the early twentieth century became a "signifier of tainted whiteness" (162) and evidence of female moral depravity.
9. Imagine listening to Matana Roberts's *Coin Coin* series when she tells the story of being lynched or Julius Eastman's performance in Peter Maxwell Davies's *8 Songs for a Mad King*, which made me physically ill when I heard it the first time.

WORKS CITED

Abani, Chris. "Ethics and Narrative: The Human and Other." *Witness*, vol. 22, 2009, p. 167+, http://witness.blackmountaininstitute.org.

———. *The Secret History of Las Vegas*. Penguin Books, 2014.

———. *Song for Night: A Novella*. Akashic Books, 2007.

Abdur-Rahman, Aliyyah I. *Against the Closet: Black Political Longing and the Erotics of Race*. Duke University Press, 2012.

Adeyemi, Kemi. "The Practice of Slowness: Black Queer Women and the Right to the City." *GLQ: A Journal of Lesbian and Gay Studies*, vol. 25, no. 4, 2019, pp. 545–67. https://doi.org/10.1215/10642684-7767767.

Ahmed, Sara. *The Cultural Politics of Emotion*. Edinburgh University Press, 2004.

———. *Strange Encounters: Embodied Others in Post-Coloniality*. Routledge, 2000.

Akiyode, Oluwole Olusegun. "Urban Safe Water and Millennium Development Goals in Lagos Mega-City, Nigeria." *Journal for Sustainable Development and Environmental Protection*, vol. 1, no. 3, 2011, pp. 41–50.

Alexander, Phoenix. "Spectacles of Dystopia: Lauren Beukes and the Geopolitics of Digital Space." *Safundi*, vol. 16, no. 2, 2015, pp. 156–72.

Alisch, Stefanie. *Angolan Kuduro: Carga, Aesthetic Duelling, and Pleasure Politics Performed through Music and Dance*. 2017. Universität Bayreuth, PhD dissertation.

Alisch, Stefanie, and Nadine Siegert. "Grooving on Broken: Dancing War Trauma in Angolan Kuduro." *Art and Trauma in Africa: Representations of Reconciliation in Music, Visual Arts, Literature and Film*, edited by Lizelle Bisschoff and Stefanie Van de Peer. Berlin: I. B. Tauris 2013, pp. 50–68.

Allen, R. L., and David L. Nickel. "The Negro and Learning to Swim: The Buoyancy Problem Related to Reported Biological Differences." *Journal of Negro Education*, vol. 38, no. 4, 1969, pp. 404–11.

Álvarez, David. "Unstable Vessels: Small Boats as Emblems of Deaths Foretold and as Harbingers of Better Futures in Figurations of Irregular Migration across the Strait of Gibraltar." *Migration by Boat: Discourses of Trauma, Exclusion and Survival*, edited by Lynda Mannik. Berghahn Books, 2016, pp. 116–31.

Amade, M'Charek, and Sara Casartelli. "Identifying Dead Migrants: Forensic Care Work and Relational Citizenship." *Citizenship Studies*, vol. 23, no. 3, 2019, pp. 738–57.

Amado, Tony. "How Did Jean-Claude Van Damme Inspire the Kuduro Dance in Africa!" *YouTube*, uploaded by Jean-Claude Van Damme, April 23, 2021, www.youtube.com/watch?v=qSHKXURWnEg.

Amanze, Ruby Onyinyechi. *Either way, you'll be in a pool of something*. 2015. Goodman Gallery.

———. *That low hanging kind of sun, the one that lingers two feet above your head, (never dying) house plants in exchange for your freedom . . . orchids in exchange for your love, who are you kissing, when you kiss a mask?* 2015. Galerie des Galeries, http://www.galeriedesgaleries.com.

Ames, Margaret. "Dancing Place/Disability." *Theatre Research International*, vol. 40, no. 2, 2015, pp. 170–85. https://doi.org/10.1017/S0307883315000048.

Aminzade, Dan Maynes. "Wesley Willis." Monzy. www.monzy.org. Accessed June 10, 2019.

Andersen, Hans Christian. *The Little Mermaid*. 1836. http://hca.gilead.org.il.

Andersson, Ruben. "A Game of Risk: Boat Migration and the Business of Bordering Europe." *Anthropology Today*, vol. 28, no. 6, 2012, pp. 7–11.

Andregård, Emmelie, and Lina Magnusson. "Experiences of Attitudes in Sierra Leone from the Perspective of People with Poliomyelitis and Amputation Using Orthotics and Prosthetics." *Disability and Rehabilitation*, vol. 39, no. 26, 2017, pp. 2619–25. https://doi.org/10.1080/09638288.2016.1236409.

"Anger Mounts over South African Miner's Fate." *Al Jazeera*, August 18, 2012, www.aljazeera.com.

Arondekar, Anjali, and Geeta Patel. "Area Impossible: Notes toward an Introduction." *GLQ: A Journal of Lesbian and Gay Studies*, vol. 22, no. 2, 2016, pp. 151–71.

Attoh, Kafui. "What Kind of Right Is the Right to the City?" *Progress in Human Geography*, vol. 35, no. 5, 2011, pp. 669–85.

Auslander, Mark. "We Can't Breathe: Performing Subjection in African American Protest Traditions." Center for Imaginative Ethnography, February 3, 2015, http://imaginative-ethnography.com/.

Baderoon, Gabeba. *Regarding Muslims: From Slavery to Postapartheid*. Witts University Press, 2014.

Bailey, Moya, and Izetta Autumn Mobley. "Work in the Intersections: A Black Feminist Disability Framework." *Gender and Society*, vol. 33, no. 1, 2019, pp. 19–40.

"The Bare-Handed Prosthetists—Raymond and Pierre Jaccard." *YouTube*, uploaded by CheminNeuf NetforGod, January 18, 2016, www.youtube.com/watch?v=z5t6h-xUXIw.

Barker, Jennifer M. "Out of Sync, Out of Sight: Synaesthesia and Film Spectacle." *Cinema and the Senses*, vol. 31, no. 2, 2008, pp. 236–51.

Baucom, Ian. *Specters of the Atlantic: Finance Capital, Slavery, and the Philosophy of History*. Duke University Press, 2005.

Belser, Julia Watts. "Vital Wheels: Disability, Relationality, and the Queer Animacy of Vibrant Things." *Hypatia*, vol. 31, no. 1, 2016, pp. 5–21.

Benjamin, Walter. "The Storyteller: Reflections on Nikolai Leskóv." *Illuminations*, edited by Hannah Arendt, translated by Harry Zohn, Harcourt, Brace and World, 1968, pp. 83–109.

Berardi, Franco "Bifo." *After the Future*. AK Press, 2011.

———. *And: Phenomenology of the End*. Semiotext(e), 2015.

———. "Chaosmic Spasm and the Educational Chaoide." *Deleuze and Guattari, Politics and Education: For a People-Yet-to-Come*, edited by Matthew Carlin and Jason Wallin. Bloomsbury, 2014, pp. 181–94.

———. *Heroes: Mass Murder and Suicide*. Verso, 2015.

Bester, Rory. "Brett Murray: Putting It Bluntly." *Mail & Guardian*, May 25, 2012. https://mg.co.za.

———. "Interview with Berni Searle for the Field's Edge." *The Field's Edge: Africa, Diaspora, Lens*, edited by Rory Bester and Amanda Carlson. Exhibition catalogue, USF Contemporary Art Museum, Tampa, 2003, http://archive.stevenson.info/.

Bethlehem, Louise. "Scratching the Surface: The Home and the Haptic in Lauren Beukes's *Zoo City* and Elsewhere." *Scrutiny2: Issues in English Studies in Southern Africa*, vol. 20, no. 1, 2015, pp. 3–23.

Beukes, Lauren. *Zoo City*. Angry Robot, 2010.

Bizos, George. *No One to Blame? In Pursuit of Justice in South Africa*. David Philip, 1998.

Bodinson, Sara, and Kelly Cannon. "Pope.L: The Artist Revisits the Site of His Iconic Crawl." *MoMA Magazine*, January 15, 2020, www.moma.org.

Bonneville, Rishi. "Angolan Kuduro Superstar Costuleta Fires Away at Pretenders." *MTV*, September 9, 2011, www.mtviggy.com.

Borelli, Melissa Blanco. "A Dance between Chaos and Complexity: Choreographing the Spasm in Music Videos." *International Journal of Screendance*, vol 6, 2016, pp. 57–77.

Born on the Fourth of July. Directed by Oliver Stone. Universal Pictures, 1989.

Boulle, Catherine. "'Madam, I Can See Your Penis': Disruption and Dissonance in the Work of Steven Cohen." *Acts of Transgression: Contemporary Live Art in South Africa*, edited by Jay Pather and Catherine Boulle. Wits University Press, 2019, pp. 60–81.

Bradley, Rizvana. "Introduction: Other Sensualities." *Women & Performance: a journal of feminist theory*, vol. 24, nos. 2–3, 2014, pp. 129–33.

———. "Poethics of the Open Boat: In Response to Denise Ferreira da Silva 'Fractal Thinking.'" *aCCeSsions*, no. 2, 2016, http://accessions.org.

Bradshaw, Melissa. "How Kwaito Became a Global Force." *The Guardian*, August 11, 2011, www.theguardian.com.

———. "Speaking the Kwaito Language." *Mail & Guardian*, August 19, 2011, http://mg.co.za.

Brand, Dionne. *A Map to the Door of No Return: Notes to Belonging*. Vintage Canada, 2012.

Brandstetter, Gabrielle. "Choreography as a Cenotaph: The Memory of Movement." *ReMembering the Body: Body and Movement in the 20th Century*, edited by Aleida Assman et al. Hatje Cantz, 2000, pp. 102–34.

Braun, Leslie. *Fast Foot Work*, http://fastfootwork.tumblr.com. Accessed May 8, 2019.

Brink, Yolandi, et al. "The Postural Stability of Children with Foetal Alcohol Spectrum Disorders during One-Leg Stance: A Feasibility Study." *African Journal of Disability*, vol. 7, 2018. https://doi.org/10.4102/ajod.v7i0.319.

Brody, Jennifer DeVere. *Punctuation: Art, Politics, and Play*. Duke University Press, 2008.

Brooks, Daphne A. *Bodies in Dissent: Spectacular Performances of Race and Freedom, 1850–1910*. Duke University Press, 2006.

Brown, Jayna. "Buzz and Rumble: Global Pop Music and Utopian Impulse." *Social Text*, vol. 28, no. 1, 2010, pp. 125–46.

Brown, Ras Michael. "'But the Mermaid Did Not Rise Up': The Death of a Simbi in the Carolina Lowcountry." *Southern Quarterly*, vol. 47, no. 4, 2010, pp. 120–50.

Bruce, La Marr. "Mad Is a Place; or, The Slave Ship Tows the Ship of Fools." *American Quarterly*, vol. 69, no. 2, 2017, pp. 303–8.

Bruckner, Johanna. "How Will I Remember Your Embrace: Episode 2, *Phylum Lava*." *Aos: Arebyte on Screen*, 2020, http://aos.arebyte.com.

Buikema, Rosemarie. "Performing Dialogical Truth and Transitional Justice: The Role of Art in the Becoming Post-Apartheid of South Africa." *Memory Studies*, vol. 5, no. 3, 2012, pp. 282–92.

Buraka Som Sistema. "Sound of Kuduro." *YouTube*, uploaded by Buraka, March 3, 2008, www.youtube.com/watch?v=4CkXhtw7UNk.

Burning Memories. "We Need to Talk about What Is Happening with Die Antwoord Now." *Medium*, March 16, 2019, http://medium.com.

Butler, Octavia. *Clay's Ark: A Patternist Novel*. Grand Central, 1984.

———. *Parable of the Sower*. Grand Central, 1993.

Buxbaum, Lara. "Representations of Xenophobia and Animalisation in *Zebra Crossing, Zoo City* and *Wolf, Wolf*." *Journal of Literary Studies*, vol. 33, no. 1, 2017, pp. 78–93.

Byrd, Courtney T., et al. "The Client's Perspective on Voluntary Stuttering." *American Journal of Speech Language Pathology*, vol. 25, no. 3, 2016, pp. 1–16.

Byrd, Jodi. *The Transit of Empire: Indigenous Critiques of Colonialism*. University of Minnesota Press, 2011.

Cervenak, Sarah Jane. *Wandering: Philosophical Performances of Racial and Sexual Freedom*. Duke University Press, 2014.

Chandler, Eliza, and Megan Johnson. "Reflections on Crip Imitations as Cultural Space-Making." *Journal of Literary and Cultural Disability Studies*, vol. 15, no. 4, 2021, pp. 383–99.

Chaney, Michael. "Animal Subjects of the Graphic Novel." *College Literature*, vol. 38, no. 3, 2011, pp. 129–49.

Chen, Mel Y. *Animacies: Biopolitics, Racial Mattering, and Queer Affect*. Duke University Press, 2012.

———. "Brain Fog: The Race for Cripistemology." *Journal of Literary and Cultural Disability Studies*, vol. 8, no. 2, 2014, pp. 171–84.

———. "Lurching for a Cure? On Zombies and the Reproduction of Disability." *GLQ: A Journal of Lesbian and Gay Studies*, vol. 21, no. 1, 2015, pp. 24–31.

Cheng, Anne Anlin. "Sushi, Otters, Mermaids: Race at the Intersection of Food and Animal; or, David Wong Louie's Sushi Principle." *Resilience: A Journal of the Environmental Humanities*, vol. 2, no. 1, 2014, pp. 66–95.

Clare, Eli. *Brilliant Imperfection: Grappling with Cure*. Duke University Press, 2017.

Clausius, Claudia. "The Temporal Theatres of Sculpture and Drama: Wole Soyinka and New York's Metropolitan Museum of Art." *Kronoscope*, vol. 7, no.1, 2007, pp. 3–31.

Cleary, Krystal. "One of Us? Disability Drag and the Gaga Enfreakment of Fandom." *Disability Media Studies*, edited by Elizabeth Ellcessor and Bill Kirkpatrick. New York University Press, 2017, pp. 177–96.

Cohen, Steven. "Limping into the African Renaissance." 1999. *Stephen Cohen: Life Is Shot, Art Is Long*, solo exhibition, January 21–March 6, 2010, Michael Stevenson, Cape Town. http://archive.stevenson.info.

Cole, Alyson. "All of Us Are Vulnerable, but Some Are More Vulnerable than Others: The Political Ambiguity of Vulnerability Studies, an Ambivalent Critique." *Critical Horizons*, vol. 17, no. 2, 2016, pp. 260–77.

Cole, Sean. "Time Bandit." Episode 713, Act One "Made to Be Broken." *This American Life*. WBEZ Chicago and PRX The Public Radio Exchange, August 7, 2020, www.thisamericanlife.org.

Cole, Teju. "Victory in the Shadows." *New York Times*, August 10, 2017, www.nytimes.com.

Coleridge, Samuel Taylor. *The Rime of the Ancient Mariner*. 1798.

Coly, Ayo A. "A Pedagogy of the Black Female Body: Viewing Angèle Essamba's Black Female Nudes." *Third Text*, vol.24, no. 6, 2010, pp. 653–64.

Comaroff, Jean, and John Comaroff. "Alien-Nation: Zombies, Immigrants, and Millennial Capitalism." *South Atlantic Quarterly*, vol. 101, no. 4, 2002, pp. 779–805.

Connerton, Paul. *How Societies Remember*. Cambridge University Press, 1989.

Connor, Stephen. "Intersensoriality." The Senses Conference, February 6, 2004, Thames Valley University, http://stevenconnor.com.

Conway-Smith, Erin. "South African President Jacob Zuma's Genitals Exposed in Another Painting (Video)." Agence France-Presse, August 28, 2012, www.pri.org.

Cooper, Helene. "Grim History Traced in Sunken Slave Ship Found off South Africa." *New York Times*, May 31, 2015, www.nytimes.com.

Cooper Albright, Ann. *Choreographing Difference: The Body and Identity in Contemporary Dance*. Wesleyan University Press, 1997.

———. "Strategic Abilities: Negotiating the Disabled Body in Dance." *Michigan Quarterly Review*, vol. 37, no. 2, 1998, pp. 475–501.

Costuleta, "Mama Kudi." *YouTube*, uploaded by IEFE Discos, October 27, 2016, www.youtube.com/watch?v=mO12k5lHGhc.

Crary, Jonathan. *Techniques of the Observer: On Vision and Modernity in the Nineteenth Century*. MIT Press, 1991.

Csordas, Thomas. "The Rhetoric of Transformation in Ritual Healing." *Culture, Medicine and Psychiatry*, vol. 7, no. 4, 1984, pp. 333–75.

Currier, Ashley, and Thérèse Migraine-George. "Queer Studies/African Studies: An (Im)Possible Transaction?" *GLQ: A Journal of Lesbian and Gay Studies*, vol. 22, no. 2, 2016, pp. 281–305.

D'Amato, Alfredo. *The Sound of Kuduro*. Photography collection, 2010, www.alfredo-damato.com.

Danticat, Edwidge. "We Are Ugly, but We Are Here." *Caribbean Writer*, vol. 10, 1996, http://faculty.webster.edu.

Davidson, Michael. *Concerto for the Left Hand: Disability and the Defamiliar Body*. University of Michigan Press, 2008.

———. "Concerto for the Left Hand: Disability (in the) Arts." *PMLA*, vol. 120, no. 2, 2005, pp. 615–19.

Davies, Telory. "Mobility: AXIS Dancers Push the Boundaries of Access." *Understanding Disability Studies and Performance Studies*, edited by Bruce Henderson and R. Noam Ostrander. Routledge, 2010, pp. 43–63.

Davis, Rebecca. "From the Spear to Umshini Wam, a Trip Less Expected." *Daily Maverick*, September 4, 2012, www.dailymaverick.co.za.

Davis, Wade. *Passage of Darkness: The Ethnobiology of the Haitian Zombie*. University of North Carolina Press, 1988.

Deffner, Sebastian, and Steve Campbell. *Quantum Thermodynamics: An Introduction to the Thermodynamics of Quantum Information*. IOP Concise Physics, 2019.

DeFrantz, Thomas. "Book Review: *Exhausting Dance: Performance and the Politics of Movement*." *TDR: The Drama Review*, vol. 51, no. 3, 2007, pp. 189–91.

———. "*This Is America*." *ASAP/J*, b.O.s. 7.3, August 27, 2018, http://asapjournal.com.

Deleuze, Gilles, and Félix Guattari. *A Thousand Plateaus: Capitalism and Schizophrenia*. Translated by Brian Massumi, University of Minnesota Press, 1987.

Dennie, Garrey. "The Standard of Dying: Race, Indigence, and the Disposal of the Dead Body in Johannesburg, 1886–1960." *African Studies*, vol. 68, no. 3, 2009, pp. 310–30.

Dent, Michelle, and M. J. Thompson. "Introduction: Falling." *Women and Performance: A Journal of Feminist Theory*, vol. 27, no. 1, 2004, pp. 7–12.

Devlieger, Patrick, and Jori De Coster. "On Footwear and Disability: A Dance of Animacy?" *Societies*, vol. 7, no. 2, 2017, pp. 1–11. https://doi.org/10.3390/soc7020016.

Die Antwoord. "Baita Jou Sabela feat. Slagysta (Official)." *YouTube*, edited by Yo-Landi Vi$$er, uploaded by Die Antwoord, November 30, 2019, www.youtube.com/watch?v=pRgUpRx1wE8&list=RD9MXKfP46A-0&index=25.

———. "Enter the Ninja (Explicit Version) (Official Video)." *YouTube*, directed by Roger Ballen, Interscope Records, uploaded by DieAntwoordVEVO, August 3, 2010, www.youtube.com/watch?v=cegdRoGiJl4&feature=kp.

———. "Fok Julle Naaiers (Official)." *YouTube*, directed by Ninja & Ross Garret, Zef Films, uploaded by Die Antwoord, March 7, 2012, www.youtube.com/watch?v=L-wpS49KNoo.

———. "House of Zef—MegaMix9000." *YouTube*, directed by Ninja, ¥o-Landi Vi$$er and Calder Greenwood, Zef Films, uploaded by Die Antwoord, March 15, 2019, www.youtube.com/watch?v=xTPLMtDGg98.

———. "I Fink U Freeky (Official)." *YouTube*, directed by Roger Ballen & Ninja, uploaded by Die Antwoord, January 31, 2012, www.youtube.com/watch?v=8Uee_mcxvrw.

———. *Ten$ion*. Cooperative Music, VVR795506, compact disc, 2012.

———. "Umshini Wam (A Short Film)." *YouTube*, written and directed by Harmony Korine, uploaded by VICE, October 30, 2012, www.youtube.com/watch?v=mtUvq82WkDY.

Douglas, Oronto, et al. "Alienation and Militancy in the Niger Delta: Petroleum, Politics and Democracy in Nigeria." *The Quest for Environmental Justice: Human Rights and the Politics of Pollution*, edited by Robert D. Bullard. Sierra Club Books, 2005, pp. 239–54.

Drewal, Henry John. "The Arts of Egungun among Yoruba Peoples." *African Arts*, vol. 11, no. 3, 1978, pp. 18–19.

Drewal, Margaret Thompson. "Improvisation as Participatory Performance: Egungun Masked Dancers in the Yoruba Tradition." *Taken by Surprise: A Dance Improvisation Reader*, edited by Ann Cooper Albright and David Gere. Wesleyan University Press, 2003, pp. 119–32.

Droogers, André. *Play and Power in Religion: Collected Essays*. De Gruyter, 2011.

Durrant, Sam. "Creaturely Mimesis: Life after Necropolitics in Chris Abani's Song for Night." *Research in African Literatures*, vol. 49, no. 3, 2018, pp. 178–206.

Eggington, Shanaaz. "Does Zef-Rap Rule? The Answer's Blowing Away the Internet." *Times Live*, February 7, 2010, www.timeslive.co.za.

The Elephant Man. Directed by David Lynch. Brooksfilms, 1980.

Ellis, Cristin. *Antebellum Posthuman: Race and Materiality in the Mid-Nineteenth Century*. Fordham University Press, 2018.

Ellis, JJJJJerome, Saidiya Hartman, and Erica Hunt. "Looking for Language in the Ruins." YouTube, uploaded by Center for African American Poetry and Poetics (CAAPP), September 29, 2020, www.youtube.com/watch?v=2bSu_ysGzVQ.

Ellis, JJJJJerome, and Alice Sheppard. *Life of Life*. Video performance. Vimeo, uploaded by James & Jerome, September 27, 2020, http://vimeo.com/462493035.

Emezi, Akwaeke. *Freshwater*. Grove, 2018.

Emzini Wezinsizwa. Created by Pixley Muziwakhe Shabangu. SABC1, 1994–2004.

English, Darby. *How to See a Work of Art in Total Darkness*. Massachusetts Institute of Technology Press, 2007.

Enwonwu, Oliver. "In Conversation with Ruby Onyinyechi Amanze." *Omenka Online*, April 10, 2018, www.omenkaonline.com.

Erevelles, Nirmala. *Disability and Difference in Global Contexts: Enabling a Transformative Body Politic*. Palgrave, 2011.

Ericson, Suzanne. "Thinking with Crocodiles, Thinking through Humans." *Issues in English Studies in Southern Africa*, vol. 23, no. 1, 2018, pp. 22–34.

Evernden, Neil. "Beyond Ecology: Self, Place, and the Pathetic Fallacy." *North American Review*, vol. 263, no. 4, 1978, pp. 16–20.

Fanon, Frantz. *Black Skin, White Masks*. Grove, 2008.

———. *The Wretched of the Earth*. Grove, 2004.

Featherstone, Mark. "Chaosmic Spasm: Guattari, Stiefler, Berardi, and the Digital Apocalypse." *CM: Communication and Media*, vol. 11, no. 38, 2016, pp. 243–68.

Ferguson, Roderick. *Aberrations in Black: Toward a Queer of Color Critique*. University of Minnesota Press, 2004.

Ferreira da Silva, Denise. "Fractal Thinking." *aCCeSsions*, no. 2, 2016, http://accessions.org.
———. "No-Bodies: Law, Raciality and Violence." *Griffith Law Review*, vol. 18, no. 2, 2009, pp. 212–36.
———. *Toward a Global Idea of Race*. University of Minnesota Press, 2007.
Fish, Frank E., et al. "Death Roll of the Alligator: Mechanics of Twist Feeding in Water." *Journal of Experimental Biology*, no. 210, 2007, pp. 2811–18, http://jeb.biologists.org.
Fleming, Julius B., Jr. "Transforming Geographies of Black Time: How the Free Southern Theater Used the Plantation for Civil Rights Activism." *American Literature*, vol. 91, no. 3, 2019, pp. 587–617.
Forrest Gump. Directed by Robert Zemeckis. Tisch Company, 1994.
Fraser, Benjamin. *Cognitive Disability Aesthetics: Visual Culture, Disability Representations, and the (In)Visibility of Cognitive Disability*. University of Toronto Press, 2018.
Fraser, Nancy. "Rethinking Recognition." *New Left Review*, vol. 3, 2000, pp. 107–20.
Fryer, Jocelyn. "Rewriting Abject Spaces and Subjectivities in Lauren Beukes's *Zoo City*." *English in Africa*, vol. 43, no. 2, 2016, pp. 111–29.
Garland-Thomson, Rosemarie. "Integrating Disability, Transforming Feminist Theory." *NWSA Journal*, vol. 14, no. 3, 2002, pp. 1–32.
———. "Introduction: From Wonder to Error—A Genealogy of Freak Discourse in Modernity." *Freakery: Cultural Spectacles of the Extraordinary Body*. New York University Press, 1996, pp. 1–19.
Geere, Jo-Anne L., et al. "Domestic Water Carrying and Its Implications for Health: A Review and Mixed Methods Pilot Study in Limpopo Province, South Africa." *Environmental Health*, vol. 9, art. 52, 2010. https://doi.org/10.1186/1476-069X-9-52.
Gelfand, Michael. "The African's Concept of Causes and Treatment of Epilepsy and Convulsions." *South Africa Medical Journal*, vol. 48, no. 20, 1974, pp. 879–81.
Gerber, David. "Preface: The Continuing Relevance of the Study of Disabled Veterans." *Disabled Veterans in History*, edited by David A. Gerber. University of Michigan Press, 2012, pp. ix–xxiii.
Gerrets, Borris. "Director's Note." *Shado'Man: A Boris Gerrets Film*. www.shadomanfilm.com. Accessed February 27, 2022.
Gilbert, Erin. "*And Fight*: Wura-Natasha Ogunji and Mary Okon Ononokpono." *Writing in Relation*, July 25, 2015, http://writinginrelation.wordpress.com.
Glissant, Édouard. *Poetics of Relation*. Translated by Betsy Wing, University of Michigan Press, 1997.
Gone with the Wind. Directed by Victor Fleming. Selznick International Pictures and Metro-Goldwyn-Mayer, 1939.
Gonye, Jairos. "Mobilizing Dance/Traumatizing Dance: Kongonya and the Politics of Zimbabwe." *Dance Research Journal*, vol. 45, no. 1, 2013, pp. 64–79.
Gorman, Rachel. "Disablement In and For Itself: Toward a 'Global' Idea of Disability." *Somatechnics*, vol. 6, no. 2, pp. 249–61.
Gqola, Pumla Dineo. "Memory, Diaspora and Spiced Bodies in Motion: Berni Searle's Art." *African Identities* vol. 3, no. 2, 2005, pp. 123–38.

Grace, Alicia. "Dancing with Lassitude: A Dramaturgy from Limbo." *RiDE: the Journal of Applied Theatre and Performance*, vol. 14, no. 1, 2009, pp. 15–29.
Greslé, Yvette. "Ruby Onyinyechi Amanze: A Story. In Parts." *Writing in Relation*, February 24, 2015, http://writinginrelation.wordpress.com/.
Guattari, Félix. *Chaosmosis: An Ethico-Aesthetic Paradigm*. Power, 1995.
Guimaraes, Chissano, and Waldney Oliveira. "Agre-G: Isto é Kuduro: Músico criador do estilo de Kuduro, O Melindro." *Vida Online*, September 27, 2010, www.opais.net. Translated by Melissa Schindler.
Gunner, Liz. "Jacob Zuma, the Social Body and the Unruly Power of Song." *African Affairs*, vol. 108, no. 430, 2009, pp. 27–48.
Hable con Ella. Directed by Pedro Almodóvar. El Deseo, 2002.
Hailu, Selome. *Home in Contemporary Black Girls' Bedrooms*. Student performance. Prof. Hershini Young's class, AADS374F: Home in Contemporary Diasporic Fiction, University of Texas at Austin, Spring 2019.
Halberstam, Jack. Introduction. *The Undercommons: Fugitive Planning and Black Study*, by Stefano Harney and Fred Moten. Minor Compositions, 2013, pp. 5–12.
Haleta, Savo. "How Many Immigrants Live in South Africa?" *Africa Is a Country*, October 26, 2018, http://africasacountry.com.
Hannigan, Mary. "Serena Williams Tramples Down Twitter Trolls and Opponents." *Irish Times*, January 28, 2016, www.irishtimes.com.
Harney, Stefano, and Fred Moten. *The Undercommons: Fugitive Planning and Black Study*. Minor Compositions, 2013.
Harries, Patrick. *Work, Culture, and Identity: Migrant Laborers in Mozambique and South Africa, 1860–1910*. Heinemann, 1999.
Harris, Cheryl. "Whiteness as Property." *Harvard Law Review*, vol. 106, no. 8, 1993, pp. 1710–91.
Hartman, Saidiya. "The Dead Book Revisited." *History of the Present: A Journal of Critical History*, vol. 6, no. 2, 2016, pp. 208–15.
———. *Scenes of Subjection: Terror, Slavery and Self-Making in Nineteenth-Century America*. Oxford University Press, 1997.
———. "Venus in Two Acts." *Small Axe*, vol. 12, no. 2, 2008, pp. 1–14.
———. *Wayward Lives, Beautiful Experiments: Intimate Histories of Riotous Black Girls, Troublesome Women and Queer Radicals*. Norton, 2019.
Haupt, Adam. "Part IV: Is Die Antwoord Blackface?" *Safundi: The Journal of South African and American Studies*, vol. 13, nos. 3–4, 2012, pp. 417–23.
———. *Static: Race and Representation in Post-Apartheid Music, Media and Film*. HSRC Press, 2012.
Hayes-Conroy, Allison, and Deborah G. Martin. "Mobilising Bodies: Visceral Identification in the Slow Food Movement." *Transactions of the Institute of British Geographers*, vol. 35, no. 2, 2010, pp. 269–81.
Head, Bessie. *A Question of Power*. Longman, 1973.
Healthgrades. "Spasms." www.healthgrades.com. Accessed November 8, 2019.

Hevey, David. *The Creatures Time Forgot: Photography and Disability Imagery*. Routledge, 1992.

Hibbs, Thomas S. "Dead Body Porn: The Grotesqueries of the 'Body World' Exhibit." *New Atlantis*, no. 15, 2007, pp. 128–31.

Holland, Sharon. *Raising the Dead: Readings of Death and (Black) Subjectivity*. Duke University Press, 2000.

Höller, Christian. "Africa in Motion: An Interview with the Post-Colonialism Theoretician Achille Mbembe." *Mute*, March 17, 2007. http://metamute.org.

Hopkins, Kevin. "Nowhere to Hide: The Case against PW Botha." *Comparative and International Law Journal of Southern Africa*, vol. 36, no. 3, 2003, pp. 289–307.

Hopkinson, Nalo. *Sister Mine*. Grand Central, 2013.

Houser, Heather. *Ecosickness in Contemporary U.S. Fiction: Environment and Affect*. Columbia University Press, 2014.

Hugo, Pieter. *Nollywood*. Prestel, 2009.

———. *Pieter and Maryna Vermeulen with Timana Phosiwa*. 2006. In *Figures and Fictions: Contemporary South African Photography*, April 12–July 17, 2011, Victoria and Albert Museum, London.

Huizinga, Johan. *Homo Ludens: A Study of the Play Element in Culture*. Beacon, 1955.

Hurston, Zora Neale. *Their Eyes Were Watching God*. Amistad, 2006.

Hutchins, Edwin. *Cognition in the Wild*. Massachusetts Institute of Technology Press, 1995.

ICRC (International Council of the Red Cross)."Anti-Personnel Landmines: Friend or Foe? A Study of the Military Use and Effectiveness of Antipersonnel Mines." www.icrc.org. Accessed June 9, 2020.

Igreja, Victor, et al. "The Epidemiology of Spirit Possession in the Aftermath of Mass Political Violence in Mozambique." *Social Science and Medicine*, vol. 71, no. 3, 2010, pp. 592–99.

Ingstad, Benedicte. "The Myth of Disability in Developing Nations." *Lancet*, vol. 354, no. 9180, 1999, pp. 757–58. https://doi.org/10.1016/S0140-6736(99)06049-3.

Jackson, Shelley. *Riddance: The Sybil Joines Vocational School for Ghost Speakers and Hearing Mouth Children*. Black Balloon, 2018.

Jackson, Zakiyyah Iman. *Becoming Human: Matter and Meaning in an Antiblack World*. New York University Press, 2020.

———. "Losing Manhood: Animality and Plasticity in the (Neo)Slave Narrative." *Qui Parle: Critical Humanities and Social Sciences*, vol. 25, nos. 1–2, 2016, pp. 95–136.

"Jacob Zuma Sings Umshini Wam." *YouTube*, uploaded by Livhuwani Mammburu, August 4, 2008, www.youtube.com/watch?v=lof6XJ8b1SU.

Jacobs, Sean. "Die Antwoord's at It Again." *Africa Is a Country*, November 11, 2011, http://africasacountry.com.

Jelloun, Tahar Ben. *Leaving Tangier*. Translated by Linda Coverdale, Arcadia Books, 2016.

Jensen, Jeff. "The End of 'Sweet Tooth': A Deep Dive with Jeff Lemire about Wrapping Up His Acclaimed Comic Book Saga." *Entertainment Weekly*, January 9, 2013, http://ew.com.

Joy, Jenn. *The Choreographic.* Massachusetts Institute of Technology Press, 2014.

Joy Division. "She's Lost Control." *Unknown Pleasures,* Factory Records, 1979.

Jutel, Annemarie Goldstein. *Putting a Name to It: Diagnosis in Contemporary Society.* John Hopkins University Press, 2011.

Kaamil, Robbyne. "Animal Captivity Is Slavery." *YouTube,* uploaded by PETA (People for the Ethical Treatment of Animals), May 28, 2015, www.youtube.com/watch?v=8PZBV8O5pfI.

Kafer, Alison. *Feminist, Queer, Crip.* Indiana University Press, 2013.

Kaviani, Fareed. "Portraits of South Africa's Bloodiest Prison Gang: The Number." *Vice,* November 13, 2018, www.vice.com.

Kazeem, Maryam. "Performances That Seek to Interrupt: Nigerian Artist Wura-Natasha Ogunji & the Craft of Spectacle." *Okay Africa,* May 28, 2013, www.okay-africa.com.

Keeling, Kara. *Queer Times, Black Futures.* New York University Press, 2019.

Kennedy, Meredith. "4 Decades Later, South African Court Rules That Activist Was Murdered." *NPR,* October 12, 2017, www.npr.org.

Kickboxer. Directed by Mark DiSalle and David Worth. King's Road Entertainment, 1989.

Kim, Eunjung. "Continuing Presence of Discarded Bodies: Occupational Harm, Necro-Activism, and Living Justice." *Catalyst: Feminism, Theory, Technoscience,* vol. 5, no. 1, 2019, pp. 1–31.

———. *Curative Violence: Rehabilitating Disability, Gender, and Sexuality in Modern Korea.* Duke University Press, 2017.

Kinderman, Peter. "Imagine There's No Diagnosis, It's Easy If You Try." *Psychopathology Review,* vol. 2, no. 1, 2015, pp. 154–61.

King, Jason. "Which Way Is Down? Improvisations on Black Mobility." *Women and Performance: A Journal of Feminist Theory,* vol. 14, no. 1, 2004, pp. 25–45.

King, Tiffany Lethabo. *The Black Shoals: Offshore Formations of Black and Native Studies.* Duke University Press, 2019.

Knoetze, Daneel. "'I Have Drawn Penises Most of My Life.'" *IOL News,* August 29, 2012, www.iol.co.za.

Knowles, Solange. "Cranes in the Sky." *YouTube,* directed by Alan Ferguson and Solange Knowles, uploaded by solangeknowlesmusic, October 2, 2016, www.youtube.com/watch?v=SoqrinhNnOM.

Kriel, Johanet. *Affirmative Aberrations in South Africa? Towards an Investigation of Possible Effects in Neil Blomkamp's "District 9" and Selected Works of Nandipha Mntambo.* 2012. University of Groningen, master's thesis.

Krueger, Anton. "Part II: Zef/Poor White Kitsch Chique: Die Antwoord's Comedy of Degradation." *Safundi: The Journal of South African and American Studies,* vol. 13, nos. 3–4, 2012, pp. 399–408.

Kuppers, Petra. "Bodies, Hysteria, Pain: Staging the Invisible." *Bodies in Commotion: Disability and Performance,* edited by Carrie Sandahl and Philip Auslander. University of Michigan Press, 2005, pp. 147–62.

———. *Disability and Contemporary Performance: Bodies on Edge*. Routledge, 2003.
Kurawa, Sabo Suleiman. "The Impact of Disability on Self and Society: An Agenda for Research on Rehabilitation of Disabled in Nigeria." *Procedia Social and Behavioral Sciences*, no. 5, 2010, pp. 1804–10.
Lee, Jin-Kyung. *Service Economies: Militarism, Sex Work, and Migrant Labor in South Korea*. University of Minnesota Press, 2010.
Lee, Rachel C. *The Exquisite Corpse of Asian America: Biopolitics, Biosociality, and Posthuman Ecologies*. New York University Press, 2014.
Lemire, Jeff. *Sweet Tooth*. Vertigo, 2009.
Leonard, Charles. "Spoek Mathambo: Afro-futurism's Heir Apparent." *Mail & Guardian*, December 14, 2012, http://mg.co.za.
Lepecki, André. "The Body as Archive: Will to Re-enact and the Afterlives of Dances." *Dance Research Journal*, vol. 42, no. 2, 2010, pp. 28–48.
———. *Exhausting Dance: Performance and the Politics of Movement*. Routledge, 2006.
Leshem, Noam. "Over Our Dead Bodies: Placing Necropolitical Activism." *Political Geography*, no. 45, 2015, pp. 34–44.
Levine, Debra. "How to Do Things with Dead Bodies." *E-Misferica*, vol. 6, no. 1, http://archive.hemisphericinstitute.org.
Linton, Simi. "Cultural Territories of Disability." *Disability. Dance. Artistry*. Dance/NYC, 2015, pp. 14–53.
Lipschitz, Ruth. "Skin/ned Politics: Species Discourse and the Limits of 'The Human' in Nandipha Mntambo's Art." *Hypatia*, vol. 27, no. 3, 2012, pp. 546–66.
Livingston, Julie. *Debility and the Moral Imagination in Botswana*. Indiana University Press, 2005.
London, Leslie, et al. "Farm Workers in South Africa—The Challenge of Eradicating Alcohol Abuse and the Legacy of the Dop System." *South African Medical Journal*, vol. 88, no. 9, 1998, pp. 108–10.
Lorde, Audre. "The Uses of Anger." *Women's Studies Quarterly*, vol. 25, nos. 1–2, 1997, pp. 278–85.
Low, Marcus. "Interview with Lauren Beukes." *GroundUp*, May 15, 2013, www.groundup.org.za.
Mabulu, Ayanda. *Umshini Wam*. In *Our Fathers*, exhibition curated by Kirsty Cockerill and Chantal Louw, August 27–September 21, 2012, The Ava Gallery, Cape Town.
Macharia, Keguro. *Frottage: Frictions of Intimacy across the Black Diaspora*. New York University Press, 2019.
———. "On Being Area-Studied: A Litany of Complaint." *GLQ: A Journal of Lesbian and Gay Studies*, vol. 22, no. 2, 2016, pp. 183–90.
Mackey, Nathaniel. "Breath and Precarity: The Inaugural Robert Creeley Lecture in Poetry and Poetics." *Poetics and Precarity*, edited by Myung Mi Kim and Cristanne Miller. SUNY Press, 2018, pp. 1–30.
———. "Sound and Sentiment, Sound and Symbol." *Callaloo*, no. 30, 1987, pp. 29–54.
Madera, Judith. *Black Atlas: Geography and Flow in Nineteenth-Century African American Literature*. Duke University Press, 2015.

Mair, Kimberly. "The Sofa's Objection: Troublesome Things and Affective Emplacements." *Feelings of Structure: Explorations in Affect*, edited by Karen Engle and Yoke-Sum Wong. McGill-Queen's University Press, 2018, pp. 12–28.

Makhubu, Nomusa. *Intertwined: A Selection of Photographs by Nomusa Makhubu 2005–2017*. Erdmann Contemporaries, 2017, www.contemporaryand.com.

———. "Politics of the Strange: Revisiting Pieter Hugo's Nollywood." *African Arts*, vol. 46, no. 1, 2013, pp. 50–61.

Malaby, Thomas M. "Anthropology and Play: The Contours of Playful Experience." *New Literary History*, vol. 40, no. 1, 2009, pp. 205–18.

Mapplethorpe, Robert. *Black Males*. Gallerie Jurka, 1980.

Martin, Michel. "'Song for Night': Highlights Hope, Despair." Interview of Chris Abani. *NPR*, October 4, 2007, www.npr.org.

Masalacism. "Titica—Kuduro's Dance Queen." *Tumblr*, December 14, 2011, www.masalacism.com.

Mason, Andy. "The Presidential Penis: Questions of Race and Representation in South African Comic and Satirical Art." *Representing Multiculturalism in Comics and Graphic Novels*, edited by Carolene Ayaka and Ian Hague. Taylor and Francis, 2014, pp. 49–68.

Mathambo, Spoek. "Control." *YouTube*, directed by Pieter Hugo and Michael Cleary, uploaded by SPOEKMATHAMBO1, February 23, 2011, www.youtube.com/watch?v=UKfwSFI8LhQ.

———. *Mshini Wam*. BBE Music, 2010.

———. "The Scare Tactics of Spoek Mathambo: Spoek Mathambo at TEDxSoweto 2011." *YouTube*, uploaded by TEDxTalks, January 31, 2012, www.youtube.com/watch?v=5X517T2muuM.

———. *Tales from the Lost Cities*. TEKA Records, February 26, 2020.

Mbembe, Achille. *Critique of Black Reason*. Duke University Press, 2017.

———. "Necropolitics." *Public Culture*, vol. 15, no. 1, 2003, pp. 11–40.

———. *On the Postcolony*. University of California Press, 2001.

———. "The Spear That Divided the Nation." *JWTC: The Johannesburg Workshop in Theory and Criticism*, June 26, 2012, http://jhbwtc.blogspot.com.

———. "Variations on the Beautiful in the Congolese World of Sounds." *Politique Africaine* 100, no. 4, 2005, pp. 69–91, www.cairn.info.

McDonnell, John. "Scene and Heard: Kuduro." *Guardian*, October 6, 2008, www.theguardian.com.

McDougall, Kathleen. "'Ag Shame' and Superheroes: Stereotype and the Signification of Disability." *Disability and Social Change: A South African Agenda*, edited by Brian Watermeyer et al. HSRC Press, 2006, pp. 387–400.

McKittrick, Katherine. *Dear Science and Other Stories*. Duke University Press, 2021.

———. *Demonic Grounds: Black Women and the Cartographies of Struggle*. University of Minnesota Press, 2006.

———. "Diachronic Loops/Deadweight Tonnage/Bad Made Measure." *cultural geographies*, vol. 23, no. 1, 2016, pp. 3–18.

———. "On Plantations, Prisons, and a Black Sense of Place." *Social & Cultural Geography*, vol. 12, no. 8, 2011, pp. 947–63.

McMillan, Christopher-Rasheem. Live performance. Black Performance Theory working group meeting, University of Arizona, 2019.

McRuer, Robert. "Cripping Sex; or Globalizing Otherness." Lecture delivered at the University of British Columbia, March 7, 2011.

McRuer, Robert, and Anna Mollow. Introduction. *Sex and Disability*, edited by Robert McRuer and Anna Mollow. Duke University Press, 2012, pp. 1–34.

Medina, Juan. *In Plain Sight*. Reuters, 2006, http://widerimage.reuters.com.

———. "Juan Medina—Cruel Sea." *Foto 8: The Home of Photojournalism*, April 12, 2006, www.foto8.com.

———. *Juan Medina—Cruel Sea*. HOST gallery, April 12–May 29, 2006, London.

Mendieta, Ana. *Untitled, Ocean Bird Washup*. Video performance, 1974.

Merali, Zeeya. "The New Thermodynamics: How Quantum Physics Is Bending the Rules." *Nature: International Weekly Journal of Science*, vol. 551, no. 7678, November 1, 2017, www.nature.com.

Milks, M. Review of *An Unkindness of Ghosts*, by Rivers Solomon. *Strange Horizons*, April 9, 2018, http://strangehorizons.com.

Miranda, Krista K. "Playing with Your Parts: Dismantling Bodily 'Wholeness' through Queer and Crip Performance." 2005. New York University, PhD dissertation.

Mitchell, David T., and Sharon L. Snyder. *The Body and Physical Difference: Discourses of Disability*. University of Michigan Press, 1997.

"Mixed Reviews over 'Umshini Wam' Painting." *Eyewitness News*, August 2012, http://ewn.co.za.

Mntambo, Nandipha. *Ukungenisa*. 2009. Digital video, 2 mins., 30 secs. *Nandipha Mntambo: The Encounter* solo exhibition, 16 April–30 May 2009, Michael Stevenson, Cape Town.

———. *Umfanekiso wesibuko* (Mirror image). 2013. Nandipha Mntambo solo exhibition, May 16–June 20, 2013, Andréhn-Schiptjenko, Stockholm, Sweden.

Moonlight. Directed by Barry Jenkins. A24, Plan B Entertainment, 2016.

Moorman, Marissa J. "Anatomy of Kuduro." *African Studies Review*, vol. 57, no. 3, 2014, pp. 21–40.

———. *Intonations: A Social History of Music and Nation in Luanda, Angola*. Ohio University Press, 2008.

Moret, A. "Nandipha Mntambo: In Her Skin." *Installation Magazine*, August 31, 2013, http://installationmag.com.

Mossman, Mark. "Acts of Becoming: Autobiography, Frankenstein, and the Postmodern Body." *Postmodern Culture*, vol. 11, no. 3, 2001. https://doi.org/10.1353/pmc.2001.0012.

Moten, Fred. *In the Break: The Aesthetics of the Black Radical Tradition*. University of Minnesota Press, 2003.

———. *Stolen Life (Consent Not to Be a Single Being)*. Duke University Press, 2018.

Muñoz, José Esteban. *Disidentifications: Queers of Color and the Performance of Politics*. University of Minnesota Press, 1999.

———. "Theorizing Queer Inhumanisms: The Sense of Brownness." *GLQ: A Journal of Lesbian and Gay Studies*, vol. 21, nos. 2–3, 2015, pp. 209–48.

Murinik, Tracy. "Berni Searle." *Nka: Journal of Contemporary African Art*, no. 13/14, 2001, pp. 74–79.

Murray, Brett. *Hail to the Thief II*. Exhibit *Hail to the Thief II*, Goodman Gallery, Johannesburg, May 10–June 16, 2012, www.goodman-gallery.com.

———. *The Spear*. Goodman Gallery, Johannesburg, 2010.

Mustakeem, Sowande M. *Slavery at Sea: Terror, Sex, and Sickness in the Middle Passage*. University of Illinois Press, 2016.

Myburgh, James. "Ahmed Timol: What the Pathologists Found (IV)." *Politicsweb*, November 7, 2017, www.politicsweb.co.za.

Naimou, Angela. "Double Vision: Refugee Crises and the Afterimages of Endless War." *College Literature*, vol. 43, no. 1, 2016, pp. 226–33.

Nario-Redmond, Michelle R., et al. "Crip for a Day: The Unintended Negative Consequences of Disability Simulations." *Rehabilitation Psychology*, vol. 62, no. 3, 2017, pp. 324–33.

National Eye Institute. "Floaters." www.nei.nih.gov. Accessed November 14, 2021.

National Museum of African American History and Culture. "National Museum of African American History and Culture to Display Objects from Slave Shipwreck Found Near Cape Town, South Africa." June 1, 2015, http://nmaahc.si.edu.

Naylor, Gloria. *Bailey's Café*. Vintage Books, 1992.

Ndopu, Eddie. "Oscar Pistorius: Salvaging the Super Crip Narrative." *Feminist Wire*, February 19, 2013, http://thefeministwire.com.

Nguyen, Vinh. "Nuoc/Water: Oceanic Spatiality and the Vietnamese Diaspora." *Migration by Boat: Discourses of Trauma, Exclusion and Survival*, edited by Lynda Mannik. Berghahn Books, 2016, pp. 65–70.

Nicki, Andrea. "The Abused Mind: Feminist Theory, Psychiatric Disability, and Trauma." *Hypatia*, vol. 16, no. 4 (Special Issue: Feminism and Disability, Part 1), 2001, pp. 80–104.

Niehaus, Isak. "Witches and Zombies of the South African Lowveld: Discourse, Accusations and Subjective Reality." *Journal of the Royal Anthropological Institute*, vol. 11, no. 2, 2005, pp. 191–210.

Nkosi, Milton. "Oscar Pistorius and South Africa's Gun Obsession." *BBC News Johannesburg*, December 5, 2015, www.bbc.com.

Nuttall, Sarah. *Entanglement: Literary and Cultural Reflections on Post-Apartheid*. Wits University Press, 2009.

Nyong'o, Tavia. *Afro-Fabulations: The Queer Drama of Black Life*. New York University Press, 2019.

Obasogie, Osagie K. *Blinded by Sight: Seeing Race through the Eyes of the Blind*. Stanford University Press, 2013.

Obbard, Kiera, and Stephanie Cork. "Skin Salvaged: Die Antwoord, Oscar Pistorius, and the Spectacle of the Flesh in the Rainbow Nation." *Journal of Popular Culture*, vol. 49, no. 2, 2016, pp. 417–32.

Ogunji, Wura Natasha. *Belongings*. Video installation, 2007. http://wuraogunji.com.

———. "*Can't I just decide to fly?*" September 6, 2014. http://wuraogunji.com.

———. "*Will I still carry water when I am a dead woman?*" April 18, 2013. http://wuraogunji.com.

———. "Will I still carry water when I am a dead woman?" *This Road*, April 25, 2013, www.goldeniron.blogspot.com.

Ogunji, Wura Natasha, and Mary Okon Ononokpono. *And Fight*. Performance at the 50 Golborne, London, curated by Erin Gilbert, June 12, 2015.

O'Hagan, Sean. "Africa as You've Never Seen It." *Guardian*, July 20, 2008, www.theguardian.com.

———. "Figures & Fictions: Contemporary South African Photography—Review." *Guardian*, April 16, 2011, www.theguardian.com.

Okeowo, Alexis. "The Spear Affair." *New Yorker*, June 8, 2012, www.newyorker.com.

Oppong, Joseph R., and Ezekiel Kalipeni. "The Geography of Landmines and Implications for Health and Disease in Africa: A Political Ecology Approach." *Africa Today*, vol. 52, no. 1, 2005, pp. 3–25.

"A Origem do Milindro Angola." *YouTube*, uploaded by Kelly Stress, June 24, 2009, www.youtube.com/watch?v=p7JJe8xboQI. Translated by Melissa Schindler.

Ovadiya, Mirey, and Giuseppe Zampaglione. *Escaping Stigma and Neglect: People with Disabilities in Sierra Leone*. World Bank, 2009.

Parker-Starbuck, Jennifer. "Shifting Strengths: The Cyborg Theater of Cathy Weiss." *Bodies in Commotion: Disability and Performance*, edited by Carrie Sandahl and Philip Auslander. University of Michigan Press, 2005, pp. 95–108.

Paterson, Mark. "Haptic Geographies: Ethnography, Haptic Knowledges and Sensuous Dispositions." *Progress in Human Geography*, vol. 33, no. 6, 2009, pp. 766–88.

Paxton, Steve. "3 Days." *Contact Quarterly*, vol. 17, no. 1, 1992, pp. 13–19.

Perez, Rodrigo. "SXSW Review: Harmony Korine's 'Umshini Wam' Starring Die Antwoord Now Online." *IndieWire*, March 16, 2011, www.indiewire.com.

Pergadia, Samantha. "Like an Animal: Genres of the Nonhuman in the Neo-Slave Novel." *African American Review*, vol. 51, no. 4, 2018, pp. 289–304.

Philip, M. NourbeSe. "The Ga(s)p." *Poetics and Precarity*, edited by Myung Mi Kim and Cristanne Miller. State University of New York Press, 2018, pp. 31–40.

Pickens, Therí A. *Black Madness: Mad Blackness*. Duke University Press, 2019.

Pope.L, William. *The Great White Way: 22 Miles, 9 Years, 1 Street*. 2001–9. *Member: Pope.L., 1978–2001* exhibition, MoMA, New York, October 21, 2019–February 1, 2020, www.moma.org.

———. *Times Square Crawl*. MoMA, 1978, www.moma.org.

———. *Tompkins Square Crawl*. MoMA, 1991, www.moma.org.

Porco, Alex S. "Throw Yo' Voice Out: Disability as a Desirable Practice in Hip-Hop Vocal Performance." *Disability Studies Quarterly*, vol. 34, no. 4, 2014. https://doi.org/10.18061/dsq.v34i4.3822.

Posel, Deborah, and Pamila Gupta. "The Life of the Corpse: Framing Reflections and Questions." *African Studies*, vol. 68, no. 3, 2009, pp. 299–309.

Prescod-Weinstein, Chanda. *The Disordered Cosmos: A Journey into Dark Matter, Spacetime, and Dreams Deferred*. Bold Type Books, 2021.

Preston, John. "Prosthetic White Hyper-Masculinities and 'Disaster Education.'" *Ethnicities*, vol. 10, no. 3, pp. 331–43.

Priestly, Mark. "Developing Disability Studies Programmes: The International Context." *Disability and Social Change: A South African Agenda*, edited by Brian Watermeyer et al. HSRC Press, 2006, pp. 19–30.

Przybylo, Ela. "The Politics of Ugliness." *eSharp*, vol. 16, 2010, pp. 1–26.

Puar, Jasbir. *Terrorist Assemblages: Homonationalism in Queer Times*. Duke University Press, 2007.

Pullman, Phillip. *His Dark Materials Trilogy: The Golden Compass / The Subtle Knife / The Amber Spyglass*. Laurel Leaf, 1994.

Ralushai, N. V., et al. *Report of the Commission of Inquiry into Witchcraft Violence and Ritual Murders in the Northern Province of the Republic of South Africa* (To: His Excellency the Honorable Member of the Executive Council for Safety and Security), Northern Province, 1996.

Redvers, Louise. "Transsexual Artist Titica Takes Angola by Storm." *BBC News*, April 12, 2012, www.bbc.co.uk.

Řezáčová, Vendula. "'The Ancestors Are Beating Us': Men, Migration and Spirit Possession in South Africa." *Modern Africa: Politics, History and Society*, vol. 4, no. 1, 2016, pp. 107–29.

Richardson, Judy. "Womanpower and SNCC." *Massachusetts Review*, vol. 52, no. 2, 2011, pp. 179–88.

Roach, Joseph. *Cities of the Dead: Circum-Atlantic Performance*. Columbia University Press, 1996.

Rocha-Gray, Rozanne. "Control. A Spoek Mathambo Music Video by Pieter Hugo & Michael Cleary. Chosen by Rozanne Rocha-Gray." *Africa.film*, http://africa.film. Accessed March 8, 2022.

Rodriguez, Hector. "The Playful and the Serious: An Approximation to Huizinga's Homo Ludens." *Game Studies*, vol. 6, no. 1, 2006, http://gamestudies.org.

Rodríguez, Juana María. *Sexual Futures, Queer Gestures, and Other Latina Longings*. New York University Press, 2014.

Sandahl, Carrie. "The Tyranny of Neutral: Disability and Actor Training." *Bodies in Commotion: Disability and Performance*, edited by Philip Auslander and Carrie Sandahl. University of Michigan Press, 2005, pp. 255–67.

Sargent, L. T. "The Three Faces of Utopianism Revisited." *Utopian Studies*, vol. 5, no. 1, 1994, pp. 1–37.

Saunders, P. J. "Fugitive Dreams of Diaspora: Conversations with Saidiya Hartman." *Anthurium*, vol. 6, no. 1, 2008, pp. 1–16.

Schmidt, Bryan. "Fatty Boom Boom and the Transnationality of Blackface in Die Antwoord's Racial Project." *TDR: The Drama Review*, vol. 58, no. 2, 2014, pp. 132–48.

Schmidt, Jennifer M. "The Girls Who Don't Die: Subversions of Gender and Genre in Recent Fiction by Lauren Beukes." *Safundi*, vol. 17, no. 2, 2016, pp. 137–55.

Schneider, Stephen. "Good, Clean, Fair: The Rhetoric of the Slow Food Movement." *College English*, vol. 70, no. 4, 2008, pp. 384–402.

Schweik, Susan M. *The Ugly Laws: Disability in Public*. New York University Press, 2009.

Scott, Claire. "Die Antwoord and a Delegitimized South African Whiteness: A Potential Counter-narrative?" *Safundi: The Journal of South African and American Studies*, vol. 26, no. 5, 2012, pp. 745–61.

Scott, Darieck. *Extravagant Abjection: Blackness, Power and Sexuality in the African American Literary Imagination*. New York University Press, 2010.

Searle, Berni. *Home and Away*. Video installation, commissioned by NMAC Montenmedio Arte Contemporaneo, Vejer, Spain, 2003.

Seshadri, Kalpana Rahita. *HumAnimal: Race, Law, Language*. University of Minnesota Press, 2012.

Shado'Man. Directed by Boris Gerrets. Pieter Van Huystee Film, 2013, www.shadoman-film.com.

"Shado'Man: IFDA Review." *Hollywood Reporter*, November 24, 2013, www.hollywood-reporter.com.

Shange, Ntozake. *For Colored Girls Who Have Considered Suicide / When the Rainbow Is Enuf*. Scribner, 1997.

Shannon, Bill. "Art, Life and the Disability Factor." *What Is What*, www.whatiswhat.com. Accessed March 8, 2022.

Sharma, Kriti. *Interdependence: Biology and Beyond*. Fordham University Press, 2015.

Sharp, Helen. *Encounters with the Breath: Nine Introductions*. Victoria University, Melbourne, 2006.

———. "The Profane Halo: Becoming Breath." 2014. Victoria University, PhD dissertation.

Sharpe, Christina. "And to Survive." *Small Axe: A Caribbean Journal of Criticism*, vol. 22, no. 3, 2018, pp. 171–80.

———. *In the Wake: On Blackness and Being*. Duke University Press, 2016.

Sheridan, Garth. "Fruity Batidas: The Technologies and Aesthetics of Kuduro." *Dancecult: Journal of Electronic Dance Music Culture*, vol. 6, no. 1, pp. 83–96.

Shildrick, Margrit. *Dangerous Discourses of Disability, Subjectivity and Sexuality*. Palgrave Macmillan, 2009.

Siebers, Tobin. "A Sexual Culture for Disabled People." *Sex and Disability*, edited by Robert McRuer and Anna Mollow. Duke University Press, 2012, pp. 37–53.

Simbao, Ruth. "A Sense of Pause: Ruth Simbao Interviews Mntambo, Nandipha." *Nandipha Mntambo: Standard Bank Young Artist Award 2011*, edited by Sophie Perryer. Exhibition catalogue. Stevenson, 2011, pp. 9–23.

Simon, Herbert. *The Sciences of the Artificial*. 3rd ed., Massachusetts Institute of Technology Press, 1996.

Sirowitz, Hal. "Zombies Are Loose." *Beauty Is a Verb: The New Poetry of Disability*, edited by Jennifer Bartlett, Sheila Black, and Michael Northen. Cinco Puntos, 2011, pp. 238–39.

Smallwood, Stephanie. *Saltwater Slavery: A Middle Passage from Africa to American Diaspora*. Harvard University Press, 2007.

Smith, Angela M. "Walk This Way: Frankenstein's Monster, Disability Performance, and Zombie Ambulation." *Literature and Medicine*, vol. 36, no. 2, 2018, pp. 412–38.

Smith, Owen. "Shifting Apollo's Frame: Challenging the Body Aesthetic in Theater Dance." *Bodies in Commotion: Disability and Performance*, edited by Carrie Sandahl and Philip Auslander. University of Michigan Press, 2005, pp. 73–85.

Smith, Russell. "In South Africa, the Music Is Hyphenated—and Pervasively Violent." *Globe and Mail*, March 23, 2011, www.theglobeandmail.com.

Snorton, C. Riley. *Black on Both Sides: A Racial History of Trans Identity*. University of Minnesota Press, 2017.

Solga, Kim. "Ghosts: Death's Double and the Phenomena of Theatre (Review)." *Theatre Journal*, vol. 59, no. 4, 2008, pp. 698–99.

Solomon, Rivers. *An Unkindness of Ghosts*. Akashic Books, 2017.

Spillers, Hortense J. "Mama's Baby, Papa's Maybe: An American Grammar Book." *Diacritics*, vol. 17, no. 2, 1987, pp. 64–81.

Springgay, Stephanie. "Corporeal Pedagogy and Contemporary Video Art." *Art Education*, vol. 61, no. 2, 2008, pp. 18–24.

Staeheli, Lynn, and Donald Mitchell. *The People's Property: Power, Politics and the Public*. Routledge, 2008.

Stobie, Cheryl. "Dystopian Dreams from South Africa: Lauren Beukes's *Moxyland* and *Zoo City*." *African Identities*, vol. 10, no. 4, 2012, pp. 367–80.

Stoller, Paul. *Embodying Colonial Memories: Spirit Possession, Power and the Hauka in West Africa*. Routledge, 1995.

———. *Sensuous Scholarship*. University of Pennsylvania Press, 1997.

Stone, Jasmine. "Artist Brett Murray Explains Why He Painted 'The Spear.'" *2oceansvibe*, May 25, 2012, www.2oceansvibe.com.

———. "Ninja: God Made a Mistake with Me. I'm Actually Black Trapped in a White Body." *2oceansvibe*, February 17, 2012, www.2oceansvibe.com.

Strukus, Wanda. "Mining the Gap: Physically Integrated Performance and Kinesthetic Empathy." *Journal of Dramatic Theory and Criticism*, vol. 25, no. 2, 2011, pp. 89–105.

Stubblefield, Anna. "'Beyond the Pale': Tainted Whiteness, Cognitive Disability, and Eugenic Sterilization." *Hypatia*, vol. 22, no. 2, 2007, pp. 162–81.

Stuckey, Daniel. "Remembering Wesley Willis, Ten Years Later." *Vice*, August 21, 2013, http://vice.com.

Swartz, Leslie. "Oscar Pistorius and the Melancholy of Intersectionality." *Disability and Society*, vol. 28, no. 8, 2013, pp. 1157–61.

Szántó, Diana. *Politicising Polio: Disability, Civil Society and Civic Agency in Sierra Leone*. Palgrave, 2020.

Thomas, Linda E. *Under the Canopy: Ritual Process and Spiritual Resilience in South Africa*. University of South Carolina Press, 1999.

Thomas, Trisha. "Identifying Body No. 421, Pulled from Migrant Shipwreck." *Edwardsville Intelligencer*, October 13, 2016, www.theintelligencer.com.

Thompson, Charis. "Afterbirth of a Nation: William Pope.L's Great White Way." *Women and Performance*, vol 12, no. 1, 2004, pp. 63–90.

———. *Making Parents: The Ontological Choreography of Reproductive Technologies*. Massachusetts Institute of Technology Press, 2007.

"Timol Inquest Hears Body Falling." *Randburg Sun*, July 25, 2017, http://randburgsun.co.za.

Titchkosky, Tanya. *The Question of Access: Disability, Space, Meaning*. University of Toronto Press, 2011.

Toit, Andries du. "Lost in Africa: *Disgrace*, Whiteness and the Fear of Desire." *A Subtle Knife: Reflections on Myth, Politics and Desire*, September 17, 2009, http://asubtle-knife.wordpress.com.

Tómas, António. "Becoming Famous: Kuduro, Politics and the Performance of Social Visibility." *Critical Interventions: Journal of African Art History and Visual Culture*, vol. 8, no. 2, 2014, pp. 261–75.

Torrey, Jesse Junr. *A Portraiture of Domestic Slavery, in the United States: With Reflections on the Practicability of Restoring the Moral Rights of the Slave, Without Impairing the Legal privileges of the Possessor; And a Project of a Colonial Asylum for Free Persons of Colour: Including Memoirs of Facts on the Interior Traffic in Slaves, and on Kidnapping. Illustrated with Engravings*. Published by the Author, John Bioren, Printer, 1817.

Touretteshero. "About." www.touretteshero.com. Accessed March 8, 2022.

Trani, Jean-Francois, et al. "Access to Health Care, Reproductive Health and Disability: A Large Scale Survey in Sierra Leone." *Social Science and Medicine*, vol. 73, no. 10, 2011, pp. 1477–89.

Truth and Reconciliation Commission. Human Rights Violations Submissions. Transcript, April 24, 1996, www.justice.gov.za.

Udobang, Wana. "Will I Still Carry Water When I Am a Dead Woman." *Wanawana*, April 24, 2013, http://wanawana.net.

Unburied. Directed by Sally Fenaux Barleycorn. Runnymede Trust and Creative Interruptions, 2019.

Unicef. "Children and Landmines: A Deadly Legacy." www.unicef.org. Accessed March 8, 2022.

US National Library of Medicine. "Muscle Twitching." Medline Plus, http://medlineplus.gov. Accessed March 8, 2022.

Venter, Zelda. "#AhmedTimol—Several Injuries 'Not Consistent with Fall.'" *IOL*, July 26, 2017, http://iol.co.za.

Verhoeff, Berend. "Autism in Flux: A History of the Concept from Leo Kanner to DSM-5." *History of Psychiatry*, vol. 24, no. 4, 2013, pp. 442–58.
Vermaak, Maryke, and Daniel Pensador. "Long after Angola's Civil War, Its Veterans Are Destitute." *Modern Ghana*, July 5, 2019, www.modernghana.com.
Vernallis, Carol. *Unruly Media: YouTube, Music Video, and the New Digital Cinema*. Oxford University Press, 2013.
Virtual Crack Distribution Services. "Titica—Kuduro Trap Extraordinaire." *Crackdistro*, February 19, 2012, http://crackdistro.blogspot.com.
Vision Health Institute. "Eye Floaters: Are They Serious?" November 4, 2015, http://visionsource-visionhealthinstitute.com.
Visiting Artist Program. "Ruby Onyinyechi Amanze." PAFA—Pennsylvania Academy of Fine Arts, www.pafa.org.
Wagner, Thomas. Review of *An Unkindness of Ghosts*, by Rivers Solomon. *SFF180: Science Fiction and Fantasy Book Reviews*, 2018, http://sff180.com.
Walker, Joanna S. "The Body Is Present Even If in Disguise: Tracing the Trace in the Artwork of Nancy Spero and Ana Mendieta." *Tate Papers*, no. 11, 2009, www.tate.org.uk.
Walter, Patrick. "Spectral Alphabets: Photography, Necropolitics, and the Marikana Massacre." *Cultural Critique*, vol. 93, 2016, pp. 1–31.
Waltz, Mitzi, and Martin James. "The (Re)marketing of Disability in Pop: Ian Curtis and Joy Division." *Popular Music*, vol. 28, no. 3, 2009, pp. 367–80.
Wa-Mungai, Mbugua. "'For I name thee . . .': Disability Onomastics in Kenyan Folklore and Popular Music." *Disability Studies Quarterly*, vol. 29, no. 4, 2009. https://doi.org/10.18061/dsq.v29i4.984.
Watt, Liese van der. "Disappearing Act." *Art South Africa*, vol. 1, no. 4, 2003, pp. 22–28. Accessed at https://archive.stevenson.info.
———. "Tracing: Berni Searle." *African Arts*, vol. 37, no. 4, 2004, pp. 74–96.
Weber, Bruce. "A Dance Company Mixes Arms, Legs and Wheels." *New York Times*, October 30, 2009, www.nytimes.com.
Weheliye, Alexander G. *Habeas Viscus: Racializing Assemblages, Biopolitics, and Black Feminist Theories of the Human*. Duke University Press, 2014.
Weil, Kari. *Thinking Animals: Why Animal Studies Now?* Columbia University Press, 2012.
Weld, Theodore Dwight, editor. *American Slavery as It Is: Selections from the Testimony of the Thousand Witnesses*. Dover, 2017.
Wilkinson, Kate. "Factsheet: South Africa's Official Poverty Numbers." *Africa Check*, February 15, 2018, http://africacheck.org.
Willems, P. A., G. J. Bastien, N. C. Heglund. "Mechanics of Carrying Head Supported Loads." Université cathelique de Louvain, Louvain-la-Neuve, Belgium. *Journal of Biomechanics*, vol. 39 (Suppl. 1), 2006, p. 360.
Williams, Patricia J. *The Alchemy of Race and Rights*. Harvard University Press, 1991.
———. "On Being the Object of Property." *Signs*, vol. 14, no. 1, 1988, pp. 5–24.
Winnubst, Shannon. "The Many Lives of Fungibility: Anti-Blackness in Neoliberal Times." *Journal of Gender Studies*, vol. 29, no. 1, 2020, pp. 102–12.

Wolchover, Natalie. "A New Physics Theory of Life." *Quanta Magazine*, January 22, 2014, www.quantamagazine.org.

———. "The Quantum Thermodynamics Revolution." *Quanta Magazine*, May 2, 2017, www.quantamagazine.org.

———. "Time's Arrow Traced to Quantum Source." *Quanta Magazine*, April 16, 2014, www.quantamagazine.org.

Wolfe, Cary. "Learning from Temple Grandin, or, Animal Studies, Disability Studies, and Who Comes after the Subject." *New Formations: A Journal of Culture/Theory/Politics*, no. 64, 2008, pp. 110–23.

Wong, Edlie L. *Neither Fugitive nor Free: Atlantic Slavery, Freedom Suits, and the Legal Culture of Travel*. New York University Press, 2009.

Woodward, Wendy. *The Animal Gaze: Animal Subjectivities in Southern African Narratives*. Wits University Press, 2008.

Woubshet, Dagmawi. *The Calendar of Loss: Race, Sexuality and Mourning in the Early Era of AIDS*. John Hopkins University Press, 2015.

Wright, Michelle M. *Physics of Blackness: Beyond the Middle Passage Epistemology*. University of Minnesota Press, 2015.

Wu, Cynthia. *Chang and Eng Reconnected: The Original Siamese Twins in American Culture*. Temple University Press, 2012.

Wynter, Sylvia. "Beyond Miranda's Meanings: Un/Silencing the 'Demonic Ground' of Caliban's 'Woman.'" *Out of the Kumbla: Caribbean Women and Literature*, edited by Carole Boyce Davies and Elaine Savory Fido. Africa World, 1990, pp. 355–72.

———. "On Disenchanting Discourse: 'Minority' Literary Criticism and Beyond." *Cultural Critique*, no. 7, 1987, pp. 207–44.

———. "Unsettling the Coloniality of Being/Power/Truth/Freedom: Towards the Human, After Man, Its Overrepresentation—An Argument." *CR: The New Centennial Review*, vol. 3, no. 3, 2003, pp. 257–337.

Young, Alex Trimble. "Settler Sovereignty and The Rhizomatic West, or, the Significance of the Frontier in Postwestern Studies." *Western American literature*, vol. 48, nos. 1–2, 2013, pp. 115–40.

Young, Harvey. *Embodying Black Experience: Stillness, Critical Memory, and the Black Body*. University of Michigan Press, 2010.

Young, Hershini Bhana. *Illegible Will: Coercive Spectacles of Labor in South Africa and the Diaspora*. Duke University Press, 2017.

Yusoff, Kathryn. *A Billion Black Anthropocenes or None*. University of Minnesota Press, 2018.

Yusuf, Mohammed. "Turning Nigeria's Disabled from Beggars to Workers." *Voa News*, June 26, 2015, www.voanews.com.

Zvomuya, Percy. "There's a Spoek on My Stoep." *Mail & Guardian*, November 4, 2011, http://mg.co.za.

INDEX

Page numbers in italics indicate figures

ABOUT THE AUTHOR

HERSHINI YOUNG is Professor of African and African Diaspora Studies at the University of Texas, Austin, and the author of *Haunting Capital: Memory, Text and the Black Diasporic Body* and *Illegible Will: Coercive Spectacles of Labor in South Africa and the Diaspora.*

CPSIA information can be obtained
at www.ICGtesting.com
Printed in the USA
LVHW111109291222
736122LV00013B/160

9 781479 81844(